A CULTURAL HISTORY OF HAIR

VOLUME 4

A Cultural History of Hair
General Editor: Geraldine Biddle-Perry

Volume 1
A Cultural History of Hair in Antiquity
Edited by Mary Harlow

Volume 2
A Cultural History of Hair in the Middle Ages
Edited by Roberta Milliken

Volume 3
A Cultural History of Hair in the Renaissance
Edited by Edith Snook

Volume 4
A Cultural History of Hair in the Age of Enlightenment
Edited by Margaret K. Powell and Joseph Roach

Volume 5
A Cultural History of Hair in the Age of Empire
Edited by Sarah Heaton

Volume 6
A Cultural History of Hair in the Modern Age
Edited by Geraldine Biddle-Perry

A CULTURAL HISTORY OF HAIR

IN THE AGE OF ENLIGHTENMENT

VOLUME 4

Edited by
Margaret K. Powell and Joseph Roach

BLOOMSBURY ACADEMIC
LONDON • NEW YORK • OXFORD • NEW DELHI • SYDNEY

BLOOMSBURY ACADEMIC
Bloomsbury Publishing Plc
50 Bedford Square, London, WC1B 3DP, UK
1385 Broadway, New York, NY 10018, USA
29 Earlsfort Terrace, Dublin 2, Ireland

BLOOMSBURY, BLOOMSBURY ACADEMIC and the Diana logo are trademarks of Bloomsbury Publishing Plc

First published in Great Britain 2021
Paperback edition published 2022

Copyright © Bloomsbury Publishing, 2022

Margaret K. Powell and Joseph Roach have asserted their right under the Copyright, Designs and Patents Act, 1988, to be identified as Editors of this work.

For legal purposes the Acknowledgements on p. xii
constitute an extension of this copyright page.

Series design: Raven Design
Cover image: Dressing for a Masquerade © Courtesy of The Lewis Walpole Library, Yale University

All rights reserved. No part of this publication may be reproduced or transmitted in any form or by any means, electronic or mechanical, including photocopying, recording, or any information storage or retrieval system, without prior permission in writing from the publishers.

Bloomsbury Publishing Plc does not have any control over, or responsibility for, any third-party websites referred to or in this book. All internet addresses given in this book were correct at the time of going to press. The author and publisher regret any inconvenience caused if addresses have changed or sites have ceased to exist, but can accept no responsibility for any such changes.

A catalogue record for this book is available from the British Library.

A catalog record for this book is available from the Library of Congress.

ISBN:	HB:	978-1-4742-3207-4
	HB set:	978-1-4742-3212-8
	PB:	978-1-3502-8560-6
	PB set:	978-1-3502-8751-8
	ePDF:	978-1-3500-8794-1
	eBook:	978-1-3500-8795-8

Series: The Cultural Histories Series

Typeset by Integra Software Services Pvt. Ltd.

To find out more about our authors and books visit www.bloomsbury.com
and sign up for our newsletters.

CONTENTS

LIST OF FIGURES	vi
GENERAL EDITOR'S PREFACE	xi
ACKNOWLEDGMENTS	xii
Introduction *Margaret K. Powell and Joseph Roach*	1
1 Religion and Ritualized Belief: Evangelical Hair *Misty G. Anderson*	17
2 Self and Society: Women Wearing Wigs *Julia H. Fawcett*	39
3 Fashion and Adornment *Lynn Festa*	53
4 Production and Practice *Sean Silver*	75
5 Health and Hygiene *Margaret K. Powell and Joseph Roach*	91
6 Gender and Sexuality: "Hairs Less in Sight" *Jayne Lewis*	109
7 Race and Ethnicity: Mortal Coils and Hair-Raising Revolutions *Heather V. Vermeulen*	135
8 Class and Social Status: Hair and Social Boundaries *Manushag N. Powell*	155
9 Cultural Representations: Hairstory *Crystal B. Lake*	171
NOTES	191
BIBLIOGRAPHY	219
CONTRIBUTORS	235
INDEX	237

LIST OF FIGURES

INTRODUCTION

I.1	*Ridiculous Taste or the Ladies Absurdity* (Published by M. Darly, 1771). Courtesy of The Lewis Walpole Library, Yale University.	2
I.2	"Flea" from Robert Hooke's *Micrographia*, Schema XXXIV (1665). Wellcome Library, London.	3
I.3	Thomas Rowlandson, *London Clergy/Country Clergy* (1786). Courtesy of The Lewis Walpole Library, Yale University.	5
I.4	Richard Newton, *Sketches in a Shaving Shop* (1794). Courtesy of The Lewis Walpole Library, Yale University.	8
I.5	*The Ridicule* (Published by M. Darly, 1772). Courtesy of The Lewis Walpole Library, Yale University.	9
I.6	*A French Hair Dresser Running through the Streets to his Customers* (Published by William Darling, 1771). Courtesy of The Lewis Walpole Library, Yale University.	11
I.7	James Gillray, *La Belle Espagnole,—ou—la Doublure de Madame Tallien* (1796). Courtesy of The Lewis Walpole Library, Yale University.	13

CHAPTER 1

1.1	Title page to an edition of *The Farewell Sermons of the Late London Ministers* (ca. 1662–1663). © National Portrait Gallery, London.	21
1.2	Robert Walker, *Oliver Cromwell* (ca. 1649). © National Portrait Gallery, London.	22
1.3	William Faithorne, *Sir Thomas Fairfax* (ca. 1646). Yale Center for British Art, Yale Art Gallery Collection. Gift of Edward B. Greene.	23
1.4	Giovanni Battista Cipriani, *John Milton* (1760). Yale Center for British Art. Gift of David M. Doret in memory of William Ferguson.	24
1.5	William Faithorne, *John Milton* (1670). © National Portrait Gallery, London.	25
1.6	George Bickham, *Enthusiasm Display'd: or, The Moor-Fields Congregation* (1739). Courtesy of The Lewis Walpole Library, Yale University.	27

LIST OF FIGURES

1.7	William Hogarth, *Credulity, Superstition and Fanaticism. A Medley* (1762). Courtesy of The Lewis Walpole Library, Yale University.	28
1.8	*The Elected Cobler* (Published by M. Darly, 1772). Courtesy of The Lewis Walpole Library, Yale University.	34
1.9	*The Mischief of Methodism* (1811). Courtesy of The Lewis Walpole Library, Yale University.	37

CHAPTER 2

2.1	William Hogarth, *An Election Entertainment*, Plate 1 (1755). Courtesy of The Lewis Walpole Library, Yale University.	40
2.2	John Simon after Giuseppe Grisoni, *Mr. Cibber* (ca. 1742). © National Portrait Gallery, London.	42
2.3	Frances Garden, *An Exact Representation of Mrs. Charke Walking in the Ditch at Four Years of Age* (1755). © The Trustees of the British Museum.	43

CHAPTER 3

3.1	*Betty the Cook Maids Head Drest* (Published by W. Humphrey, 1776). Courtesy of The Lewis Walpole Library, Yale University.	55
3.2	William Hogarth, *The five orders of Perriwigs as they were worn at the late Coronation, measured Architectonically* (1761). Courtesy of The Lewis Walpole Library, Yale University.	59
3.3	*What is this my Son Tom* (1774). Courtesy of The Lewis Walpole Library, Yale University.	63
3.4	Philip Dawe, *The Macaroni. A real Character at the late Masquerade* (1773). Courtesy of The Lewis Walpole Library, Yale University.	65
3.5	*The Extravaganza. or the Mountain Head Dress of 1776* (Published by M. Darly, 1776). Courtesy of The Lewis Walpole Library, Yale University.	67
3.6	*The Ladies Ridicule* (Published by M. Darly, 1772). Courtesy of The Lewis Walpole Library, Yale University.	68
3.7	After J.H. Grimm, *The French Lady in London, or the Head Dress for the Year 1771* (1771). Courtesy of The Lewis Walpole Library, Yale University.	70
3.8	*Bunkers Hill or America's Head Dress* (1776). © The Trustees of the British Museum.	71
3.9	*Beautys Lot* (Published by William Humphrey, between 1760 and 1810). British Cartoon Prints Collection, Library of Congress, LC-USZ62-115001.	73

CHAPTER 4

4.1	John Kelly, *Pattern Book of Worsted Samples* (1763). © Victoria and Albert Museum, London.	80
4.2	"Of a Louse" from Robert Hooke's *Micrographia*, Schema XXXV (1665). Beinecke Rare Book and Manuscript Library, Yale University.	84
4.3	Silk ribbon and watered silk from Robert Hooke's *Micrographia*, Schema III (1665). Wellcome Library, London.	86

CHAPTER 5

5.1	Thomas Rowlandson, *A Doleful Disaster, or Miss Fubby Fatarmin's Wig caught Fire* (not before 1813). Courtesy of The Lewis Walpole Library, Yale University.	91
5.2	*[Hairdressing]* (Published by J.S. Bretherton, 1787). Courtesy of The Lewis Walpole Library, Yale University.	93
5.3	Thomas Rowlandson, *An Old Maid in search of a Flea* (1794). Beinecke Rare Book and Manuscript Library, Yale University.	96
5.4	Thomas Rowlandson, *[I]s this, your Louse [?]* (1787). Courtesy of The Lewis Walpole Library, Yale University.	98
5.5	*Bunters Hill or May Day* (Published by J. Lockington, 1776). Courtesy of The Lewis Walpole Library, Yale University.	101
5.6	Thomas Rowlandson, *Dressing for a Birthday* (1790). Courtesy of The Lewis Walpole Library, Yale University.	102
5.7	Thomas Rowlandson, *Dressing for a Masquerade* (1790). Courtesy of The Lewis Walpole Library, Yale University.	102
5.8	Thomas Rowlandson, *Bug Breeders in the Dog Days* (1806). Beinecke Rare Book and Manuscript Library, Yale University.	107

CHAPTER 6

6.1	*Oh-Heigh-Oh. or a View of the Back Settlements* (Published by M. Darly, 1776). Courtesy of The Lewis Walpole Library, Yale University.	111
6.2	Claude Du Bosc and Claude Du Guernier, Frontispiece, Alexander Pope's *The Rape of the Lock* (1714). Beinecke Rare Book and Manuscript Library, Yale University.	112
6.3	Samuel Wade, "Let Wreaths of Triumph now my Temples twin, / The Victor cry'd, the glorious Prize is mine," from Alexander Pope's *Works*, vol. 1, Plate IV (1757). Beinecke Rare Book and Manuscript Library, Yale University.	113
6.4	Henry Fuseli, *The Dream of Belinda* (ca. 1780–1790), oil on canvas. Collection of the Vancouver Art Gallery, Founders' Fund, VAG 34.12. Photo: Rachel Topham, Vancouver Art gallery.	114

LIST OF FIGURES

6.5 *Mademoiselle de Beaumont, or the Chevalier D'Eon* (1777). Courtesy of The Lewis Walpole Library, Yale University. — 116

6.6 Locket (1775–1800). © Victoria and Albert Museum, London. — 120

6.7 *The Optic Curls. or the Obligeing Head Dress* (Published by M. Darly, 1777). © The Trustees of the British Museum. — 123

6.8 *The Flower Garden* (Published by M. Darly, 1777). Courtesy of The Lewis Walpole Library, Yale University. — 127

6.9 Emma Crewe, *Flora at play with Cupid*, Frontispiece, Erasmus Darwin's *Loves of the Plants* (1791). Courtesy of The Lewis Walpole Library, Yale University. — 129

6.10 Henry Fuseli, *Flora attired by the Elements*, Frontispiece, Erasmus Darwin's *The Economy of Vegetation* (1791). Courtesy of The Lewis Walpole Library, Yale University. — 130

6.11 *The Vis a Vis Bisected or the ladies Coop* (Published by M. Darly, 1776). Courtesy of The Lewis Walpole Library, Yale University. — 131

6.12 Mattina Darly, *A Speedy & Effectual preparation for the next World* (1778). Courtesy of The Lewis Walpole Library, Yale University. — 132

CHAPTER 7

7.1 *The Monkey who had seen the World,* Fable XIV, illustration from John Gay's *Fables* (1727). Beinecke Rare Book and Manuscript Library, Yale University. — 136

7.2 *The Toilette* from William Hogarth, *Marriage a-la-Mode,* Plate IV (1745). Courtesy of The Lewis Walpole Library, Yale University. — 138

7.3 Philip Dawe, *Can you forbear Laughing* (1776). Courtesy of The Lewis Walpole Library, Yale University. — 140

7.4 William Dent, *Abolition of the Slave Trade, or the Man the Master* (1789). © The Trustees of the British Museum. — 144

7.5 James Sayers, *Mr. Burke's Pair of Spectacles for short sighted Politicians* (1791). Courtesy of The Lewis Walpole Library, Yale University. — 146

7.6 *Gorgon* (Published by E. Hedges, 1784). Courtesy of The Lewis Walpole Library, Yale University. — 147

7.7 James Gillray, *ALECTO and her Train, at the Gate of Pandæmonium: —or—The Recruiting Sarjeant enlisting JOHN BULL, into the Revolution Service* (1791). Beinecke Rare Book and Manuscript Library, Yale University. — 148

7.8 James Gillray, *The Dagger Scene: __or__ The Plot discover'd* (1792). Courtesy of The Lewis Walpole Library, Yale University. — 150

7.9 Isaac Cruikshank, *A Right Honorable alias a Sans Culotte* (1792). Courtesy of The Lewis Walpole Library, Yale University. — 151

7.10 James Gillray, *Doublûres of Characters; _ or _ striking Resemblances in Phisiognomy* (1798). Courtesy of The Lewis Walpole Library, Yale University. 152

7.11 Anne-Louis Girodet-Trioson, *C[itizen] Jean-Baptiste Belley, Ex-Representative of the Colonies* (1797). Musée National des Châteaux de Versailles et de Trianon, Versailles, France. Photo by Leemage/Corbis. Getty Images. 153

CHAPTER 8

8.1 William Thornhill, *John Sheppard* (1724). © National Portrait Gallery, London. 156

8.2 William Blake after William Hogarth, *Beggar's Opera*, Act III (1790). Courtesy of The Lewis Walpole Library, Yale University. 157

8.3 *Jack Shepherd Drawn from the Life* (Published by John Bowles, 1724). © The Trustees of the British Museum. 158

8.4 Philip Dawe, *A Hint to the Husbands, or the Dresser, properly Dressed* (1777). © The Trustees of the British Museum. 161

8.5 B. Cole, *Captain Bartho. Roberts with two Ships, Viz. the* Royal Fortune *and* Ranger, *takes 11 Sail*, illustration from *A General History of the Pyrates* (1724). Beinecke Rare Book and Manuscript Library, Yale University. 165

8.6 B. Cole, *Blackbeard the Pirate*, illustration from *A General History of the Pyrates* (1724). Beinecke Rare Book and Manuscript Library, Yale University. 166

8.7 B. Cole, *Ann Bonny and Mary Read convicted of Piracy*, illustration from *A General History of the Pyrates* (1724). Beinecke Rare Book and Manuscript Library, Yale University. 169

8.8 Double portrait of Elizabeth Canning and Mary Squires the Gypsy (*The London Magazine*, May 1754). Courtesy of The Lewis Walpole Library, Yale University. 169

CHAPTER 9

9.1 The figure of Curiosity from Isaac Fuller's English edition of Cesare Ripa's *Iconologia* (London, 1709). Wellcome Library, London. 179

9.2 "Schema V" from Robert Hooke's *Micrographia* (1665). Wellcome Library, London. 182

9.3 Portrait of Charles I in which his hair was thought to include copies of the psalms. Reproduced by permission of the President and Fellows of St John's College, Oxford. 186

9.4 A lock of Edward IV's hair (Recovered by members of the Society of Antiquaries in 1774). By kind permission of The Society of Antiquaries of London. 188

9.5 Example of Victorian hairwork. Wellcome Library, London. 189

GENERAL EDITOR'S PREFACE

A Cultural History of Hair offers an unparalleled examination of the most malleable part of the human body. This fascinating set explores hair's intrinsic relationship to the construction and organization of diverse social bodies and strategies of identification throughout history. The six illustrated volumes, edited by leading specialists in the field, evidence the significance of human hair on the head and face and its styling, dressing, and management across the following historical periods: antiquity, the Middle Ages, the Renaissance, the Age of Enlightenment, the Age of Empire, and the Modern Age.

Using an innovative range of historical and theoretical sources, each volume is organized around the same key themes: religion and ritualized belief, self and societal identification, fashion and adornment, production and practice, health and hygiene, gender and sexuality, race and ethnicity, class and social status, representation. The aim is to offer readers a comprehensive account of human hair-related beliefs and practices in any given period and through time. It is not an encyclopedia. *A Cultural History of Hair* is an interdisciplinary collection of complex ideas and debates brought together in the work of an international range of scholars.

Geraldine Biddle-Perry

ACKNOWLEDGMENTS

The Editors wish to offer special thanks to the Lewis Walpole Library (LWL) of Farmington, Connecticut, for providing images free of charge, and to the LWL staff, especially Susan Walker and Kristen McDonald, who promptly and patiently answered every request. We are also grateful to the staffs of the Yale Center for British Art and the Beinecke Rare Book and Manuscript Library, especially Anne Marie Menta, for their kind assistance. We thank the editors and staff at Bloomsbury, including Anna Wright, Pari Thompson, Yvonne Thouroude, and Katherine Bosiacki, for their attentive help. Frances Arnold, Editorial Director for Visual Arts, and Geraldine Biddle-Perry, Series Editor, have kept faith with the project from the beginning, and we are grateful for their expert guidance. We thank Janice Carlisle for her help in preparing the Bibliography.

Introduction

MARGARET K. POWELL AND JOSEPH ROACH

What is Enlightenment? To this question the philosopher Immanuel Kant famously answered: Enlightenment is people daring to be wise. By that he meant people having the maturity and courage to think for themselves as individuals, living in a society that allows others to do the same. Kant's definition of Enlightenment is both affirmed and contradicted by the cultural history of hair, 1650–1800, the period known by scholars today as the "long" eighteenth century. On the one hand, by the time Kant wrote in 1784, empiricism, or proof by scientific experiment rather than by appeal to traditional authorities or received ideas, had firmly established itself in philosophical theory and laboratory practice. Over a century earlier it had already inspired the motto of the Royal Society (founded in 1660): *nullius in verba*, or "don't take anybody's word for it." On the other hand, irrational behavior about hair, along with hair itself, simultaneously reached all-time highs. The Enlightenment saw the most extravagant developments of hair fashion in any period of history, including the proliferation of wigs for men and fantastic hairdos for women (Figure I.1). The popularity of these extravagancies proved that many people were anxious to express themselves by means of their hair without necessarily bothering to think things through for themselves before doing so. Although the laws of fashion may seem to operate as inevitably as the physical laws of nature, they always depend on the word of someone, real or imagined, to exert the gravitational forces of emulation, discrimination, and discipline. In the chapters that follow, the contributors understand hair in the Enlightenment, also known as "The Age of Reason," as both a material fact of nature and social magic.

Under the sway of empiricism, enlightened science looked at hair objectively, literally putting it under the microscope, itself a recent invention. In 1665 Robert Hooke, Curator of Experiments for the Royal Society, published his meticulously illustrated *Micrographia*, featuring the magnified images of vermin, including one of a louse, itself covered with tiny hairs, grasping a strand of human hair with its well-adapted little claws (see Chapter 4 below, Figure 4.2) and another, on a spectacular fold-out plate, depicting a common flea. The microscope discovers what neither the unaided eye nor the unprompted imagination can apprehend: otherwise invisible hairs cover the bodies of these monsters, the flea's six bristling legs rooted in hairy pods, its proboscis mustached by bulging fur balls (Figure I.2). While studying the physical properties of hair descriptively and rationally, scientists such as Hooke set aside many of the superstitions and religious doctrines that made hair seem magical to people in traditional societies worldwide. These included beliefs in the sacredness of hair as the home of occult spirits. They also included taboos against cutting hair, or wearing hair shorn from the heads of others. Since Medusa and Samson at least, hair has, in this sense, remained at once mystified and forbidden. The poet Alexander Pope ridiculed such taboos in the representative mock-heroic satire of the age, *The Rape of the Lock* (1714), which serves as a touchstone for several of the

FIGURE I.1: *Ridiculous Taste or the Ladies Absurdity* (Published by M. Darly, 1771). Courtesy of The Lewis Walpole Library, Yale University.

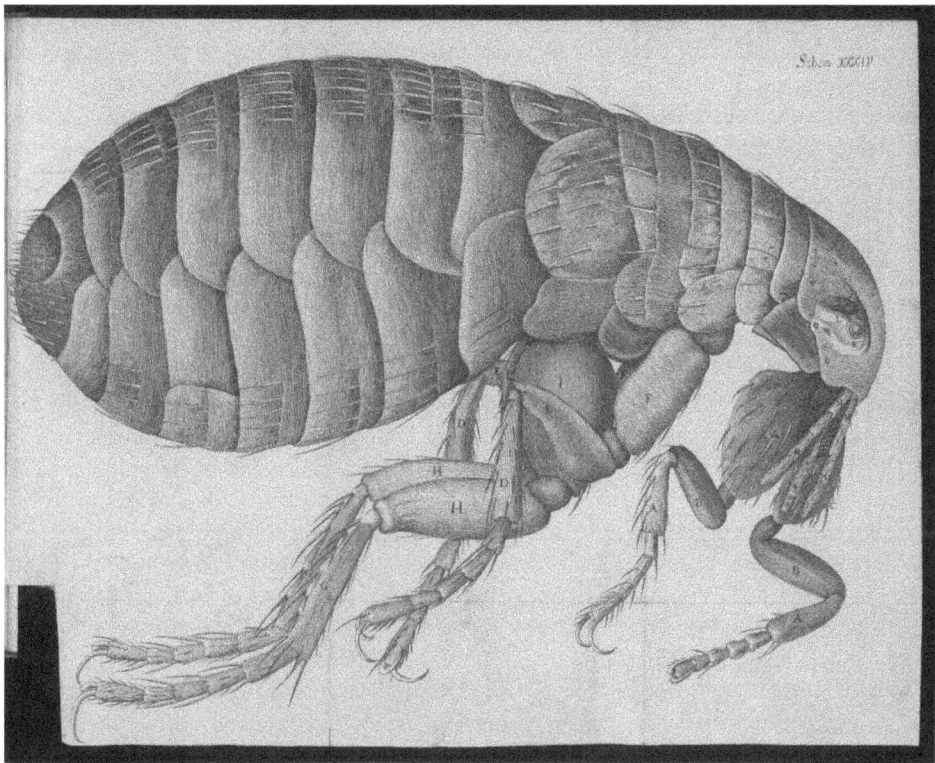

FIGURE I.2: "Flea" from Robert Hooke's *Micrographia*, Schema XXXIV (1665). Beinecke Rare Book and Manuscript Library, Yale University.

chapters in this volume. The poem tells us a good deal about the ways in which Pope's contemporaries attached value to hair. Of the real-life feud that broke out when Robert Lord Petre (or the "Baron" in the poem) snipped a lovelock from the head of Arabella Fermor (or "Belinda"), the poet constructed a fantastically exaggerated narrative, filled with hair-dwelling Sylphs and Gnomes, supposedly outraged by the violence done to their habitat. "What mighty Contests," the speaker of the poem reasons facetiously in response to all the upset, "rise from trivial Things."[1] Far from being trivial in its consequence, the episode of the purloined lock inspired Pope to produce the most celebrated and quoted poem of his age. The poet spotted a trend: in the Enlightenment, social hair could be as charismatic in its own way as sacred hair once was and every bit as mighty.[2]

Meanwhile, the successes of empirical experimentation encouraged the growth of instrumental reason, the application of scientific discoveries to practical arts and trades. Modernizing specialists such as physicians, professional hairdressers, and manufacturers of woolen goods, for instance, applied the newly acquired knowledge to a range of innovations in medical treatment, hair care, and textile production. The number and prominence of hairdressers grew, and the increasing recognition of their technical expertise created a demand not only for primping but also for publication: while treatises, manuals, handbooks, and illustrative prints abounded, so did mocking poetry, prose, and graphic satires. Natural philosophers also applied scientific principles to great projects of classification, distributing hair along with all kinds of flora and fauna into detailed taxonomies. But even at its most instrumentally rational, hair research could revert to pseudoscience under the pressure of unexamined stereotypes and bigoted presuppositions. The classification of peoples by race, for instance, grew apace during the age of Enlightenment. Observable differences in the kinds of hair typical of people from different parts of the world morphed spuriously from demonstrable empirical fact into new superstitions about racial difference. Racist taxonomists went so far as to place some types of human hair into the category of animal "wool." Less egregious but still dubious notions about the meaning of hair defined human persons on the bases of gendered identity and social class. Nor did religion abdicate to secular fashion all of its long-standing authority over hair.

The chapters in this volume—covering Religion and Ritualized Belief, Self and Society, Fashion and Adornment, Production and Practice, Health and Hygiene, Gender and Sexuality, Race and Ethnicity, Class and Social Status, and Cultural Representations— concern themselves with the Enlightenment in Britain and some of its colonies. This focus honors the special expertise of the contributors and the precedents of their previous collaborations on the subject of hair in the long eighteenth century. Another ensemble of authors would have produced a different volume, but not, we believe, wholly different. They would have been obliged, as we have been, to treat the subject of hair seriously in light of its most important and representative meanings: spiritual, psychological, ornamental, commercial, medical, sexual, ethnic, social, cultural, and philosophical. Of course on numberless occasions in normal life, then as now, hair meant nothing at all; but these instances, available to be known by commonsense inference alone, obviously escaped documentation by historical records. What the records do show, as the contributions to this volume attest, is an increasingly robust preoccupation with hair over the course of the long eighteenth century. They show the norms and the deviations, the obsession and the neglect, the pleasures and the pains, and the artistry and the folly. In aggregate, they prove that hair, whatever its length, was big in the Enlightenment.

In Chapter 1, Misty G. Anderson argues that evolving traditions of "Religion and Ritualized Belief" in the seventeenth and eighteenth centuries resist the tidy containment of religion in its own hermetic category. She writes: "The rhetorical force of distinctions between the secular and the sacred that construct the field of 'Enlightenment' philosophically prove to be much less clear, and even to collapse when we look at the social connections and affiliations that hair signified." The ascetic rigors of what she calls the "Puritan hair," for instance, once associated with the Parliamentary Roundheads (so called because of their bowl-cropped dos), were compromised over time among the clergy by recourse to the flowing locks of the romanticized Cavaliers. This ecumenical-tonsorial compromise, Anderson shows, produced "Evangelical Hair" in the mid-eighteenth century. She notes how the foreshortened "hyacinthine locks" of Adam in Milton's *Paradise Lost* contrast with Eve's waist-length tresses, "in wanton ringlets waved." Evangelical hair, she argues, no less eroticized, fell somewhere in between Adam's and Eve's. The charismatic preaching of Methodist evangelicals, namely John Wesley, Charles Wesley, and George Whitefield, relied in part on the special appearance of what Anderson calls "Methodist hair," worn long and flowing to the shoulders and kept white with powder and/or natural aging to convey the image of the biblical prophets. Anderson goes on to untangle the complexities of Methodist hair in her reading of *The Spiritual Quixote* (1772) by Richard Graves. The protagonist is Geoffrey Wildgoose, whose self-fashioning attempts to style himself a Methodist (in defiance of the unbidden

FIGURE I.3: Thomas Rowlandson, *London Clergy/Country Clergy* (1786). Courtesy of The Lewis Walpole Library, Yale University.

ministrations of his fractious barber) turn on getting his natural hair cut to just the right length—not too long, not too short—in imitation of the charismatic preacher George Whitefield. *The Spiritual Quixote* makes fun of Wildgoose as the comic eccentric, as obstinate in his folly as the original title character in Cervantes, for resisting the prevailing customs of his own time. In Wildgoose's case, the hero is funny because he rejects the near-universal adoption of false hair by men in almost all walks of life, including the ecclesiastical, as caricatured by Thomas Rowlandson in *London Clergy / Country Clergy* (Figure I.3). Railing against moral decadence, the protagonist foolishly refuses at all costs to take up the most popular solution to problem hair, sacred or secular, in the age of the Enlightenment: the periwig.

Indeed, wigs of various shapes and sizes signaled the social identity of the wearer by association with specific trades and professions. This is still the case with judges, barristers, and until recently, the Speaker of the House of Commons; but in the long eighteenth century, the wig made not only the man but also fine distinctions between and among diverse types of men. False hair was not unknown in earlier periods, including the Elizabethan: in his advice to the Players, Hamlet deprecates a "periwig-pated fellow" for overacting his part (*Hamlet*, 3.2.9). But for wigs in the period 1650–1800, the past was but prologue. In *Plococosmos: Or the Whole Art of Hair Dressing* (1782), the hairdresser and natural philosopher James Stewart, looking back on the specialization of wigs that began with their systematic introduction into Britain during the reign of Charles II a hundred years earlier, itemizes different kinds of wigs across the classes except for the very poorest and specifies their functions as signposts of the self in society:

> As the perukes became more common, their shape and forms altered. Hence we hear of the clerical, the physical, the huge tie peruke for the man of the law, the brigadier, or the major for the army and navy, as also the tremendous fox ear, or cluster of temple curls, with a pig-tail behind. The merchant, the man of business and of letters, were distinguished by the grave full-bottom, or more moderate tie, neatly curled; the tradesman by the snug bob, or the natty scratch; the country gentleman, by the natural fly and hunting peruke. All conditions of men were distinguished by the cut of the wig, and none more so than the coachman, who wore his, as there does some to this day, in imitation of the curled hair of a waterdog.³

Stewart's period-specific taxonomy suggests not only how hairstyles, like clothes, make the man but also why a man appearing in public without a wig might reasonably feel naked.

In Chapter 2, "Self and Society," Julia H. Fawcett confirms that wigs were worn to express public selfhood at a time when men were more likely to wear false hair than women. Fawcett's countervailing purpose, however, is to show how several women who did wear wigs struggled without much success to benefit from their powers of public self-definition. "Peppered through the eighteenth-century archive," she writes, "are a few anxious anecdotes about women who defied their society's fashion trends and gender expectations and elected, either for a moment or throughout their lives, to wear a wig." Like men, women sometimes donned wigs after cutting their hair close to rid themselves of an infestation of head lice; but Fawcett's case studies feature stories about women who made their wigs a problematic self-expression of what men and other critics wanted to see.

Fawcett begins with the actor Colley Cibber and his daughter Charlotte, who secretly donned her father's periwig on a childhood lark. Cibber had established his public persona in large measure through the fame of the wig he first wore onstage as the character of Sir Novelty Fashion in his own play, *Love's Last Shift* (1696), and then further enlarged when Sir Novelty was elevated into Lord Foppington in Sir John Vanbrugh's sequel, *The Relapse* (1698). The actor's prominence in the role helped to popularize the newly coined word *bigwig*. Charlotte symbolically foreshadowed her actual estrangement from her father when she became his professional rival later in life—and, as Fawcett argues, first discovered her life-long selfhood as a gender renegade—when she slipped into a closet and put on Lord Foppington's full regalia, periwig and all. In her second case study, Fawcett recounts the strange disguise adopted in a pinch by the actress George Anne Bellamy. Trying to enter the city of Edinburgh incognito, she cut off all her hair in order to prevent her fans from recognizing her. Compelled by popular demand to perform, however, she reluctantly resorted to wearing a wig in order to appear disguised as herself.

She did so not to make herself into what she wanted to be but into what her public wanted, her false hair suppressing, not expressing, her true self. Fawcett's next case study concerns the intimate production of gendered selfhood through one of the strangest uses of false hair in the Enlightenment period: the merkin. Worn more often by women than by men, the merkin was a pubic wig. It could be attached by spirit-gum and worn over the shaved pudendum to hide symptoms of venereal infection or to aid in the eradication of infestation by *Pthirus pubis* ("crabs"). In Fawcett's retelling of Alexander Smith's obscene anecdote of 1714, a Roman Catholic cardinal misidentifies a prostitute's merkin and presents it piously to the pope as the relic of St. Peter's beard. This remarkable passage in the cultural history of hair aligns itself satirically to the superstitious sanctification of hair that Alexander Pope contemporaneously ridicules—and retails—in *The Rape of the Lock*. Fawcett concludes by returning to the example of Belinda's doomed quest for autonomous selfhood in Pope's poem. She interprets the severed lock, which Belinda wishes somehow restored to her, as a kind of magical wig, not one that the bereft heroine any longer possesses but one that, through no fault of her own, still possesses her by the mere fact of its shaming absence.

Important as its role in individual self-expression was, hair did more general social work as well. Cultural and intercultural distinctions, such as those between "polite" and "rude" or "civilized" and "barbaric," for instance, could turn on the question of hair's location as well as its specific physical properties. Eighteenth-century voyages of encounter and exploitation brought back a wealth of new knowledge about peoples and their customs, often reported negatively, particularly with regard to hair. Perhaps the most vivid fictional instance of such discrimination appears in Jonathan Swift's account of the revolting Yahoos, hirsute in face and upper body, hairless below, in Part IV of *Gulliver's Travels* (1726). Enlightened opinion was often conflicted about hairstyles, and fashion reflected its contradictions. As wigs came in, for instance, beards went out. Following ancient Roman precept, imputations of barbarity grew along with facial hair, and there were practical reasons for that development, as Lynn Festa suggests in Chapter 3, "Fashion and Adornment": the look of actual hair growing on the face might openly clash with that of false hair sitting atop the head. The near-obligatory style of close shaving of men's faces took hold generally across Europe in the period as the fashion for wig-wearing spread, even to the perspiring heads of agricultural laborers in the fields and workmen at building sites. Festa examines the multiple contradictions in the meaning of hair fashions manifested by each of the varied authorities she cites—consumers, expert producers (such as hairdressers and wigmakers), performers, writers, and graphic satirists: fashion adorns, but it also disciplines; fashion conserves, but it also innovates; fashion spends without profit in some ways, but it also drives the engine of commerce in others. Festa argues that hair as a product—grown without cost to the wearer, treated with panache by the expert, and located prominently in plain sight—lent itself particularly well to fashionable novelty. "The ease with which hair could be re-fashioned," she writes, "made it a primary sign of the accelerating tempo of material life associated with the consumer revolution." At the apex of production and consumption, at least of human hair, towered the headdresses women of leisure and the up-dos of the dandies known as "Macaronis," who were walking fashion plates noted for their ambiguous gender but ostentatious clarity of style. Expertise and ostentation alike provoked satirical lampoons, as in *Sketches in a Shaving Shop* (Figure I.4) and *The Ridicule* (Figure I.5).

FIGURE I.4: Richard Newton, *Sketches in a Shaving Shop* (1794). Courtesy of The Lewis Walpole Library, Yale University.

Human hair, however, was not the only hair that mattered in the vast consumer revolution associated with the period of the Enlightenment. In fact, it was arguably not the kind of hair that mattered most. In Chapter 4, "Production and Practice," Sean Silver begins with the obvious, but occasionally underappreciated, fact that the economy of Britain historically depended on the manufacture, merchandizing, and export of woolen goods, especially so in the long eighteenth century. He acknowledges the well-researched relationships of the imperial trade in raw materials and finished goods, but he also insists on the importance of trade based on the prolific commercial production of hair: "The story of incipient industry, of the transformation of England from a feudal kingdom of artisanal handicrafts to a global superpower with emerging factory-style production," he argues, "must focus instead on the native production of sometimes homely goods, like British woolens." Starting with the sweepingly protectionist Wool Act of 1699, which shut down exports from the colonies, he recounts the growth of an industry that employed perhaps one million Britons by the mid-eighteenth century. They participated in a lucrative process that produced and moved a valued commodity "from sheep, to shop, to ship," leading Silver to conclude that England was a "hair economy" in the period and beyond. In fact, the Wool Act was not repealed until 1867. Increasingly, skilled weaving enlarged its operations into economies of scale, perfecting the process of turning hair into cloth, broadcloth earlier in the period giving way to worsteds and stuffs as manufacture became more complex. Silver calls this knowledge "Fiber Science," which grows apace into "Textile Science" in the period. Here the kind of theoretical knowledge produced by the Royal Society, from the moment Hooke used his microscope to examine

FIGURE I.5: *The Ridicule* (Published by M. Darly, 1772). Courtesy of The Lewis Walpole Library, Yale University.

fine cloth fibers, intersects with the story of the rise of the hair-production industry. Natural philosophers found in fibers and textiles an incomparable metaphor for the material complexity of the mechanistic universe: "Weaving and cloth-making alone," Silver notes, "produced a wide range of surface effects merely through the careful arrangement of barely visible microstructure, beginning with particles of almost no properties at all—single fibers of wool, flax, cotton, or silk—and weaving them into resplendent, two-dimensional surfaces of varying thickness, stiffness, and tactile qualities." The conceptual revolution of seeing the large-scale phenomena of the world as the aggregate of many smaller-scale mechanical operations between particles, Silver points out, was analogized by the Royal Academician William Petty to the workings of a loom. Petty, the son of a weaver, pointed out that the real inner workings of a loom consist of the wool itself, a "complicated machinament made of threads," and he conceived them as a model of the mechanical systems and networks of the physical world, indeed the universe itself. As capitalized wool production upheld an entire national economy with its invisible hand, so the transformation of hairs into textiles became a dominant metaphor for expressing the complexity of a heretofore unseen world. But craftsmen and natural philosophers alike could see the actual relationship of the physical and economic worlds with their own eyes, watching humble thread spun into pure gold, and they didn't need to take it on the word of anyone.

Instrumental reason found other applications in the burgeoning hair-care industry. Professional hairdressers, physicians, druggists, and quacks of all kinds sought or touted improved remedies for age-old diseases of the hair. They especially concerned themselves with fighting communicable afflictions, made all the more virulent by the growing density of urban populations. In Chapter 5, "Health and Hygiene," we, the editors, bring together written and pictorial evidence to show that few people in the period could escape the experience of feeling like "their heads were on fire," for kings as well as beggars knew the itchy torment inflicted by hair-dwelling vermin. We also show that the remedies against infestation could be worse than the affliction. Normally covered in powder and saturated with greasy pomatum, infected hair and skin suffered further insult from poisons and corrosives intended to eradicate the voracious bloodsuckers—head lice above, crabs below, and fleas all over. Meanwhile, everyday hair care for uninfected persons developed apace in ambition and scope, and the proliferation of hair-care professionals is a remarkable feature of the long eighteenth century. As hairdressers grew more numerous, prominent, and confident, they published "treatises" on the "science" of hair health and hygiene, and their publications provide a valuable source of knowledge about their procedures, methods, and materials as well as their theoretical assumptions about the material properties of hair itself. At the same time, the hairdressers became the butt of ridicule in printed and graphic satires, which, as in *A French Hair Dresser Running through the Streets to his Customers* (Figure I.6), mocked their pretensions as well as those of their clients, offering another kind of evidence towards the reconstruction of the cultural history of hair in the Enlightenment.

In Chapter 6, "Gender and Sexuality," subtitled "'Hairs Less in Sight': Some Vibrant Ideas of Gender," Jayne Lewis opens with Pope's smutty allusion to Belinda's pubic hair in *The Rape of the Lock*. The poet stealthily insinuates these "Hairs Less in Sight" in the reader's imagination while keeping them out of the characters' view. Introducing (in)visibility as a problem underlying ideas of gender in the Enlightenment, Lewis continues her account with a gloss on hair as a general Idea. The word *Idea* (with a capital "I") in this context means an abstract philosophical "category of being" as contrasted to *ideas*

FIGURE I.6: *A French Hair Dresser Running through the Streets to his Customers* (Published by William Darling, 1771). Courtesy of The Lewis Walpole Library, Yale University.

(small "i"), meaning more locally contingent thoughts, conceptions, or notions. Lewis writes: "To get at how hair might have engendered eighteenth-century ideas of gender as 'Ideas' that shaped matter by participating with it, we should [first] look outside the psychosocial, cultural, and economic register to hair's treatment in a changing history and philosophy of nature." In point of fact, science could discover no discernible difference between male and female hairs as matter. "Hair" itself could therefore be said to exist as an Idea apart from localized ideas of sex and gender, and hair's properties could engage the attention of natural philosophy on that general basis. Lewis enumerates those properties—"matter's indirectly tangible qualities of fluidity, flexibility, resilience, and freedom"—and traces them to technical discussions by their wide-ranging scientific explicators. Royal Society founding member Robert Boyle, for instance, likened the physico-mechanical "spring" of air (as atmosphere) to the flexible resilience of hair. Other scientists explored hair's electrical conductivity and tensile strength, which show no gendered difference as general properties. Anatomical investigation, however, found that the sexes differed in the likelihood that hair would grow deep inside the body, especially in the female organs of reproduction, and of course everyone can see that men's and women's hair typically differs in external locality, with men possessing greater potential to add it to their faces and lose it from their heads. The intellectual push and pull between *Idea* and *ideas* in Lewis's account thus disclose fascinating theories of hair's origin and nature. Ancient tradition likened hair, along with the fingernails, to excrement, offering yet another reason, as if one were needed, for the clean-shaven to despise barbarians. More modern theories understood hair to be a remarkable extension of living tissue that possesses unique powers of growth without sensation, more like vegetable matter than animal flesh. As vegetation, authorities believed, hair continued to grow despite the death of its host; but it could also, therefore, be managed on the heads of the living as tractably as the plantings that composed the groves and glades of a landscape garden. Existing as a big Idea poised on the threshold between life and death, then, hair provided enlightened arts and sciences with "an animate medium of unlimited ideational life," as Lewis puts it; but it did so without ever relinquishing its important role in the formulation of more particularized but still powerful ideas of sexual difference.

In addition to experimentation, empirical science prioritized classification. In Chapter 7, "Race and Ethnicity," Heather V. Vermeulen provides a subtitle, "Mortal Coils & Hair-Raising Revolutions: Styling 'Race' in the Age of Enlightenment," to prepare the reader for her harrowing documentation of a most malignant kind of "style." For her purposes, style means systemized racism founded on spurious taxonomies. She shows how taxonomists deployed differences in the properties of hair to classify human beings of African descent as belonging to a species closer to, or actually among, the animals. Taxonomists attributed "hair" to Europeans and "wool" to Africans, a canard that stubbornly persisted into nineteenth-century tracts, where racists used it to justify slavery and incite racial fears. Vermeulen meditates on the phobic meanings of different kinds of hair among the self-terrorized plantocracy in the West Indies and their political supporters in Parliament. Edward Long's notorious *History of Jamaica* (1774), for instance, cites "wool" on the heads of the slaves as the source of a kind of tonsorial contamination because he thinks it has inspired the ridiculous fashion for big-haired *têtes* among the wives of his planter friends. To the extent that such a degraded style is not African, it is French, which is almost as bad, as Gillray's *La Belle Espagnole* suggests (Figure I.7), with xenophobia keeping pace in a race to the bottom of the human spirit. In an age when one of the

FIGURE I.7: James Gillray, *La Belle Espagnole,—ou—la Doublure de Madame Tallien* (1796). Courtesy of The Lewis Walpole Library, Yale University.

greatest theatrical effects was David Garrick's fright wig in his production of *Hamlet*, Vermeulen notes, hair had a prominent role in the representation of the passion of terror. The vivid graphic satires that she educes confirm the pervasive importance of hair in connection with the emotion of fear at the time of the French and Haitian Revolutions and the many smaller-scale slave revolts in the Caribbean and Louisiana. Horripilation appears willy-nilly in response to the hydra-headed Medusas that stand in for the specter of a bloody Reign of Terror in the slave colonies, which would be even more terrible than the original. Hair, Vermeulen concludes, creates a practical and imaginative "Contact Zone," where Europeans confront racial others along the frontier created by their own taxonomic hallucinations, corrupt guarantors of a resilient ignorance that remains to the present day the greatest failure of Enlightenment.

Not all frontiers marked arbitrarily by hair, however, separated people into races. In Chapter 8, Manushag N. Powell makes the popular images of infamous criminals the centerpiece for her general discussion of hair as a critical register of "Class and Social Status." From the jail-break artist Jack Sheppard on land to the pirate Edward Teach at sea, Powell starts at the bottom of the social scale and works her way up to show how prominently eighteenth-century status hierarchies featured hairstyle. Among men, beards threatened social disqualification, a motive for censure not in any way diminished by the fact that the most terrifying criminal of the age came to be known metonymically by his wildly unkempt and notoriously flammable facial hair—"Blackbeard." Among women, long hair worn unbound (as the two most famous female pirates, Anne Bonny and Mary Read, wore theirs) corresponded to the imputation of "looseness" in matters of sexual conduct and consequent social abjection (along with popular notoriety). Among servants, expectations included high standards of personal grooming as well as skilled attentiveness to the care of their masters' hair. Among masters, obligations included expensive treatments such as powdering, a considerable outlay and a readily legible status symbol. Powell points out that in the narratives and performances of social inversion, whereby the criminal becomes the hero, such as Daniel Defoe's *A Narrative of all the Robberies, Escapes etc. of John Sheppard* (1724) and John Gay's *The Beggar's Opera* (1728), the grooming of the felon is as fine as his gentlemanly manners. But such is the illuminating irony of fiction: social hierarchy likes to imagine itself momentarily upside-down, as in pastorals or carnival masquerades, in order to reaffirm its unchallenged entitlement to the actuality of remaining right-side up.

The division of social formations into high and low as well as inside and outside occupies much of the effort expended by cultural production, but at the same time, the category of the social does not contain all the work that culture does. In the concluding essay, Chapter 9, "Cultural Representations," subtitled "Hairstory," Crystal B. Lake touches on a number of the philosophical issues raised by the other contributors, especially the material properties of hair as a substance and the effects of those properties on the way in which it is perceived, investigated, valued, and preserved. Beginning with a rhetorical question from David Hume's *Dialogues Concerning Natural Religion* (1779), in which one of the speakers in the dialogue asks if anything can be learned about the generation of a man from observing the growth of a hair, Lake argues for the central place of hair in Enlightenment cultural representations, especially philosophical ones. Hair commends itself to philosophers because of its liminal position as a "biocultural" phenomenon, "poised between the human and the animal, the exterior and interior of the body, the living and the dead." To be liminal is to hover on a threshold, teetering "betwixt and between" two fundamentally different states of being. For Lake, the liminal position of hair is precisely the quality that inspired the generation of what she calls "hairstories"—histories and natural histories that turn on the most persistent of all philosophical issues, the relationship of spirit and matter. Lake's analysis helps to explain the special attention devoted to hair by empirical science, and she takes a detailed look at the importance of hair in Robert Hooke's *Micrographia* (1665). She also notes its importance to the collectors of the Royal Society of Antiquaries (founded 1717). Antiquarianism encouraged the veneration of talismanic hair as a rational project. The durability of hair, its survival long after the rest of the body has decomposed, renders it efficacious to archeological investigation in a special way: less perishable than flesh, but more intimate than bones, hair from a corpse as revered as that of an English king proved intellectually as well as emotionally energizing to the antiquarian excavators of the Enlightenment and thereafter. They understood that durable hair stands on the threshold of past and present, history and memory, as well as spirit and matter.

The chapters that follow engage the cultural history of hair in the period of what may well be its greatest prominence. Although the consumers, producers, artists, scientists, and philosophers who assured its preeminence during the Enlightenment did not always dare to be wise about the subject, they rarely failed to be seriously engaged. Despite the growth of skeptical science, religion still invested spiritual power in hair, so much so that the charismatic leaders of emerging denominations styled their tonsures as pointedly as their homilies. Secular selfhood developed apace in political philosophies and artistic representations, but it rendered itself instantly and wordlessly expressible (or concealable) by coiffure. Ornament flourished on the heads of fashionable women and men to a degree heretofore unprecedented and still unrivalled, adding a brisk trade in goods and services to the great consumer revolution, including the consumption of written and graphic satires of hair-related follies. The increase in the number and professionalism of hairdressers abetted a rising awareness not only of hairstyle but also of hair health, stocking the booksellers' shelves with trade publications. Race, class, gender, and sexuality intensified their visibility as categories of identity due to the taxonomic importance attached to the quality and location of hair. Natural philosophy found in hair a material substance of unique properties, including its category-defying neutrality, which recommended it to general philosophical reflection and practical experimentation. Last but not least, even as natural philosophers elevated hair into a metaphor for the complexity of the cosmos, instrumentalist entrepreneurs enlarged technologies of turning animal fibers into textiles to proto-industrial scale, raising an artisanal trade into a transoceanic monopoly. When mighty contests ensue, no cause is trivial (*pace* Pope), and the contributors to this volume endeavor to show why hair is no exception.

CHAPTER ONE

Religion and Ritualized Belief: Evangelical Hair

MISTY G. ANDERSON

Long before Tammy Faye Bakker's teased up bob, Jan Crouch's gravity-defying mane, or the self-proclaiming toupée of Ernest Angley, evangelical hair was a thing. It's fair to say that hair's religious and political journey through the Reformation and into the modern world began when Martin Luther let his hair down in 1521; after burning Pope Leo's papal bull, denouncing indulgences and private mass, and writing *The Judgment of Martin Luther on Monastic Vows*, Luther grew out his Augustinian tonsure. While Luther's hair may not have been especially fabulous, it was a sure and visible sign of the Reformation and the cultural fact that Christian hair would, for some time to come, signify religious identification across a Protestant to Roman Catholic spectrum of meanings, with the tonsure at one pole and an infinite variety of delight and disorder at the other.

The particular "thing-ness" of hair itself as of the body but not in it provided an arena for doctrinal debates about sensation, pleasure, and worldliness. What did it mean, for instance, to be in this world but not of it? How should Christians read Paul's confusing declaration in 1 Corinthians 11:6 that a woman should have her head covered in church or cut it all off, even though that would be both a shame and shameful? Stranger yet, how should they read his pronouncement a few lines later that the hair itself is a woman's glory and her covering? In the Bible, hair is the source of Samson's strength, the towel with which a weeping woman dries her tears from the feet of Jesus, and the means to police women. Hair occupies a liminal space in the Christian religious imagination, residing somewhere between the human and the superhuman; it is both perfectly natural and hopelessly excessive. Men's hair, which occupies the most attention in religious debates and conflicts about hair in the long eighteenth century, sits on the sensual paradox of Christianity, torn as it is between incarnation and asceticism.

The larger debates about pleasure, happiness, and choice that frame the significance of hair from a Christian point of view heat up with the Reformation, which makes matters of individual conscience the new standard for religious identity. The rhetoric of conscience grounds the subject known as the modern individual, whose freedom of choice and capacity for conscious choice is celebrated and defended by theories of liberalism.[1] The discourse of freedom can, however, be reduced to consumer and fashion choices. The "unavailability of personal style" that Jameson argues is the key feature of postmodernity's mediated pastiche harkens back to and runs through the limited protest that hair has provided.[2] As Srinivas Aravamudan avows in "Subjects/Sovereigns/Rogues," texts have many ages; so do hairstyles, and the hermeneutic if not defiantly nonlinear temporality of

Christian experience makes the recursiveness of hair lengths and styles a kind of second coming. What I am calling "evangelical hair" draws on both the Greek *euangelion*, "good news," and Luther's Latinization, *evangelium*, the churches appearing after the Protestant Reformation. This dual formation of the evangelical as both the proclamation of good news (always already yet to come) and the sign of difference or rupture captures the semantic volatility of hairstyles. Understanding the discursive as well as recursive significance of hair, as both *langue* and *parole*, in the uncomfortably but necessarily shared modern territories of religion and politics, helps us see how eighteenth-century evangelical hair functioned as both a signifier in formation, growing, and changing, and a sign of the primitive or backward-looking believer who makes the enlightened modern possible. The believer's hair, whether Puritan, Leveller, or Methodist, differentiated the faithful from a consuming modernity. At the same time, the big, wide, and rapidly changing world of eighteenth-century fashion mediated the sociable, messianic call of consumer capitalism, in which sporting the next great look, style, or "do" could mean that you might have "it," that "pronoun aspiring to the condition of a noun […] the easily perceived but hard-to-define quality possessed by abnormally interesting people."³ Taking religion and hair this seriously might help us trace the braid of sensuous, ascetic, and religious meaning that began with the tonsure, worked through the Roundheads, then the Methodists, and eventually, gave us televangelist hair. Rhetorics of personal affect, freedom, and autonomy from papal control that defined Protestant, post-Reformation hair quickly made clear that one's hairstyle, especially for men, was subject to more than occasional conformity. As Puritan and later Methodist protests became hairstyles, the look that was supposed to be the sign of the most deeply held commitments proved to be yet another imitable style.

PURITAN HAIR

The Restoration only exaggerated what had been true since James (VI of Scotland and I of England) began sporting his natural locks: the court was home to both luxury and luxurious hair. The courtly locks of the Stuarts before and after the English civil wars suggested an erotic excessiveness that sparked Puritan protests, including low-church bowl cuts for men and modest caps for women. The stakes of these Puritan and courtly styles were so high that even talking about someone's hair in the seventeenth century was potentially actionable. The widely invoked insult "roundhead," a reference to the close-cropped hair of Parliamentarians who fought against Charles I, was a punishable offense in Cromwell's New Model Army.⁴ Roundheads were most often Puritans of various denominational stripes, often Presbyterians with a few of the more radical factions such as the Levellers and the Diggers. But the significance of hair was neither straightforward nor merely a matter of style. We know that some covenanters (Scottish Presbyterians) like the Rev. Alexander Peden wore wigs that would have looked like a full head of natural hair. At least one survives at the National Museum of Antiquities of Scotland, Edinburgh, showing extreme wear in the spots where Rev. Peden's hat was pulled on and off.⁵

The short version of seventeenth-century British hair is that short hair (on men) meant Puritan allegiance, until Laud stole the style. The classically Puritan case against long hair came from Puritan divines and doctrinaire stylists like Thomas Hall, who denounced men's hair "when it is so long that the godly are thereby grieved, the weak offended and the wicked hardened."⁶ The full title of Hall's treatise is worth reproducing in all its glory: *The Loathsomnesse of Long Haire: or, a Treatise Wherein you have the Question stated, many Arguments against it produc'd, and the most materiall Arguments for it retell'd and answer'd, with the concurrent judgement of Divines both old and new against it.*

With an Appendix against Painting, Spots, Naked Breasts, &c. As a preface, Hall included the cautionary verse, "To the Long-hair'd Gallants of these Times," attributed to "R.B." (probably Robert Bolton), which urges:

> Go Gallants to the Barbers, go,
> Bid them your hairy Bushes mow.
> God in a Bush did once appear,
> But there is nothing of him here.
> Here's that he deeply hates: beside,
> That execrable sin of Pride;
> Here also is that Felony:
> Nay, Is not here Idolotry?
> Such Bushes daily intervert
> The time that's done to th'better part:
> [...]
> Those pour sweet powders rather strow
> Upon the ground on which you goe,
> Than let them be so vainly spent
> Upon an haughty Excrement.
> Forget not that your selves are dust,
> And the Times tell your Heads they must
> Their powders into Ashes turne,
> And teach their Wantonnesse to Mourne.

This cautionary verse and call to humility compares the lavish and unholy "bushes" of Cavaliers to the burning bush through which God spoke to Moses. His connection between hair and "excrement" refers both to the idea that hair is a form of excrement and to the use of excrement as a popular cure for baldness in the seventeenth century. For these and other reasons, Hall would probably have disagreed with that truism from the American South, "the higher the hair, the closer to God."

The psychological boundary that hair represents, in both its vitality and its morbidity, breaks open in Hall's footnote about a click-bait-worthy new Polish hairstyle, "Enough to make all Lands afraid, / And your long dangles stand on end?" A tightly packed "L" of marginalia, in the manner of the Geneva Bible, *The Pilgrim's Progress*, and many other Puritan texts, glosses the tale:

> most loathsome and horrible disease in the haire, unheard of in former times; bred by modern luxury & excess. It seizeth specially upon women; and by reason of a viscous venomous humour, glues together (as it were) the haire of the head with a prodigious ugly implication and intanglement; sometimes taking the forme of a great snake, sometimes of many little serpents: full of nastiness, vermin, and noisome smell: And that which is most to be admired, and never eye saw before, pricked with a needle, they yield bloody drops. And at the first spreading of this dreadfull disease in *Poland*, all that cut off this horrible and snaky haire, lost their eyes, or the humour falling downe upon other parts of the body; turned them extremely. (n.p.)

Hall attributes the story of the Polish stigmatic snake-dos to puritan Robert Bolton's *Hercules Saxonia*; it also appears in *Mr. Boltons last and learned worke of the foure last things: death, judgement, hell, and heaven* (London, 1633). The story is a compact blend of a Medusa tale, manufactured stigmata, and anxiety about excessive, serpentine coifs and the hair products that held them up. The phallic headdresses of these Polish women did not need to await Freud for analysis; the powerful effects, including blindness and mysterious bodily ailments, track along with the mortifying power of Medusa and the reversal of the power of the gaze that she represents. Grammatically, the hairstyle is represented as a "disease," not a choice, but the damage is done to those who cut off the hair, reeking with pomatums and blood. These Polish serpentine styles damn excess on the heads of men as well as women as messy, smelly, and on the side of death.

The most important reversal in the seventeenth-century history of hair was, however, the Roundheads themselves. Short hair as a Puritan objection to Cavalier and courtly style met with its own counterreformation just a few years after Hall's treatise when Archbishop William Laud instructed all clergy via a 1636 statute to wear their hair short. Many Puritans, especially higher ranking ones such as Sir Oliver Cromwell and Sir Thomas Fairfax, rebelled against this Church of England edict and grew their hair. Many others followed these "Roundhead" leaders and grew their natural locks, thus quickly confusing the visual economy of hair length and religiopolitical allegiance (Figures 1.1 and 1.3).

Andrew Marvell, Cromwell's protégé, poet, and eventual MP, is another case of long Parliamentarian locks. But the paradox of Roundheads with long hair is nowhere clearer than in the portraits by Samuel Cooper and Robert Walker showing Oliver Cromwell's head, richly adorned with his own long hair, an image that was also used on various medals (Figure 1.2).

The ups and downs of Puritan styles help to contextualize Milton's complex personal and aesthetic relationship to hair. The earliest image we have of Milton (Figure 1.4), as Stephen Dobranski observes, is the poet at ten years of age "with closely cropped auburn hair," which suggests "he was exposed to Parliamentarian ideas as a young man; according to Milton's widow, her late husband's schoolmaster, 'a puritan in Essex,' had 'cutt his haire short' (Aubrey 2)," in keeping with the cropped Puritan style of the early seventeenth century.[7] Portraits of the adult Milton, including the William Faithorne engraving, show him in long and presumably natural hair (Figure 1.5). Milton lived through the period of changing hair lengths for the faithful, which, by the actual Restoration, had thoroughly confused the issue, even as the term "roundhead" persisted.

More significant for the history of evangelical hair, however, are Milton's characters, particularly Adam, Eve, Lycidas, and Samson. Lycidas's "oozy locks" and hair imagery running throughout *Paradise Lost* connects, as Dobranksi has argued, pagan myth, pastoral tradition, and Christian symbolism. Milton's choice to lead with hair in the skewed blazon of Adam, then Eve, has been a source of critical controversy at this tangled intersection of meanings:

> His fair large front and eye sublime declared
> Absolute rule; and hyacinthine locks
> Round from his parted forelock manly hung
> Clustering, but not beneath his shoulders broad:
> She, as a veil, down to the slender waist
> Her unadorned golden tresses wore
> Dishevelled, but in wanton ringlets waved
> As the vine curls her tendrils, which implied
> Subjection, but required with gentle sway,
> And by her yielded, by him best received,
> Yielded with coy submission, modest pride,
> And sweet reluctant amorous delay.[8]

FIGURE 1.1: Title page to an edition of *The Farewell Sermons of the Late London Ministers* (ca. 1662–1663). © National Portrait Gallery, London.

FIGURE 1.2: Robert Walker, *Oliver Cromwell* (ca. 1649). © National Portrait Gallery, London.

Adam's long but not too long hair, while hardly the ear-revealing cut preferred by hard-core Puritans and conservative headmasters, is decisively shorter than Eve's, signifying what John Rogers has called "exceedingly fragile evidence" to support gendered hierarchy.[9] Catherine Belsey argues that Eve's hair, "at once God given and dangerous," signifies her sexuality and Milton's ambivalence about it, though Dobranski makes a strong case for the Satanic gaze that sets up the picture through the already fallen voyeurism that is the

FIGURE 1.3: William Faithorne, *Sir Thomas Fairfax* (ca. 1646). Yale Center for British Art, Yale Art Gallery Collection. Gift of Edward B. Greene.

FIGURE 1.4: Giovanni Battista Cipriani, *John Milton* (1760). Yale Center for British Art. Gift of David M. Doret in memory of William Ferguson.

FIGURE 1.5: William Faithorne, *John Milton* (1670). © National Portrait Gallery, London.

condition of seeing the prelapsarian Eden.[10] Between life and death, their hair is both vital in its eroticism and a marker of death, the *momento mori* they carry with them, prior to the tree of knowledge, in the midst of the *felix culpa*, and after the losses of age.

As wigs for men came into fashion in the Restoration, their significance unfolded against Puritan anxieties about display, pride, and luxury, which set the terms of the conversation well beyond Puritan circles. Pepys worried about his decision to shave his head and switch to the wig as a choice that might be too noticeable in church. He seems a bit disappointed that it wasn't:

> To church, where I found that my coming in a periwig did not prove so strange as I was afraid it would for I thought that all the church would presently have cast their eyes all upon me, but I found it no such thing.[11]

Pepys assumes that his church would not welcome his new periwig yet would also find it visually irresistible. Neither proves to be the case. Hair as a sign of religious devotion in the Restoration *habitus* proves to be ambiguous at best after revolutionary years of being called into the service of social connections, religious differences, and political affiliations. Enter Pepys at church, his head full with periwig and pomade, signifying nothing. The confusion or perhaps exhaustion of the meanings of hair generated by seventeenth-century Puritanism predicted some of the ways that hair would be both divine and divinely problematic for the long eighteenth century. An image of paradise, a Protestant paradox of the physical and the spiritual, a denominational signifier, a tool of political protest, and a secular fashion statement, hair was strained to the breaking point with competing meanings by the time of Charles II's restoration, which began with Charles in his natural hair and ended with the monarch in a black wig.[12] In a world with Roundheads, Quakers, royalists, old rakes, and young evangelicals, hair could mean a few things at once.

METHODIST HAIR

When the Methodist movement first emerged in Britain in the 1730s, its association with three reasonably good-looking young men, John Wesley, Charles Wesley, and George Whitefield, eroticized the movement from the start, even before they became "the people call'd the Methodists." Appearing in an age of growing mediation and mechanical reproduction, images as well as news reports and sermons of the early Methodists circulated widely and spread their sense of style. Whitefield, who was only eighteen when he rose to fame as the "boy preacher," is represented in Figure 1.6 as an object of female attention.

While the focus is on Whitefield's shapely legs, he is also the only man in the print without a hat, revealing his wavy hair, perhaps a wig but more likely at this age his natural hair, following the example of John Wesley. While still part of the Holy Club at Oxford, Whitefield earnestly reports that he began to fast twice a week, deny himself "Fruits, and the like," and "thought it unbecoming a Penitent to have his Hair powdered."[13] He was seventeen. His *A Short Account of God's Dealings with the Rev. George Whitefield*, a somewhat premature autobiography, appeared in 1740, when Whitefield was twenty-five. Satires of "the people called the Methodists" emphasized their youth and their congregants' possible confusion between spiritual worship and fandom. Even if we lay the satires aside, it is still clear that Methodism rose to national visibility led by young men with great hair.

FIGURE 1.6: George Bickham, *Enthusiasm Display'd: or, The Moor-Fields Congregation* (1739). Courtesy of The Lewis Walpole Library, Yale University.

Methodist hair, exciting as it was for many, presented a crisis of meaning in the context of hair's longer political and religious history. Were Methodists Puritans or were they not? Did their long hair suggest courtly or post-Laudian dissenting sympathies? Were they even a denomination or just very pious Anglicans? For most of the eighteenth century, just what "it" (Methodism) was, was a very unsettled matter, and their long hair only echoed that crisis of meaning. Hogarth's *Enthusiasm Delineat'd* and *Credulity, Superstition and Fanaticism* raise the possibility that Methodists are Roman Catholic through a hair visual (Figure 1.7).

Within the Methodist church, probably meant to be Whitefield's Tabernacle in London, St. Moneytrap preaches and puppeteers with so much vigor that his wig comes off, revealing a Jesuit's tonsure. The association of Methodism with Catholicism was not new. It seems to have originated in the Oxford Holy Club's interest in frequent communion and a doctrinal understanding of the Eucharist as a sacramental and mystic event, not the rational "remembrance" that Tillotson, in his 1684 *A Discourse Against Transubstantiation,* and Hoadly, in his *A Plain Account of the Nature and End of the Sacrament of the Lord's-Supper* (1735), described. The Methodist emphasis on the blood of Christ in many of their hymns furthered the connection with Catholicism and made their para-church identities seem suspicious to more conservative Anglicans. Where Wesley's natural hair came out of a matrix of post-Puritan meanings about long and short hair, the tonsure is unambiguous; the shaved head is the sign of true otherness and national threat beneath the Methodist veneer. The natural hair of the man in the foreground

FIGURE 1.7: William Hogarth, *Credulity, Superstition and Fanaticism. A Medley* (1762). Courtesy of The Lewis Walpole Library, Yale University.

stroking a young woman with a Fanny Phantom doll (in *Enthusiasm Delineat'd* it is a Christ icon) suggests that the Methodist trend for natural hair is part of a sensuality that runs through "experimental Christianity," as Wesley wished the movement to be known, where feeling, sensation, and long natural hair all end in lasciviousness.

The tonsure, which links Methodists to a range of anti-Catholic literature, including convent pornography, suggests that the simplicity and even austerity of Methodist appearance was a front, a costume, disguising a sensual, appetitive, sexual being beneath. Anstey's *New Bath Guide* features a falsely pious Methodist named Roger (a name used often in anti-Methodist satire) who persuades Prudence to have sex, which she first thinks is a dream:

> For I dream'd an Apparition
> Came, like Roger, from Above
> Saying, by Divine Commission
> I must fill you full of Love.
> Just with Roger's Head of Hair on,
> Roger's Mouth, and pious Smile;
> Sweet, methinks, as Beard of Aaron
> Dropping down with holy Oil.[14]

Roger's hair identifies him as a Methodist, even if the imagery and his hair turn carnally sensual. In the print *Dr. Rock's Political Speech* (1743), a quack pedals cures in the foreground while holding a phallic object, while Whitefield (squinting) and Wesley (with his signature natural hair) preach to the crowd in the background. The lengths and the cuts of evangelical hair generated more possibilities for signifying through hairstyle. In *Memoirs of a Woman of Pleasure*, one of Fanny's kinkier lovers, Mr. Barvile, wears his hair as "we are told the Roundheads wore in Oliver's times."[15] His bowl cut, clerical dress, and interest in flagellation mark him not just as a sexual suspect but as a religious suspect, largely through his hair. Evangelical hair, whether short or fully grown out into Methodist glory, is the open secret of their sensuality, written into the somatic intensity of "heart religion" and the role of the responsive, somatic body to the irresistible call of God and grace.

Hair length and its variability become a queer feature of Methodism's ability to remake the self, perhaps even to reimagine gender identity. "Queer" Methodists pop up in a range of anti-Methodist literature that represented the group as tricksters and sensualists engaged in secret orgiastic fellowship (it did not help that one of the conventional Methodist meetings was called the "Love Feast"). Hester Anne Roe (later Rogers) cut her hair short when she became a Methodist preacher. Her short hair mapped her identity as a preacher (a male role) while also asserting the possibility of transformation—regeneration, in the evangelical vocabulary—through personal style. As Roe wrote in her journal shortly after cutting off her hair, "I *will* lie in thy hands as passive clay."[16] The infamous Mary/George Hamilton tears her hair and beats her breasts when she is deserted by her female Methodist lover, only to transform herself into a male Methodist preacher, an identity in which her longer hair was an asset and her access to more "Methodistical sisters" simplified. Gender identity, sexuality, and religious nonconformity were tangled up in hair in these representations.

WESLEY'S HAIR

No Methodist, it seemed, had better hair than the movement's founder John Wesley. Of his own long hair he wrote: "As to my hair, I am much more sure, that what this enables me to do, is according to the Scripture, than I am that the length of it is contrary to it."[17] Benson, his early nineteenth-century editor, adds to this observation the note that "Mr. Wesley wore his hair remarkably long and flowing on his shoulders" even though his mother was concerned it harmed his health. He kept his long hair, however, because cutting it "would occasion some increase of his expenses, which he could not afford, without giving less to the poor." Wesley harkens back to Puritan principles and an ascetic rejection of primping, yet that call back to the past routes through the Roundhead style and lands on the counter-counter-reformation of the long-haired champions of the Protectorate, defying Laud and letting their hair grow.

Wesley's long hair, which he eventually trimmed back a bit, seems to have been as much about a sense of style as it was about saving money. Henry Abelove notes that Wesley kept himself neat and fastidiously clean, with special attention to his hair, which he wore long, natural, "parted in the middle, combed straight back, and curling slightly at the bottom. To some of his fellow gentlemen the hair seemed almost too arranged, too pretty. An undergraduate who saw him on the last occasion he preached at Oxford commented, for instance, on how 'very exactly' it was parted."[18] Wesley, it seems, knew how to use his hair to advantage as a visual call to public intimacy and attention. A Yorkshireman recalled the "blessed morning" he heard Wesley preach: "Soon as he got upon the stand, he stroked back his hair, and turned his face toward where I stood, and I thought fixed his eyes on me."[19] The star-struck Yorkshireman didn't record what Wesley said. Instead, he recalled seeing Wesley, locking eyes, and watching him stroke back his hair; before he heard a word, Wesley "made my heart beat like the pendulum of a clock."[20]

Walpole and others spotted a glamorousness about Wesley and his hair that they connected to the theater. Early visual satires show Wesley and other Methodist figures on crickets (small street-performer platforms) with arms waving. Theatrical, performative preaching seems to have been the satirists' main target, but again and again, natural hair, usually long, was the chief prop, the visual signal that the figure is a Methodist. When Walpole met Wesley at Bath, he noted in a letter to Chute dated October 10, 1766 that "Wesley is a clean, elderly man, fresh-coloured, his hair smoothly combed, but with a little soupcon of curl at the ends. Wondrous clever, but as evidently an actor as Garrick."[21] The association with Garrick registers the celebrity effect that Wesley now generated; he had what Joseph Roach described as "it," the magnetic, polymorphous allure that signaled "strength *and* vulnerability, innocence *and* experience, and singularity *and* typicality among them."[22] The hair was the primary signifier of Wesley's celebrity for friends and foes. Robert Southey, in his *Life of Wesley*, assures his readers that:

> no one who saw him, even casually, in his old age, can have forgotten his venerable appearance [...] When you met him in the street of a crowded city he attracted notice, not only by his band and cassock and his long hair, white and bright as silver, but by his pace and manner, both indicating that all his minutes were numbered, and that not one was to be lost.[23]

Nehemiah Curnock, a nineteenth-century editor of Wesley and historian of Methodism, recorded the recollection of a man who saw Wesley in St. Anne's parish:

> One of our friends in Buxton tells me that his grandfather distinctly remembers seeing John Wesley come out of one of the white cottages, and walk across the burial ground to the church. "dressed in a white surplice and his beautiful white hair brushed back." He looked, he said, like an angel.[24]

The figure of an angelic and venerable Wesley, regal rather than elderly, with "beautiful" white hair is an image of natural glamour. The report suggests the visual terms in which Wesley's style managed the "inward" and the "outward man" that was central to Methodism's "experimental" doctrine. Angelic, even bridal, his curated image is meant to be readable as a signifier of his inward state. The authenticity of "natural hair" anchors this economy of inward and outward as an "inward truth" on outward display.

The carefully curated and coiffed presentation that Wesley maintained and encouraged his followers to emulate produced a Methodist style as a matter of doctrinal identity. The tome *Minutes of several conversations between the Rev. John Wesley, A.M. and the preachers in connection with him. Containing the form of discipline established among the preachers and people in the Methodist societies* (London, 1779) became the basis of what was known as the *Methodist Discipline,* and included Wesley's pronouncement that "A Preacher ought not to wear powder in his hair, or artificial curls."[25] Like the young Whitefield, he took a stand against excess that, while not precisely Puritan, sympathized with their critique of luxury if not length. The otherwise politically conservative Wesley reflected on the excesses of King George II, by then in his seventies, for wearing "A huge heap of borrowed hair, with a few plate of gold and glittering stones upon his head! Alas, what a bauble is human greatness!"[26] Hair in this narrative reclaims its "natural" status, distinct from wigs and powders, which signify decay and death.

Wesley's initial arguments against luxury (including haircuts) led later Methodists to single out hair powder in the April 1796 issue of *The Arminian Magazine,* the primary Methodist periodical, through the lens of the bread shortages. The article argues that the unsavory advent of hair powder as a fashion (via ballad singers and prostitutes) led many into temptation without thinking about the consequences:

> but the present scarcity of BREAD has opened their eyes, and they are now fully convinced that the use of Hair-Powder is one great cause of this awful calamity. John Donaldson, Esq, in his Letter on the subject, to the Right Hon. William Pitt, observes, That the number of Hair-Dressers in this kingdom have been stated at 50,000, and that supposing each of them used only one pound of flour a day, on average, it amounts to 1,825,000 pounds in one year; or upwards of five millions of quarter loaves, at the usual allowance of three pounds and a half of flour for a quarter loaf.[27]

The article bemoans the likely total of flour and starch expended on hairdressing, which it estimates as enough to make over thirty million loaves of bread once one counts at-home use. After the bread riots in France and the wartime British shortages and scares, worrying about hair powder and bread took on some heft in the 1790s. Daniel O'Quinn reads in the philanthropic Mr. Harmony's tag line "provisions are so scarce" in Inchbald's *Everyone Has His Fault,* which opened in January of 1793, the trace of that concern, including the spectre of unrest among the poor, on the eve of war with France.[28] *The Arminian Magazine* takes the general problem of potential bread shortages and reads it back into religious objection grounded in social justice: "2,290,000 Pounds, British money, thrown away within the last twelve months, to the great loss of the Poor [...] may be considered as one of the chief reasons of the present high price of BREAD!"[29] Any Methodist (or citizen) concerned about national security and hunger had no business with powdered hair.

Wesley's interest in hair went beyond the personal and the doctrinal. He put forward several theories of hair in his work, particularly in *An Extract from A Survey of the Wisdom of God in Creation,* in which he explains that hair is hollow, that fear can turn it white overnight, and that though they appear to be round, some hairs are square or triangular. Wesley also specialized in stories of miracle hair growth, either on corpses or on elderly people who experienced some kind of healing. In the November 1791 issue of *The Arminian Magazine*, a Mr. Adam Clarke gives an account of Margaret Horne, a woman in her seventies, who underwent electric shock treatment (another of Wesley's interests), which made her hair grow ten inches a night. Six people attested to this "token of God's mercy" with their signatures.

Though Methodist ministers often referenced Jesus's words of comfort in Luke and Matthew that God has numbered the hairs of the believer's head and will not allow them to be harmed, anti-Methodist mobs and rioters went for the hair. John Cennick, in his *An Account of a Late Riot at Exeter* (1745) describes in detail and with multiple examples a mob attacking a group of Methodists by grabbing their hair, defiling the wigs of those who wore them, latching on to the natural hair of the others, and throwing them into open sewers (gutters), "where they roll'd them without Regard to Age or Sex, pulling their Hair, robbing them of their Wigs, and Hats, cruelly beating them beside, till some were almost kill'd and stifled."[30] Curnock's edition of Wesley's *Journals* reports that a mob, mistaking a group of Methodists for Dissenters (which, technically, they were not, yet), latched on to hair as a way to drag them through ditches and kennels: "Some of them they trampoled in the mire and dragged by the hair, particularly Mr. Mackford, who came with me from Newcastle."[31] But even in these violent situations, Wesley's hair at least seemed to exert its own powerful and protective halo. During a riot that erupted in Darlaston, Wesley was dragged "by the hair" into the middle of a mob as he attempted to seek shelter in a house. Wesley recalls the event as a version of the crucifixion, with the crowd calling out "knock his brains out; down with him, kill him at once" and then "Bring him away! Bring him away!" in an overt echo of "Crucify him! Crucify him!"[32] A shopkeeper, playing the part of Pilate, washes his hands of responsibility. As the mob grew bolder, they tried to grab onto his waistcoat, collar, and other articles of clothing, but he evaded them. Wesley numbers the most remarkable of the experiences in his entry for October 20, 1743:

> 3. That a lusty man just behind struck at me several times with a large oaken stick; with which, if he had struck me once on the back part of my head, it would have saved him all farther trouble. But every time the blow was turned aside, I know not how; for I could not move to the right hand or left. 4. That another came rushing through the press, and raising his arm to strike, on a sudden let it drop, and only stroked my head, saying "What soft hair he has!"[33]

Wesley's amazing, soft hair saves his life in this round, turning the aggressive blow of an attacker into star-struck hair petting. The serendipity of being in front of the mayor's house as the violence reached its peak (Wesley's next point) may have also had something to do with his deliverance.

As great hair became a visible and reproducible Methodist style, it also raised the question of how Wesley's helpers were to signify their identity without too obviously copying their leader. As Henry Abelove notes, helpers could be conspicuous for imitating Wesley's natural do or for failing to do so:

> Natural hair was unusual; it was a style very hard to make attractive, and anyway it had been virtually preempted by Wesley. One helper, whose hair was short and curly, very unlike Wesley's, wore it naturally and drew a hostile reaction from a Bristol man, who had come to hear the preaching. "A thick head of curled hair," the Bristol man said, disgusted, "resembling a mop." Another helper (a clerical sympathizer, really) whose hair was rather like Wesley's, wore it naturally and got charged with seeming "to ape Mr. John in the mode of wearing his hair."[34]

Many would-be Wesley coifs only managed to seem bedraggled. "The Methodist. A Poem, by ___ Author of the Powers of the Pen, and The Curate" reports on a preacher in Moorfields, a Wesleyan helper newly recruited by Satan:

> *Lean* is the *Saint,* and *lank,* to shew
> That *Flesh and Blood to Heav'n can't go;*
> His Hair like *Candles* hangs, a sign
> How bright his *inward Candles* shine.[35]

The parodic clumps of long hair trope Methodist "inward light" as greasy candles and mock the process of the relation between the inward and the outward man, which Methodists used to talk about cultivating spiritual devotion. Again, hair is the visible sign of the Methodist, but here it is reduced to a failed imitation of Wesley by a young and probably blond preacher. *The Elected Cobler* (Figure 1.8), one in a series called *Darly's Comic Prints* (1771), shows a working man who has felt the evangelical call and has experienced "election," a kind of spontaneous call to preach as well as the Calvinist notion of salvation being only available to the few "elect" of God, blurring the line between the Calvinist-Whitefieldian-Methodist connection and the more Lutheran Wesleyan Methodism's emphasis on grace. The theological distinctions, however, get lost in the stringy hair.

The cobbler's ill-fitting jacket and inelegant, blocky shoes are unfashionable, while the hair framing the open mouth gives the figure his garish appearance. Again, as in many other prints, the evangelical preacher is on a cricket, the street performer's tool, which blurs the distinction between religious devotion and theatrical performance. That blurred boundary explains why George Stevens ended his *Lecture on Heads* with a Methodist preacher. The popular theatrical entertainment featured papier-mâché heads with various wigs on them and comic impersonations of different types, performed in synch with some limited puppetry. Earlier figures include Sir Languish Lispy, whose wig is so large that he is classed as "the Doubtful Gender," and a Quaker, represented by his "two hats contrasted, and two heads contrasted," hair invisible thanks to a large "umbrella like covering, to keep off the outer light, to strengthen the light within." The final sketch is a mash-up of Whitefield and Wesley, with both Whitefield's wall-eye, about which satirists were consistently cruel, and Wesley's hair. The preacher is identified as "one of the righteous over much" who,

> with one eye [...] looks up to Heaven to make his congregation think he is devout, that's his spiritual eye, and with the other eye he looks down to see what he can get; and that's his carnal eye; and thus, with locks flowing down his face, he says, or seems to say, or at least, with your permission we'll attempt to say for him—Bretheren! Bretheren! Bretheren![36]

The long, flowing locks, coupled with the call to the audience, signified Methodism satirically reduced to bad Whitefield jokes and Wesley's fetishized hair.

THE TEMPORALITY OF EVANGELICAL HAIR

Geoffrey Wildgoose, the main character in *The Spiritual Quixote*, by Richard Graves (1773), is a case study in the temporal confusion involved in Methodist hair, especially as the movement grew in the 1760s and 1770s. Wildgoose experiences Methodism as a style and seeks to embody it, beginning with his hair and the "plain blue coat" that was

FIGURE 1.8: *The Elected Cobler* (1772). Courtesy of The Lewis Walpole Library, Yale University.

the preferred uniform of Wesley's helpers. But Graves figures Wildgoose's reproduction of Methodist style as a recourse to the past, in which distinctions between movements and moments threaten to collapse. Wildgoose first discovered Methodism after resenting a slight from the local parson and plunging himself into more Puritan readings in a fit of pique:

> Thus Mr. Wildgoose, in imitation of our primitive reformers, and those other worthies in the frontispieces of those books of the last century with which he had been lately conversant, who wore their own hair according to the fashion of the times; that he might resemble those venerable men, even in his external appearance, Mr. Wildgoose, I say, since his retreat from the world had suffered his own hair to grow for some months. Though, perhaps, there might also be something of convenience in this at first, to avoid the impertinence of his officious barber, who, whilst he was working the lather into his stubbed hair, would take upon him to insinuate some sociable advice to his patient, which was more irksome to Mr. Wildgoose in his present gloomy situation, even than the rough instruments and heavy hand of this rustical operator. This alone, therefore, would have been a sufficient reason for his omitting to be shaved, and nourishing his own hair, which, though it was now thick enough to keep him warm, yet as it did not extend below his ears, he made but an uncouth appearance to those who had been used to see him in a decent periwig.[37]

Wildgoose's textual self-fashioning depends on visual cues from the frontispieces of the Puritan books he is reading (Cromwell, Bunyan, Milton, and perhaps Marvell). These are the Roundheads turned long-hairs. But Wildgoose's first motivation is escaping a nosey barber who gives unsolicited advice about his recent fight with the curate. The fight, in which Wildgoose snubs the curate, is fueled by Wildgoose's guilty fear that the parson knows of his sexual liaison with his mother's maid. Though Wildgoose is "convicted" by the sermon, guilt, not a warmed heart, launches his quixotism. At the beginning, he is temporarily caught between the forces of national and personal history, neither Roundhead nor *au courant* Methodist until his hair grows a few more inches. Graves uses Wildgoose's liminal mane to point out the affectation involved in his experience of Methodism. Graves sees the movement as quixotic and, as such, with a "mimetic disposition of mind [...] a desire of imitating any great personage, whom we read of in history, in their dress, their manner of life."[38]

Graves situates Wildgoose's choice to imitate Wesley as quixotic eccentricity, comparing him to a man who adored ancient heroes and wore a helmet instead of a nightcap "till one night it unfortunately fell off his head, and demolished his chamber-pot."[39] Methodist fashion (especially hair) points up the alienability of history as a style and its inevitable slide into fictions about history. Cause and effect are alienated as signs begin to circulate independent of their histories and contexts. When Wildgoose visits the Bell Inn, the storied birthplace of George Whitefield, he is rejected by Whitefield's own mother, who complains, "Squire Fielding, forsooth, in that romancing book of his, pretends that Tom Jones was harboured here, we shall be pestered with all the trampers that pass the road." What began as Fielding's joke on Methodist origins (Whitefield made a point to compare himself to Jesus, who was also "born in an Inn") gets a second hearing as fiction and fact change places. After more verbal abuse from Whitefield's mother, Wildgoose and Tugwell (his Sancho Panza) are taken in by an honest barber, "whose less affluent circumstances inspired more gentle manners, and made him civil to the meanest customer."[40] It is poetic justice that a barber houses them and allows them to hold their

Methodist meetings in his dining room, showing more Christian charity and kindness than Mrs. Whitefield, even though he has little to gain from cutting Wildgoose's hair. The barber eventually offers to make Wildgoose a fine, flowing, white wig "as he had done for Mr. Whitfield," which Wildgoose rejects but which, in the Shandean flow of the novel, leads to Wildgoose's "A Dissertation On Periwigs," which moves from the Stuarts, who first use wigs at masques and then adopt them as courtly fashion, to the general public's adoption of the wig, to the absurdity and volume of modern periwigs. Wildgoose brings the point back to a defense of his own hair, to which Mrs. Sarsnet and Miss Townsend had objected as ungenteel:

> as the chief intent, of hair, considered as ornamental, seems to be to give a softness to the features, by rising in an easy manner from the forehead, and falling loosely down upon the parts which it was designated to cover, I own I had rather see the worst head of natural hair, than the most accurate wig that ever adorned a barber's block.[41]

Wildgoose's defense of natural hair implies that his own is or is on its way to being Miltonian, "falling loosely down" upon whatever needs covering. But Graves comically interpolates Eve into the gender trouble of Milton's defense of hair as both pure and ornamental. This gender-bending hair both rises, as from Adam's forelock, and falls well below Adam's, which stops at "his shoulders broad" to cover the parts that need covering, like Eve's veil. Once again, hair for Wildgoose is interstitial, a mixed sign of both his confusion of motives and the religious ambiguity of hair, long or short, in the eighteenth century.

Wildgoose's chief reasons for his preference (and his hope that wigs should be "banished from the genteel part of mankind") in this dissertation is not luxury per se but that wigs lead to moral decay. He alludes to Miss Townsend's experience with her would-be attacker, an old debauchee, who "puts on a fine flowing Adonis or white periwig […] commences beau again," and, when he cannot convince a "modest woman," turns to a "mercenary wretch," spends his money, and falls into ruin. In his retelling, it is the age confusion generated by wigs and the way they enable old rakes in their adventures that is the problem, a reading of their function as phallic supplement that surprises his listeners. After his "sermon on periwigs," Miss Townsend exclaims that she "never apprehended there was so much sin, though there might be a great deal of folly, under the wig of a beau: but you will persuade one to believe that, in a literal sense, the hairs of our head are all *numbered*, and that it is unlawful either to increase or diminish them on any account."[42] Wildgoose, confident that he has now converted his listeners and quietly pleased at Miss Townsend's attentions, prepares to leave for Bristol, but not without having raised the question of Methodism's content for Graves' readers. What exactly *is* Methodism, beyond the association of a few verbal constructions, plain blue coats, and long hair? Graves answers this question as gently as he asks it by bringing Wildgoose back into parish life, where the styles of Methodism, sartorial and verbal, give way to the care of the parish. That stewardship takes as its model an agrarian, class-based social order, a conservatism not lost on the reader who has seen the varieties of community and the revolutionary possibilities in their collected energy, which is the real threat that Methodist hair represents. Long hair and catchphrases are easy to isolate and mock, but substantial cross-class activism is not. Methodism carried that threat with it as the largest new denomination in Britain, ever with the memory of the rise of the Puritans and the political possibility Methodism could turn revolutionary. By the 1770s, it was becoming clear enough that it wouldn't, but with the working-class constituency and the Jacobins just over the horizon, how could one be sure? Marat, Napoleon, Coleridge, and the young Wordsworth with their natural hair and enthusiasm (political and poetic) suggest the plausibility of the "radical Methodist" image, in spite of Wesley's relative conservatism and royalism.

The Mischief of Methodism (1811) sets up a similarly gentle representation of Methodist identity and difference in troubled times, parodying both Methodist style and its Anglican counterpart. The similarities strike the imagination as fast as the differences do in the print shown in Figure 1.9. Both men are in clerical black, both share the same table, have the same hats hung on the wall, smoke their pipes, and drink from identical glasses. The differences come down primarily to hair and body size. The young Methodist, bright-eyed, lean, and with long, stringy hair, enthuses "When I preach at my Chapel you would be astonished to see how full it is. Why do you know the Tradesmen forsake their shops, Lawyers their Clients, and Physicians their sick." His John Bullish fellow clergyman, carbuncled, ample, and bewigged, replies "That's bad! That's bad! I manage things better in my Parish. When I Preach every man minds his own business." The joke here, despite the title, is on the Anglican's disengagement, with the Methodist serving as straight man. The wig, by 1811, also looks dated, even if the Methodist's hair fails to achieve fabulousness. History, moving on, is on the side of the Methodists. The Methodist discourse of "experimental religion," inward light, and longer natural hair is closer to the emerging zeitgeist of modernity, to Romantic constructions of genius, selfhood, spirituality, and experience, and to the direction men's hairstyles were headed. While Byron would not likely welcome the association, Romantic poets and Methodists

FIGURE 1.9: *The Mischief of Methodism* (1811). Courtesy of The Lewis Walpole Library, Yale University.

alike sought to signify, through their hair, a project of experimental engagement with stimuli that foregrounded individual affective response and the cultivation of an inward self; Methodists framed this process in terms of the conversion experience and further growth toward Christian perfection, while Romantics deified creative genius, discovered through aesthetic response and contemplation.

Evangelical hair, construed broadly through the Restoration and the eighteenth century, expressed the devout (male) subject's difference from modernity and separation from its worldliness through what is arguably the most ambiguous signifier of the body. Most of the biblical references available to guide the style choices of the faithful were ambiguous rather than fabulous. One notable exception, Revelation 1:14, presents an image so spectacular that imitation would be blasphemy. John Wesley may have approached it, but we only glimpse this through the descriptions of his followers; to cultivate the look deliberately would be to erase the difference between the creator and the creature. It is a post-apocalyptic Christ, the first human figure in John of Patmos's vision, who emerges from the golden candlesticks as "one like the Son of man." This slight ambiguity, "one like," holds the viewer at a distance, reading both the divinity of the vision and John's difference from it: "His head and *his* hairs *were* white like wool, as white as snow; and his eyes *were* as a flame of fire [emphasis added]." Wool, snow, and fire: simile is all in this moment of unveiling. It marks the difference between truly divine hair and the limits of human apprehension, even prior to imitation. Hair as both nature and artifice, as both truth and fashion, embodied the anxiety of evangelicalism itself in its appeal to "primitive" Christianity and to its founding narratives that might reveal lost ways of being in the world. That visionary, dreamlike hair, doomed to remain on the cusp of a collective imagination and realized only in postlapsarian imperfection, was, nonetheless, shaped by and gave shape to the modern semiotics of hair.

CHAPTER TWO

Self and Society: Women Wearing Wigs

(A Short History of a Long Eighteenth-Century Problem)

JULIA H. FAWCETT

The Age of Enlightenment witnessed a dramatic renegotiation of the relationship between self and society. Political theorists like Thomas Hobbes, John Locke, and (later) Jean-Jacques Rousseau debated what the individual self owed to his or her society, and whether that society corrupted or improved that self. Economists like Adam Smith and Bernard Mandeville argued about whether individuals acting in their own self-interest benefited their society. And writers as well as their critics weighed the traditional preference for poetry that marked its membership in a particular literary society through its adherence to an already-established form against an emerging push for poetry as the original expression of an individual self.[1] But in popular parlance many of these debates between self and society converged in conversations about a subject that seemed—in comparison to politics, economics, and literature—decidedly less heady: hair.

In her award-winning essay on eighteenth-century men's wigs as both costume pieces and cultural signifiers, Lynn Festa explores the hairpiece as an essential part of the uniform required for admission into the public sphere. Festa draws on Jürgen Habermas's description of an increasing separation of private life from public discourse in the late seventeenth and early eighteenth centuries, and on C.B. Macpherson's suggestion that men demonstrated their fitness for public discourse (and their freedom from private biases) by purchasing and possessing—but never becoming too attached to or controlled by—the consumer products that surrounded them. At first glance, Festa argues, the wig seems a perfect symbol of the possessive individual, one who consumes rather than being consumed by the souvenirs of his society. Because it protected men from head lice and concealed the symptoms of syphilis (which often resulted in hair loss), the wig signaled a man's unwillingness to allow his body to infect or be infected by his neighbors' bodies and, metaphorically, his unwillingness to allow his private interests to infect his

---

I would like to thank Sarah Elliott Novacich for her help and advice with this chapter.

FIGURE 2.1: William Hogarth, *An Election Entertainment*, Plate 1 (1755). Courtesy of The Lewis Walpole Library, Yale University.

public discourse.[2] Such symbolism is evident in the wigs that English barristers wore (and still wear) in order to signal their objectivity in the courtroom; in James Boswell's embarrassment that his idol Samuel Johnson, "it must be confessed," should appear occasionally in "a little old shriveled unpowdered wig, which was too small for his head," exposing the private pate of the great public man;[3] and in the subtle critique that William Hogarth offers in *An Election Entertainment* (1753) (Figure 2.1) when he pictures his crooked politicians with wigs disturbingly askew. Yet because men's wigs were usually made from the hair of lower-class country girls (who sold it for a paltry profit), the wig soon took on a more sinister symbolism, reminding its wearer of the extent to which men's bodies necessarily depended on or were inseparable from other, less masculine bodies. The wig suggested, in Festa's words, "an intimation that we may be possessed by things as much as they are possessed by us."[4]

Festa devotes little time to the hairpieces of eighteenth-century women and what these hairpieces may have suggested about women's arguably more fraught negotiations between self and society, the public and the private spheres. The omission is understandable: unlike men, most women in the eighteenth century wore their own hair (though they often embellished it with powder, props, and elaborate plaits and piles). If men signaled their independence from personal biases and their entrance into the public sphere through the putting on of a periwig, we might interpret women's bare-headedness as barring them from participation in the public sphere—or, at the very least, ensuring that when they did participate, their "natural" bodies were always visible and their private opinions always transparent. By wearing their own hair, women reassured their onlookers that no matter how far from home their bodies wandered, their hearts (and their hairdos) were always in the right place.

Yet as feminist critiques of Habermas have made clear, the relationship between women's selves and their societies was never quite so simple—and peppered through the eighteenth-century archive are a few anxious anecdotes about women who defied their society's fashion trends and gender expectations and elected, either for a moment or throughout their lives, to wear a wig.[5] In this chapter, I will look briefly at a few of these anecdotes for what they might reveal about the negotiations between self and society among eighteenth-century English women—and about the unlikely role that the wig played in such negotiations. If the donning of a wig made a private man public, I ask, what implications did it have for a woman, whose claims to publicity were even more problematic? Or to put it another way: if the wig was a costume piece that called up questions about whether men's bodies owned or were owned, what anxieties arose when it appeared upon the body of a woman? Did it mark that body as possessive in and of itself, or as possessed by its society? How, in other words, did eighteenth-century culture deploy the wig in order to contemplate not only how men's but also how women's private bodies might (and might not) enter into the body politic?

I want to answer these questions by turning to three different kinds of artifacts—performance records, a prose pamphlet, and a poem—that describe three different kinds of women—two socially mobile celebrities, a lower-class prostitute, and an upper-class debutante—who used different kinds of wigs to tease out the relationships between their selves and their societies. Each of these narratives depicts the donning of a wig as transformative, the moment that the woman's body shifts from a purely private to an inescapably public entity. But each also betrays some ambivalence about whether this newfound publicness cheapens or rarifies that body—a body which becomes, interestingly, at once basely material and impossibly mythic, at once scatological and eschatological. By examining the descriptions of these fashion *faux pas* as preserved in the written record, we can better understand not only the significance of hair to eighteenth-century culture but also the tense negotiations between private and public, self and society, tangled up in this seemingly trivial thing.

GREAT OFFENSES: THE PRIVATE MANE ON THE PUBLIC STAGE

If one were to list the most famous follicles of eighteenth-century England, surely Lord Foppington's bouffant would make the cut (Figure 2.2). The big wig made its debut in 1696, when the actor, playwright, and (later) manager of Drury Lane Theater, Colley Cibber, wore it to play the part that would make his career: the fop Sir Novelty Fashion in Cibber's comedy, *Love's Last Shift*. It gained celebrity when Sir Novelty reappeared as the newly crowned Lord Foppington in John Vanbrugh's sequel, *The Relapse*, in which it enjoyed a grand entrance on its own sedan chair. The wig stayed in the spotlight throughout Cibber's long career on the stage, in which it often accompanied him not only in plays but also in his perambulations about town and even in a few of his portraits. And it had its reprise on the head of Colley Cibber's four-year-old daughter Charlotte Charke (née Cibber), who—as she relates in her 1755 autobiography—purloined the periwig from its perch early one morning and paraded it across the town.

FIGURE 2.2: John Simon after Giuseppe Grisoni, *Mr. Cibber* (ca. 1742). © National Portrait Gallery, London.

The image of Charke's diminutive body struggling beneath the weight of her father's great white wig (Figure 2.3) seems in one sense an apt metaphor for eighteenth-century women as individual possessions struggling for the status of possessive individuals. Indeed, before we can ask of women the question that Festa asks of men—did they possess or were they possessed by the accoutrements that adorned their bodies?—we must first ask

FIGURE 2.3: Frances Garden, *An Exact Representation of Mrs. Charke Walking in the Ditch at Four Years of Age* (1755). © The Trustees of the British Museum.

whether women in eighteenth-century England could be said to possess their bodies at all. The answer is somewhat complicated. English laws of coverture stipulated that any property inherited by women under eighteen belonged to their fathers or male guardians, and any property inherited by married women belonged to their husbands.[6] This included the property of their bodies: English law had long categorized rape as a property crime rather than a sexual crime, its victim the husband or father whose property in the woman's body had been compromised in the assault.⁷ As Tim Stretton has pointed out, however, individual case law often upheld the rights of women to sue for property rights in civil court.⁸ And from the mid-fifteenth century both theorists and practitioners of the law had begun to question rape's categorization, their discussions culminating in the legal scholar Sir Matthew Hale's declaration (composed at the end of the seventeenth century, though not published until the beginning of the eighteenth) that rape was a sexual crime and that women (at least those of "good fame") possessed their own bodies.⁹ Despite Hale's treatise, however, men could not be prosecuted for raping their wives, and the burden of a woman who reported a rape to prove her "good fame" meant that few men were accused and fewer convicted.

These debates over whether or not a woman could possess a self or the property that that self acquired found their flashpoint on the English stage, where Charke followed in her father's footsteps. For one thing, Restoration and eighteenth-century audiences seemed to demand and delight in battles of the sexes in which the male and female protagonists competed for the upper hand (picture the famous proviso scene from William Congreve's *Way of the World*, 1700).¹⁰ For another, since Charles II had dismissed the law banning women from the public stage in 1660, actresses and female celebrities could earn good money by displaying and comporting their bodies on the public stage. Many commentators regarded the actresses as little more than prostitutes, their bodies the public property of those spectators who had purchased, with their tickets to the performance, the prerogative to gaze upon or grope at the bodies of the performers.¹¹ And yet, as Felicity Nussbaum has written, these members of women's second oldest profession often earned more than many men in English society and so demanded (and often achieved) the right to self-possession.¹² We might regard England's first actresses not as prostitutes but rather as the princesses and priestesses of a secular age. The same fame and self-display that sexualized also spiritualized them, debasing them as prostitutes in one breath and proclaiming them celebrity idols in the next.

It is perhaps not surprising, then, that we should discover two of the most famous eighteenth-century scenes of women wearing wigs in the autobiographies of famous eighteenth-century actresses: Charke's *Narrative of the Life of Charlotte Charke* and *An Apology for the Life of George Anne Bellamy* (1785), written by a friend of Cibber's granddaughter most celebrated for her roles as a sentimental tragedienne.¹³ I will turn to Bellamy's performance momentarily, but for now I want to ask why commentators both in the eighteenth century and today have so often regarded Cibber's wig-donning as a public declaration while describing Charke's as a private confession.

For the contrast, certainly, is striking. When it appears in Cibber's autobiography, *An Apology for the Life of Colley Cibber* (1740), the big wig is inside and backstage, a personal trademark with which Cibber negotiates a possibly homosexual or possibly homosocial relationship with a wealthy spectator, Colonel Henry Brett. Brett claims he wants to borrow the wig to help him win a wife, and yet Cibber's language hints at more private desires:

> And though, possibly, the Charms of our Theatrical Nymphs might have had their Share, in drawing him [backstage]; yet in my Observation, the most visible Cause of his first coming, was a more sincere Passion he had conceiv'd for a fair full-bottom'd Perriwig, which I then wore in my first Play … In a word, he made his attack on this Perriwig, as your young Fellows generally do upon a Lady of Pleasure; first, by a few, familiar Praises of her Person, and then, a civil Enquiry, into the Price of it.¹⁴

Cibber's comparison of the wig to a woman is telling, for it seems to portray women not as possessors of but, rather, as analogues to the wigs traded between men. Even more telling is the contrast between Cibber's own suggestion of the scene as a private moment (occurring backstage, inspiring "sincere Passion," hinting at sex and "Pleasure") and his readers' interpretation of it as a public declaration. In a parody of the *Apology* published in 1740, an anonymous critic chastises Cibber for his sycophancy ("Fye, *Colly*, Fye; have some small Regard to Decency; you cou'd go no higher than this if your *Patron* were of the *Feminine Gender*") only to complain that Cibber reveals very little of himself: "Colley Cibber," he writes, "is not the Character he pretends to be in this Book, but a mere *Charletan*, a *Persona Dramatis*, a *Mountebank*, a Counterfeit *Colley*."[15] In his comprehensive 2004 study *The Gendering of Men*, the literary historian Thomas A. King cautions us not to regard Cibber's relationship with Brett as a confession of homosexuality but suggests we read it instead as a ploy for political power—albeit one that relies on the "residual pederasty" of a patronage system that, by 1740, had become obsolete.[16] No matter how much "sincer[ity]" or "Passion" Cibber puts on his periwig, his readers both then and now tend to regard his hairpiece as the prop with which he negotiates his relationship to the public.

When the wig reappears on the head of Cibber's daughter, however, scholars and readers tend to see it less as public declaration than as private confession. This reaction is surprising since, though Charke admits she shares her father's "passionate fondness for a periwig," she stages her wig scene as a public parade: it takes place outdoors, where she seems (unlike Cibber) to invite the crowd that "assemble[s]" about her; and her language marks it in many ways as her entrée into the public life of a celebrity.[17] "Having, even then, a passionate fondness for a periwig," Charke writes of her four-year-old self:

> I crawled out of bed one summer's morning at Twickenham, where my father had part of a house and gardens for the season, and taking it into my small pate that by dint of a wig and a waistcoat I should be the perfect representative of my sire, I crept softly into the servants' hall, where I had the night before espied all things in order, to perpetrate the happy design I had framed for the next morning's expedition [...] By the help of a long broom I took down a waistcoat of my brother's and an enormous bushy tie-wig of my father's, which entirely enclosed my head and body, with the knots of the ties thumping my little heels as I marched along with slow and solemn pace. [I] walked up and down the ditch bowing to all who came by me. But, behold, the oddity of my appearance soon assembled a crowd about me, which yielded me no small joy.
>
> When the family arose, till which time I had employed myself in this regular march in my ditch, I was the first thing enquired after and missed, till Mrs Heron, the mother of the late celebrated actress of that name, happily espied me, and directly called forth the whole family to be witnessed of my state and dignity.[18]

Charke here employs her father's wig as the crowning costume piece in the one-woman coming-out party by which she declares herself part of a public. While her father describes his wig as it works in the backstage spaces behind the curtain, Charke parades her wig "up and down the ditch bowing to all who came by me" and taking "no small joy" in the crowd that gathers to watch her. While Cibber uses the wig to compare himself to or declare his affinity for a "Lady of Pleasure" and the activities that occur behind closed doors, Charke explicitly calls up her public role in the "state and dignity" that the wig afforded her. And while Cibber describes his wig as giving him a small part in the domestic negotiations between a man and his future wife, Charke deploys her hairpiece to identify herself as a celebrity like her father, her brother, and the "late celebrated actress" whose mother discovers her in her ditch.

Yet no matter how much Charke's language describes her wig as the uniform of her public persona—and no matter how much scholars have interpreted her father's backstage bouffant as a political statement—her contemporaries and biographers have read Charke's hairpiece as an emblem of her private self. Perhaps the most egregious example is the editor of *The Gentleman's Magazine*, who published uncredited (and unauthorized) excerpts of Charke's *Narrative* a few months after the original appeared, changing her "I" to the more obviously gendered "she" and deploring her "Early Fondness for Mens Cloaths and low Employments."[19] But such practices continue today: by excerpting Charke's *Narrative* in her 2003 collection *The Literature of Lesbianism*, for instance, Terry Castle marks this passage as proof of Charke's sexuality.[20] By labeling her transvestitism as either an inner proclivity toward a masculine identity or a deep desire for her father's love, similarly, scholars such as Erin Mackie, Cheryl Wanko, and Felicity Nussbaum imply that we must read Charke's published *Narrative* as a private confession.[21]

These readings suggest the complex entanglements of public and private that the wig takes on whenever it tops a feminine body. Women's relegation to the private sphere infects even this symbol of the public man until it ceases to suggest the women's repudiation of her private interest and comes to symbolize her revelation of private desires instead. For William Hogarth or for James Boswell, the male wig contained the self, allowing a man to enter the public discourse of his society unencumbered by private interests. For the author of the *Laureat*, Cibber's wig acts as a costume and a cover, transforming him into a *"Persona Dramatis"* and a *"Counterfeit Colley."* But for Charke, no matter how oversized and unnatural the "enormous" wig appears on her "little" body, it will always be read as expressing and uncovering her (emotional, sexual, private) self. What these readings do, essentially, is to transform a costume piece that allowed a man to protect or disguise his personal biases into one that forces a woman to reveal them. What's more, they mark Charke's public persona as always already the possession of someone else: as a sexualized persona defined by the object (whether male or female) she chooses to love, or as a gendered persona defined by the father she tries (and fails) to "perfect[ly] represent."

Thus while the wig on the man's head acts as a public uniform—akin, for instance, to the cloak that marks one as a clergyman and signals his professional duties—spectators who see that same wig atop a woman's body interpret it as an expression of her private desires. This eagerness with which both past and present readers hang private lives on women's wigs helps to explain one of the most inexplicable anecdotes of *An Apology for the Life of George Anne Bellamy*, in which the eponymous heroine uses a wig not to enter public society but, rather, to be seen as herself. The anecdote begins when Bellamy, on her way to Holland to join one lover, is intercepted by another (the actor West Digges), who diverts her to Edinburgh, where he is employed. Edinburgh is, unfortunately, the one city Bellamy wanted to avoid, fearing that her recognizability as an actress in a city so close to London will reveal her to the creditors and jilted lovers looking for her there. So when she finds herself in Edinburgh—and set up in a boardinghouse directly across the street from the theater, no less—"I took a pair of scissors, and cut my hair off, quite close to my head, to prevent my being solicited to appear in public."[22] The disguise backfires when the London newspapers announce Bellamy's absence and her fellow boarders start to get suspicious. "The next day," Bellamy continues:

> Mr. Bates, joint proprietor of the Edinburgh theatre with Mr. Dawson, and acting manager, acquainted Mr. Digges, that it would be useless to open the doors, unless he could induce me to appear on the stage [...] Our journey had been expensive. I had but little money left, and Mr. Digges less; for the bills I had upon Holland were of no use to me here. In this situation, there was no other alternative but my conforming to Mr. Bates's wishes.[23]

The problem, of course, is that by cutting off her trademark long blond locks Bellamy has made herself unrecognizable. And so she takes a seemingly unorthodox step: she dons a wig meant not to cover but rather to enhance her personal identity. "The loss of my hair was the greatest bar to my appearance," Bellamy explains. "However, for the first time, I had recourse to false; and ... I was obliged to have clothes made at great expense."[24]

Bellamy's anecdote thus takes for granted and even uses to its advantage the double standard that Charke's makes clear: that spectators would always read a woman's hair as a natural extension of herself, even when it was admittedly "false" hair harvested from the body of someone else. At the same time, it suggests that no matter how much fame or fortune an actress claimed, she could never fully claim her own body. Instead, that body became possessed by the objects (like the wig) that not only adorned but came to define it, and by the spectators who reserved the right to read those objects and to penetrate that self (describing it unequivocally as a transgender self, as a lesbian self, as a recognizable self). Bellamy cannot travel to a new place without appearing on stage before its public, who, because they pay her for displaying her selfhood before them, leave her "no other alternative" but to "conform" to their expectations of what her body should look like, where it belongs, and how it should be. If the wig on a man's head discouraged these spectators' scrutiny, the same wig on a woman's head seemed to enhance it. And so while Cibber, Johnson, and Hogarth pay their wigmakers for a disguise that will admit them into public society, Bellamy must purchase at "great expense" the privilege of being recognized as herself.

HAIRS LESS IN SIGHT: THE MERKIN AND THE PUBIC PUBLICNESS OF THE POOR

It may, of course, be argued that these two examples of Charke and Bellamy are unhelpful because atypical: it is difficult to draw too many conclusions from the wigs that one woman borrowed from her father and that another resorted to as an antidote to a very bad hair day. But there was one type of wig that seems to have been worn primarily by eighteenth-century women rather than their male companions: the merkin, a patch of hair pasted to the pubic region to replace hairs shorn or shed. Like the man's wig, the woman's merkin began as a health precaution. Women wearied of the constant itching and scratching inflicted by lice would shave and replace their natural hair with a removable tuft. And like the wig, the merkin concealed the symptoms of syphilis—an occupational necessity for prostitutes trying to reassure potential clients of the soundness of their product.

The impropriety of discussing these hairs less in sight helps to account for the relative scarcity of merkins in eighteenth-century England's literary and cultural artifacts, as well as in the histories of those artifacts offered by modern scholars. Much of what we know about merkins comes to us from snide jokes and sideways smirks inserted into the era's more marginal texts. The *Oxford English Dictionary* traces the term *merkin* as far back as 1617, when it appeared in a bit of doggerel. By 1796, it was commonly used enough to earn a place in *Grose's Classical Dictionary of the Vulgar Tongue*.²⁵ One of the most interesting and most extensive eighteenth-century instances of the word, however, comes from a three-volume pulp piece by Alexander Smith, first published in 1714 under the lengthy title *A Compleat History of the Lives and Robberies of the Most Notorious Highway-Men, Foot-Pads, House-Breakers, Shop-Lifts, and Cheats, Of both Sexes, in and about London, and other Places of Great-Britain, for above fifty Years last past: Wherein their most secret and barbarous Murders, unparallell'd Robberies, notorious Thefts, and unheard of Cheats, are expos'd to the Publick.* Predictably, given the nature of the work, Smith's promise to "expose" the highwaymen's crimes "to the Publick" becomes, fairly quickly in the book's opening pages, a celebration of those same crimes—and an attempt to "expose" instead the foolishness of those taken in by the "Foot-Pads, House-Breakers, Shop-Lifts, and Cheats" who serve as the book's anti-heroes.

Smith opens the second volume with an anecdote about a "daring Robber" named "Dick Dudley" who, having fled to Rome to escape the wrath of his victims, donned "the Garb […] of a Pilgrim" and "Desir'd to be admitted to the Pope's Presence for his Benediction, but more truly in Hopes of getting Money out of him."²⁶ The Cardinal refuses to admit Dudley to "his Holiness" unless he brings a relic to prove his piety:

> So, taking his Leave, after rambling about the City, he heard of an old fat Hostess had been lately hang'd for poisoning one of her Guests, and that she was deliver'd to the Chyrurgeons to be anatomiz'd. This put a strange Whim in his Hand; which was, to get the hairy Circle of her Merkin […] This he dry'd well, and comb'd out, and then return'd to the Cardinal, telling him, he had brought St. *Peter*'s Beard, which he bought for a great Price of the Fathers of the Sepulchre. The Cardinal admir'd this Relique, and looking earnestly on it, clapp'd it on his Chin, saying, *If it was true, it was a Jewel worth a Kingdom*; and immediately introduc'd him to his Holiness […] and the *Pope* put it upon his Mouth, as the Cardinal had done, and in a Manner worship[ped] the Merkin.²⁷

On its surface Smith's anecdote reiterates the same kind of anti-Catholic sentiment circulating throughout England during much of the eighteenth century, as it portrays the Catholic interest in relics as an abnormal obsession with bodies, akin to prostitution or even to necrophilia. Kissing what they think to be the beard of St. Peter, both the Cardinal and the Pope inadvertently reenact the sexual activities by which the merkin's original owner once earned her keep. Praising the relic as "*a Jewel worth a Kingdom*," they call up both the origins of the merkin ("jewel" was often used as a euphemism for vagina) and the economic extravagances with which Protestants often charged Catholics. If the Cardinal judges the discarded merkin of a dead prostitute as "*a Jewel worth a Kingdom*," what economic disasters might befall England should Catholics be allowed the throne?

Beneath this anti-Catholicism, however, lies an intense anxiety about what might happen when a body part becomes detached from its body, when a characteristic gets detached from its character or a possession "anatomiz'd" to be no longer part of a possessive self. What the "Hostess's" merkin and the relics for which it is mistaken share, in other words, is that they are objects that were once possessions of a private self but that have now passed into the public domain, to be kissed and caressed by anyone who happens upon them. For the Hostess, the publicness of her body parts is unequivocally sexual: she no longer possesses her body because it is a body that anyone may purchase (or at least may lease) to do with what he pleases. Its publicness stems, in other words, from its gross materiality: it is no longer part of a self because it is only, after all, a body.

For the Cardinal, the publicness of the merkin is spiritual: (what he believes to be) St. Peter's beard can be and must be publicly caressed and publicly displayed because of its spiritual significance. It is no longer part of a self because it is so much more than a body. With this Smith reduces the cult of personality so essential to Catholic conceptions of sainthood (and, we might add, at the basis of secular conceptions of celebrity) to a property dispute: Catholicism is regrettable because it turns private bodies into public symbols and as such makes them into little more than prostitutes.

In the eighteenth century, Smith's anecdote implies, there are two and only two ways for women's hair to pass into the public sphere: it might be used in common and so sexualized, or it might be worshipped as rarefied and so spiritualized. (Interestingly, however, even when the hair becomes spiritual in Smith's anecdote it must also become masculine, the woman's merkin transmuted into a man's beard.) In both instances, the link between the woman's body and her self is severed; her body becomes, one way or another, the interpretable object and undisputed possession of a number of powerful men.

Smith's narrative of the merkin's journey from the labia of a whore to the lips of a pope thus calls up the narratives of female celebrities like Charke and Bellamy, who were regarded as sexual objects or as national treasures (and often as both at once). It calls up, too, the etymology of the word merkin as it entered the English lexicon about a century before Smith placed it in the mouth of the pope—and not too long before the structural transformation, according to Habermas, of the bourgeois public sphere. The *Oxford English Dictionary* lists two possible origins for *merkin* as signifying "a pubic wig": the word descends from "Malkin," which was both the name for "a lower-class, untidy, or sluttish woman" and also (and relatedly) a nickname for the common English name of Mary. Both definitions of malkin associate the wig-wearing woman with the kind of "Hostess" that Smith describes, a common prostitute whose body belongs to all men who can pay its (minimal) price. But as a derivative of Mary, malkin/merkin also calls up the originators of that name: Mary Magdelene—a whore turned holy—and Mary Mother of Jesus—the only woman whose birth was wholly nonsexual, wholly holy. Not only in Bellamy's wig or in Smith's anecdote but in the very origins of the word *merkin* itself, in other words, we see the entanglement of the sexual and the spiritual—the woman's possession by man and her possession by God—the two possibilities for publicness knotted up in the way she wears her wig.

ANY HAIRS BUT THESE: BELINDA'S HAIRCUT AND THE WIG ASCENDANCY

These three bewigged women—Charke, Bellamy, and the unnamed Hostess—provide a new and important context for what we might call the most famous barbershop quintet of the Enlightenment era: the five cantos of Alexander Pope's *The Rape of the Lock*, which appeared in its complete version the very same year that Smith's pope publicly puckered up.[28] The poem relates the true (though exaggerated) tale of Miss Arabella Fermor, immortalized in the poem as the belle Belinda, who has one of her locks cut off by a lascivious Baron after he sneaks up behind her at a card party. Pope parodies his age's hypocritical emphasis on chastity and on superficial reputation (at the expense of true virtue) in his mock-epic depiction of the "rape" as devastating both to Belinda's self and to the society she inhabits.

We don't often think about Pope's mock-epic as a work about a wig, but of course that is precisely what the lock becomes by Canto V, after the baron has surreptitiously separated it from Belinda's body. Having summoned her sylphs, ladies, and supporters to avenge her loss and attack the Baron on her behalf, Belinda, seizing him, makes her demands: "*Restore the Lock!* she cries; and all around / *Restore the Lock!* the vaulted Roofs rebound."[29] What Belinda wishes, in other words, is a wig like Bellamy's, one that might resemble her own hair and thus return her to her self.

And like Bellamy's wig (like Charke's, like the posthumous Hostess's), Belinda's wig is irreducibly material and impossibly immortal. In this, it joins so many of the images of a poem that, as scholars have long remarked, derives its mock-epic humor primarily from the twinned strands of the sexual and the spiritual woven throughout its couplets.[30] The sylphs, for instance, are charged both with "guard[ing] with Arms Divine the *British Throne*" and with "curl[ing the] waving Hairs" of British ladies; Belinda at her toilette takes on the air of an "inferior Priestess, at her Altar's side"; and Bibles demand equal status as puffs and patches, both on Belinda's dressing-table and in Pope's couplets.[31] The "Hairs" that Belinda unwittingly sacrifices are undeniably sexual, a point made not only by Pope's labeling of the Baron's barbarism (or barber-ism?) as a "rape" but also by Belinda's lament that he did not decide to take "hairs less in sight" instead.[32] But they are also spiritual—or at the very least epic—as Pope compares them to the "Triumphal Arches" and "Imperial Tow'rs" that have, like them, succumbed to steel.[33]

And like the Hostess's hairs, Belinda's, too, are destined for heaven: amid the post-haircut chaos of Canto V, the Muse to which Pope addresses his poem gazes at the heavens and glimpses "A sudden Star" followed by "a radiant *Trail of Hair*."[34] The poem's final couplets seal the lost wig's fate: "Then cease, bright Nymph, to mourn thy ravish'd Hair," Pope comforts his creation:

> Which adds new Glory to the shining Sphere!
> Not all the Tresses that fair Head can boast
> Shall draw such Envy as the Lock you lost.
> For, after all the Murders of your Eye,
> When, after Millions slain, your self shall die;
> When those fair Suns shall sett, as sett they must,
> And all those Tresses shall be laid in Dust;
> *This Lock*, the Muse shall consecrate to Fame,
> And mid'st the Stars inscribe *Belinda*'s Name![35]

Here Pope entreats Belinda not to mourn "the Lock [she] lost," since it has been "consecrated to Fame" among the stars of the sky. Once base and material—even suggestively sexual—the lock has now shuffled off its mortal coil and become a little piece of heaven.

The entanglement of sexual and spiritual in *The Rape of the Lock* is hardly a new idea among studies of Pope's poem, nor is the sense that this entanglement turns Belinda into an aesthetic object with about as much agency as the patches and powders on her table or the ringlets on her head.[36] In examining Belinda's lost lock alongside Charke's patriarchal periwig, Bellamy's "false" fringe, and the dead madam's merkin, however, I mean to suggest the long and twisted history that women's wigs take on over the course of the eighteenth century and to expose Pope's lines as part of a larger cultural trend that extended well beyond Belinda's cropped lock. Unlike men's wigs, women's wigs did not induct them into public discourse or promise them possessive individualism, but instead seemed to tie them to the private sphere or to punish them should they move beyond it. The ascension of Belinda's tresses from the sexual to the spiritual, like the ascension of Bellamy's or Charke's curls to the stage (or to the crest of a ditch) or the ascension of a prostitute's pubic hairs to the mouth of the pope, does not "restore" this small piece of Belinda's body to her possession. Indeed, Pope cannot celebrate the lock's immortality without dwelling, ever-so-briefly, on the impending absence of the woman who wore it: "your self," he tells Belinda, "shall die." Belinda's self and her subjectivity thus disappear beneath the hungry gazes of spectators who view her lock not as her possession but, rather, as the key to their own sexual pleasure or spiritual redemption.

Thus Belinda's heavenly hairdo, like those of the other women in her wig-wearing cohort, succeeds only in alienating her further from the body that English law had only begun to recognize as her own. And so, like the wig that overwhelms Charke's diminutive body or the false hair that upstages George Anne Bellamy's celebrated self, Belinda's lock outlasts and overshadows her subjectivity. Politics, economics, literature, and the law of eighteenth-century England may have proclaimed the rights of the individual self as important to and even constitutive of a well-structured society. They may even have been moving, ever so slowly, towards a recognition of women's right to an individual selfhood. But the woman's wig, it seems, had a very different tale to tell.

CHAPTER THREE

Fashion and Adornment

LYNN FESTA

The age of Enlightenment begot the most extravagant of hairstyles, as if the era's celebration of reason spawned fashionable excesses that defied purpose or use. Between 1650 and 1800—a period bookended in Europe by two revolutions in which the English and French monarchs lost their heads—fashions in hair rose to vertiginous heights and were toppled. In Britain, Europe, and the American colonies, the popular practice of wearing wigs led some men to shave their scalps and don artfully constructed heads of hair, while women's modes of dressing their locks oscillated between simplicity and elaborate artifice over the course of the century, achieving their greatest heights in the 1770s and 1780s, the heyday of big hair.[1] In an era of seismic political, social, and economic upheaval, the revolutionary force—and tyrannical power—of fashion revealed both the liberating possibilities of self-transformation and the human subjection to the current mode. Serving both as instruments of self-fashioning and as sartorial signs of rank, occupation, political affiliation, sexuality, and gender identity, hairstyles register history in unexpected ways. As tangible manifestations of the changing modes of self-presentation that police the theatricality of everyday life, shifting fashions in hair made visible—and thus enabled reflection about—fundamental alterations in the categories of gender, sexuality, class, sociability, and political authority that governed personal and collective identities during the age of Enlightenment.

As its etymological origin in the Latin *facere* ("to make") suggests, fashion is not simply the adornment of an essential body—the ornamental addition of a decorative supplement—but, rather, constitutive of personal and collective identities. Hair, as Margaret Powell and Joseph Roach have argued, is a "performance ... that happens at the boundary of self-expression and social identity, of creativity and conformity, and of production and consumption."[2] Simultaneously integral to the self and an ornamental extra, hair raises questions about the way the outward fashioning of the body represents—and refashions—the identity it ostensibly proclaims. Its visibility makes hairstyle one of the most prominent markers of individual identity and of social status. "Among all the exterior ornaments and articles of dress," the hairdresser David Ritchie proclaims in his 1770 *Treatise on the Hair*, "the hair justly claims the preference over the others […] it is esteemed even as an index to the mind, and is the object that attracts our attention the first of all others."[3] Even as fashions in hair proclaim the identity of the wearer, even serving as an "index to the mind," they construct who and what one is understood to be. As hair moves from the elaborate baroque twists and turns of the late seventeenth-century full-bottom wig to the relatively compact levity of mid-century rococo, from the dazzling excesses of the towering headdresses popular in the 1770s to post-Revolutionary neoclassical sobriety, it exposes the ways aesthetics, taste, and style express political and social change on the register of the body. Eighteenth-century fashions in hair are one site on which individuals sought to negotiate the relationship between personal and corporate identities, as the rigid hierarchies of the *ancien régime* codified in formal dress and hairstyle give way to the more idiosyncratic modes of self-expression in the face of political revolution and the emergence of Romantic ideals of individuality.

Although hair is manipulable in a way that enables it to be treated like an item of dress, it is not simply a detachable accoutrement appended to a clearly demarcated essential form but an extension of the organic body. Whereas "any other ornament or part of dress" is "changeable at will," the 1767 *Dissertation upon Head Dress* observes, "Hair is at all times a real ornament to the human person, without which it is ever looked upon as imperfect."[4] Notwithstanding its integral importance, hair, unlike other bodily members or organs, can be easily cut or removed altogether. The difficulty in treating hair as fully separable from the body and its importance to our appearance raise a set of crucial questions: When is an ornament essential? How and when does the outward display refashion inward being? In an era in which men shaved their scalps and donned locks gleaned from other heads and in which women consecrated hours to the construction of elaborate hairstyles, the artificial comes to redefine the natural. If the accessory has such power, what happens to the essence?

Fashion involves a quasi-voluntary subjection to the cultural regulations that align intimate grooming practices with collectively determined norms. It thus participates in the civilizing processes famously analyzed by Norbert Elias, as "polite" behavior and refined appearance encode and enforce divisions between cultured and savage, not only marking the thresholds of individual bodies but also policing the boundaries of the body politic.[5] Yet human subjection to the whims—indeed, tyranny—of fashion makes a mockery of the exalted pretensions of the age of reason: "'if an inhabitant of the Cape of Good Hope were to behold the stiff horse-hair buckles, or the tied wigs, of our Lawyers, Physicians, Tradesmen, or Divines,'" the eponymous central character of Richard Graves's *Spiritual Quixote* pronounces, "'they would appear as barbarous and extraordinary to them, as the sheep's tripes and chitterlins about the neck of a Hottentot do to us.'"[6] Although practical concerns such as ease of access to an itchy scalp doubtless influenced the wig's popularity, fashions in hair defy explanations grounded in use, function, and even conventional ideas of beauty.

Fashions in hair were shaped by shifts in the eighteenth-century economy, as global trade and a burgeoning capitalist marketplace thrust an unprecedented array of affordable wares and services onto the marketplace, creating—and feeding—the appetite of the newly prosperous bourgeoisie to appear *à la mode*. In the course of the long eighteenth century, fashion ceased to be the exclusive preserve of the aristocracy, as the middling sort and even apprentices and servants acquired the means to affirm their newfound status through sartorial choices that alternately created, upheld, and undermined social distinction. Prints such as *Betty the Cook Maids Head Drest* (Figure 3.1) crystallize the class anxieties channeled through fashion. The servant's extravagantly dressed hair simultaneously marks the aspirations that carry her beyond her rank and mocks the aristocratic women who sported vegetables and fruits in their lavish coiffures. Transforming comestibles into ornaments, tools into decoration, useful items into mere spectacle, this image converts the badges of Betty's servitude—the broom and the mop, the turnspit and the spuds, carrots, and vegetables—into items of adornment, a reminder that fashion, like the collection in Walter Benjamin's account, invites us into a world where people are unprovided for, but

FASHION AND ADORNMENT 55

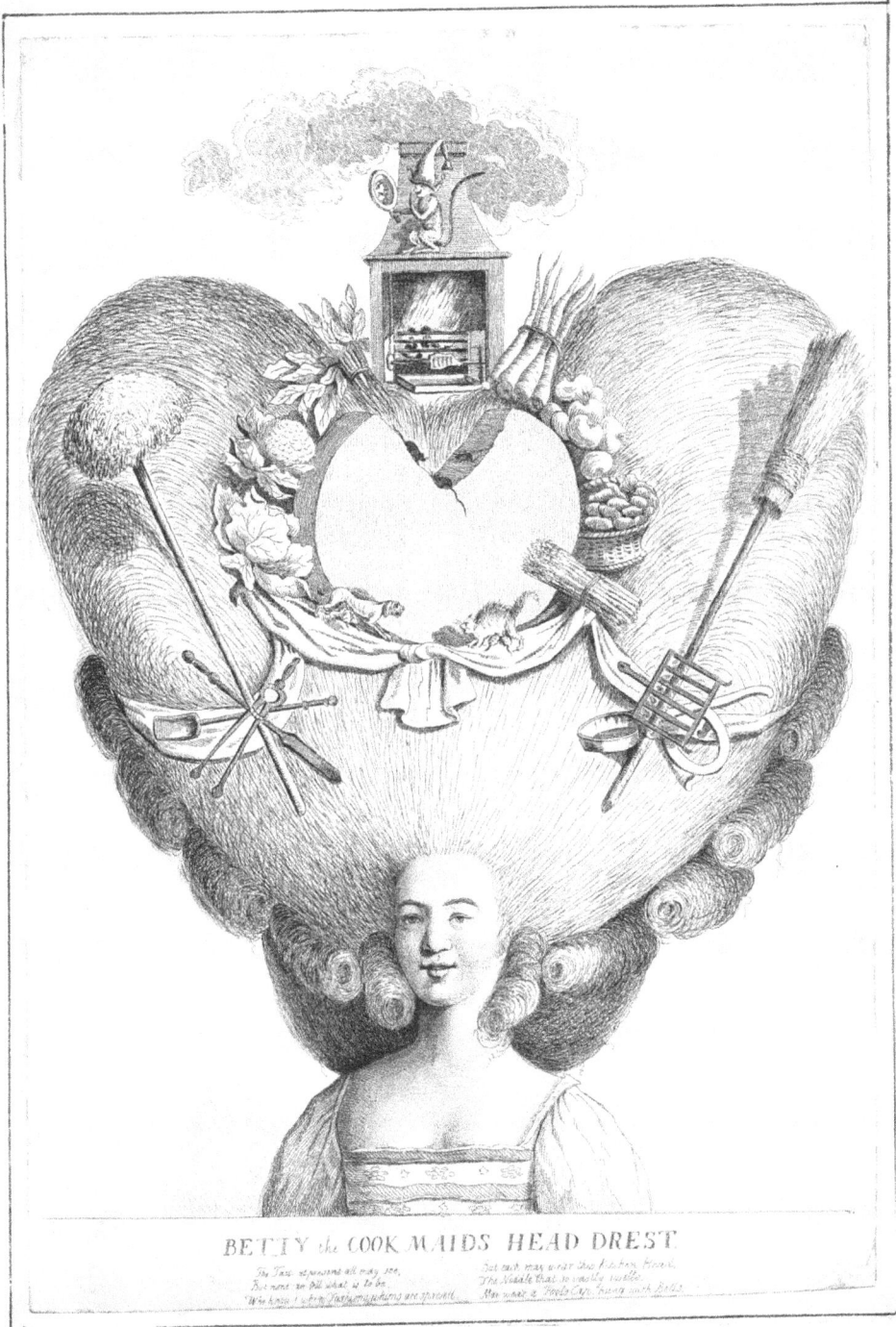

FIGURE 3.1: *Betty the Cook Maids Head Drest* (Published by W. Humphrey, 1776). Courtesy of The Lewis Walpole Library, Yale University.

"things are freed from the drudgery of being useful."⁷ The caption—"who knows when Fashion[']s whims are spread, / But each may wear this Kitchen Head"—indicates that fashions may trickle up from below and level social hierarchies. Even as the emulation of aristocratic fashion by thrusting *nouveaux riches* threatened signs of customary hierarchy, the growing cultural authority of the middling sort enabled them to recast fashionable excesses as signs of aristocratic decadence in contrast to respectable bourgeois moderation. Sartorial distinction itself operates as a form of class struggle: the imitation of styles veers between Veblenesque emulative consumption, in which the social-climbing lower classes ape the styles of their "betters," on the one hand, and subversive or parodic appropriations that menace the upper class's monopoly on the cutting edge, on the other.

The ease with which hair could be refashioned made it a primary sign of the accelerating tempo of material life associated with the consumer revolution. Since "changing or accessorizing hairstyles was a more economical way of keeping in the fashion than buying material to make up new items of clothing," hairstyles could be easily updated and as easily dated.⁸ Over the course of the century, a growing number of fashion periodicals, almanacs, and ladies' pocketbooks—often originating in Paris or London—propagated metropolitan styles through expanding print networks to the provinces and colonies, fostering an appetite for novelty even as they produced a sense of the contemporaneous.⁹ This insatiable appetite for the latest mode was understood to be an engine of the nation's commercial prosperity. Through Britons' "darling Folly, Fickleness, / In Diet, Furniture and Dress," the philosopher Bernard Mandeville argues in his 1714 *Fable of the Bees*, "That strange ridic'lous Vice, was made / The very Wheel that turn'd the Trade."¹⁰ The private vice of luxury becomes a public virtue that guarantees economic growth, as mercurial tastes create consumer demand. Fashion, in short, conjoins history to commercial modernity.

Fashion was *never* a simple question of personal adornment. It was used, as Kate Haulman puts it, "to discipline relations that had the power to enforce or compromise other social arrangements."¹¹ During and after the English civil wars of the mid-seventeenth century, hairstyles reflected political as well as religious divisions, as the royalist Cavaliers, with their extravagant manes, were pitted against the short-cropped "Roundheads" affiliated with Parliamentary forces.¹² (See Chapter 1, "Religion and Ritualized Belief," Misty G. Anderson on "Evangelical Hair.") The prevailing mid-century masculine fashion of long hair and lovelocks led to intense religious debates on the gender-bending implications of hairstyles and the vanity of worldly things. Flowing locks, Puritan writers claimed, elided an ostensibly natural difference between men and women. Yet writers at times struggle to explain why the long hair that is a sign of modesty in women betokens licentiousness in men. Since hair grows naturally and is easily cut, it is difficult to base arguments about tonsorial propriety on the organic body. In his 1650 screed against bodily alteration for the purposes of self-adornment, *Anthropometamorphosis*, John Bulwer makes an exception for long hair. Those who argue men *must* wear their hair short, he observes, "*had need prove that* Adam *had scissors, and cut his Haire in Paradise.*"¹³

The contentious debates over whether men may wear their hair long and whether women may be shorn are swept aside by the controversy over the growing popularity of the wig in the latter half of the century. Modern scholarship generally follows contemporary opinion in attributing the wig ascendancy in France to the vanity of a bald Louis XIII and a balding Louis XIV (this despite the fact that the Sun King wore his own hair into the 1670s, well after the fashion had taken hold), while Charles II is said to have imported the elaborate sartorial styles of Versailles, including the long flowing full-bottom wig, to England with the 1660 Restoration.¹⁴ Wigs were, however, fashionable prior to that time. Already in 1654 the Puritan Thomas Hall is penning screeds against the peruke as a blasphemous alteration of god-given attributes, blasting those who use "Periwigs and false haire" to make themselves "even what please themselves ... correct[ing] Gods handywork" in shame at his "workmanship in their owne haire."¹⁵ Pitting prideful interest in self-adornment against the Christian values of chastity, modesty, and humility, many divines correlate outward appearance with the corruption of the soul. The wig, the late seventeenth-century Nonjuring polemicist Charles Leslie inveighs, is "not an ornament, but a deformity ... like the horrid and hideous head of a snake-hair-twisted Gorgon."¹⁶ Although some theologians object to wigs as a form of cross-dressing, railing against men who "wear the long hair of Women in Perriwigs,"¹⁷ polemicists were, Haulman argues, also anxious about the way men's subjection to the vicissitudes of hairstyles compromised masculine authority by exposing their investment in the desire of others, signaling "an uncontrolled, Eve-like appetite for women and a desire for their attention. Such a need to be seen and judged attractive gave the intended audience great power."¹⁸

In the American colonies, settled largely by Puritans, the dictates of these polemicists held sway. With the exception of the wealthy and the middling sort, most American men wore their own hair. Wigs became an essential part of the French and British male wardrobe, however. In Britain, they were worn by all classes of men: aristocrats, merchants, clerics, soldiers, physicians, apothecaries, and apprentices (whose articles routinely provided for "one good and sufficient wig yearly"¹⁹). The universality of the practice bewilders the Swede Pehr Kalm, who in 1748 is astonished to note that wigs were worn by "farm-servants, clodhoppers, day-labourers, Farmers, in a word, all labouring-folk [...] Few, yea, very few, were those who only wore their own hair." When a puzzled Kalm asks the English "the reason for the dislike of ... their own hair," he is told "it was nothing more than the custom and *mode*."²⁰ Such tautological explanations for fashion do not address the broader sociological forces that brought the practice into being.

For although the wig, to be sure, serves practical needs—hygiene, comfort, or the time saved by having the hair dressed off the head—function does not fully explain the fashion. Why, at a moment of intense social and political change, does the visual uniformity of the wig become an unswerving sign of masculine authority? The fashion for wigs, in Marcia Pointon's influential account, stems from its capacity to homogenize male appearance. The wig's undeviating form, she argues, provisionally allowed "conflicting discourses of gender, of masculinity, of sexuality and of class to be stabilized even if not resolved," enabling men across different segments of society to consolidate a unified masculine identity in an emerging public sphere.²¹ The rows of identically bewigged masculine figures featured in eighteenth-century portraiture, Pointon argues, stand in implicit contrast with "the grotesque disorder into which—without the perpetual replication of these ordered and dignified representations of the idea of social man—it would disintegrate."²² Scenes of riotous carousing by Hogarth, Gillray, and Rowlandson feature men whose wigs have slipped or been knocked off, using the exposed head to offer a terrifying glimpse of the unreconstructed bare body and the gross disorder held at bay by the accoutrements of civilized self-presentation. A wardrobe malfunction of a scandalous order, the removal or dislodging of a wig reveals the fragility of the objects that lock the symbolic order into place.

And wigs were by no means sturdy objects. They fell off during vigorous activities and were easily damaged; the curl or buckle could be ruined by the rain—an expensive loss given the exorbitant price of wigs. Full-bottom wigs required up to ten heads of hair and cost, in 1700, upwards of £50, a princely sum.²³ The anonymous author of the 1676 *Coma Berenices; or, the Hairy Comet* laments that vain men "give as many pounds for a Periwig, as would almost make up a stock to set up a poor Apprentice."²⁴ Such gratuitous expenditure underwrites the wig's symbolic value, for the inconvenience, expense, and labor involved in the construction and maintenance of hairstyles proclaim the wearer's wealth and leisure. If the inconvenient bulk of the full-bottom wig declares exemption from labor, however, it also impedes participation in vigorous manly activities. The impracticality of these massive, cumbersome wigs renders them the object of theatrical satire in Restoration plays. The wig of Sir Novelty Fashion in Colley Cibber's 1696 *Love's Last Shift; or, The Fool of Fashion*, is famously carried onstage in its own sedan chair.

Both the expense and the inconvenience of such immense perukes led to a proliferation of smaller wigs in the early decades of the eighteenth century, including the tyewig (in which the hair was drawn back in a queue), the cadogan (in which unbraided hair was looped back on itself), the bagwig (which protected hair and clothing by enclosing the queue in a silk or velvet bag), the bob wig (a short wig without a queue), and the inexpensive scratch (a partial wig, fitted to the back of the head, over which men combed their front hair). Smaller wigs were also less expensive. Costing between 10s 6d and £1 15s, they were composed of human hair, animal hair (horse, goat), feathers, and even fine steel wire.²⁵ That the hair was culled from the bodies of other nations, ranks, genders, and even species means that the wig, as Pointon puts it, incarnates "the dilemma of a masculinity that required the artificial covering of the head as a sign of virility, station and decency but that was simultaneously threatened by the connotations—religious, moral and sexual—of the only item that could secure that signification."²⁶

Codified by wealth, occupation, rank, and generation, wigs express not only generic gentlemanly status but also profession or social role. In the prologue to David Garrick's 1775 *Bon Ton: or, High Life above Stairs*, the wig is said to be as sharp a delineator of character as speech:

> *FASHION in ev'ry thing bears sov'reign sway,*
> *And words and periwigs have both their day; ...*
> *The* Tyburn *scratch, thick club, and* Temple *tye,*
> *The parson's feather-top, frizz'd broad and high!*
> *The coachman's cauliflower, built tiers on tiers!*
> *Differ not more from bags and brigadiers,*
> *Than great St. George's or St. James's stiles,*
> *From the broad dialect of Broad St. Giles.*²⁷

Simultaneously homogenizing and creating distinctions, wig styles advertise wealth, profession, and social role. The fashions described in Garrick's catalogue express—and impose—identities, for the correlation of wig with profession or trade makes the adornment not purely elective. The proliferation of wigs enabled one to alter appearance at will, making material objects experimental expressions of an inward identity increasingly understood as malleable. "Never before had men had such a wide choice of hairstyles—styles which could be changed as quickly and as often as one wished, depending on the number of wigs one could afford."²⁸ William Hogarth would famously satirize this plenitude and its classificatory function, recasting wig styles as the Vitruvian architectural orders in his 1761 *The five orders of Perriwigs* (Figure 3.2): the "Episcopal" (clergy), the "Old Peerian or Aldermanic" (nobles and city officials), the "Composite or Half Natural,"

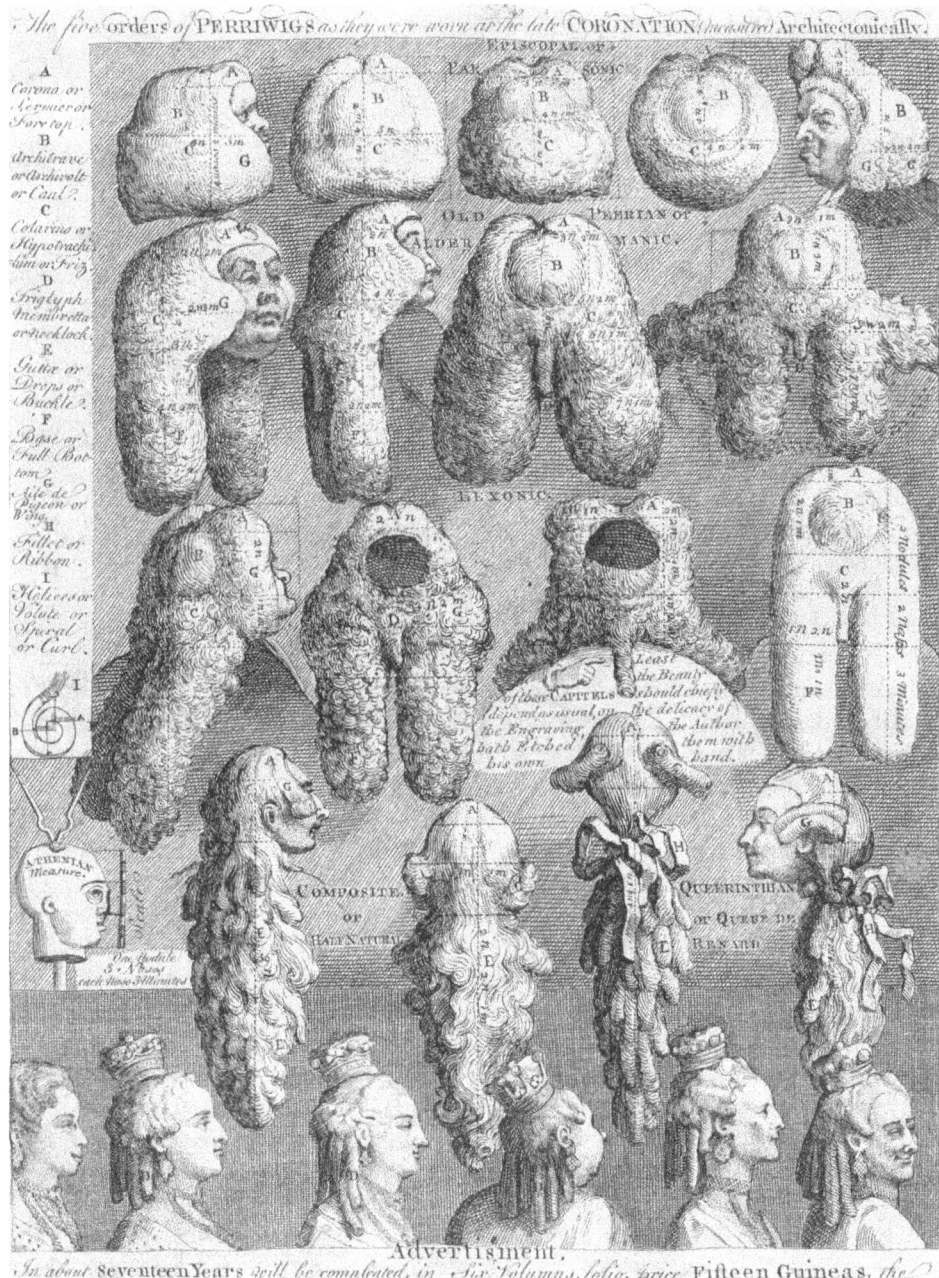

FIGURE 3.2: William Hogarth, *The five orders of Perriwigs as they were worn at the late Coronation, measured Architectonically* (1761). Courtesy of The Lewis Walpole Library, Yale University.

and the "Queerinthian," each presented through a selection of profiles and faces that aligned accessory with essential character type. Both the parody of the Vitruvian orders and the wigs' resemblance to genitalia undercut the high seriousness that attended the wig as a signifier of masculine authority.

Once ossified into seemingly fixed signs, wigs stand for—and threaten to supplant—the identity of the individual or body beneath. George Alexander Stevens demonstrated the capacity of the accessory to impose identity in his popular stage performances, described in his 1764 *Lecture on Heads*, where he transformed dummy heads into characters by swapping wigs and headgear: "Behold," he declaims of a bare head, "how simple a thing Nature is! But, behold," when bedecked with a wig, "how luxuriant is Art! What importance is now seated on these brows!"[29] The object overtakes the subject, as the emblem usurps the identity it is meant to represent. "Who, in this enlightened age," one writer mockingly inquires in the 1780s, "would put the least confidence in a physician who wears his own hair, were it the finest in the world? A wig, certainly, can't give him science, but it gives him that appearance, and that is every thing now-a-days."[30]

The very proximity of head and hair leads to recurrent jokes about the effect of one upon the other. The "Chinese" observer who offers an account of British customs in Oliver Goldsmith's *Citizen of the World* marvels that the English have placed "all wisdom" in the wig: "To appear wise, nothing more is requisite here, than for a man to borrow hair from the heads of all his neighbours, and clap it like a bush on his own."[31] The ease with which the ostensibly fixed insignia of professions could be appropriated by any with the cash to buy them fostered fears about the ability of individuals to misrepresent their identities by acquiring the fashionable accessories that proclaimed them to be something other than what they were. "There are Numbers of beings in and about this Metropolis who have no other identical Existence than what the Taylor, Milliner, and Perriwig-Maker bestow upon them," Robert Campbell writes in his 1747 *London Tradesman*.[32] The malleability of outward appearance makes it possible that nothing lies behind the outward signs of identity. Thus fashions both fostered a sense of uniqueness and conformity. As Elizabeth Wilson observes, "to dress fashionably is both to stand out and to merge with the crowd, to lay claim to the exclusive and to follow the herd […] Despite its apparent irrationality, fashion cements social solidarity and imposes group norms."[33]

The simplicity and authenticity celebrated by the mid-century culture of sensibility made nature itself into a fashion on both sides of the channel. When George III chose to wear his own hair upon ascending to the throne in 1760, the wig gradually began to fall out of style. By 1765, the decline in wig-wearing led the master peruke-makers to petition the king regarding "the almost universal decline of the trade, occasioned by the present mode of men in all stations wearing their own hair" and by the "*French* hair-dressers continually pouring in upon this nation."[34] (The "company of body-carpenters" mocked the barbers by creating a petition begging his Majesty "to wear a wooden leg himself, and to enjoin all his servants to appear in the royal presence with the same badge of honour.") The poet William Cowper notes that a friend must be "considerably a Gainer in […] Appearance by being disperiwigg'd. The best Wig is that which most resembles the natural Hair, why then should He that has Hair enough of his own, have recourse to Imitation?"[35] The emphasis on natural hair and on more sober, ostensibly "manly" styles belongs to the more austere aesthetic that emerged in the closing decades of the century, what J.C. Flügel famously calls "the great masculine renunciation."[36]

This profound shift in male self-fashioning is shaped by both national and class-based interests, as mockery of style channels political hostilities between nations and socioeconomic rivalries within them. Although the French were the acknowledged leaders of fashion throughout the eighteenth century, the culture of sensibility and liberalizing political currents in France fostered Anglomania (or the rage for things English), leading to the Gallic embrace of the less formal styles, more sober colors, and less elaborate hair favored by the British at mid-century. By contrast, devotion to French tastes in Britain is characterized as an aristocratic proclivity that sunders the upper from the patriotic middling and working classes. Critics depict French fashion as a form of unreason that compromises the austere self-possession purported to characterize British manhood. All English, a "Persian philosopher" proclaims in a 1773 issue of *The Lady's Magazine*, "live in a kind of servitude [...] subservient to caprices which are unworthy of rational creatures [...] Nothing can satisfy these malcontents: their active minds have no sooner invented new *agremens*, than they destroy them with the same precipitation."[37] Fashion compromises autonomy, by subjecting one to the vicissitudes of style governed by the dictates of others—above all, the French. Worse, such interest in adornment was depicted as a threat to British manhood, inasmuch as "luxury was what corrupted and effeminated states and empires and ensured their decline."[38] The blind adulation of French style, Samuel Fawconer argues in his 1765 *Essay on Modern Luxury*, has led to a corruption of national character: "we may observe one sex to advance in masculine assurance, as the other sinks into unmanly delicacy."[39] The wig was one of the most visible signs of male subjection to the effeminizing forces of fashion and luxury. Texts and prints pit a staid republican manhood—the solidity of identity guaranteed by an unchanging appearance—against the foppish craving for novelty and an over-investment in the wrong kind of material things. Attention to the vicissitudes of fashion suggested a mind trained on trivialities, an investment in the sensual over the reasoned.

If the wig raised questions about masculine authority, so too did the beard—or rather, its absence. Among Europeans, beards almost universally disappeared in the eighteenth century, "one of the few times in history that almost total beardlessness was ever practised," as if the lavish quantities of artifical hair crowning men's heads demanded a commensurate reduction in facial hair.[40] Or perhaps vice versa: as the hairdresser David Ritchie notes in 1770, "perukes [...] were not much in use till beards were extinguished."[41] The correlation between the adoption of the wig and shaving may stem from the fact that natural facial hair clashed with "manufactured curls, and placed limits on the variety of wigs one might choose."[42] Partaking of the clean lines and smooth planes celebrated by neoclassical aesthetics (although to be sure many Greek and Roman statues feature bearded men), the clean-shaven visage may be understood as a reflection of an Enlightenment investment in sociability, as if the beardless countenance that hides nothing from view bespeaks an open mind and heart. The associations of the beard with martial masculinity may have led to its rejection by a culture of polite male refinement, while the waning belief in Renaissance humoral medicine attenuated long-standing connections between the beard and virility.[43] Technical refinements in the production of steel, as Alun Withey has argued, may also have played a role, enabling the manufacture of razors able to hold a fine edge and yield a close shave.[44] Although the removal of facial hair was sometimes derided as feminizing—it softened the visage and implied men's subjection to women's purported preference—it was also a mark of civilization in contrast to the hirsute savage. Yet the beard proves to be a conflicted sign. While a beardless countenance signifies civility, the *need* to shave continues to serve as an important sign in distinguishing Europeans from purportedly "beardless" American and Asian men.[45] Towards the end of the century, Jean-Jacques Rousseau's celebration of the beard as the ornament of natural man gradually leads writers like Jacques-Antoine Dulaure to call for a rejection of superficial fashions and a resumption of the beard "to recall to men's minds their ancient dignity."[46]

This late-century interest in both natural hair and beard stands in stark contrast to a brief efflorescence in the 1770s of earlier, more flamboyant styles in the figure of the Macaroni. Initially referring to a group of aristocratic dandies who returned to Great Britain from the Grand Tour with Continental manners, gestures, and styles that "exceeded the ordinary bounds of fashion," the term Macaroni was soon applied to "all ranks of people, indifferently, who fell into this absurdity."[47] The Macaronis donned stylized clothing with flamboyant patterns, stripes, and pastel colors, wearing enormously tall toupées with side curls, often topped with a tiny hat, "of an inch in the brim, that do not cover, but lie upon the head, with about two pounds of fictitious hair, formed into what is called a club, hanging down their shoulders as white as a baker's sack."[48] The engorged "club" of hair converts the wig as a token of civic masculinity into an obscene parody of itself, exposing the artificiality of the signifiers that enable individual men to come together as equals in the public sphere. In the figure of the Macaroni, the fashions that secured masculine authority are reduced to mere ornament.

Yet the "merely" ornamental wields immense power. As the caption of a 1774 mezzotint—*What is this my Son Tom* (Figure 3.3)—suggests, Macaroni fashion threatens to alter the body beyond recognition. In the print, an "honest Farmer" recoils in shock at his newly stylish son, prodding the diminutive hat topping Tom's extravagant coiffure with his riding whip, either to dislodge the hat that his son ought to have doffed, or to verify his son's identity. Pitting cosmopolitan urbanite against rustic farmer, the mannered style of the youthful dandy against the squire's bluff—even crude—demeanor, the print exposes a contest between generations waged not only in sartorial choices but in codes of politeness and civility. As Amelia Rauser has argued, the farmer is no ideal himself; rather, the print invites a reconciliation of extremes.[49] If refinement depends upon a progressive model of civilization, fashionable excess suggests a decadent decline, as the caption indicates: "Our wise Forefathers would express / Ev'n Sensibility in Dress; / The Modern Race delight to Shew / What Folly in Excess can do." Whereas "Our wise Forefathers" saw dress as an outward token of sensibility and a stable identity, such reliable signifiers have been distended beyond recognition in a pursuit of novelty that bears no kinship to use or identity. The lavish quantities of hair and the Lilliputian hat, the tottering heels, and the tasseled decorative sword, all present objects evacuated of their useful functions and repurposed as pure style. In the process, the fashionable body raises questions about both gender and sexuality. In various satires, the commodity supplants the body and in the process threatens to strip away grammatical gender. "To what sex does the thing belong?" one ditty inquired. "'Tis call'd a Macaroni."[50]

This radical revaluation of subjects and objects alike lies at the heart of the many satires, both visual and textual, of the Macaroni. Dedicated to the secretary of the Macaroni Club and modeled on Pope's *Rape of the Lock*, Ellis Pratt's mock-Georgic *The Art of Dressing the Hair* promises to explain how "with various Art the tortur'd Curls to place, / Confirm their Structure, and dispose with Grace; / The Puff to manage with exactest Care, / And pour the Snow-white Show'r on ev'ry Hair." The poem not only offers directions on the production of style; it takes up the thorny question of who or what, if anything, controls the irrational flux of fashion. Pratt's Macaronis "in secret Conclave mix; / The Laws of Dress, the Change of Fashion [to] fix. / If pondr'ous *Clubs* shall from behind depend, / Or

FIGURE 3.3: *What is this my Son Tom* (1774). Courtesy of The Lewis Walpole Library, Yale University.

Queues in formidable Length descend."⁵¹ The judicial responsibilities of the eighteenth-century public man have devolved into conspiratorial plots to dictate the unnatural contortions of fashion, as men who should be engaged in politics instead expend their energies on the management of trivial things.

The Macaroni's ostensibly "improper" investment in material goods exposes him to insinuations not only about his gender identity but also about the connection between sartorial and sexual object choice. Although men earlier in the century were vilified for what was understood to be an excessive interest in their *toilettes*, foppishness was originally associated with a heterosexual desire to attract women: "Many a Lady has fetched a Sigh at the Toss of a Wig," Addison observed in *The Tatler* in 1710.⁵² By contrast, the Macaroni's investment in wardrobe and hair was said to betoken a *lack* of sexual interest in women and even, at times, to indicate a sexual preference for men. The titular Macaroni in Robert Hitchcock's 1773 comedy is characterized by a solipsistic absorption in his own image that stands in contrast to the predatory heterosexuality of the libertine Lord Promise, who mocks the Macaroni's dependence "upon dress and fashion—I despise both—Even my pleasures are different from yours—I am wholly devoted to the charms of beauty, you, to those hourly discovered by your looking-glass."⁵³

Alluding to the Pantheon, a London venue for masquerade balls, *The Macaroni: A real Character at the late Masquerade* (Figure 3.4) plays with the porous threshold between "real" character and "fancy" dress. The overt theatricality of the preening Macaroni annihilates any claim to nature or to the values of authenticity so central to the culture of sensibility. In offering us the preparation *before* entry onto the stage of the masquerade, the print toys with the cleavage of public and private, exposing the labor of fabrication. By setting the scene in the dressing room, the print converts what Powell and Roach (following the sociologist Erving Goffman) call the "back region" work area, where the "front region" outward performance is produced, into a theatrical space, hinting that there may be no organic figure anterior to its artificial materialization.⁵⁴ Although the multiple mirrors so prominently featured in the print underscore the Macaroni's ostensible narcissism, they reflect nothing: here fashion constitutes subjects rather than expressing depths. In the print, the theatrically posed body solicits the gaze, converting the male body into a spectacle. Although desires are concentrated on the commodities that figuratively and even literally make up the self, the image subtly registers the correlation of Macaroni style with sexual subculture in the cat carved into the back of the chair in the background, a possible coded reference to the catamite.⁵⁵

Such references, however, remain in the background. What is foregrounded in the print is the visual spectacle of the cosmetically pieced-together body, not least the dramatic and ostentatiously false hairstyle. In giving pride of place to fashionable accessories, the Macaronis, as Miles Ogborn has argued, "threatened to show that the modern self was an illusion made of commodities and fantasies with no real, knowable substance."⁵⁶ Yet by wearing his superficiality on his sleeve, as Amelia Rauser has argued, the Macaroni's overt declaration of artifice becomes an acknowledgment of the importance of artifice and manufactured personae to the civility of the public sphere: "manners and up-to-date fashion did not cloak character with artifice, but in some way constituted it."⁵⁷ Even in the recesses of the dressing room, one poses for an unseen gaze that governs one's identity. Yet even as these prints mock the Macaroni's modes of self-representation, they register performances of stylish eccentricity that belie fashion's tyranny, as experiments with identity become the object of a meta-theatricalizing and self-aware display.

FIGURE 3.4: Philip Dawe, *The Macaroni. A real Character at the late Masquerade* (1773). Courtesy of The Lewis Walpole Library, Yale University.

If hair proved to be central to debates over masculine authority and self-presentation, it also registers the shifting status of women. Women's hair rose and fell over the course of the long eighteenth century. Although at the beginning of the period hair was worn in buns or dressed close to the head, as in the tightly curled style known as a *tête de mouton* or sheep's head, by the 1770s hair was teased into immense ornamented confections that sometimes towered more than a foot over women's skulls.[58] These changes in hairstyles are tightly bound up in transformations in gender norms and, especially in Britain and the American colonies, in the values assigned to—and the challenges made to—the ideals of domestic womanhood.

The emergence of professional hairstylists during the period proves to be a signal threat to domesticity, for if "the ceremonies and rituals that surround [hair's] dressing, cutting and collection act as a safeguard against transgression and as a marker of the maintenance of the social order," they also become the site on which social norms can be challenged.[59] Thus the periodical writer Joseph Addison in a 1711 *Spectator* worries about the incursion of "male *Abigails*" into ladies' boudoirs, as the pursuit of fashion transforms the mores governing the domestic sphere.[60] Addison is troubled by the "light, fantastical Disposition" that leads women to a "heedless Pursuit after [...] glittering Trifles," preferring the modest demeanor of the retiring domestic women. Shallow fashionable women in Addison's account consider "only the Drapery of the Species, and never cast away a Thought on those Ornaments of the Mind, that make Persons Illustrious in themselves, and Useful to others." Yet harbored in Addison's censure is a recognition of the fact that women dress *for one another*, circumventing the male gaze: they are, he notes, "perpetually daz[z]ling one another's Imaginations."[61] Hairdressing and other fashionable practices on these terms become a medium for dynamic and empowering creative expression by women: a form of self-fashioning, a source of pleasure, an advertisement of a crafted identity, a means of sexual attraction. "Every woman of fashion," Gilchrist writes in 1770, "ought indisputably to enjoy the liberty of pleasing her own fancy."[62]

And that liberty increasingly took the form of towering mounds of hair that would attain Promethean heights in the final third of the century. In the 1760s, hair began to be dressed in an egg-shaped dome from a quarter to half the length of the face; by the 1770s, headdresses had quadrupled in size. At a moment in which courtly society in France was under new public pressures and in which the losses in the American war had brought Britannic morale to a new low, women's hairstyles went very high. To create these immense confections, natural and artificial hair was combed up over wire scaffolding or over large pads made of wool, felt, and gauze, coated with a gum-like paste called pomatum, composed of the fat of bears or calves, and covered with colored powder. Amidst the curls and rolls, the hairdresser placed feathers, garlands, flowers, and fruits, as well as sentimental scenes incorporating figurines of beloved family members and friends, and miniature reenactments of historical events such as military victories and the first balloon ascension.[63]

The print satires of these fashions simultaneously revel in and censure the excesses they depict, acknowledging the allure of what they condemn. The headdress reaches hallucinatory proportions in plates such as *The Extravaganza, or the Mountain Head Dress of 1776* (Figure 3.5), where the ostrich plumes, garlands, fruits, and nesting birds sprout forth in a giddily garish display. Notwithstanding the presence of vegetation, the headdress has no pretensions to nature: the ornamentation transforms the hair from an ancillary adornment—the supplement of an organic body—to an autonomous object. The immense headdress dwarfs the female face, reducing the person to an appendage of the

FASHION AND ADORNMENT 67

FIGURE 3.5: *The Extravaganza. or the Mountain Head Dress of 1776* (Published by M. Darly, 1776). Courtesy of The Lewis Walpole Library, Yale University.

thing, and exposing the "literal autonomy of fashion beneath which the wearer is reduced to impersonality."[64] If earlier writers were anxious that fashion *conceals* true identity, these images suggest that it may obliterate the figure altogether. "Because a little ornament heightens the splendor of beauty," *The Lady's Magazine* complains in 1773, women

> have concluded that by multiplying their ornaments, they could not fail of increasing their charms in proportion. [...] All the productions of nature have either been placed or imitated in the different parts of their dress. [...] Their personal charms appear as it were annihilated by this astonishing luggage [...] so that the woman [...] has vanished out of our sight.[65]

Yet the moralists' cautionary pleas are themselves obliterated by the hedonistic excess of the image, which permits the beholder to revel in unchecked fancy under the alibi of reform. In such images, we encounter a tonsorial sublime that explodes the received outlines and proportions of the body. Such wild constructions, Henri Focillon has argued, are intrinsic to the impulses that underwrite fashion. Although, Focillon contends, "fashion may attempt to respect, and even to expose, the proportions of nature," it will more often "submit form to incredible transmutations; it will create hybrids. [...] The body becomes but the pretext, the support and sometimes only the material for utterly gratuitous combinations."[66]

In practice, however, these fashions created discomfort and practical difficulties. The staggering height of many headdresses made it difficult to ride in carriages or to maneuver through doorways—the object of satire in prints such as *The Ladies Ridicule* (Figure 3.6),

FIGURE 3.6: *The Ladies Ridicule* (Published by M. Darly, 1772). Courtesy of The Lewis Walpole Library, Yale University.

where the sedan chair has been modified to accommodate a lofty headdress. Because of the labor involved in constructing such "heads," they were sometimes prepared the day before they were required and even left unopened for extended periods.[67] "Such was the labour employed [...] that night-caps were made in proportion to it [the headdress], and covered over the hair," the diarist Mary Frampton observed of 1780 hairstyles. "Twenty-four large pins were by no means an unusual number [...] on your head."[68] Vermin nested in the heads, necessitating long head-scratchers or *grattoirs* and flea-traps to mitigate the itching. Movement itself could be difficult. In her *Mémoires*, one of Marie Antoinette's ladies-in-waiting noted that dancing was "a kind of torture," with "a coiffure a foot high, surmounted by a bonnet called *pouf*, upon which feathers, flowers and diamonds were piled up, besides a pound of powder and pomade which the least movement caused to fall upon the shoulders; such a scaffolding rendered it impossible to dance with pleasure."[69]

Yet the sheer exuberance of these styles, as Diana Donald observes, explodes Veblen's insistence that women's fashionable appearance merely serves to advertise masculine wealth. Indeed, Donald argues, eighteenth-century moralists insist that fashion was "the instrument of female dominance, the means by which men were entrapped and emasculated."[70] Numerous prints depict men dodging colossal coiffures and male hairdressers climbing up ladders to adorn towering headdresses, suggesting an imperiled masculinity daunted by and in the service of female fancies. And while images such as *The French Lady in London, or, the Head Dress for the Year 1771* (Figure 3.7) vilify the fashionable excesses of England's Gallic adversary and satirize women's subjection to imported sartorial extremes, it is notable that the female form dominates the image, as the man—along with the cat, the parrot, and the dog—recoils in terror. The gentleman's hat has tumbled to the floor, along with a scroll featuring George Alexander Steven's *Lecture upon Heads*, both indicating that men are by no means exempt from the codification of fashion. The headdress dwarfs even the Peak of Teneriffe, depicted in the background painting, punning on the Teneriffe lace of which the bonnet is composed even as it suggests that women's adornments have superseded the order of nature.[71] Hairstyles such as *Bunkers Hill, or America's Headdress* (Figure 3.8) depict ant-like male soldiers trudging up the side of a coiffure rescaled into a colonial landscape, suggesting that the colonial cause—or perhaps Britain's own military commitment—are as hollow and as fleeting as the ephemeral headdress.

Such hairstyles not only represented political scenes but were themselves fiercely politicized. The famous coiffures of Marie Antoinette were theatrical powergrabs, lethal weapons in courtly warfare that advertised alliances and proclaimed the wearer's influence over the king. Yet they also became a site of immense contention, for the costly jewels and feathers that bedecked the head of the French queen drained the royal coffers and excited outrage among the populace. Thus Marie Antoinette's famous 1778 *coiffure à La Belle Poule*, which commemorated France's entry into the American Revolution with a headdress featuring a fully rigged replica of the aforementioned frigate, was so lavish and expensive that it became a staple in prints vilifying the queen's "presposterous extravagance."[72] Fashion, on these terms, could not be disassociated from broader political and social debates and even turmoil.

And however many forms of vegetation were incorporated into these elaborate confections, there was little appearance of nature in the final result. The pomatum used in perukes and headdresses hardened into a shell that—in one 1767 writer's words—"would wholly have deadened the utmost velocity of a pistol-shot." Lamenting that "so flexible a body as hair is, is drove and forced into such forms as is inimitable with so stiff a substance as wire," the author praises the "movement" and "easy play [...] that tells me, it is neither

FIGURE 3.7: After J.H. Grimm, *The French Lady in London, or the Head Dress for the Year 1771* (1771). Courtesy of The Lewis Walpole Library, Yale University.

FIGURE 3.8: *Bunkers Hill or America's Head Dress* (1776). © The Trustees of the British Museum.

wire, wood, nor stone, upon the head; but hair, or something like it."⁷³ Increasingly, hairdressers encourage women to gravitate towards the "natural." William Barker in ca. 1785 will argue for fashions that express a sense of self. "Uniformity of the head-dress ... may be justified in the army," Barker notes, but "why such a ridiculous and unmeaning uniformity should obtain among the ladies [...] is beyond my comprehension [...] The ladies never had such opportunities of improving in their ideas of natural elegance in hair-dressing as at present," he observes, directing the reader to the works of Joshua Reynolds and Angelica Kauffman for more natural models, in which curls are no longer "imprisoned [...] [and] smothered with a profusion of powder."⁷⁴ Such proclamations suggest a yearning for liberty: for a fashion expressive of individuality and—perhaps oxymoronically—of nature.

Such "natural" styles grow in popularity in the wake of the French Revolution. "Natural hair," as Nina Rattner Gelbart puts it, "had become a political symbol, the free-flowing mane of the sans-culottes as powerful as their red caps."⁷⁵ The aristocratic connotations of the wig meant that supporters of the French Revolution on both sides of the Channel shed them, and the towering women's headdresses likewise disappeared, supplanted by simple hairstyles, such as masses of curls bound with a ribbon and sometimes decorated with beads, feathers, or flowers. In the wake of the Terror, hairstyles *à la victime* and *à la sacrifié* imitated the shorn locks of those destined for the guillotine. Under the Directory, male hairstyles were modeled on Roman portrait busts, with the "Titus" cut—short hair combed forward over the temples and forehead—popular first among men as a sign of "republican virility" and subsequently among women.⁷⁶ In Britain, earlier styles held sway into the 1790s, but a succession of bad harvests coupled with a need for new revenue led the prime minister William Pitt to impose a tax on hair powder in 1795 that inflicted the death blow on the wig in Britain.⁷⁷ Yet the age of artificial hair was not entirely over: wigs continued to be worn by judges and lawyers, on the one hand, and servants, on the other. Declarations of political liberty notwithstanding, sartorial choice is rarely free.

This chapter has sought to trace fashions in hair across the long eighteenth century. The immense vicissitudes—from wigs to natural locks, from towering headdresses to demure cropped manes—suggest that little is stable, including the body. Yet, as Elizabeth Wilson has argued—in a reversal of Roland Barthes's insistence that fashion "substitutes for the real body an abstract, ideal body"—it is precisely the "way in which fashion constantly changes" that "actually serves to fix the idea of the body as unchanging and eternal."⁷⁸ This fixity is apparent in the countless prints that convert the fashionable body into a *momento mori*, a reminder of the corruption of the flesh and the damnation that awaits those who dance to a worldly piper. In images like *Beautys Lot* (Figure 3.9), the dramatic contrast between the lavishly dressed hair and the skull beneath the skin admonishes the viewer to eschew vanity in favor of higher spiritual concerns. The extravagant mane of fashionable hair—real? artificial?—capping a skull from which the flesh has been whittled away reveals how fashion, as Walter Benjamin puts it, "couples the living body to the inorganic world," offering a "bitter colloquy with decay whispered between shrill bursts of mechanical laughter."⁷⁹ Yet the exuberant and endlessly inventive hairstyles featured throughout the century suggest an energetic life force that perhaps defeats Benjamin's deathly mirth. For if the extremes of fashionable hair point to the limits of the era's celebration of reason, the extravagant styles attest not only to frivolity of fancy but also to pleasure in the body as an aesthetic object in its own right. And if the plasticity of the hair menaces the fixed relation between identity and outward sign, fashion holds out the creative possibility of yielding to and becoming something other than what one

FIGURE 3.9: *Beautys Lot* (Published by William Humphrey, between 1760 and 1810). British Cartoon Prints Collection, Library of Congress, LC-USZ62-115001.

already is. In an era often described as the age in which modern versions of individuality came to hold sway, hair served as an integral element of bodily appearance that could, nevertheless, be utterly transformed, its liminal status marking it out as the perfect object to mediate between the human attempt to express one's own nature and the growing powers of art and techne central to the Enlightenment.

CHAPTER FOUR

Production and Practice

SEAN SILVER

The following chapter explores the importance of hair and hair production to the early Enlightenment sciences in England. It is motivated by recent insights that late seventeenth- and eighteenth-century sciences were largely consumed with the analysis of natural materials: the natures of earths and metals, the properties of liquids and air, animal structures, and the qualities of such materials as are used in construction, such as wood and fibers from animals and plants. Fabrics were particularly central. By the beginning of the Enlightenment, England had long held a dominant position in the production and manufacture of woolens. Broadcloth was England's signature export, and even the rise of new materials like silk and cotton could not drive English manufacturers from their perch. But when fabrics were brought into the laboratory, the lessons that were learned were not lessons about the better production of cloth. Something else was produced, a set of insights about the world as a woven one. This, then, is the thesis of this chapter: that the material context of early modern empiricism in England produced a constellation of emergent concepts—complexity among them—which hearken explicitly to the physical affordances of hair. This chapter discusses these related developments.

In pursuing this goal, I braid together three narratives:[1] a mildly revisionary account of the English economy as depending crucially on the processing of wool and other fibers, the rise of materials science in seventeenth-century England (including its exquisite attention to the affordances of hair), and the emergence of certain metaphysical or explanatory concepts that seize on hair as figure and instance. My approach, in knitting persons to things to concepts, leans on arguments by scholars such as Ian Hacking, Steven Shapin, and Bruno Latour; by these accounts, it is not enough to do a history of ideas simply as a treatment of words in their textual sites. We should also make an effort to re-embed concepts in the material conditions (the networks or complex systems) from which they emerged. Complexity means "woven," and uncovering the early history of complexity, of the braidedness of the world, means therefore returning to seventeenth- and eighteenth-century British textiles. It was in these researches, halfway between thinking and doing, that the ground was laid for a number of advances in the empirical sciences—not least the chemical revolution, which has been recognized (after insights by Thomas Kuhn) as perhaps the most crucial transformation in early modern science.[2] Could theories of complexity have developed without hair? Surely. But this chapter argues that complexity only emerged in its early forms through hair as a crucial material resource.

THE HAIR ECONOMY

I begin with the English economy in an era of empire. The story of British woolen manufacture, of the entire commodity chain from domestic shepherding to the export of finished cloth, often gets overlooked in stories of the eighteenth century. Especially in the transatlantic context, the narratives we tell tend to focus on one of two things: the adoption of the plantation system in the English colonies to grow, process, and export raw materials, or the influx of finished consumer goods into London and other metropolitan centers.[3] On the one hand, British expansion into new territories in the Caribbean can largely be explained by land-hungry and labor-intensive crops such as sugar, coffee, tea, and cotton, which were grown in the colonies only to be shipped to England for processing and consumption.[4] This story is a crucial one—for it is the story of slave labor and the establishment of global asymmetries which are with us still. The disparities in power and privilege between plantation-owners and exploited laborers foreshadowed an early prehistory of the global south and global north; these are often graphically realized in one or more visually striking *triangles of trade*, each of which seems to close an economic circuit: African slave labor is shipped to America; the sugar, tobacco, and cotton produced by that labor is shipped to England; textiles, rum, and manufactured goods are returned to Africa to purchase more labor; and so on. This is one popular story of empire, not least because (by one influential account) the excess capital released by the plantation system kick-started modern capitalism.[5]

On the other, the striking wealth that pooled in places like London, Paris, and the Netherlands triggered the upsurge of new practices in the purchase and display of luxury goods. Luxury objects began to be purchased as objects of social display and class standing.[6] These included movables such as crockery, curtains, paintings and engravings, personal ornaments, and so on—but also addictive substances like tea, sugar, and tobacco. Some of these objects were produced in England, with a native design tradition developing by the second half of the eighteenth century;[7] others were imported as finished goods, sometimes produced in Europe and sometimes imported from points farther east. Taken together, these patterns of consumption are called the *consumer revolution*, the metropolitan labor of conspicuous consumption which shadows the earliest forms of commodity capitalism. New forms of consumerism and its commodities show up in art forms like stageplays and novels issuing from London and other urban centers;[8] the very consumer culture recorded in plays and novels is also the culture of the people visiting the plays or reading the novels as acts of consumption.[9] So: the continual despoliation of native ecologies and the exploitation of indentured and slave labor are neatly balanced by new preferences in the food people ate, the ornaments they displayed, and the clothes they wore.[10] Narratives like these are well attested and remain attractive partly because they locate empire, and the consumerist habits funded by empire, as outgrowths of cycles of dependence on addictive substances such as sugar and tobacco—not to mention addictive substances like novels, purchasing power, and other trappings of middle-class life.[11]

Somewhat lost in the twin stories of colonial violence and luxury consumption is, however, an alternative, mostly compatible narrative tracing the rise within England of preindustrial manufacture. The story of incipient industry, of the transformation of England from a feudal kingdom of artisanal handcrafts to a global superpower with emerging factory-style production, doesn't involve flashy commodities and novel materials imported from abroad; it focuses instead on the native production of sometimes homely goods, like British woolens.[12] These, nevertheless, were the engine of early British imperial growth. The contemporary literary imagination, like our own, tends to focus on the returns of empire, with the silks, spices, gems, and fragrances that ended up in Londoners' pockets or on their tables. However, the many accounts of voyages abroad (as, for instance, in Richard Hakluyt's *Voyages and Discoveries*[13]) remind us that woolens were the native export overwhelmingly traded for the range of objects ending up in the metropole. By Lawrence Stone's classic account, England "clothed the Northern European peasant, and in return absorbed a great proportion of the products contrived by Europe's technical skills and imported from the East and South."[14] Wool, one merchant insisted in 1645, was "Englands Golden Fleece," the "Most substantiall and staple Commodity that our Countrey affords for the maintenance of Trade."[15] Expansion in places like India and the American eastern seaboard meant a striking increase in imports of cottons (especially of bright, color-fast calicoes) yet wool production continued its dominance; agricultural writer Arthur Young estimated the annual output ratio of finished products at about twenty of wool to one of cotton.[16] "All the World wears it," Daniel Defoe in 1719 insisted, "all the World desires it, and all the world envies us the Glory and Advantage of it."[17]

British economic policy was structured to protect and exploit this dominance, ensuring British command of the entire commodity chain of wool and wool products, from sheep to shop to ship. The sweeping Wool Act of 1699[18] set the tone for transatlantic policy, drastically restricting the sale and transportation of wool fibers, yarns, and finished cloth. Among the first in a complex series of protectionist instruments, the Wool Act forced producers and manufacturers in the colonies to funnel wool through English textile mills and to English markets. Not only did this policy mean that taxation revenue was generated at each stage of the production and transportation of goods, but also that the relatively labor-intensive arts of producing raw materials were shipped overseas, while the technically demanding labor of manufacturing finished goods was centralized at home. While opinions vary as to whether these policies altogether helped or harmed the English economy, they were central to what was to be called *mercantilism*—the general, centripetally oriented strategy that was the rule for England's transatlantic and colonial dealings.[19] And it signaled Britons' investment in woolens, not only as a crucial economic sector but as a cultural identity; a traditional component of what it was to be British, for the commodity chain, from the fleece to the finished cloth, was in fact a complex web, knitting together countryside and urban center. As John Smith insisted in 1757, in his magisterial source-book *Memoirs of Wool*, "The Wool of England is, in effect, considerably Part of the Land of England; and the Land of England is, in a manner, ENGLAND ITSELF."[20]

I make the point about Britain's cloth, about the basis of its economy in the processing of animal hair, to emphasize that imperial England was not only the culture of novel goods and luxury consumption. By the mid-eighteenth century, perhaps one million inhabitants of England were directly employed in the production of woolens.[21] The long eighteenth century had already witnessed the general cashiering of the domestic system of manufacture; now it was becoming one of the first large-scale positive-feedback economies, where centralization of production in factory-style centers allowed manufacturers to buy materials in bulk, hire workers on a piece-basis, and sell directly to wholesalers.[22] This is a different England than that captured by either the colonial or consumer narratives—for transformations triggered by woolen manufacture in pre- and early-industrial England have been compellingly linked to the first major welfare programs, the rise of a permanent urban poor, and even instabilities in family structure and marriage rates.[23] Though luxury consumption is largely what is registered in London magazines like the *Spectator* or on the London stage, a close look at England's economy tells a different story. For England was the world's leader in the processing and export of cloth. In short, England was a hair economy. And remembering this asks us to look at empire differently; it asks us to attend to the properties of hair. This is the work of the next section.

FIBER SCIENCE

More than any other craft in eighteenth-century England, weaving depended thoroughly on the deliberate manipulation of vanishingly small particles for its phenomenal effects. Engraving, watchmaking, and locksmithing differently specialized in the arrangement of small parts; cookery, painting, and chemistry differently combined materials. But weaving and cloth-making alone produced a wide range of surface effects merely through the careful arrangement of barely visible microstructure, beginning with particles of almost no properties at all—single fibers of wool, flax, cotton, or silk—and weaving them into resplendent, two-dimensional surfaces of varying thickness, stiffness, and tactile qualities. Understanding woolens as an aspect of England's imperial ambitions will therefore require a shift of scale, which is another way of saying that it will require a different lexicon and an understanding of laws of a different order. It requires shelving large-scale macroeconomic models and sweeping historical plots in favor of the very smallest of manipulated materials and the most singular of narrative threads: the properties, powers, and qualities of single, spun, and woven wool hairs.

Finished British woolens were of two general types.[24] The first was *broadcloth*, sometimes simply called "woolens." This was for many years England's signature export, and the techniques by which it was made were centuries old by the time the first English overseas colony was founded.[25] Shorter, "short-staple" wool is chemically treated for pliability, carded to clean and disentangle it, and then spun on a wheel into yarns. Short-staple wool comes from sheep specifically bred to deliver fleeces of short, fine hair; the Cheviot sheep, which thrived on the poor soils of Northumberland, Wales, and Ireland, was particularly prized for the wool it fed to the broadloom. Because a loom binds threads together at right angles to one another, weaving demands two sorts of threads: *warp* yarns, which run longitudinally, and *weft* or *filling* yarns, which run at right angles to the warp. Each of these is prepared separately for its own properties—the filling yarns generally thicker and more elastic than the stiff, slippery warp. Prepared separately, and differently wound, warp and weft are made to meet in the broadloom, where they are woven into cloth. The extra width of the broadloom, which is half again as wide as a standard loom, is where the cloth gets the name, but the width is not reflected in the finished material. Instead, the raw cloth as it comes from the loom is taken to the fulling mill, where it is submerged in a hot, soapy chemical bath and passed under water-powered trip-hammers. Here, it is squeezed and crushed; the extra working shrinks the weave and binds the wool fibers in a microstructural process called felting. The finished cloth is stiff and smooth, naturally repels water, and can be cut or scraped without requiring hemming.

Broadcloth technology was more than a thousand years old by the time its production chain dominated the British economy. But broadcloths, partly because of technological improvements and changes in style, were slowly phased out by fabrics called *worsteds* or *stuffs*. The making of worsted fabrics is similar to broadcloth; wool fleeces are processed into yarns and fed into the loom. But the microstructural logic of worsteds is importantly different. In their simplest forms, worsteds depended on long-staple wool, from sheep differently bred to produce long, coarser fleeces; the Romney Marsh and Lincoln Down sheep were prized for the long, springy wool they produced. After being sheared, long-staple wool is cleaned, chemically treated, and combed, in the aim of making it even straighter (and hence longer) than it comes from the sheep; the long, slippery fibers are then spun into yarns which, just as with woolens, are woven into cloth. The crucial difference is what happens next. Unlike broadcloths, worsteds are not milled but are taken directly from the loom and finished. The fabric that results is less good at repelling weather and less resistant to damage than broadcloth. But because the finished surface is not felted, the fabrics are capable of being woven with yarns individually dyed, hence retaining sharp, visually striking patterns (see Figure 4.1, a sample book of worsteds from 1763). Moreover, worsteds can take advantage of mixtures of materials in a way that woolens can't; fabrics such as inexpensive linsey-woolsey, which crosses a woolen weft with linen warps, were capable of attaining qualities not belonging to either fiber alone. Taken together, then, these features were a crucial part of the rise of a native tradition of domestic design, encouraging new dyeing techniques and novel weaves. It was worsteds, rather than woolens, that led the innovations in industrial production in the nineteenth century.[26]

Each stage in the production of wool cloth feeds forward, each step remembering the last and anticipating the next. The selection of wool fibers itself looks all the way forward to the finished cloth in which those fibers will be constituted. The very value of the sheep to the wool-shepherd's trade is in the qualities of the sheep's hair: the waviness of sheep's wool lends it elasticity, while fibers' microscopic serratures, their saw-like scales, help them to bind to their neighbors.[27] This means that different sorts of cloth prefer kinds of wool sheared from different breeds of sheep. The felted surface of broadcloth, tightly matted from the repeated blows of the hammer, benefits from the shorter fibers of short-staple wool, like those from the shorter, curlier, and finer fleeces of the Cheviot or Hampshire Down sheep; indeed, it was largely these breeds, and the thin soils on which they thrived, that were responsible for the initial advantages that the British woolen industry enjoyed.[28] Worsteds, on the contrary, rely on the greater tensile strength of threads spun from long-staple wool, as, for instance, the coarser, but much longer, wool fibers of Romney or Lincoln Down breeds.[29] So, one way of describing the shift from broadcloth to worsteds has to do with the finished product; worsteds more easily lent themselves to innovation in weaving, dyeing, and combining of materials. But the story may also be explained as the effect of evolutionary changes and breeders' decisions within the domestic flock; faced with a shortage of meat, the British shepherding industry shifted its focus from the kind of sheep that could supply fine, short-staple wools, to those bred for mutton, which incidentally produced longer wool fibers.[30] By this account, large-scale shifts in British cloth production developed in step with an oversupply of cheap long-staple wool, with its fibers more suited for worsteds than broadcloths.[31]

The first scientific studies of wool, undertaken in the first years of the Royal Society, occurred in the context of wool as a crucial economic and cultural commodity. The Royal Society of London for Improving Natural Knowledge was formed in 1660, upon the Restoration of the Stuart dynasty to the throne of England. Committed to an experimental program, including the compiling of natural histories, the Royal Society was founded in the hope of delivering new insights about the natural world—especially to pay off in practical lessons about artisanal crafts. At the core of this project was a circle of Oxford thinkers who were also practitioners, in one way or another: John

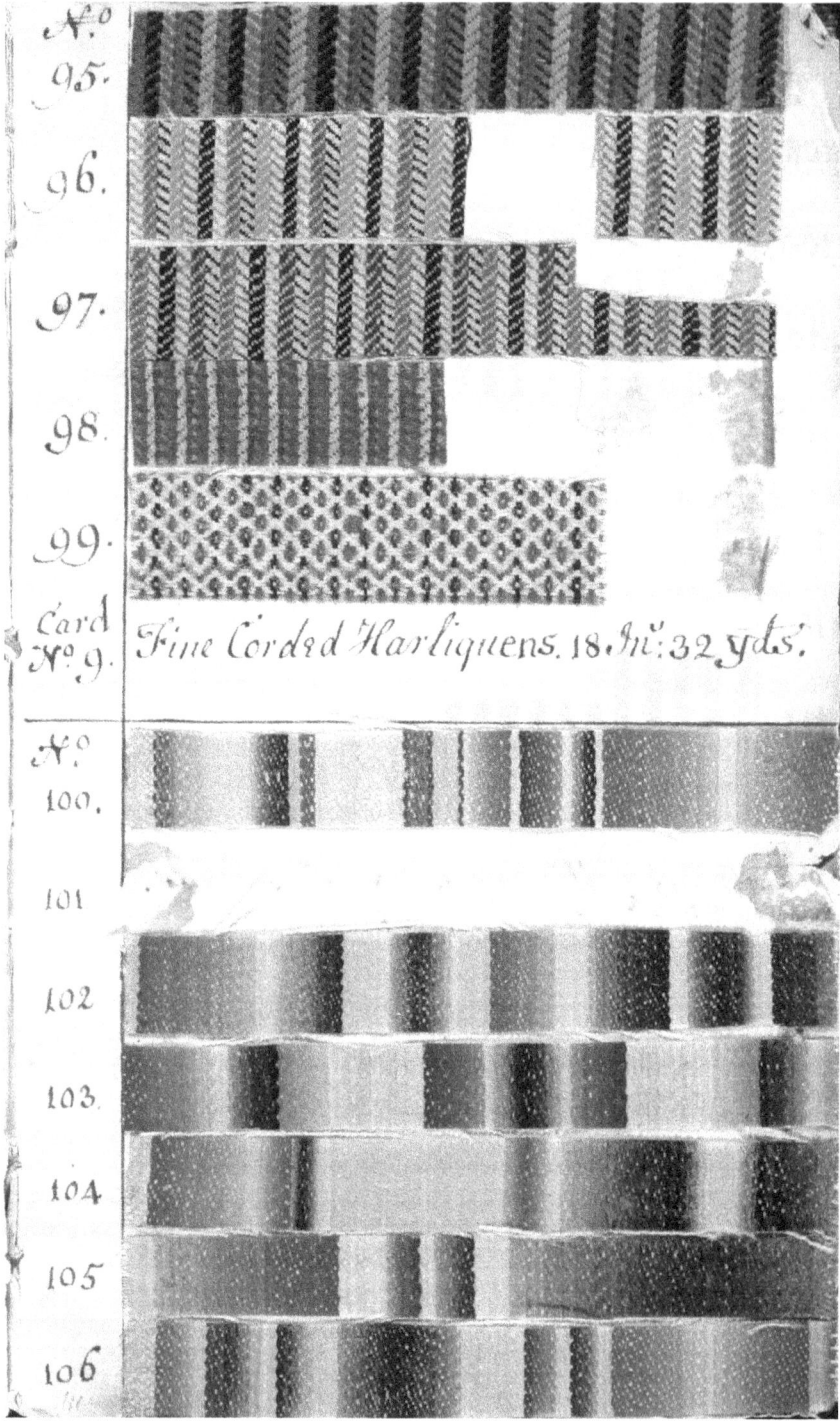

FIGURE 4.1: John Kelly, *Pattern Book of Worsted Samples* (1763). © Victoria and Albert Museum, London.

Locke was a physician, Robert Hooke an instrument-maker trained as a limner, Robert Boyle a studied and practicing chemist, and William Petty the son of a clothier who had been apprenticed to the sea as a merchant. Each was a mechanist, who sought to explain large-scale phenomena analogically through small-scale, quasi-mechanical relations between individual particles. Each had already evinced an interest in materials and applied sciences, and was, therefore, influential in steering the emerging empirical sciences—what would blossom into modern scientific practice.[32] And each was at least ostensibly committed to the Royal Society's mandate and practical program. However, when it came to wool, they were to glean very few practical insights; they produced no new dyeing processes, nor gadgets for spinning or weaving. By and large, innovations in the woolen industry were developed in the workshop, or in flocks and fields, with the pace of change rapidly accelerating in the later eighteenth century.[33] Rather, the lessons learned in the Restoration laboratory were of the general features of complex materials, especially regarding emergent properties, the ways that phenomenal effects (like strength, color, or sheen) can be produced by combining simple entities which have none of those properties. While these discoveries had little to add (at least in the short term) to the keeping of sheep or the making of cloth, they were crucial in theorizing the world as a complex one—that is, as a world of sensory qualities made up of the connections and interlockings among swarms of insensible particles.

Among the earliest, most practical studies of wool submitted to the Royal Society were a pair of histories by the young William Petty. Petty's papers were interested in the world of weaving in a relatively literal sense, for each of his essays (on weaving in 1661 and dyeing the year after) capitalized on the trades he had learned in his childhood. Petty's father was a manufacturer in the domestic system of weaving, and Petty had been raised among wool.[34] His "History of Clothing" leans on this practical experience to offer a comprehensive description of the wool trade; it traces a chain of production from raw material to finished cloth. It is attentive to fine-grained stages (from shearing, to carding and combing, spinning, preparation of yarns, weaving, dressing, and dyeing) even while attending closely to the processes themselves. And it succeeds, throughout, in linking finished effects to the microparticulate affordances of material wool, describing weaving as the physical and chemical manipulation of barely perceptible fibers. The finished products may appear simple; the flat sheen of broadcloth might be celebrated for its uniformity. But these effects descend from a complicated set of practices, and Petty took as his task to analyze—to unloose or untwist—these processes.

Petty describes the chemical and physical processes that prepare the fleece for the spinner's wheel; he describes the spinning itself and the different ways of preparing the yarns for their different tasks. But the sublime object of his description is clearly the broadloom, and it is here that the burden of his task becomes clear. From sheep to yarn, Petty's narrative simply traces a commodity chain; it follows, by the trope already available in his moment, a single thread: shearing, washing, carding, spinning. But in the loom, his strategy changes. A loom, as Petty describes it, is hardly a thing of wood, iron, and brass. His prose allows the wooden and steel frame of the loom to vanish, revealing in its place the lattice-like tangle of spun fibers that is the purpose of the tool to produce. The loom, he writes, is a thing of wool, a "complicated machinament made of threads." Confronted by this tangle of lines, he finds his description becoming "extralocal," enmeshing processes that are not, strictly speaking, in their proper order, for Petty's task has become one of weaving together the many trades, techniques, and influences that account for well-woven cloth. Warp chains, filler yarns, harness, shuttle, and slay; to describe these, he remarks, is "the most curious enquiry in the whole business of weaving."[35] Rather than describing them as objects, he explains uses, purposes, and tasks. It is as though the many processes of the twisting, washing, and treating of yarn are all made to meet in one complicated node, the densest center of his description. I would say that the loom activates a dense network of persons and things, of techniques, substances, machines, and artisans, but calling this a "network" gets the language wrong. For network, itself a metaphor drawn from fibers, would have to wait another two centuries to be deployed in quite this way. Petty calls this a *complication*, a weaving or braiding together; the loom binds together persons and things in one complex system.

Petty's solution to the complexity of cloth, to the way that its features emerge through foldings, is to trace large-scale effects (like the working of the loom) to relationships between small-scale particles. At one level of scale, there is the finished cloth, which is complicated from individual threads. Its properties are produced by weaving, a sort of "connexion [...] made only by alternating the figure of the threads so joined [...] by alternate crooking them out of one straight line into many semi-circles or other curve lines, alternately convex and concave."[36] The filler thread is made to pass over, then under, alternate yarns of warp. At a second level, the elements of the threads themselves are already folded together, the microscopic threads evincing a similar batch of relationships as the macroscopic cloth. "Spinning," Petty supposes, "is a sort of connecting parallel bodies (suppose cylinders) by changing their figures alike, from strait to screws: for all twisted threads are screws."[37] These screw-like figures are what Petty, coining a word, calls the "contortuplications" of wool fibers; much like the threads in a complex web, Petty is imagining tortured foldings at a microscopic scale, linking fibers each to each.[38] The individual wool fibers, Petty insists, "are indeed threads of themselves," and he is comfortable registering the level of scale by the number of threads that are gathered together—from individual contortuplicated fibers, to the threads or yarns spun from them, to cloth that might be complicated from thousands of individual threads, millions of fibers. The rule is analogy; as fiber is to thread, so thread is to its cloth, and vice versa. Each depends upon the mechanical twists and folds of simpler entities to produce new qualities in combinations.

Complexity is just one of a family of neologisms springing into being from the hair culture of seventeenth- and eighteenth-century England; others include filament and thread (as in the threads of a screw).[39] Of these, complexity is the most wide-ranging. We have already seen that the loom, under Petty's eye, is "complicated"; the loom is a "complicated machinament made of threads." Complicated, strictly speaking, isn't only Petty's word; it turns up in English a few times in the decades immediately preceding Petty's "History of Cloth."[40] But, in Petty, the word receives a new urgency. "Complicated," like "complex," descends from a Latin construction meaning woven, braided, or plaited together.[41] It is because simple materials are divided, differently treated, and then recombined that the weaver's task is one of complication; it is for the same reason that "complexity" provides a way of thinking. It comes to mean the wovenness or braidedness of the world: not just cloth but any situation or object of thought which is experienced as being woven together out of simpler components. Ideas are entangled in worlds of practice (a concept partly captured by complexity itself). I am tempted to say that concepts are not cut from whole cloth—except that complexity clearly is. It takes its rise from materials science in the hair economy of early modern England.

TEXTILE SCIENCE

Fabrics have been conceptually interesting because they do not easily succumb to philosophy. They are the stuff of technique (on the supply end) and fashion (on the consumption end).[42] As a concept born in the weaver's shop, complexity does not emerge from clean, a priori philosophizing; cloth is not the kind of universal idea that would be called *simple*. The distinction is between a world of simple forms and complex networks, between common (and hence universal) ideas, and the products of time, place, and history. The distinction comes to the fore in the work of John Wilkins, Petty's senior and sometime mentor, whose magnum opus was a dictionary of philosophical ideas. In Wilkins's system, simple ideas are common notions that are shared by people across wide ranges of times and places; they might include actions like *writing* and *dyeing*, relations like *parent* and *child*, or things like *sun* or *stone*. Complexity emerges when philosophers wade into the mangle of everyday materials, matching linguistic and conceptual resources to the world's wide variety of actually occurring things—especially the things of human commerce and art. Stooping from universal ideas, the philosopher encounters the mangle of practice.

Such actually occurring things, which are different for every time and place, include the tools that artisans use, which are "every day multiplying," and *"Kinds of Stuffs,"* that is, fabrics, which are everywhere different. A partial list, true to Wilkins's moment, includes: "Baise, Flannel, Serge, Kersey, Grograin, Tammy, Tabby, Sattin, Plush, Velvet, Tiffany, Lawn, Douless, Canvas, Buckrom, &c. Diaper, Damask, &c." The list is meant only to indicate what such a list might look like; it is striking for the casual familiarity Wilkins has with a range of fabrics that to the modern reader are probably as foreign as our fabrics would have been to him. Categories like these, because of their very complexity, are conspicuously of the moment; precisely because stuffs are combinations of certain kinds of weaves with certain sorts of materials, they are the contingent products of particular times and places. And if they are made to fit with philosophical systems, he continues, it will only be as ideas "of a more *mixed* and *complicated* signification," things of a "more complex nature."[43] They are the kinds of things emerging from the highly contingent, extralocal networks Petty is at great pains to report in his "History." And while single words might, therefore, very well suffice for relatively unchanging notions, like "sun," or for relatively stable kinds, like "gold," kinds of cloth will require a different nomological system. The distinction between "Diaper" and "Damask" might very well do among contemporary experts familiar with the trade, or even for people casually buying and consuming a range of fashions, but it hardly signifies for the rest of us, whether outside the trade or the cultural moment. Nor was this insight lost on Wilkins. Complex ideas, like kinds of cloth, must instead be expressed "periphrastically," spelling them out through the simple components that make them up. In Wilkins's compact formulation, they are to be recorded by "matter and figure," the materials and weaves that add up to particular fabrics.[44] Thus does the complexity of the object insist on the complexity of its description.

Philosophically speaking, complexity emerges when philosophy makes contact with contingency. But historically speaking, complexity emerges when philosophers start troubling themselves about materials like woolen cloth. In its etymology, which was still very much alive for Wilkins, we can hear the burden of the culture from which complexity emerges. Wilkins's use of the word records, as if by accident, the difficult disentanglement of a concept from its context, *complicated*, then *complex*, clearly vibrating for Wilkins between their literal and metaphorical senses. He is speaking of cloth, of the way that it is woven together, literally and figuratively. But he means to name the way that ideas are likewise hybrids of simpler ones. For cloth offered a lesson in the ways that precise arrangements of different kinds of particles (in Wilkins's language, descriptions of "figure" and "stuff") could produce effects that belonged neither to the material nor to the arrangements. It is as concepts such as these that the fiber arts offered lessons in materials—not as tips or techniques which were immediately returned to manufacture but as ideas in the realm of pure research and even metaphysical philosophy.

Robert Hooke's *Micrographia* (1665) is the most visually magnificent document in early Royal Society materials science—and it is preoccupied with the microstructure of fibers. Perhaps the best-known image from Restoration microscopy was the 35th plate from Hooke's *Micrographia*, titled "Of a Louse" (Figure 4.2). It is clearly an engraving of a parasite (which Hooke in his caption extends to a meditation on kingship and parasitism). But Hooke's description, and even his approach, to the striking structure of the louse depends upon lessons learned in studying the structural qualities of fibers. It isn't just that Hooke's microscope reveals a creature adapted for clinging to hair and to hair's dark environment. It is also that Hooke's approach to parsing the natural world depends upon lessons derived from the structural qualities of woven goods.

Hooke's interest in the louse is unsurprising, for his preference is for natural objects of all sorts over manufactured ones. "There are," Hooke remarks, "but few *Artificial* things that are worth observing with a *Microscope*."[45] This is because, for Hooke, what can be learned from a thing is limited to its causes, so viewing a razor's edge or the point of a needle through a lens only brings into view the failures of art to produce a perfect edge or a sharp point. Hooke favors "natural forms," which "are some so small, and so curious, and their design'd business so far remov'd beyond the reach of our sight,

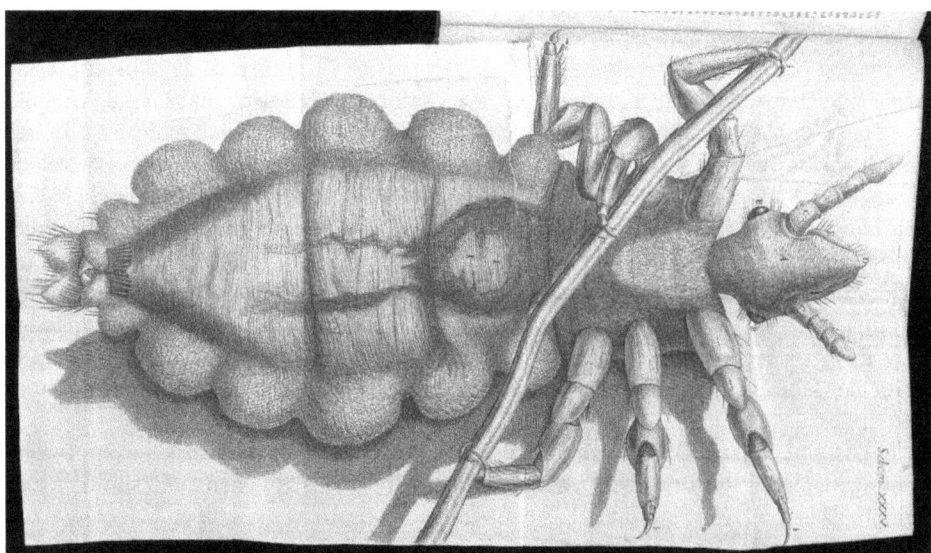

FIGURE 4.2: "Of a Louse" from Robert Hooke's *Micrographia*, Schema XXXV (1665). Beinecke Rare Book and Manuscript Library, Yale University.

that the more we magnify the object, the more excellencies and mysteries do appear."[46] In naturally occurring things, magnification reveals a system of small, interacting parts, which together reveal something of the divine idea which created them. The exception, in *Micrographia*, is cloth. Hooke's very celebration of the superiority of natural materials comes as part of an apology for the time he is lavishing on woven goods. For it is through cloth that Hooke establishes a relationship between eye-level phenomena and those microstructural interactions that can be revealed by the microscope—a pattern that he perpetuates throughout *Micrographia*. Qualities observed by the eye are, by this account, explicable by appeal to complex relationships, especially mechanical relationships, between sub-visible particles.

Hooke subscribed to a general metaphysical system that was just becoming mainstream; this is the Lucretian tradition of atomism known, after Robert Boyle's formulation, as "corpuscularianism." These systems, although not directly observable, offered novel ways of imagining relationships between sensory phenomena and objective causes. Boyle's corpuscularianism, for instance, postulated a world composed of vanishingly small particles of universal matter, so fundamental as to have virtually no qualities at all.[47] Fleetingly little, invisible, they are distinguished only by size, shape, impenetrability, and motion. Blind and in darkness, they can only occupy space and hook to one another. But it is, of course, these combinations that are the crucial thing. Corpuscles themselves have their own form and shape, but objects are corpuscles joined in such a way that their mutual orientation and positioning produces a new, composite entity, with a new shape and new possibilities of combination that are not present in its component particles.[48] Imagining how this could happen required a series of analogical leaps, continually relying on processes which were already familiar. Engraving, watchmaking, and locksmithing differently specialized in the arrangement of small parts; cookery, painting, and the apothecary's trade differently combined materials. And each of these crafts turns up in Hooke's thought, and in the thought of Robert Boyle, John Locke, and others in the same circle. But weaving and cloth-making alone, to reiterate, produced a wide range of surface effects merely through the careful arrangement of barely visible microstructure, beginning with particles of almost no properties at all—single fibers of wool, flax, cotton, or silk—and weaving them into two-dimensional surfaces of varying thickness, stiffness, and tactile qualities. It is for this reason that weaving became philosophically important—for it offered a means of mapping the relationships between eye-level phenomena and invisible, metaphysical cause.[49]

Crucial to the liberation of fabrics into a metaphor is Hooke's study of watered silks (Figure 4.3). It is here that he observes, in a rigorous way, the emergence of complex properties from relationships between simple things. Watering silk cloth causes it to take on a variegated sheen; "if the right side of it be looked upon," Hooke remarks, it will appear "to the naked eye, all over [...] waved, undulated, or grain'd, with a curious, though irregular variety of brighter and darker parts." This effect is intentionally added to the cloth, but it is not achieved merely by adding the curiously variegated, brighter and darker parts. Rather, this quality is added to the cloth through an intricate process of wetting, folding, and pressing, which Hooke is at some pains to detail. When taken from the loom, the material's weft-threads are "onely *bent round* the warping threads." After being dampened, and carefully pressed face to face under heat and pressure, however, the weft threads become "creas'd or angled in another kind of posture then they were by the weaving." Thus does the familiar phenomenon of watered silk "proceed [...] onely from the variety of the *Reflections* of light, which is caus'd by the various *shape of the*

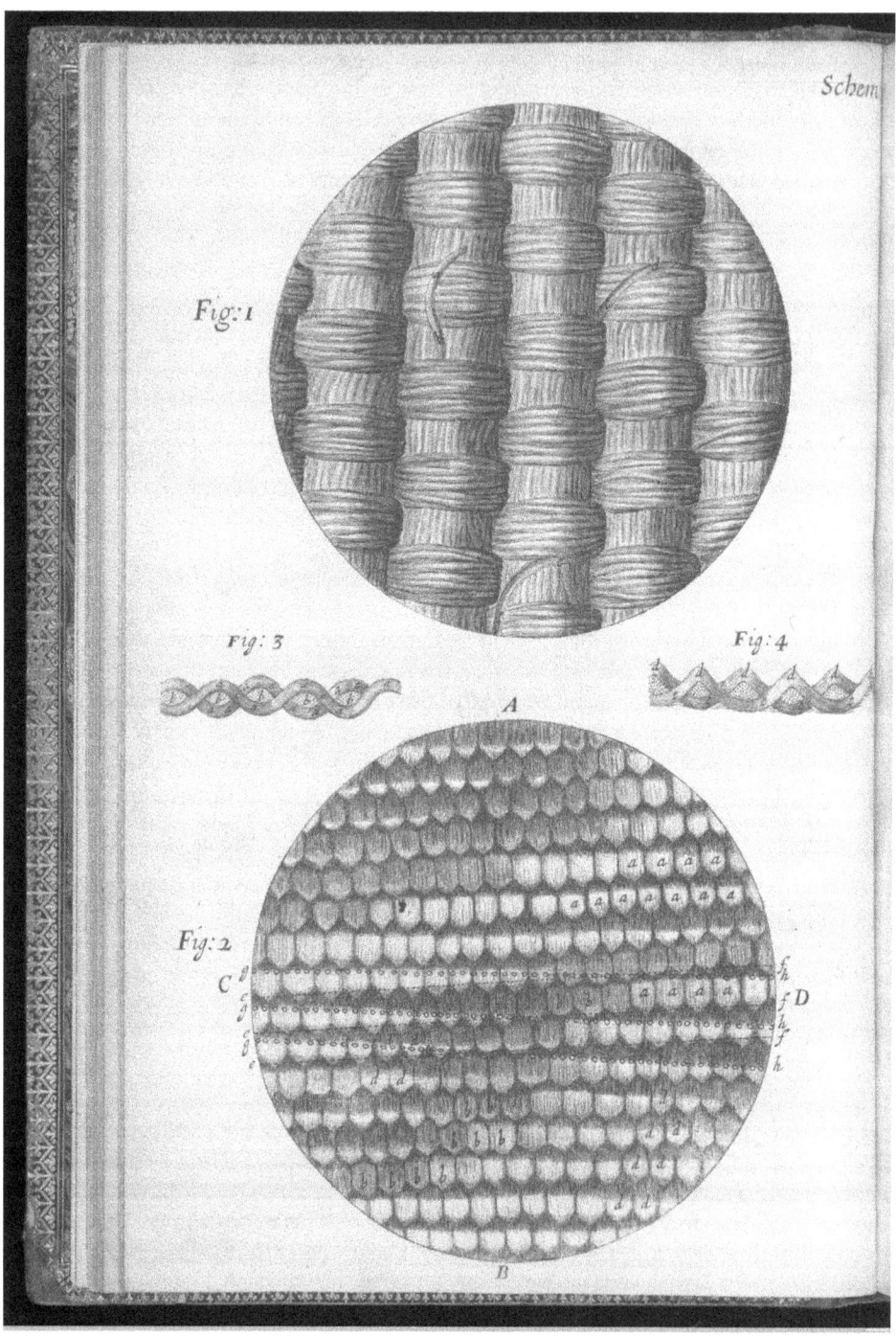

FIGURE 4.3: Silk ribbon and watered silk from Robert Hooke's *Micrographia*, Schema III (1665). Wellcome Library, London.

Particles, or little protuberant parts of the thread that compose the surface."⁵⁰ The crucial thing is that large-scale effects are achieved through geometrically simple variations in microstructure. It is not the threads themselves that evince these properties; the threads, taken individually, are nearly clear and almost colorless. It is the threads, brought in to precise conjunction, which together produce the effect. The work of the microscope is to translate phenomenal spectacle into microstructural cause.

Lessons learned from cloth end up informing Hooke's treatment of other natural materials which are not outwardly like textiles at all. In fact, the observation most explicitly about fibers—number 32, "Of Hair"—is precisely where he liberates woven cloth into an explanatory mechanism. Although Hooke begins by examining the properties of hair, human and animal, he proceeds to an extended explanation of the properties of skin. The leap is possible not simply because hair and skin are associated by proximity, nor merely because hairs grow from skin. The weaving of hair, Hooke supposes, explains the properties of skin, which the microscope finds to be "constituted of an infinite company of small long *fibres* or hairs […] here and there twisted, as twere, or interwoven […] exactly jointed and contex'd."⁵¹ Hooke imagines that the elasticity of skin is due to its net-like weave; the skin of animals "consists of a great many small filaments, which are implicated, or intangled one within another […] almost no otherwise then the hairs in a lock of Wool, or the flakes in a heap of Tow." Even "filament," a newly coined term from the Latin for *spinning*, is drawn from the art of weaving, for weaving has emerged as a master metaphor for the construction of natural materials.

It is through routes such as these that weaving is transformed from a craft into an explanatory figure. Over the course of his *Micrographia*, Hooke becomes increasingly confident deploying cloth as a figural resource.⁵² A cloth woven from spun particles, skin's complexity (the "implication" or "intangling" of fibers), the patterned microstructure of seaweed or a sea sponge: its complexity, its wovenness from fiber-like particles accounts for the properties of each. It is only with such a structure as cloth, Hooke supposes, that the skin of an animal "should be able to suffer so great an extension any ways."⁵³ It is as though Hooke's watered silks have left an immeasurably fine smear upon the objective lens of the microscope, casting their weave over everything that comes under his instrumentally augmented eye. Clothing is not a second skin; skin, like everything else, is a second clothing, woven and dressed.

Fabrics may even have performed a more subtle, phenomenological function, governing how Hooke saw, and therefore engraved, natural forms, like sea-sponges, or the 14th plate, an engraving of seaweed at high magnification. The regularity of its microstructure owes something to the engraving, included on the same page without explanation, of what appears to be a swatch of wool worsted. This image is an anomaly; William Petty would call it "extralocal." Also on the same plate, as the second figure, is a drawing of the surface of a rosemary leaf—its upper surface (just visible in the top of the circle) doubled over onto the underside; this he compares to "a curious quilted bagg of green Silk […] Nature in this, as it were, expressing her Needle-work, or imbroidery." Perhaps the third figure, the swatch of worsted, was part of an earlier version of *Micrographia*, where Hooke returned to fabrics as analogies for spontaneous or emergent forms; possibly it was included here as a thought or comparative sketch comparing the regularity of the seaweed to the regularity of woven fabrics. But the inclusion here of this unmentioned engraving points to the deeper logic continuing to coordinate his conception of the natural world; it registers the orbital drag or mutual magnetism of weaving, as an idea, drawing two natural materials to the woven one that explains them. From cloth made from spun particles, to skin as the "implication" or "intangling" of fibers, to the patterned microstructure of seaweed or a sea sponge: weaving accounts for the properties of each.

SELVAGE: COMPLEXITY

A selvage is the stitching added to the raw end of cloth when the weaving is done. In this spirit, less of tying up loose ends than of defining a border, I offer a brief, local glance at the immediate aftermath of the complexity concept. This is in the work of John Locke, the philosopher for whom complexity had the greatest direct impact. Robert Hooke, pursuing a continued interest in wool and wool fibers, undertook an extensive study on the making of felt.[54] This he delivered as a lecture to the Royal Society in 1666, the year after *Micrographia* appeared, but unlike the book, which was received enthusiastically, his research on the felt-hat industry received little applause. Hooke's treatise is of interest in part because of its excruciating attention to detail—but it is not detail of the corpuscularian, microstructural sort. It lavishes attention on twists of the craftsman's hand, the singing of his bow as he fluffs loose particles of wool in the fleece, or the pressure he places on a batt (a loosely compacted layer of wool) to compress it into hardened cloth. In its focus on craft, it outdoes even Petty's "History of Cloth," and perhaps for this reason, studies of cloth and cloth-making reached a dead end. Although Hooke prepared a manuscript for the press, it was never printed, and Hooke turned his attention to other, immanently pressing matters, like the rebuilding of London after the Great Fire.

It was at about this same time, however, that Locke moved to London and joined the Royal Society, where he picked up the thread dropped by Hooke, Petty, and their colleagues. Locke's innovation would be to adapt their corpuscularian metaphysics into a system of mental contents, of a faculty of understanding presiding over little, nugget-like mental objects called "ideas."[55] Our idea of the sun might seem like one of the simplest possible ideas—but in fact it is, Locke would in 1671 aver, the "complication of many simple Ideas together," a "collection of these several simple ideas round, bright, hot."[56] And while "complex" and "complication" had a prior life in Latin and French-language philosophy, Locke was using it for the first time in a new way.[57] He had picked up the vocabulary of complication as what binds together simple components—a lexical turn that would persist. Such ideas as "beauty, gratitude, a man, an army, the universe," Locke would by 1691 insist, "I call complex," for, like the sun, each of these ideas is itself composed of other ideas: each is "complicated" from ideas so simple they evade definition. Thus is the basic work of the understanding, the way that we learn about the world in order to anticipate and manipulate the world in which we move, borrowed from the lingo of a handcraft. In short, Locke has given us an intellectual system in which the mind's work is akin to an extended, perpetual weaving. This is how the concept of complexity descends to us—where it forms a cornerstone of analytical approaches to practical and theoretical problems.

The Enlightenment generally thought of knowledge about created things and knowledge about natural ones as distinct. There were, on the one hand, the mysteries of nature and the perfection of divine design, and there was, on the other, the intentional activity of the artisan and the imperfect productions of the hand. But, as a term referring to the deliberate, intricate combinations which happen in the loom, complexity reminds us of the extent to which early modern metaphysics and theories of nature were inspired by and embedded in artisanal practices. Similar arguments might be made of the special techniques of medical chemistry, of the ink and dye trades, of mining and smelting, and of the general production of working materials, but when it comes to imagining phenomenal properties, no trade was more crucial to imagining the invisible workings of the world than the weaving of hair into cloth.[58] Early modern materials offered the laboratory its world and its vocabulary, and so Enlightenment theory was indebted, both for its rhetorical figures and for its conceptual structure, to artisanal practice. Complexity, and its constellation of related concepts, was profoundly linked to this world of craft and the kinds of models that artisanal labor made possible to imagine.[59] As a lexicon and a related way of viewing the world, complexity was woven on the loom.

CHAPTER 5

Health and Hygiene

MARGARET K. POWELL AND JOSEPH ROACH

During the Enlightenment nothing threatened hair health more dramatically than fire. In a candle-lit age, powdered wigs brought dry hair into proximity with open flame. As predicted by the cause-and-effect logic of empirical science, combustion naturally followed. The graphic satirist Thomas Rowlandson captured the drama of such a conflagration in *A Doleful Disaster, or Miss Fubby Fatarmin's Wig caught Fire* (1813) (Figure 5.1). Although the interior décor and the costumes of the ensemble are conventionalized in the routine manner of a domestic conversation piece, the artist omits no grotesque detail of the action precipitated by the emergency. The protagonist, her head aflame, screams and flails, kicking over a chair. Her panic sets in motion a farcical sequence of events depicted as happening simultaneously. The room fills with

FIGURE 5.1: Thomas Rowlandson, *A Doleful Disaster, or Miss Fubby Fatarmin's Wig caught Fire* (not before 1813). Courtesy of The Lewis Walpole Library, Yale University.

would-be firefighters. A servant douses the victim with water from a fish-themed bladder. A uniformed officer upsets the tea things by pulling off the table cloth to smother the flames. And characteristically of Rowlandson's gendered depiction of social upset, several strained bodices burst their seams all at once, spilling their contents unrestrainedly in the fleshy equivalent of a choric shriek.

Such a fiasco need not have been typical to be compellingly allegorical of the ways in which eighteenth-century society viewed hair. First, there was its overall importance. More personally connected to the wearer than clothing and yet more reliably prearranged than countenance, hair represented a primary means of staking a social claim, for better or worse, on the occasion of first impressions. Second, there was its widely understood vulnerability to misfortune. The beholders of *A Doleful Disaster* may not themselves have experienced their hair going up in flames, but, given the prevalence of afflictions of the scalp at that time, they very likely had known an itch that made them feel as if their "heads were on fire."[1] Third, there was the sense of hair as a general problem: What to do with it? That was so because of the many troubles it caused the people who tried to grow it, purchase it, do it, clean it up, let it down, comb it out, cut it off, medicate it, and, rarely but urgently, extinguish it. Durable in human experience over time, these troubles live on also in works of history and literature. Nowhere do they appear more prolifically than in the hairdressers' advice, medicinal remedies, anecdotes, poems, novels, graphic satires, diaries, and letters of the Enlightenment.

Specifically, the hairdressers' treatises explain how to keep hair healthy and deal with problems as they arise; the collections of medical remedies propose solutions to problems that hairdressers could neither prevent nor cure; the literary works suggest what it means to care for hair or neglect it in a society that knows its importance; the satirical prints, especially those by Thomas Rowlandson (1756–1827), inspire laughter at the ludicrous and sometimes painful predicaments it creates; and finally, the unique source of the diary of Samuel Pepys (1633–1703) records in confessional detail what it felt like to have issues of hair care take over the most intimate relationships in his household.

THE NATURAL PHILOSOPHY OF HAIR

A variety of diseases afflicted the hair and head, of course, then as now: clinical observations of folliculitis, dermatitis of the scalp, and psoriasis, all generally diagnosed as "scurvy," appear in the historical record of the period. As hair grew brittle, its ends "forked" (split). As it grew oily, it clogged pores and raised pimples. As it became infested, it had to be close cropped or shaved clean. Wig-wearers reasonably feared contagion when they donned hair shorn from unknown heads. Inherited baldness defied remediation regardless of effort. Hair loss from other causes, including smallpox and syphilis, worried the afflicted. Dandruff annoyed sufferers and repelled their associates. Numerous publications touted remedies for diseases of the hair and scalp, and professional hairdressers promised to prevent them. Exceptionally dirty hair provoked comment and censure, while fashionable grooming occupied a good deal of time for those who could afford it.

Affording hair care likely meant suffering hairdressers' treatments of teasing, frizzing, curling, powdering, and greasing with oil or pomatum, a perfumed unguent derived from animal fat, of which "bear's grease" was a highly prized source. The treatments themselves raised questions about health, not least of which was damage done by the

FIGURE 5.2: *[Hairdressing]* (Published by J.S. Bretherton, 1787). Courtesy of The Lewis Walpole Library, Yale University.

heat and pressure of the curling iron. Contemporaries knew that scorching wrecked the hair, but some also believed that fashion justified the sacrifice, as claimed by the hortatory verses that accompany a 1787 satirical print titled *Hairdressing* (Figure 5.2):

> Alas by some degree of woe
> We ev'ry bliss must gain.
> The heart can ne're a transport know
> That never felt a pain.

Impositions on their clients notwithstanding, experts spoke about the management of hair with the innovative authority of empiricist philosophy behind them. Earlier conceptions of hair as magical had been veiled in superstition of the sort that Alexander Pope ridiculed in *The Rape of the Lock* (1712), with its fantastical choruses of Sylphs and Gnomes. Now less likely to rely on received lore, authorities tested physical hypotheses with rational methods. "Hair dressing is not altogether a practical part of science," opined *The New London Toilet* (1778), "for unless theory is joined to it, the hair dresser will never make any proficiency in his business."[2] What sort of theory? In his *Treatise on the Hair* (1770), Peter Gilchrist, citing the modern discovery of the circulation of the blood, bases his explanation of healthy hair on a free ebb and flow of the "the vital liquor" that is "conveyed through the hair by a small and almost imperceptible tube," one equipped with a tiny valve for the purpose.[3] An exceptionally learned hairdresser like James Stewart, writing in his compendious *Plocacosmos: Or the Whole Art of Hair Dressing* (1782), understood his role as a natural philosopher as well as a historian of hair. His data range from prescientific lore ("the ancients held the hair to be a sort of excrement, fed only with excrementitious matter") to microscopic examination of damaged hairs to investigate the vexing problem of split ends.[4] Addressing "forked" hair in clinical terms, Alexander Stewart in *The Natural Production of Hair* (1795) sensibly urges an emergency trimming if there isn't time for more laborious treatment, lest "all the Hair will sustain great injury from the points being thus split."[5] For all their philosophy and skill, however, no amount of expert precaution could avert every affliction or accident. Moreover, the Enlightenment's philosophy of hair hygiene, for all its awareness of its own modernity, differed in profound ways from that which prevails today. "Those who bathe," cautions Peter Gilchrist solemnly, "should never wet their hair, unless it be requisite on account of their health."[6] Typical of his colleagues, Alexander Stewart recommended waterless cleaning by coordinated applications of powder (typically refined from starch) and pomatum to keep the lustrous balance of dryness and oiliness to the benefit of both hair and scalp. He also defended the more labor-intensive solution of burning off split ends a few at a time as superior to the quick-fix of cutting them.[7] Although hairdressers universally recognized careful combing as key to hair hygiene, they cautioned that combing every day turned the hair gray.[8] Nevertheless, lapses of hair hygiene among people who could afford to keep themselves clean by the standards of the day were widely enough recognized as aberrant to become a subject of satirical censure as well as professional disapproval; but they were also known to be widespread and deeply engrained in individual behavior as well as socioeconomic circumstances.

Jonathan Swift's "excremental" or "scatological" group of poems, for instance, begins with "The Lady's Dressing Room" (1732). One woman's carelessness regarding hair hygiene occupies a prominent place in this satire, which proceeds as if following a check-all-the-boxes visit by a health inspector. In the first stanza, Celia's lover Strephon steals into her dressing room and finds it empty. He uses the occasion of her absence to take inventory of her wardrobe, accessories, and necessaries. Her name means "heavenly" but his discovery of her shocking personal habits disillusions the swain who has heretofore thought her so. As Strephon holds Celia's filthy smock up to the light of day, discovering the stains made by her underarms, he intervenes with the speaker and reader of the poem to suppress the reported observation that would logically come next:

In such a Case, few Words are best.
And *Strephon* bids us guess the rest;[9]

At first nothing seems to be left to innuendo in Strephon's report of his examination of the next items of his "Inventory," the disgusting implements on Celia's vanity, beginning with the most damning, her combs:

Now listen, while he next produces
The various Combs for various Uses;
Fill'd up with Dirt so closely fixt,
No Brush cou'd force a way betwixt;

> A paste of Composition rare,
> Sweat, Dandruff, Powder, Lead and Hair.[10]

Combs with teeth of different fineness were used to clean hair of different lengths and degrees of entanglement. But Celia's combs will clean nothing, fouled as they are with her bodily wastes, old powder, and lead-based face makeup, the whole mess congealed into a paste and knotted in a rancid hairball. The best authorities decried such abuses. William Moore, in *The Art of Hairdressing* (1780), concluded an excursus on failures of hair care by mincing no words about hygiene:

> Lastly, the keeping the Head clean, which is of such consequence, that the neglecting of it, the Head gets so dirty, and full of Pimples, that worse often follows, such as Vermin, scabby Heads, and Hair falling off; and if it does not, it will weaken the Roots, so that it will come off in Time, and leave a very thin Stock that can't be increas'd if ever so tenderly used after.[11]

The sense of the treatises on hair is that hygiene is an expression of enlightenment itself. In her account of Swift's "The Lady's Dressing Room" in *Designing Women: The Dressing Room in Eighteenth-Century Literature and Culture* (2005), Tita Chico analyses the system of Strephon's observations as representative of the empiricist methods of eighteenth-century natural philosophy, each item on the inventory moving by association from the identification of the object to its use and from its use to the woman herself—from comb to hair to Celia. Chico shows how Swift thus invokes the prestige and satirizes the limitations of finding enlightenment by such experimental procedures.[12] Strephon's induction leads him to a hypothesis about Celia's hair that is self-evidently valid as far as it goes in the absence of Celia herself, which is presumably the best evidence. But as with gravity and the weight of air, which are intangible except for their invisible influences, sometimes the phenomena under investigation reveal themselves to science only by deduction. The natural philosopher in this case has likely deduced but fails to mention the full implications of a comb that is so clotted with debris that it will no longer clean. Strephon bids us guess the rest: not only is Celia absent from her dressing room; she has taken her lice with her.

Swift's contemporaries and satirical successors knew that the most pervasive and persistent issues concerning hair health and hygiene arose from infestation: lice, scabies (burrowing mites), and fleas. In *An Old Maid in search of a Flea* (1794) (Figure 5.3), Thomas Rowlandson depicts the most readily available treatment for a common problem. At her bedside the woman exterminates her tormentors one at a time while her cat looks on as if innocent of its role.

As in painting, so it is in poetry. In Swift's next "excremental" poem, "A Beautiful Young Nymph Going to Bed" (1734), the speaker narrates the progress of an aging demimondaine named Corinna as she undresses herself at the end of a day's work. With the removal of each item of clothing, she reveals her decrepitude, as Strephon incrementally exposes Celia's slovenliness one possession at a time; but in this poem, Swift's speaker makes infestation explicit. After a catalogue of revolting images of running sores and diseased body parts, in which every item represents a subtraction, he ends with an account of an addition—the ardent visitors brought in to her rooms by her lapdog, as he and they are the only ones left who in any way care for her: "And *Shock* her tresses fill'd with Fleas."[13] Her case may have been extreme, but her visitors belonged to a family that is ancient, wide-ranging, and very successful.

FIGURE 5.3: Thomas Rowlandson, *An Old Maid in search of a Flea* (1794). Beinecke Rare Book and Manuscript Library, Yale University.

SOCIABLE VERMIN

Many customs and beliefs of the Enlightenment period differ from what we know about those of antiquity, the Middle Ages, the Renaissance, and modernity; but, biologically speaking, bloodsucking pests haven't changed that much. Hematophagous ectoparasites, gorging themselves at the site of their bites, regurgitate and defecate the contents of their blood meal back into the wound they have made. Along with their vomit and feces may come a number of even more unwelcome infusions. In the case of *Yersinia pestis*, the rat flea, the most unwelcome indeed is bubonic plague. In the case of *Pediculus humanus humanus*, the body louse, it is typhus. But in the case of *Pediculus humanus capitis*, head lice, and *Pthirus pubis*, pubic lice (popularly known as "crabs"), it is injected allergens that cause a persistent itch. While not life-threatening in themselves, "pediculosis," the infestation, and "pruritus," the itch, are personally embarrassing, socially objectionable, and utterly maddening.

Some general distinctions obtain. Body lice make themselves most noxious as vectors of infectious diseases. Hair lice, wherever on the body they may be found, *are* the infection, transmitted by direct body-to-body contact or, with greater difficulty, by passing through shared headgear or other articles of clothing. Unlike fleas, lice cannot jump, only crawl. With a life cycle spent entirely in the hairy regions of their hosts, they deposit eggs that hatch in seven to ten days, with another ten days required for the hatchlings to mature and lay eggs of their own. "Nits" are the white eggshells that they leave behind attached to individual hairs. Once separated from their hosts, head lice will die within a day. Coevolved over millions of years of interspecies transfer among primates, such parasites came to need human blood to survive, and now they will suck no other. Unmotivated to separate themselves from their source of food and shelter, therefore, such parasites, while ready and willing to migrate person to person (and even more to reproduce), have proved difficult to evict. Ineradicably conjoined with their hosts over time, they live on also in cultural representation as the most intimately familiar of nuisances.

In Tobias Smollett's *Roderick Random* (1748), for example, the eponymous hero imagines his hair to be hosting a large number of guests, "whose visit I did not at all think seasonable; neither did they seem inclined to leave in a hurry, being in possession of my chief quarters, where they fed without reserve at the expence of my blood." He likens them to a colony settling on his head, and he quickly accepts a friend's advice to preempt its "naturalized" establishment by getting his hair cut short.[14] He does not need to name the guests, so familiar are they to the general reader; nor does he need to explain the remedy—keeping his hair close cropped or shaved clean. Thinking of lice under the socioeconomic metaphor of colonization allows Smollett to orient his picaresque narrative. Infection transcended geographical location as well as social position. A popular miscellany poem first appearing in 1737, "The Louse in Imitation of the Flea," narrates the progress of a louse, who is the first-person narrator, on a journey through the heads of ten hosts drawn from the various occupations and classes of society. The speaker of the poem, The Louse, was born on a beggar woman who prostitutes herself to and infects a lawyer, who communicates The Louse to a judge; he, to his wife; his wife, to her lover; her lover, to a gamester; the gamester, to a coquette, who, to rid herself of The Louse and its companions, cuts off her hair and has her maid throw him into the street, where a rag-picker scavenges the cuttings and carries him back to the slum to die where he was born.[15] Not even kings escaped visitations, or at least the imputation of them. Satirizing George III, Peter Pindar (John Wolcot) brought forth the mock-heroic

Lousiad (1786–1795), in which the hero makes a startling appearance in Canto I at the very invocation of the poem:

> The Louse I sing, who, from some head unknown,
> Yet born and educated near a Throne,
> Dropp'd down (so will'd the dread decree of Fate)
> With Legs sprawling on the Monarch's plate[16]

Thomas Rowlandson illustrated the scene in a satirical print (Figure 5.4). While the princesses recoil at the scandal, the outraged king interrogates the cowed servants one by one, *Is this your louse?* But the joke is that no head escapes the implication of lousiness, even the head of state.

Very short hair was a style abetted throughout the period by the fashion of wig-wearing. Close cropping or clean shaving offered a first-line defense against infestation, especially but not exclusively for men. Short hair is obviously easier to clean as well as to inspect, and an infested wig may be set aside until the lice starve, or it might also be boiled for good measure. Short hair is also easier to comb, and fine-tooth combs were a second line of defense against infestation, rousting out the adult lice and culling the nits. That is why Celia's careless habits mattered to Swift's readers, on the one hand, and Roderick's diligent precautions to Smollett's, on the other. Alternatively, the hairdressers touted

FIGURE 5.4: Thomas Rowlandson, *[I]s this, your Louse [?]* (1787). Courtesy of The Lewis Walpole Library, Yale University.

various concoctions of grease or oil-based pomatum as a repellent as well as a cleansing agent. And they had good reasons for doing so. The drier the head (in today's sense, cleaner), the more accommodating it is to lice, which have difficulty attaching their eggs to oily follicles. In *The Natural Production of Hair*, Alexander Stewart explains that the key to the healthy management and proper growth

> is to keep it clean, from dirt and vermin, &c. as they effectually prevent its growing; nits being of such a clammy nature, that nothing is yet found out, sufficient with labour to extricate them from the Hair, and when they are in great numbers upon the Hairs, as I have seen them, they not only prevent its growth, but by eating out all the substance it contained, so that it becomes in comparison, like the withered branches of a decayed tree, for they even eat the Hair into a powder, therefore there is nothing so good as keeping the head clean, the Hair moist with fresh pomatum, for either young or old.[17]

He goes on to recommend bear's grease as the precaution of greatest efficacy, but in its absence (the bears had to be imported from Norway), other pomatums will do. Noting that bear's grease is "finer" than any of the alternatives, however, William Moore reassures his readers that it will not, as some clients fear, whiten their hair. Bears, he allows, do indeed turn white but only in the winter due to the extreme cold.[18]

No regime of prevention, however, stood proof against a virulent social disease like lice. Most people in the period seem to have kept as clean as they could afford to. But nonconformity put everyone else at risk. Such was the case, for instance, when the egregious Topham Beauclerk infected all the guests at a holiday party at Blenheim in the 1770s. Lady Louisa Stewart narrates the story of this one-man epidemic:

> The elegant and accomplished gentleman [was] what the French call *cynique* in his personal habits beyond what one would have thought possible in anyone but a beggar or a gipsy. He and Lady Di made part of a great Christmas party at Blenheim, where soon after the company were all met, they all found themselves as strangely annoyed as the Court of Pharaoh were of old by certain visitants—"*in all their quarters*"—It was in the days of powder and pomatum, when stiff frizzing and curling, with hot irons and black pins, made the entrance of combs extremely difficult—in short, the distress became unspeakable. Its origin being clearly traced to Mr. Beauclerk, one of the gentlemen undertook to remonstrate with him, and began delicately hinting how much the ladies were inconvenienced—"What!" said Beauclerk, "Are they so nice as that comes to? Why I have enough to stock a parish."[19]

Sociopathic in his filthiness, Beauclerk invaded the throng as an uncontainable vector, threatening a wave of pestilence with every tête-à-tête, while the women's complicated hairdos, fixed in place for the duration of the holiday, offered vulnerable objectives to the occupying swarm.

At this time the women in Beauclerk's set wore their hair piled fashionably high with extenders curled into comb-defying headdresses. At the base of these structures at the crowns of their heads, the hairdresser inserted a heart-shaped "cushion," which was puffed up like a pillow to add body to the hairdo and held in place with special "cushion pins." The hair, natural or acquired, could then be frizzed and piled over and around the cushion, which might remain pinned in place for days or even weeks. The professionals who created these structures well knew their vulnerabilities. "It should be made clean," Stewart, the natural philosopher-hairdresser, cautions with regard to the cushion, "and delicately neat, or else, being placed on the warmest part of the head, it may breed and prove troublesome."[20] Stewart did not need to specify what kind of trouble would stem from breeding or what it was that would likely breed.

Roderick Random's comparison of the lice on his head to colonists in a "naturalized" (that is, well established) colony illuminates the remarkable plantation of all manner of foreign things, living and dead, into the fantastic *têtes* of the period. The graphic satirists had to outdo themselves in exaggeration to keep a step ahead of the hairdressers, who installed such impedimenta as model ships and birdcages with live birds along with plumes and ornaments in their actual creations. The anonymous print *Bunters Hill or May Day* (1776) (Figure 5.5) shows the full-blown colonization of the coiffure at the height of the big hair craze. Surmounted by a sow and her piglets, the hair teems with life down to the roots. The misspelled allusion to the battle of Bunker Hill (1775) suggests that the "naturalized" colonists are about to rise in revolt and occupy the high ground. The fear that hairdos will be overrun by objectionable aliens finds its most harrowing affirmation in reformer John Donaldson's story of the lady who woke one morning to discover that during the night a female rat had not only made its nest in her hair, but also "brought forth her young."[21] It is to be hoped that she did not also bring forth any fleas.

What could be done by way of defense? Blood-baited flea-traps provided the third line of defense against infestation, and they could be deployed against lice as well. The trap consisted of a hollow cylindrical tube, typically carved out of ivory or fashioned from silver, with perforations along its length. The hollow of the tube was filled with a combination of human blood (as the bait) and a sticky substance such as fat or honey (as the trap).[22] The last line of the ladies' defense—the deployment of which seems more like a public acknowledgment of surrender—was the long-handled head scratcher. Two satirical prints by Rowlandson, *Dressing for a Birthday* (1789) (Figure 5.6) and *Dressing for a Masquerade* (1790) (Figure 5.7), depict many of the activities related to hair and hair hygiene discussed above. Everyone in both scenes, mistress and servant alike, seems to be having a lot of fun preparing to party hard, but the details disclose that serious precautions are in place as well. In the left foreground of the "Birthday Party," three maids minister to a large woman whose clean-shaven head is about to receive a fantastic headdress festooned with fruits and topped by plumes: her total baldness is a strong measure against *Pediculus humanus capitus*. On the right, a young woman whose full head of natural hair is curled and powdered seats herself so that her *friseur* can put his finishing touches on the extender that drops down her back. Her velvet choker could conceal a flea trap worn as a lavaliere. At least the dogs that sport in both scenes suggest that prudence might prompt general vigilance on that score.

In the center of the "Masquerade," a be-plumed masker with one breast bared admires her headdress in a mirror, while on the left a girl waits expectantly while her hairdresser combs out her thick brown tresses. Behind her, an older woman disguised as a nun (perhaps a duenna?) stands by, holding a long-necked jar suitable for containing an unguent. Other jars wait within reach on the table. Offering the two prints as companion pieces, Rowlandson shows how heavily labor-intensive hair care was as part of dressing up in the eighteenth century. Altogether six maids and three hairdressers busy themselves in the service of the party-goers, and the dishabille on view implies that the staff is still short-handed. Throughout the period, hair care defined the relationship of servants and masters in an intimate way, and in no source is that relationship better documented than in the daily personal records of an official in the admiralty office during the reign of Charles II.

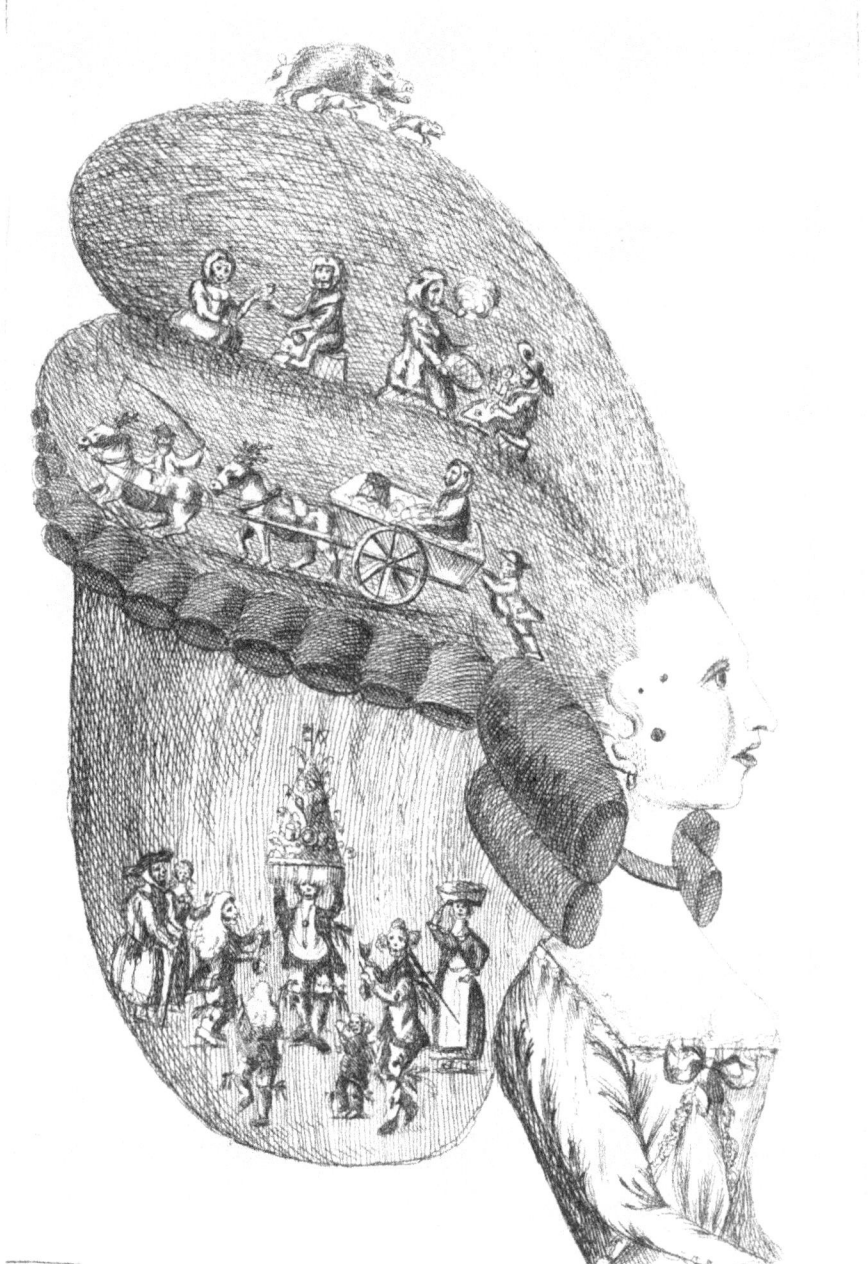

FIGURE 5.5: *Bunters Hill or May Day* (Published by J. Lockington, 1776). Courtesy of The Lewis Walpole Library, Yale University.

FIGURE 5.6: Thomas Rowlandson, *Dressing for a Birthday* (1790). Courtesy of The Lewis Walpole Library, Yale University.

FIGURE 5.7: Thomas Rowlandson, *Dressing for a Masquerade* (1790). Courtesy of The Lewis Walpole Library, Yale University.

A LOUSY HUSBAND

The Diary of Samuel Pepys gives us as detailed an account as we have of the place of hair health and hygiene in the daily life of an Enlightenment subject. No detail of his daily routine was too small for Pepys to confide in his diary, which he kept from 1659 to 1669. That includes details of his grooming. As part of an overall orientation to the most important matters relating to hair at the moment in fashion history when periwigs came into vogue, Pepys offers a personal narrative of one man's efforts to keep "neat"—free of vermin as well as fashionably tonsured—as he endeavors to rise in the bureaucratic ranks of the navy office, at court, and about town. More poignantly, he also recounts how the likelihood of infestation contributed to the overall environment of his household and influenced the relationships within it. Specifically, he returns to issues of hair hygiene when he recounts key scenes from his troubled marriage to the beloved but long-suffering Elizabeth Pepys, including details of the affair that nearly wrecked it.

In the struggle against vermin, the punctilious admiralty clerk began the contest with an unusual advantage. A rarity among men or beasts, he did not taste good to fleas. Traveling with Dr. Timothy Clarke, physician to the king's household, Pepys slept in the same infested bed with him during their journey. Enjoying much ribaldry together as fellow civil servants (Clarke was more senior), they made a most amusing discovery, as Pepys records: "We lay very well and merrily. In the morning, concluding him to be of the eldest blood and house of Clerkes, because that all the fleas came to him and not to me."[23] At that time the rat flea still remained unsuspected as the vector of the world's most dreaded infectious disease. The diarist's relative immunity from its bites may have, unknown to him, saved his life during the Great Plague of London in 1665 (*SP*, 10:337). Four years later he had another close call when he backed into a candle flame while gossiping with Lady Hinchinbrooke and set his wig on fire (*SP*, 9:322). Head lice, however, presented Pepys with a threat to his well-being of a different sort.

Pepys cared for his hair. Even though taking precautions against infestation by having his hair cut close made sense to him, as it increasingly did to most men and some women over the course of the long eighteenth century, he repeatedly tells his diary how reluctant he is to part with his naturally flowing locks (*SP*, 2:97). After back-and-forth discussions during the year 1662–1663, he and Elizabeth decide that he should have his hair cut and a peruke made out of it (*SP*, 4:343). Reluctantly but philosophically, he has Chapman, his wigmaker, do this service for him, and at the same time he shops for a wig made from someone else's hair. Where cleanliness is concerned, he realizes, two heads of detachable hair are better than one (*SP*, 4:362). Worrying about the provenance of the purchased hair, however, he makes careful inquiries about the donor (*SP*, 4:350). A scion of the empiricism of the Royal Society and an observant witness to the great pestilence of 1665, he worries that contact with the bodies or clothing of plague victims may communicate the disease. Later, he sets aside a prized wig when he finds he has reason to suspect its origins:

> Up, and put on my coulour silk suit, very fine, and my new periwig, bought a good while since, but I darst not wear it because the plague was in Westminster when I bought it. And it is a wonder what will be the fashion after the plague is done as to periwigs, for nobody will dare to buy any haire for fear of infection—that it had been cut off the heads of people dead of the plague. (*SP*, 6:210)

But even after he has it cut close to accommodate his wigs, his hair requires fine-combing every night. The purpose of the combing is to discover and remove adult lice and any nits. Having a servant perform this service becomes a cherished bedtime ritual along with the washing of his hands and face.[24] Cleanliness necessitates vigilance. When Pepys's groomer finds lice in his hair, he has them counted and sorted by size (*SP*, 9:24). When he suspects a boy servant of bringing lice into the house and infecting him, he orders an examination of the boy's head, which proves negative: "so how they came, I know not; but presently did shift myself, and so shall be rid of them, and cut my hayre close to my head" (*SP*, 9:424). But changing rooms and cutting his hair were only part of the domestic decontaminating process that he is obliged to carry out, as he remorsefully discloses to his diary.

As a serial philanderer, Pepys conducted his most flagrant and destructive affair when he seduced Deborah Willet ("Deb"), a favorite household servant and his wife's companion, who came to work for the childless couple in the autumn of 1667. Pretty, intelligent, and fresh from boarding school, Deb won the hearts of both of them. At first they treated her almost like a daughter. She traveled with the family, sleeping in the same room with them both and keeping affectionate company with Elizabeth; but Samuel developed feelings for Deb of a different kind.

Hair care provided the inciting incident to the heartbreaking but exciting domestic drama that then ensued. As she settled into the household, Deb took on the task of combing Pepys's hair at bedtime. He soon came to look forward to this intimate ritual more than ever. Her ministrations inflamed, if they did not ignite, his interest in her, while other contributing circumstances stoked the fire. Play-going constituted another of Pepys's pleasurable rituals. Even at a dull play the sight of pretty actresses rarely failed to excite his libido. On the wintry afternoon of January 11, 1668, as was now his custom, he took both his wife and Deb to see John Fletcher's *The Wild Goose Chase* at the King's Theatre. The play disappointed him, but he warmed to the backstage gossip shared by actress Mary Knepp, another of his amours. He took particular note of Knepp's salacious update about the king's complicated adulteries with three other actresses—Nell Gynne, Moll Davies, and Elizabeth Farley—who were, under the king's sponsorship of the company, servants in his royal household, whatever other roles they played on the stage or off. Pepys's starchy disapproval of "a prince so devoted his pleasure" neither conceals his envy nor dissuades him from emulation. The *Diary* continues:

> Thence home, and there to the office and did some business; and so with my wife for half an hour walking by moonlight and, it being frosty weather, walking in the garden; and then home to supper, and so by the fireside to have my head combed, as I now often do, by Deb, whom I love should be fiddling about me; and so to bed. (*SP*, 9:20)

The spark had landed in the tinder, and it began to smolder. By bedtime on March 31, Pepys has added overtly sexual kissing and fondling to Deb's tonsorial "fiddling." Elizabeth seems to suspect something is going on because that evening she becomes uncharacteristically angry with Deb over the relatively trivial problem of the girl's clumsy penmanship, while Pepys, in public solidarity with his wife, feigns displeasure. Behind closed doors, however, he expresses himself otherwise: "I seemed angry with [Deb] too; but going to bed, she undressed me, and there I did give her good advice." The "advice" includes taking her on his lap, playing with her breasts, and touching her thigh (*SP*, 9:143). Worse is to come. On October 25, his escalating liberties with his mate's trusted companion leads to a scene of discovery in *flagrante delicto*: "and after supper, to have my head combed by Deb, which occasioned the greatest sorrow to me that ever I knew in this world; for my wife, coming up suddenly, did find me imbracing the girl with my hand sub su coats; and endeed, I was with my main in her cunny. I was at a wonderful loss upon it, and the girl also" (*SP*, 9:337). Keeping his hair clean, he has fouled his nest.

Over the next several months, a deeply wounded Elizabeth reacts variously. She creates scenes of silent reproach, uncontrollable tears, aggrieved rages, and finally the refusal to wash or groom herself until Deb is evicted from the household. Ruefully, Pepys complies. Deb's nightly combing ceases, but despite his avowals to the contrary, the affair continues even after she moves out. On January 12, 1669, Elizabeth, waiting until bedtime, attempts a physical assault on her husband, wielding red-hot tongs from the fireplace. Truly alarmed at this violent revision of his beloved evening ritual, Pepys persuades her to put down her pincers and come back to bed. After several hours of pleading, he finally soothes her to sleep, but not to unqualified forgiveness, with tender words (*SP*, 9:14). Now his misery knows no limit, and neither does his self-pity. Not only has he turned his household upside down and imperiled his marriage by his incendiary infidelity but now, in the absence of Deb's nightly nit-picking, it's his scalp that's on fire.

After suffering an increasingly maddening itch for a week, he finally works up his nerve to ask Elizabeth for her help:

> So to my wife's chamber, and there supped and got her [to] cut my hair and [to] look [at] my shirt, for I have itched mightily these six or seven days; and when all came to all, she finds that I am louzy, having found in my head and body above twenty lice, little and great; which I do wonder at, being more than I have had I believe almost these twenty years. (*SP*, 9:424)

Here Pepys, the lousy husband, reveals much about his attitudes and practices relating to hair hygiene over two decades. Dealing with lice meant keeping regular score, monitoring not only their number but their size. But more importantly, Elizabeth and Samuel both now demonstrate how well they know that caring watchfulness is the price of domestic cleanliness in more ways than one.

The vermin create for the Pepys household not only a nuisance but an environment. Living with them as intimately as with one another, the human agents locate and occupy their relative places among them on their little chain of domestic being. Lice draw the parties together in the service of hygiene, for richer or poorer, for better or worse, but cleanliness of hair and scalp seems more like the ultimate epiphenomenal benefit of a crucial interpersonal ritual than the singular end of one. Elizabeth first withholds her own cleanliness in protest but she ultimately—and pointedly—effects the delousing of her errant mate. Both women perform this rite on an alpha male, mirroring the submissive grooming behavior in other primates. But Elizabeth can now lay claim to a certain degree of redeeming power, however limited, over his suffering and penitent body. He bade Deb momentarily usurp her role; now Elizabeth takes over Deb's for good. She performs this humble ritual for Pepys at the moment of her greatest influence over him, as their marriage enters a new phase of seriousness even as the diary comes to an end. He has pledged improvement. She has set aside the tongs. At bedtime on January 21, still itching, he takes tender note of her slowly yielded but sincere forgiveness: "So late up, silent and not supping, but hearing her utter some words of discontent to me with silence; and so to bed weeping to myself for grief—which she discerning, came to bed and mighty kind; and so, with great joy on both sides, to sleep" (*SP*, 9:422). Two nights later, she does his hair.

DESPERATE REMEDIES

Other people who suffered from infestation had much harder luck with it than Pepys. Not everyone could count on helping hands or a change of linen, especially those who populated the teeming slums or lived rough on the streets. Of all the miserable depredations Tim Hitchcock catalogues in *Down and Out in Eighteenth-Century London* (2004), he names lice as the most painful to the beggars and street people whose condition he documents. Let the harrowing story of the death of Mary Whistle in the workhouse in St. Giles in the Fields stand for many others. Hitchcock puts together published accounts with Whistle's autopsy to reconstruct the circumstances of her final days. Whistle starved to death, uncared for in the workhouse dormitory, lingering for eleven weeks in an infested bed, literally eaten alive. Appalling even for the time, her case inspired sympathetic protests in prose and verse: "Her Hair was matted with the Vermin so, / The like before no one did ever know."[25] When lice flourish unchecked, they breed in cascading generations, limited in their expansion on the body they infest only by the supply of fresh blood. For unfortunates like Mary Whistle, the supply lasted months, nourishing the parasites that beset her even as she wanted sustenance herself.

Yet even those who lived in the worst squalor had ways to fight back. At the most primitive level of delousing, there was retaliation in kind. Reviewing the membership of "The Beggar's Club" in 1709, Ned Ward reports on one wretch who entertains the crowd gathered around him by eating the lice he finds on his own person, "conveying the little prisoners between his finger and his thumb from his neck to his mouth in order to bite the biters."[26] Other strategies commended themselves to those with better means and more scruple. Again, Rowlandson finds a vividly graphic way to narrate the most telling scene. In *Bug Breeders in the Dog Days* (1806) (Figure 5.8), an infested couple, who might have suggested to theater-goers a parodic version of Macbeth and Lady Macbeth, do not rub blood off their hands but scratch themselves in the places where they itch the most. The snuffed candle on the bedside table suggests that the night wears on but that sleep is impossible. The man in the bed has already futilely fanned his burning head, which he has tried and failed to protect with a nightcap. The nightcap, worn tight, was a key item in recommended treatment and prevention. But it was only one element in the onerous project of extirpating vermin from the head or crotch.

The hairdressers suggested some relatively mild countermeasures. Alexander Stewart's recipe called for "the best rum" applied to the scalp at night once a week.[27] William Moore specified "Stavesacre Root," a traditional insecticide derived from the delphinium plant.[28] But the popular circulation of prescriptions for much harsher treatments suggests that they were also in use and probably more widely so across classes. *The Complete Vermin-Killer* (1777), which distinguishes between head lice and "crab" lice, offers a quite frightening array of remedies, in ascending order of rigor and danger. The first is relatively benign: boil fresh butter mixed with pepper into a salve; cut off all the hair; rub the salve liberally on the head; cover it with a nightcap. The others are more harrowing, demonstrating by their likely side-effects the desperate need for relief:

> Boil Rats-bane in spring Water. When it is pretty well boiled, keep the Water for use. Rub it occasionally on the head; put on a cap, and tie it close. This must be used with the utmost care, and the hands washed clean after, for it is a strong poison.[29]

Rats-bane consists of arsenic, the ingestion of which leads to internal bleeding, blindness, and heart failure. But in this remedy, it is to be diluted in water. *The Complete Vermin-*

FIGURE 5.8: Thomas Rowlandson, *Bug Breeders in the Dog Days* (1806). Beinecke Rare Book and Manuscript Library, Yale University.

Killer goes on to suggest a similar application of "three-pennyworth of Quicksilver [mercury]," but without the broth. A heavy metal, mercury vapor poisons the blood and nerves, ironically causing a symptom called "formication," the illusion that bugs are swarming over the body. The final vermin-killing nostrum is to cover the scalp with lye, a corrosive, which would likely burn off all the skin in the treated area along with the lice.[30] The severity of the proposed remedies suggests the urgency of complaints.

The image of a scalp "on fire" returns this account of hair health and hygiene to where it began with Rowlandson's *A Doleful Disaster*; but rather than the unusual accident of a wig aflame, it is the everyday reality of infection and the inventive (though alarming) variety of its remedies that affirm the important place of hair care in the period of the Enlightenment. The pervasiveness of problem hair in popular publications—technical and imaginative, printed and graphic—shows a high degree of interest among literate consumers. The expansiveness of the comedy associated with problem hair attests to the public recognition not only of its suitability as an object of satirical ridicule but also of some measure of sympathetic identification, for the number of individuals who never experienced the sort of episode that hairdressers called "troublesome" must have been few. In his well-staffed household, for instance, Pepys worked diligently at keeping his hair clean and fell short anyway. At the same time, disturbing glimpses of diseased hair among the very poor suggest that the number of those who did not know the experience of being free of such troubles must have been many. In the workhouse, Mary Whistle died neglected, but she didn't die alone. But then Topham Beauclerk, who could afford cleanliness, gloated over his filth instead.

Perhaps the most remarkable single development in the Enlightenment period of the cultural history of hair is the number and prominence of the experts now devoted to its care. The hairdresser, ridiculed by satirists but pursued by consumers of his services, became a kind of celebrity professional. William Barker, who came to preeminence doing the hair of starring actors and actresses—David Garrick, Sarah Siddons, Frances Abington—wrote in his *Treatise on the Principles of Hair-dressing* (ca. 1785) about the rise of his profession during the eighteenth century: "nor was it till lately ever brought into such repute as to employ so great a number of professors."[31] That its professors sought to elevate its repute by making claims for its status as a liberal art or science is demonstrated by the words that recur in the titles of their publications: "treatise," "principles," and "art." That these titles often refer to self-published promotions for the author's practice does not diminish the ambition of their claim. They obviously could count on the wide and continuing interest of a public that cared for its hair and was glad to be enlightened about it.

CHAPTER SIX

Gender and Sexuality: "Hairs Less in Sight"

Some Vibrant Ideas of Gender, 1714–1795

JAYNE LEWIS

For the Hair, either natural or artificial, may be dress'd to produce in us different Ideas of the Qualities of Men.

> David Ritchie, *A Treatise on the Hair: Shewing its Generation, Means of its Preservation, Causes of its Decay. How to recover it when lost* (1770)

Oh hadst thou, Cruel! Been content to seize
Hairs less in sight, or any Hairs but these!

> Alexander Pope, *The Rape of the Lock* (1714)

In a rare enjambment, Pope hands his shorn Belinda the most transparent double entendre in *The Rape of the Lock*. "What else could this mean except pubic hairs?" wonders the poem's twentieth-century iconographer Robert Halsband. "And who else could seize them except an earthly lover?"[1] Writing to his friend Charles Ford in 1714, John Gay proposed that Ford might, as Aeneas did Venus, recognize Belinda's living prototype Arabella Fermor "by her Locks" and mischievously urged him to "think not of Hairs less in sight or any Hairs but these."[2] Charles Gildon too exulted in a couplet that, "with admirable Address, made *Arabella F—m—r* prefer the Locks of her Poll, to her Locks of another more sacred and secret Part" even as it paid "a Compliment to those parts of the Lady, to let the World know that the Lady had Hairs elsewhere, which she valu'd less."[3] Feminist critics of our own day often pardon Belinda's hyperbole in light of a scale of cultural "valu[e]" that compels women into false relation with their own bodies, making the hair of a woman who has been dead for almost three hundred years a lively topic in ongoing debates about the body's place in modern sexual politics and the social construction of gender.[4] But nobody doubts what Pope must have wanted his readers to "think"—indeed "know"—when they saw his Belinda speak of "Hairs less in sight."[5]

Leaving aside the spiritual and supernatural connotations that both Gildon and Gay facetiously attached to Belinda's (and Fermor's) unseen "Hairs," what would happen if we refused to fix those hairs in physical space?[6] Our ideas about what hair meant to eighteenth-century Britons are bound up with ideologies of substance and doctrines of visibility. But in certain spheres of eighteenth-century thought, hair was so ubiquitous that it was no longer meaningfully localized within any individual body. For instance, in contemporary taxonomies abetted by the modern microscope and other emergent technologies of vision, "Tufts of Hair" were to be found "on each Joint" of the caterpillar and, on the turkey, a "bushy Tuft like Horse-hair." Even the spider's back is so "beset with Hairs [that] the three Parts of the Body [are] in this Creature strangely confus'd"— as, by the bye, "they are also in a Crab."[7] Ubiquity and hypervisibility removed hair from view as a marker of bodily difference while hair's integrity as a specific substance dissolved into a figure of speech: do spiders or caterpillars or turkeys "really" have hairs? In his paradigmatic text *Micrographia* (1665), Robert Hooke trained his microscopic eye upon the "Haire" of a nettle only to find "a multitude of small and slender conical bodies, much resembling Needles or Bodkins"; moreover, "tho [these] appear'd very cleer and transparent, yet I could not perceive whether they were hollow or not, but to me they appear'd like solid transparent bodies."[8]

Threaded through implements of female domestic and social life, Hooke's idiom of "appear[ance]" turns "hair" from a fully discernible object into a speaking instance of what Ian Hacking terms "representationalism," Hacking's now canonical point having been that once Democritus attributed reality to "imperceptible particles," nothing perceptible can transcend the status of an appearance.[9] The eighteenth-century taste for "fictitious hair" in the form of wigs and conspicuously crafted up-dos made human hair overtly representational in this sense.[10] Did that make hair, as hair, visible or invisible? It is easy to forget that depilation was as common as bag wigs or the "Towers and Topknots" that crowned so many middling and aristocratic female heads.[11] Then too, most wigs were bleached in the open air and many quoted the clouds, while women's dressed hair, largely invisible to its wearers (Figure 6.1), could reach dizzying heights—"above thirty Degrees," in Joseph Addison's estimation.[12] Approximating the sublime, "high hair" pressed against the very edges of perception, collapsed into pun, as in Mary Darly's *Oh-Heigh-Oh* caricature of 1776, or disappeared into tinted clouds of powder that themselves began to dissipate only with the notorious imposition of Pitt's hair powder tax in 1795.

What might hair's invisibility and the limits of perceptible form have to do with the way enlightened persons thought of human bodies as female or male, endowed with corresponding, gender-specific vulnerabilities, virtues, powers, and destinies?[13] Belinda's rebuke to the "cruel" Baron who has just caused half of her own hair to vanish makes 1714 (the year Pope published the second, augmented edition of his 1712 *jeu d'esprit*) a convenient point of entry into this question, especially insofar as *The Rape of the Lock* tracks hair's disappearance into ideas, and ideals, of gendered identity. New engravings by Louis Du Guernier and Claude Du Bosc so downplayed Belinda's lock that by the time of its celebrated ascent to the heavens at the end of Canto V that "radiant *Trail of Hair*" looks nothing like hair, even the (surely) metaphorical kind that astronomers had long assigned to comets. It is far more likely to lead the mind to a girl's ribbon or some Medusan serpent (Figure 6.2).

Yet when they deflected the supposed subject of Pope's poem, its earliest illustrators read that poem aright. The eventually "dissever'd" tress whose absence Pope's title establishes makes no appearance whatsoever in Canto I, while in the remaining four it is absorbed either into the linguistic operations of Pope's verse or into "Ideas rising in [the] Mind" (*RL*, 3.142)—"Ideas" whose superficiality it seems to mirror in an inversion of Lockean ideation.[14] Throughout the eighteenth century, new illustrations of *The Rape*

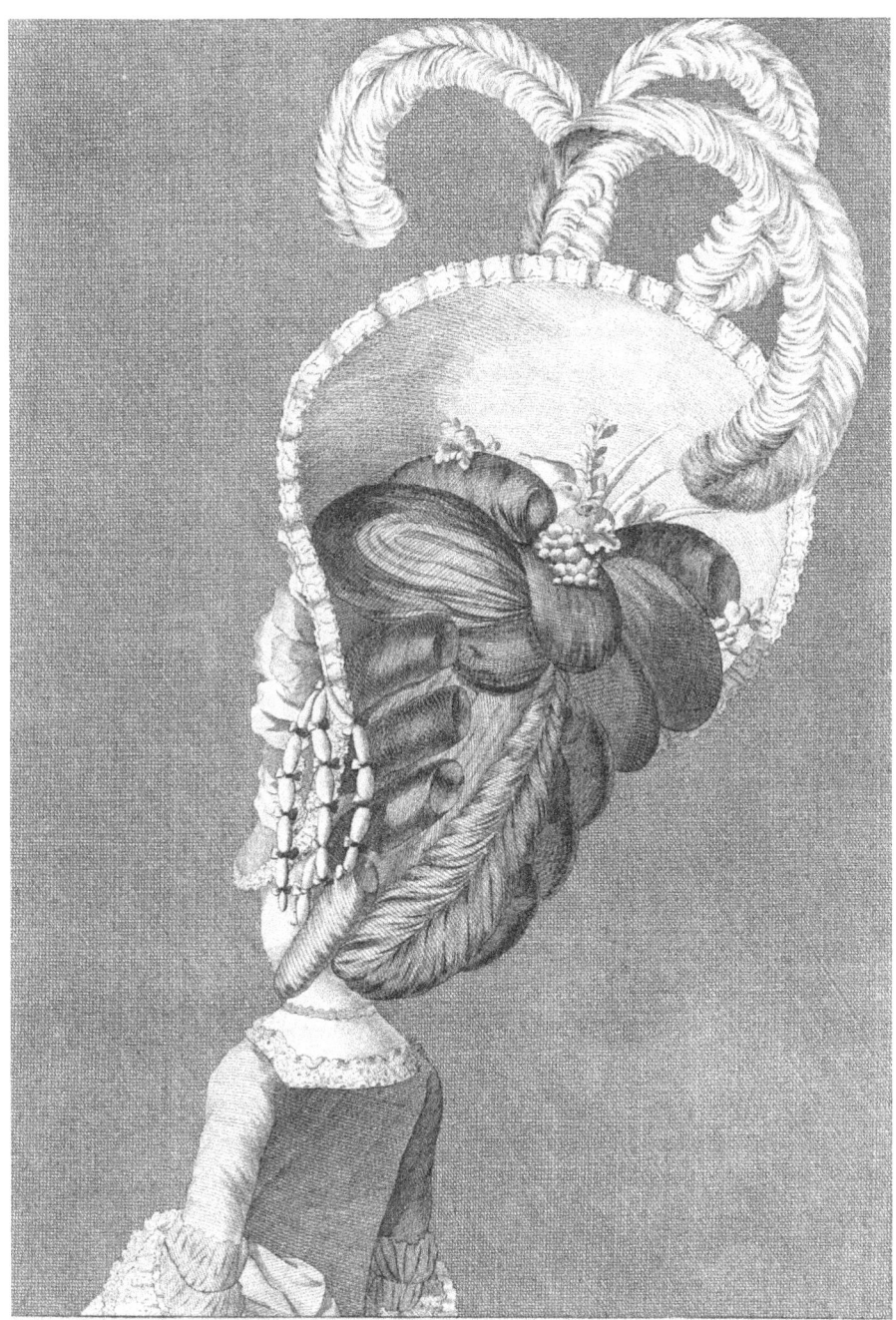

FIGURE 6.1: *Oh-Heigh-Oh. or a View of the Back Settlements* (Published by M. Darly, 1776). Courtesy of The Lewis Walpole Library, Yale University.

FIGURE 6.2: Claude Du Bosc and Claude Du Guernier, Frontispiece, Alexander Pope's *The Rape of the Lock* (1714). Beinecke Rare Book and Manuscript Library, Yale University.

FIGURE 6.3: Samuel Wade, "Let Wreaths of Triumph now my Temples twin, / The Victor cry'd, the glorious Prize is mine," from Alexander Pope's *Works*, vol. 1, Plate IV (1757). Beinecke Rare Book and Manuscript Library, Yale University.

of the Lock continued to move "the Lock" itself to the periphery of the visual field when they thought to show it there at all. And although heads—as they do in Samuel Wale's 1757 engraving (Figure 6.3)—often bend irresistibly in the direction of Belinda's hair, the line of otherwise imperceptible force that passes through that hair transforms it from an object of perception into a medium of open-ended collective fantasy. Artists like Thomas Stothard much preferred to picture the fanciful penumbra of sylphs that surrounds Belinda's head. The aptly surnamed William Lock interwove her hair with butterflies, the most ephemeral figures to be found in the natural world.

The elusiveness of Belinda's hair obviously underscores the *vanitas* tradition that Pope's idealized Clarissa sanctions when she reasons that "frail Beauty must decay / Curl'd or uncurl'd, since Locks will turn to grey" (*RL*, 5.25–6). But as the convoluted logic of Clarissa's syntax suggests, Belinda's curls are also inextricably entangled with the world of "Ideas" and the life of thought that they engender. By the time of Henry Fuseli's 1790 *Dream of Belinda* (Figure 6.4), a transparent cowl has come to envelop Belinda's hair, ingeniously displaying that hair's concealment in the gossamer of dream. Here no "Hairs" are "less in sight" than the ones on our heroine's head; it's only those in the mind, Fuseli hints, that we can truthfully be said to see. When those ideas are ideas about gender, what might this possibly mean?

FIGURE 6.4: Henry Fuseli, *The Dream of Belinda* (ca. 1780–1790). Oil on canvas. Collection of the Vancouver Art Gallery, Founders' Fund, VAG 34.12. Photo: Rachel Topham, Vancouver Art gallery.

VIBRANT IDEATION

Much has been said about hair's eighteenth-century meanings in relation to both sex and gender. Tapping the insights of twentieth-century psychoanalysis, sociology, and anthropology, those who have commented on hair find that it upheld and substantiated gender difference in a period when men wore wigs that fixed them firmly within a social and professional taxonomy based on uniformity, stable identity, personal property, and the affirmation of civic identity. Women usually wore their "own" (albeit dressed) hair and were, correspondingly, typically excluded from all of these grids of visibility. Exemplary treatments of this problem by Marcia Pointon and Lynn Festa commission psychoanalysis, psychoeconomic theories of commodity fetishism, and anthropologies grounded in the dialectic of purity and danger to foreground hair's essential sameness regardless of its wearer's sex.[15] In turn, hair's indiscriminacy threatens the very uniform symbolic order that hair makes visible, mixing alienability with possession, adiaphora with grammars of distinction. From this perspective, hair is best understood as a *thing* and indeed as the peculiarly modern kind of thing that the eighteenth-century *friseur*-turned-man-of-letters Alexander Stewart deemed "a very considerable article in commerce."[16] The forms of desire that hair-as-thing arouses are mimetic and above all ambivalent, given hair's true position on countless boundaries whose threatening fluidity it also exposes. Individuals and social actors, physical bodies and cultural semiotics, life and death, disease and health, subjects and objects: as hair moves from head to head or takes various specific shapes upon a single head—above all, as it is severed from particular bodies—it melts fixed binaries, arousing anxiety in the eighteenth-century persons we imagine. To us, the living, hair reveals all of these oppositional pairs in both their ill-gotten cultural authority and their true reversibility.

Of all the socially instantiated boundaries that hair-as-thing makes visible, the most concerning would seem to be the one dividing female from male. Conceived as biomaterial, hair denies sexual difference insofar as, in Festa's unimprovable assessment, there would appear to be "no material differences between male and female hair."[17] Given that hair-as-thing is a thing indifferent, the gendered identity that it asserts must be irreducibly performative. So foretell Joseph Roach and Margaret K. Powell in their study of "social hair" as "magical hair" that as such manipulates appearances in a cultural game whose contemporary metonym was Garrick's stage as it synchronized wigs with character.[18] The resulting idea that character is assumable, disposable, fictional, and contingent resonates with distinctions between sex and gender that seem to have emerged in the Enlightenment. In the historical models supplied by such scholars as Londa Schiebinger, Dror Wahrman, and Thomas Laqueur, gender difference was, at least for a few scintillating decades, detached from the "one [bodily] sex" that earlier males and females shared and negotiated through the kinds of play exemplified in the passing of wigs from men's heads to those of women.[19] To take two favorite mid-eighteenth-century examples: When the cross-dressing actress Charlotte Charke "tak[es] it into my small Pate, that, by Dint of a Wig and a Waistcoat I should be the perfect Representative of my Sire" or when the intersex Chevalier d'Eon (1728–1810) is pictured with two hairstyles, one male and one female (Figure 6.5), gender is projected onto a world of surfaces.[20] There it can be adjusted, renegotiated, and parsed as one prop among several in the social, cultural, and linguistic performance influentially theorized by Judith Butler.[21] In the examples just cited, d'Eon is represented as wearing two (half-)heads of hair without having done so in the physical world, while in fact we see only a verbal representation of Charke's representation of her

FIGURE 6.5: *Mademoiselle de Beaumont, or the Chevalier D'Eon* (1777). Courtesy of The Lewis Walpole Library, Yale University.

"Sire"—one that itself frontloads a mental representation that she first took "into [her] Pate." But if we unsee the graphic medium that conveys the idea of it to us, hair (as in J.C. Flügel's *Psychology of Clothes*) appears to be a subspecies of apparel with all of the slippages, ambivalences, signal crossings, and good fun that accrue to that medium of expression.[22]

The ludic readings that hair-as-thing attracts uphold a strong narrative arc along which we can chart culture-based gender's plummet into naturalized and essentialized sex. Here we drop through the exuberant effeminacy of the Macaronis of the 1760s and 1770s into the tragic fixity of naturalized sex (and sexual difference) after the French Revolution. This disastrous trajectory corresponds to the retirement of "fictitious hair"—the wig—as an accoutrement of all but the professional and exclusively masculine classes of barrister, clergyman, and physician and the emergence of its "natural" counterpart as a marker of postrevolutionary and specifically British identity. Nobody supposes that renatured hair ignored politics or history; if nothing else, it updated the Puritan "roundhead" as a badge of freedom. But like the parallel demise of female "frizzing," the wig's decline and the fall of the headdress implicated hair in the reification of sexually different bodies. Recent cultural criticism understands this reification to be a political, social, and symbolic process—an assumption which has the further advantage of revealing the hierarchical and oppressive power relations believed to underwrite it.

Despite the Enlightenment penchant for mixing female hair with model boats, bows, birdcages, and all manner of bric-a-brac, the resulting *exposés* are most likely to focus on the fictitious hair that migrated across men's heads, downplaying the "real" hair that grew out of those of women. The more visibly acculturated it is, the more firmly hair supports a core assumption in a vast body of feminist scholarship on "it," where hair's "presentation and manipulation [...] wherever it grows, has been fundamental to embodied social and symbolic practices that inscribe it with meaning."[23] Such formulations have acquired the force of empirical fact, even as some of this force may come not from their accuracy but, rather, because they have supported necessary political critique and an ongoing reassessment of the relationship between women's bodies and their meanings in culture.

The inscription model underwrites the enduring conceit that hair—"it"—has a mind and even a life of its own, one that mysteriously persists well beyond that of the bodies on which it appears. In *The Rape of the Lock*, a "dissevered" tress should betoken bodily vulnerability and all flesh's sorry destiny. Instead, it seems to live on, and in so doing reinforces myths of specifically female power and virtue that can be traced back through Milton's unfallen Eve to Callimachus's Berenice.[24] Pope's engagement with these myths made his poem a touchstone in eighteenth-century thinking not just about but with and through hair. Where an earlier poet such as Donne or Milton might have braided these myths into long religious traditions that put hair at a point of transition between spiritual and physical levels of reality, the enlightened poet shows them to be manmade and a threat to Belinda's moral life, leaving her thereby feminized body the unenviable job of propping them up.[25] But Pope also perpetuates the very poetics of sexual myth that he mocks and elucidates, as his poem's own robust afterlife bears witness.[26]

The rational thesis that hair-as-thing but spuriously refutes material reality may be traced to enlightened Britain's Puritan and sectarian "before," with its grim insistences on the "unloveliness of love-locks" and its contention that hair both false and dressed sinfully denies mortality. "The powder forgets the dust," ranted Thomas Hall.[27] Likewise, over the eighteenth century, a waxing fashion for mourning jewelry that literally holds the hair of the departed in the material world tries to override matter's defining feature of decay, as does a rash of hairdressing manuals teaching "how to recover [hair] when lost." Even hair's increasingly obvious responsiveness to fashion masks death in the embrace of transience.[28] In all of these instances, hair "lives" only insofar as it shows culture imposing meaning, both spiritual and moral, on inert matter. What makes such matter consistently "effeminate," whether it appeared on men's heads or on those of women, is its vulnerability to this process, its demonstration that only culture makes matter meaningful and thereby extends its life.

All of this makes perfect sense from the skeptical and materialist perspective that the Enlightenment itself has left us. But what if hair itself really does live independently and forever? What if the *faux* longevity that culture appears to impress upon it were not imposed—were not, in fact, even *faux*? What if hair, while still substantial, turned out to be "not of a decaying substance that labels man 'here today and gone tomorrow'"?[29] The same natural philosophers, Pope's contemporaries, who were for the first time seeing hair up close and everywhere occasionally arrived at this very conclusion. In their investigations, hair's relative immortality as an objectively independent life form is established not through ornament, code, and illusion but instead through the bodies of dead women, in which and out of which it apparently continued to grow. For instance, Hooke printed a 1680 letter concerning a woman who had been buried in Nuremberg for 43 years:

> [When her casket was exhumed,] through [its] clefts [...] much Hair was thrust out, and had grown very plentifully, in so much that 'tis believ'd that the whole Coffin may for some time have been all covered with Hair. The Cover of this Coffin being removed, the whole Corps appeared perfectly resembling an Humane shape [...] but from the very Crown of the Head to the Sole of the Foot covered over with a very thick set Hair, long and much Curl'd. Which strange sight (they never having seen the like before) much amazed the Sexton and his Companions; but he after a little viewing of it going to handle the upper part of the Head with his Fingers, found immediately all the shape of the Body to fall, and left nothing in his Hand but a handful of Hair [...] This Hair was somewhat rough at first, but afterward it grew very much harder, and of brown red Colour.[30]

"Inclosed Papers" included a physical "Sample" of the "thick set Hair" that was soon filed away in Gresham College's repository, where it was "found to be stiff, red, somewhat curled, but rotten Hair." But with so many verbal prompts to sensation at hand—curl, color, texture—the reader of this letter can only envision the "amaz[ing]" curl as substantive and dynamic even as the body in which it grows literally "fall[s]" away. The hands and eyes of living virtuosi replace that body as the condition of hair's ongoing capacity for change, a capacity now supported by acts of communication and collaborative witness— "transaction"—represented both in and by the text. In the pages of the Royal Society's *Transactions* themselves, hair thus construed sparked "some Anatomical Observations on Hair" by the physician Edward Tyson. These were unorthodox, and included the speculation that, while hair seems to be bound up with animal life, it might instead be an "Animal Vegetable." After all, hairs "as Plants may be transplanted, and made to grow in a Soil they did not at first," they also seem to move around on and in their new "Soil."[31] Does it matter that it is a female body that hosts the on-living hair, ultimately losing its own definitive "shape" and leaving nothing but a (man's) "handful of hair"? To eighteenth-century redactions of this account it did. Selecting it for a 1740 abridgment of the Royal Society's seventeenth-century *Transactions*, the Oxford don John Lowthorp stressed that the "*Hairy Corps*" was that of a woman but perforce replaced the missing hair sample with enhanced reflections of his own. These led him to confirm Tyson's speculation that hair might be an "Animal Vegetable." It also led him to look for hairs less in sight: "Though the outward surface of the Body be the usual place where [hair] grows," Lowthorp wrote, "yet hath it been sometimes found on the Tongue, upon and in the Heart, in the Breasts, and Kidneys [...] but there is scarce any inward part more subject to it than the *Ovarium* or Testicles of Females."[32]

Here, hairs less in sight are not necessarily pubic, and if they are meaningfully gendered, that meaning is multiform, variable, fixed only at the moment of communication and collaboration that introduces hair into the mind. Indeed, in several of the *Transactions* that Lowthorp contributed to the Royal Society in his own voice, the unseen "Hairs" that he had most in mind were certain "large Lock[s] ... variously entangl'd" that appeared to grow in the muck of women's wombs while, upon dissection, ovaries "swelled as big as a man's Head" seemed to be "filled with a purulent matter and Hair" that "resembled somewhat some of the *Hair* of the Skin."[33] These hirsute globules spattered when fried and under the microscope looked sometimes transparent, sometimes iridescent. And they almost always came from the insides of women ("a Gentlewoman, aged about 39 Years," a "Woman here in Town," a "Woman lately Dissected, who was the Day before her Death with great difficulty delivered of a dead Child").[34]

Still identified with the female form, hair previously not seen sponsored unorthodox conceptions of a prolific but otherwise unimaginable nature, spontaneous and irrational. The sight of "Hair *within* gave a Suspicion to some, that [it] possibly might be the parts of a corrupted Embryo [emphasis added]," Lowthorp noted. "But I rather think not." He would "rather look upon it as a Lusus Naturae," where Nature, "endeavouring to form something, and being disappointed of an Animal, produced a Vegetable."[35] Opinions naturally differed: "Some philosophers as call these extraordinary appearances *Lusus Naturae* [...] take Refuge in Words," observed another virtuoso, "if they mean by *Lusus Naturae*, the Sport or Recreation of Nature, they accuse her who does nothing in vain [...] as delighting to make monstrous, deformed, useless, and mischievous Things."[36]

Eighteenth-century fascination with Nature's apparent powers of self-formation (and self-deformation) as revealed through hair anticipates recent feminist critiques of linguistic and social constructionist models of identity that fail to acknowledge the active role that matter might play in determining its own identity. "Conative" with its human observers, such matter is, in Jane Bennett's phrase, "vibrant."[37] Others posit what Karen Barad theorizes as the inextricable "entanglement of matter and meaning." Though derived from descriptions of particle interaction in quantum physics, "entanglement" is a pleasingly hairy word, understanding the identity of any body to emerge through an "interagential" process of wavelike "diffraction" rather than through the assignment of significance and value to material objects by acculturated linguistic subjects who remain separate from it.[38]

Enlightenment investigators of female hairs less in sight did not merely anticipate the resurgence of vibrant matter or register their own "entangle[ment]" with the objects they investigated. Because the nonlinear life of reflexive thought is also visibly part of their representations, they bring something to the table that even the new feminist materialism overlooks: collaborative ideation as a condition of a stable form's visibility. Pope registers as much at the end of *The Rape of the Lock* when Belinda's lock takes flight and her attendant sylphs "behold it kindling as it flies" (*RL*, 5.131) even as the crackpot astrologer John Partridge is promised that he too "shall view i[t] in cloudless Skies, / When next he looks thro' *Galilaeo*'s Eyes" (*RL*, 5.137–8). As Claire Colebrook supposes, novel forms of ideation thrive and even take on objective reality when new technologies—emergent "systems [...] that are never fully alive"—redefine the relationship between material and immaterial worlds. The best example of the resulting potential to reinstantiate reality, however, is to be found in the reflexive spring of "literary language," which "by deforming the syntax and grammar that enables efficient, striving, and self-maintaining life [...] frees human thought from its own rhythms and propensities."[39]

Barad finds that the entanglement of human agency with the life of matter becomes visible along the line of the "agential cut."[40] In eighteenth-century Britain, hair severed from the body made such cuts visible as a component of meaningful matter, not only under the microscope or in the telescope but in new "objects of remembrance" such as the mourning lock, which, in Christiane Holm's evocative reading, achieved its sentimental meaning only through its paradoxical suspense between matter and culture: "The cut edge of the hair in the material medium of remembrance marks the act of remembrance as the very moment when its natural status was transformed into a cultural status."[41] "Memory miniatures" were indeed diminutive, their details difficult to make out with the naked eye. But if we magnify them electronically, as is now possible (Figure 6.6), we

FIGURE 6.6: Locket (1775–1800). © Victoria and Albert Museum, London.

discover not just the fusion of "cut edge" with "material medium" but a dynamic principle of design in which a single lock of hair has obviously been woven into the illusion of multiplicity. This illusion is conceptually compatible both with a unified, objective, and itself invariant formal order and with organic matter's fate in time, as evidenced in hairs sprung from the very bind that they create.

Twenty-first-century viewing technologies transpose the eighteenth-century literature of hairwork as it interwove the techne of writing with those of hairdressing or the manipulation of hair in the laboratory. In these texts, hair's vibrancy arises not because of culture's designs on matter nor because of a power inherent in matter but because of their entanglement within a common medium. When hair registers the presence of this medium, it serves as a prompt to unrestricted thought.

Especially thought of gender difference. "Pittoresque prompt" was the phrase that the artist Jonathan Richardson coined to convey the kind of meaning that the "hyancinthin" hair of Milton's Adam acquires for Milton's reader when he or she comes upon the blind poet's slippery representation of our first parents in *Paradise Lost*—a representation doubly mediated through a satanic observer and Milton's epic narrator. Richardson grafted his own suppositions onto Milton's double-glazed portrait of originary sexual difference when he paraphrased Milton's famous contrast between the "hyacinthin Locks" that "round from [Adam's] parted forelock manly hung" and Eve's "unadorned golden tresses" that "in wanton ringlets waved" (4.302–5): "He had Bright Black Hair, She fair Yellow; Both Curl'd, tho' His, parted A-top, hung not below his Shoulders, Her's to her Waist; and let us Suppose it in Loose Natural Wavings playing about her Face." Speculating about what Milton might have meant by depicting Adam's hair not, in fact, as "Bright Black" but rather as "hyacinthin," Richardson decided that the floral adjective was meant to suggest "what Images [are] to be set before us," in this case brightness and blackness. Such "Helps to Conceive" guarantee that "a Lively *Pittoresque* Imagination with Poetical Good Sense will furnish the Possessors of these Qualities with Something."[42] Significantly, such "Qualities" belong as much to the idiosyncratic "*Pittoresque* Imagination" that will always come up with "something" as they do to the otherwise invisible object at hand. Meanwhile, it is Eve's "Loose Natural Wavings playing about her Face" that make the ideational process of assigning sexual identity itself perceptible, a condition of matter's meaning that leaves room for that meaning to alter without matter itself losing its shape at any given moment.

In the reading praxis that Richardson models, hair neither grounds nor undermines sexual difference. Rather, it provokes a multiplicity of ideas about how bodies, be they human, plant, or animal, might positively differ from one another as they dynamically interact with different minds in representational space. It's with this potential in mind that the celebrated Georgian hairdresser of letters David Ritchie's 1770 *Treatise on the Hair* proposed that "the Hair, either natural or artificial, may be dress'd to produce in us different Ideas of the Qualities of Men."[43] To get at how hair might have engendered eighteenth-century ideas of gender *as* "Ideas" that shaped matter by participating with it, we should thus look outside the psychosocial, cultural, and economic register to hair's treatment in a changing history and philosophy of nature. While this resource has not been tapped in recent analyses of hair's relationship to gender in the Enlightenment, it asserts a (literally) vital ontological unity between hair's material and immaterial dimensions, one that gives hair a dynamic affinity with the similarly suspended literary medium.

Here, materiality and immateriality are not seeming opposites whose differences hair ultimately denies. They are, instead, aspects of a single, differently appearing reality whose unity hair, conspicuously passing through such media as air and language, realizes in human experience. Such experience can take the form of ideas, imaginings, and conceptions as easily as it can that of sense impression, social practice, and cultural performance. If sociable body worlds were, however insecurely, gendered in the ways that recent critics have elucidated, gender figures differently in the other world of vibrant ideality—a world where hairs less in sight can reconcile form with fluidity, letting women be women even when they cannot be told from men.

THE SPRING OF THE HAIR

Hair's seeming return to nature in the 1790s distracts attention from its value throughout the eighteenth century as a form that conveys nature's invisible powers and with them matter's indirectly tangible qualities of fluidity, flexibility, resilience, and freedom. Robert Boyle figured air's physico-mechanical "spring" by likening it "to many slender and flexible hairs; each of which may indeed, like a little spring, be easily bent or rolled up."[44] He also began to suspect that an "electric [body] [...] acquires an atmosphere" when he noticed the "false locks of hair" on "two beautiful ladies who wore them" and "observed that they could not keep them from flying to their cheeks, and from sticking there." Another beauty testified that "she had sometimes met with [such] troublesome locks; but all that she could say farther was, that they seemed to fly most from her cheeks when they had put into a stiff curl, and when the weather was frosty."[45]

Well into the 1790s, experimental "electricians" were still favoring ladies' "troublesome locks" when they sought both to conceptualize and to communicate electrical currents that themselves resembled "golden hair"; at the sight of a woman "combing her hair in frosty weather in the dark," for example, George Adams saw "sparks of fire to issue from it." When he asked the woman to comb her sister's hair while standing on a wax platform, Adams was "surprised to find her whole body electrified" and that "her hair was strongly electrical."[46] Both volumes of Erasmus Darwin's *Botanic Garden* (1789–1791) were alive with the flowing, "slender hair" found both in the polymorphous and delightfully perverse reproductive organs of plants and—variously "bristling," "whistling," and "radiant"—on the heads of the supernatural beings that Darwin employed to make a previously imperceptible, spiritually animated vegetable world conceivable.[47]

In all of these rapidly spreading branches of natural philosophy, as in the dissections of Lowthorp and his fellow anatomists, hair's ubiquity makes it less a thing to be seen or even (vibrant matter) to be seen *by* than an instrument to be seen through and with. Mary Darly's *Optic Curls* of 1776 (Figure 6.7) literalizes—and feminizes—this surprising potential. Considered very strictly as biomaterial, women's hair could not be told apart from that of men. But it remained mysteriously distinctive in its formal propensities: in its growth patterns and liabilities, in its habitual responses to time and physical environment. According to many an eighteenth-century observer, unlike that of men, the hair that appears on women's bodies is seldom lost, tends not to grow on the face, and is far more likely to turn up deep inside the body. Alexander Stewart thus pondered "the Hair or beard upon the face or faces of men to which women are but very little liable to, and those who are consequently of a strong, masculine nature, nor are they liable to baldness at all, as men are." A penumbra of new ideas about gendered bodies arose from these thoughts, for example, the one that "Men retain much more blood than women, which so overheats the excrements that nourish, or ought to nourish, and support the Hair, that

FIGURE 6.7: *The Optic Curls. or the obligeing head dress* (Published by M. Darly, 1777). © The Trustees of the British Museum.

they are daily diminished thereby, and in time will wear off the whole Hair [...] whereas the female sex, from the age that they are properly stiled woman, are greatly reduced in their growing strength."⁴⁸ Gendered differences were intrinsic to human hair in the same way that womanhood could not be separated from "prope[r] stil[e]"— consistent manner of behaving and thinking were required if identity was to be perceived.

Manner was contingent. Ritchie maintained that

> Women retain [hair] longer than men; for tho we see many men bald, hardly one woman is without some violent cause; some by pinning to the top of the head through the skin [...] or by straining the hair hard back from the forehead, in moving the eyebrows [...] but it appears not to be natural for them to be bald as men.⁴⁹

Under the shadow of the "violent cause" that might conceal them, the differences of women's hair show hair's treatment to be part of its nature—not because culturally dictated fashions and meanings are imposed on it but because matter and meaning are entangled in and through it. John Quincy's popular 1736 medical dictionary found that, "whatsoever the efficient cause may be, why a man has a beard, and a woman none, it is certain that the final cause is for the distinguishing the male from the female sex, which otherwise could hardly be known if both were dressed in the same habit."⁵⁰ Other gendered differences took shape only in words wrested: "Physicians distinguish the hair into several kinds, and give it divers denominations; but this only in Greek and Latin, the hair of the head they call capillus, that of a woman particularly, coma, from Greek komer, to dress and adjust; and that of a man caesaries, from coedendo, because often cut."⁵¹

Gendered differences in hair's manner of appearing allowed fixed sexual differences to coexist with fluidity under the same idea of nature. In Hogarth's delicate idealization of "the many waving and contrasted turns of naturally intermingling locks [which] ravish the eye with the pleasure of the pursuit, especially when they are put in motion by a gentle breeze," it is easy to spot the gendered roles of spectatorship and objectification. But what makes these ravishing locks "especial[l]" is the "gentle breeze" that puts them "in motion" in the first place, and is common to both beholder and beheld. In such renderings, hair's flow, curl, and wave made perceptible a dynamic, resilient, but formally consistent nature, at the same time honoring continuity between nature so conceived and the physical bodies on or in which hair happened to live. If Hogarth appears to have had female hair in mind, it is not because the "naturally intermingling locks" that he evokes have been objectified by the eye that pretends to be ravished by them but because they are part of a web of formal associations that seems to radiate from Hogarth's memory of Milton's Eve. "Written with a view of fixing the fluctuating Ideas of Taste," Hogarth's *Analysis of Beauty* (1753) picked for its epigraph Milton's serpent that "curl'd many a wanton wreath, in sight of Eve, / To lure her eye."⁵² The citation implicates Eve's eyesight in the sight of her hair—which hair is not in fact visible here at all, except in the mirror of the serpent's body.

When eighteenth-century stylists of women's hair assumed Nature's own "power of forming the hair into graceful ringlets on the shoulders, or to bend in waves round the temples," they advanced an idea of femininity as a mode of expression—one whose medium, like masculinity's, is hair.⁵³ But if hair is a common medium expressing varying modalities, that medium must still be something. Today, we might decide that hair "is" a compound of keratin and dead skin cells or a variable composition of sulphur and carbon—vocabularies, thus perceptions, at best but nascent in the Enlightenment. Many scholars spotlight contemporary references to hair as an "excrement," heartened by the word's associations with transgressive, boundary-crossing waste. Buffon, however, observed that while "the ancients held the hair to be a sort of excrement [...] the moderns have found that every hair may be truly said to live, to receive nutriment, to fill and distend itself like the other parts of the body." Goldsmith concurred: "The ancients indeed held the hair to be a sort of excrement [...] but the moderns have found that every hair may be truly said to live, to receive nutriment, to fill and distend itself like the other parts of the body."[54]

The modern idea of hair's natural extension into a life of its own was not incompatible with Edward Tyson's notion—sparked by a "lump of greasy hair" whose presence inside the solid body of a dead woman he could not explain—that hair is "the nature and production of air in human bodies, living or dead."[55] This was not a new idea either. In Elizabeth Tudor's barber Thomas Vicary's 1577 *True Anatomye of Mans Body*, for example, hair is "a superfluity of members, made of the grosse fumes of a smoke passing out of viscous matter, thickened to the forme of heyre." Consequently, "by the colour of the heyre is witnessed and knowen the complexion of the braine" such that "heyre" tells us less about the what, more about the where and how "the fumosities of the brayne might ascende and passe lightlier out."[56] In the Restoration, Daniel Sennart's *Art of Chirurgery* proposed that hair might be generated "not only from some kind of fuliginous vapors, but from a matter that is even more solid." If all that is vaporous here threatens to condense into "matter," Sennart was really after some relationship between the two that could explain the appearances of things. In this he was aided by an anecdote from de Serbis's *Anatomy of the Hair*, in which de Serbis "saw and touched the dead body of a Woman buried in the way called Appia (just opposite unto the way where Cicero was buried)." Noting that "in this Carcass there was a good store of Hair, adorned and tied up with a Golden Fillet," de Serbis allowed the "Carcass" to putrefy until it was "resolved into its first principles," revealing that hair is "generated by the formative or pilifick faculty that is by the Creator implanted in some certain parts." So conceived, hair sponsors the possibility of infinite difference. Differences temporarily stabilize when matter attaches to impressions (for example, of "a great variety of colors in the hair") and ideas ("Men have beards, Women have none").[57]

In Johnson's 1755 *Dictionary*, hair appears to be neither an excrement nor a solidifying vapor. It's a "tegument." This identity emerged through new technologies of vision, for "when we examine the hairs with a microscope, we find that they have each a round bulbous root which lies pretty deep in the skin and which draws their nourishment from the surrounding humours." Nor "is" a hair a single entity: "each hair consists of five or six others wrapt upon a common tegument or tube." Thus the "tegument" that seems to be hair merely wraps other hairs in infinite subdivisibility.[58]

When figured—thus conceived—as an integument, even animal hair can be thought of as a citizen of the material yet ever-etherealizing world of plants. As such, it changes from matter made meaningful by cultural values and symbolic practices into a force actively mediating between material and immaterial levels of reality as well as between organic and inorganic states of existence. The perfumer and ladies' hairdresser John Mather reckoned that, in its "infinite variety," hair "grows as plants do out of the earth; each has its separate life and distinct economy" with the result that it "may exist although the body be starved, and even will continue to grow long after death."[59] Moving toward the perception that all "hairs" are "species or varieties of one vegeto-animal plant," others "ingeniously compare[d hairs] to Polypody, or some other plant growing upon an old tree, which continues to grow after the tree is dead, as they did before, because they have a proper life distinct from the form or anima of the tree out of which and in which they grow."⁶⁰ "Hairs are not part of the body," agreed Gibson's *Anatomy of Human Bodies*, "and therefore have no animal life; yet they have a vegetative life, and that peculiar to themselves, and not owing to the life of the body."⁶¹ Hair's "vegetative life," while bodily, seems also to be "owing" to no "body" at all.

Such perceptions bind hair and plant life through metaphor itself. Hair belongs to the plant world not only because it is an "organ of insensible perspiration" but also because of its inherently figural properties: "Hairs of men, horses, sheep, &c. are composed of long, small, tubular fibres, or smaller hairs, encompassed with a rind or bark, and from this structure, a split hair appears like a stick, shivered by beating." A "stem" that pierces "the surface of the skin," hair depended on mediation to reveal its apparitional affinity with vegetation: "what, to the naked eye, appears only a single hair, to the microscope seems a bush."⁶² Even Uvedale Price's *Essay on the Picturesque* confirmed that "in many points the hair has a striking relation to trees." After all, "they resemble each other in their intricacy, their ductility, the quickness of their growth, their seeming to acquire fresh vigour from being cut, and in their being detached from the solid bodies whence they spring."⁶³

As if it were, itself, a metaphor, the hair of fashionable women was dressed to bring this other life of matter, at once violent and transformative, into view. Hannah More wryly sketched eleven country women who "had amongst them, on their heads, an acre and a half of shrubbery, besides slopes, grass-plats, tulip-beds, clumps of peonies, kitchen gardens, and green-houses."⁶⁴ Often staging full-fledged pastoral scenes— one headdress "of prodigious height" culminated in "precipitous hills, enameled fields, silver streams, foaming torrents, symmetrical gardens, and an English park"—the heads of urban women were no less diverting, as Mary Darly showed when she plotted fantastic gardens on top of female heads (Figure 6.8).⁶⁵ Since "the grass of the field or any flower or shrub" could be thought to be "of the self same nature," women's hairdressers were trained to think of themselves as landscapers who, "after having been liberal with his sweet waves around the face and fore part of the neck," should leave "just room enough behind the shoulder to plant in a wanton ringlet."⁶⁶

Hairscaping seemingly strives to master and discipline wayward female bodies. Indeed, for "the lovely Hebe of eighteen," William Barker recommended that "the chaste hand of taste, guided by judgment, should be employed to check its wildness, and conduct with elegance each waving lock, into that maze of irregular charms it is so prompt of itself to form, when inclined to curl."⁶⁷ But before the "chaste hand of taste," there is the curl "prompt of itself to form," and before that (at least in Barker's sentence), there is the goddess Hebe, who in John Gay's translation of Ovid's *Metamorphoses*, restores Iolaus to manhood after he has been transformed into a tree: "the soft Down began / O'er his smooth Chin to spread and promised Man."⁶⁸ A curl "prompt of itself to form" is reflexive, dynamic, reversible. It opens into new ideas about sexual identity. Reviving Vicary's "fumosity," figures *in* the head can thus fuse with the ones that turn up on top of it. "Notions" and "thoughts" were popular curl styles throughout the middle of the century, and the frizzing technique that produced them was often called "perplexing."⁶⁹ Horace Walpole toyed with hair's place on both sides of the skull when he sent his friend George Montague a popular recipe "to make a fine head of hair" urging him to "take your own head and [...] dig as large a hole as you can conveniently in the skull and water it ... add now and then a handful of bean flowers; then when you have agreed for a head of hair to your mind, take it up by the roots ... always observing the exposition it grew in upon the former skull."⁷⁰ Walpole and his friends were not copying or appropriating

FIGURE 6.8: *The Flower Garden* (Published by M. Darly, 1777). Courtesy of The Lewis Walpole Library, Yale University.

women's vegetal hairstyles, instead, they were working in and through hair to realize its multisexual potential in the notionally externalized life of the mind.

To such flights of fancy, graphic representations of women's dressed hair often added a second layer of reflexivity, opening the possibility of oblique critique of the social and symbolic structures that limit thought about what matter might mean and about how even imagined meanings might matter. Consider Emma Crewe's frontispiece for Darwin's *Loves of the Plants* (Figure 6.9), the second (if first published) half of Darwin's two-volume *Botanic Garden*. Here, idealized femininity shades almost imperceptibly into an etherealizing material world. Cupid's raffish cap contrasts with idle Flora's floral headdress, which is identified both with the image's outmost periphery—the part of it by definition invisible to the figures in the frame—and with its diagonal axis, which runs from Flora's hair to the tipped basket of flowers at her feet. As Alan Bewell observes, "in the elaborately excessive hairstyle of Flora" Crewe presents nature as "primarily decorative and ornamental."[71] Yet the ambiguity of the line separating Flora's efflorescent hair from the overtly representational features of this image also provokes dynamic reflection, activating an open-ended dialectic between sensation and idea that makes multiple manners of embodiment conceivable without denying the material specificity of bodily forms.

The reflexive spring that animates Crewe's image becomes explicit in Fuseli's corresponding illustration for *The Economy of Vegetation*—the first, more technological and "scientific" volume of *The Botanic Garden* (Figure 6.10). Here Cupid literally holds a mirror up to Flora, his earthly chapeau now at once mythologized and naturalized in his headdress of flames and wings while Crewe's torrent of blossoms has been, in effect, buzz-cut. Flora's handmaiden, meanwhile, has acquired both a job—hairdresser—and springy ringlets that seem to grow through a fashionable hat into butterfly wings. The dynamism of this image, framed as it is with more floral "hair," is to be found not only in its representationalism but in what is common to all five heads of hair: their blending with the communicative breeze—the attiring element that seems to be blowing in a readerly directly from left to right through the scene.

There can be little doubt as to the sexes (or genders) of the bodies we see in these tableaux, but the hair upon them discloses these bodies' hidden unity. This unity is expressed in a diversity of shapes, styles, and manners but its stylistic penchants are revealed only with the natural and artistic media that convey them to the mind's eye. Torqued by such media, they appear as unlimited ideas. Women's hair could be arranged into another such medium. The Victorian hairworker Alexanna Speight affectionately recalled a female milliner whose bestselling hats were "composed of certain elastic springs" that "gave way when a lady went into her coach or chair, without discomposing the form, as it rose immediately to its original height when the lady got out of her coach."[72] Darly's caricature of a "vis-à-vis bisected" inside "the Ladies Coop" (Figure 6.11) also invites us to imagine the spring of the hair. The hair on the heads of the two women bends them forcibly toward each other, making apparent an invisible axis of force through the center of the image. One head of hair is festooned with flowers, the other with vegetables, at once recapitulating fashion's botanical tropology and releasing its hidden theme of etherealizing transformation. Like the craze for springs, Darly's image reflects *on* new possibilities for bodily freedom even as it reflects what limits them.

FIGURE 6.9: Emma Crewe, *Flora at play with Cupid*, Frontispiece, Erasmus Darwin's *Loves of the Plants* (1791). Courtesy of The Lewis Walpole Library, Yale University.

FIGURE 6.10: Henry Fuseli, *Flora attired by the Elements*, Frontispiece, Erasmus Darwin's *The Economy of Vegetation* (1791). Courtesy of The Lewis Walpole Library, Yale University.

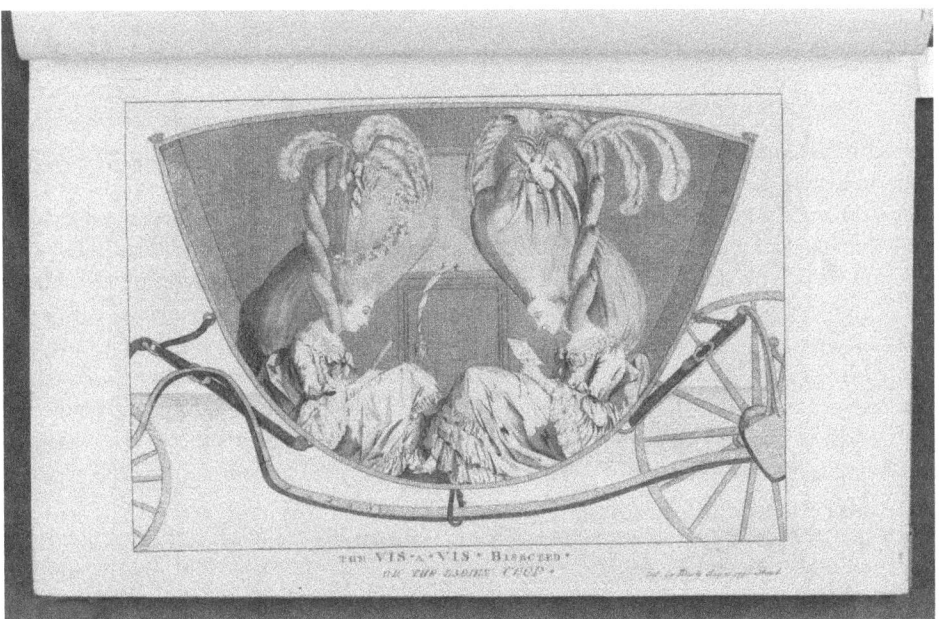

FIGURE 6.11: *The Vis a Vis Bisected or the ladies Coop* (Published by M. Darly, 1776). Courtesy of The Lewis Walpole Library, Yale University.

Frances Burney's 1776 novel *Evelina* engages Darly's exactly contemporary image in delightful conversation. When Burney's ingénue protagonist makes (and records) her maiden voyage to the hairdresser for a round of hair-frizzing, more happens than the subjection of a female body to the denaturing tortures of fashionable metropolitan culture: here too is the spring of shareable reflective life. "I have just had my head dressed," the as yet "unpolished" Evelina writes to her guardian Mr. Villars:

> You cannot think how oddly my head feels; full of powder and black pins, and a great cushion on the top of it. I believe you would hardly know me, for my face looks quite different to what it did before my hair was dressed. When I shall be able to make use of a comb for myself I cannot tell, for my hair is so much entangled, *frizled* they call it, that I fear it will be very difficult.[73]

Hairdressing seems to create new dependencies designed to turn Evelina into a cultural object unable to recognize or act "for myself." But it is also "through" her hair that Evelina at once masters and distances "modish" forms. In conveying what Villars "cannot think," Evelina reclaims her own hair as an idea to embody what she herself *can* think. Her representation of her thought—"how oddly my head feels"—fuses feeling's subject and object in the single figure of oddness, discovering an interior ("full") outside and teasing verbs of cognition ("think," "know," "believe," "tell," "fear") until they reveal their dynamic continuity with sensation, image, and language. Evelina's own word for what has occurred ("entangled") thus coexists in volatile tension with what "they call it" ("*frizled*").[74]

Evelina's bewigged grandmother, Madame Duval, lacks such reflexive capacity precisely because "her" hair does not grow out of her own head. Early on, a prankster has dumped her into a ditch and "stole all my curls." The "villain," Evelina writes, eventually restores "a great quantity of hair, in such a nasty condition, that I was amazed she would take it."[75] But because she can only see hair as a thing, Madame Duval has no choice but to "take it." Evelina's vibrant ideation frees her to leave it, if she wants. She expresses this freedom through her capacity for "amaze[ment]," a freedom that elevates her even above the culturally empowered men in the novel, from the brutally masculine Captain Mirvan, who holds all "hair-pinches" in contempt, to her own effete father, who turns her away upon the arrival of his hairdresser. In time, this potential endows the curves and tendrils of Evelina's own writing with an almost electrical force as she imparts "particulars" that "would make you hair stand an [sic] end to hear them."[76] Evelina's frizzing also makes her a comic, modern, acculturated iteration of Milton's Eve, "wanton ringlets" (or "loose natural Wavings") and all. Only a few years before Burney published her first novel, an "English Periwig Maker" doubted that "had this lovely creature been under the hands of a modern hair-dresser, […] there would have been any danger of her pining away with desire; she would instead have said 'avert the mirror!'" Evelina averts the mirror[77] without throwing it away. As did Mary Darly's daughter Mattina in a memorable, if perplexing, 1777 sketch. *A Speedy & Effectual preparation for the next World* (Figure 6.12) has been thought to satirize a woman of the mind, Catherine Macaulay, setting her before a dressing table that brings that of Pope's Belinda to mind. Hair is well in sight: it appears on three heads, though nowhere so conspicuously as on that of the aging bluestocking. Darly establishes a visual line from the mirror in front of her female subject through the slant of her hair to the figure of death behind her. A fashionable hearse appears in her hair to reinforce this association: we do not need a Clarissa to warn of locks that turn to gray.

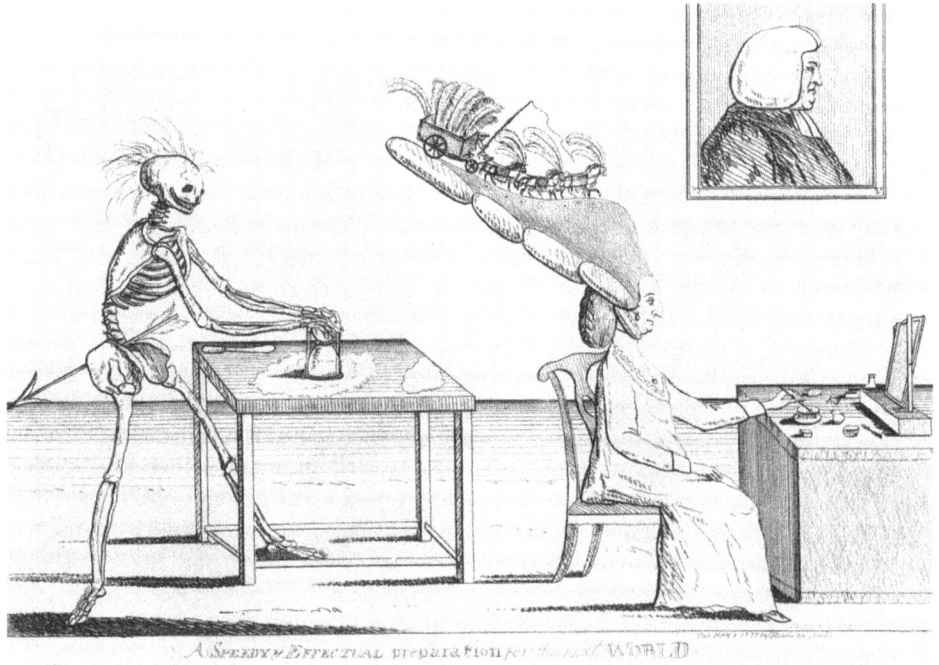

FIGURE 6.12: Mattina Darly, *A Speedy & Effectual preparation for the next World* (1778). Courtesy of The Lewis Walpole Library, Yale University.

Darly, to borrow Belinda's word, is "cruel." But she also identifies the woman at her table as an artist; if she is making a "preparation" with a hairbrush, that could easily be the kind of hairbrush with which painters seize autonomy from the world they represent. Like the formal limitations of Mary Darly's "Coop," the image's representational matrix becomes perceptible in the horizontal lines of shadows on the floor as they intersect the vertical lines establishing various articles of furniture. Death, meanwhile, sprouts the very hair so often pictured growing out of female bodies and is unmistakably feminized by it. Even as it identifies female hair with death, Darly's "speedy and effectual preparation" also fuses it with velocity and even life—hair springs from Death's skull as dynamically as it did out of the head of the Royal Society's hirsute female corpses. By contrast, the bewigged clergyman in the inset picture, usually supposed to be Thomas Wilson, wears false hair that marks his profession but also excludes him from the perverse dynamism that absorbs even mortal, finite bodies into an ongoing exchange of energy and vitality. How easy it is to imagine Death releasing some spring that will pop that slanted coiffure forward and catapult Wilson and his narrowly significant wig into kingdom come.

Darly's "preparation for the next World" presents hair as an animate medium of unlimited ideational life. The spring of the hair in such surreal images refutes the linear and ultimately dispiriting narratives we find when we look too long at hair as a cultural object. Such narratives instead bend into possibilities that can never be wholly seen but whose envisioning yields insight into what the bodies on which it lives might—and might not—be. It is a possibility whose time has, perhaps, returned in the emergent idioms of postmodern science. Ten years ago, Stephen Hawking's 2016 determination that "black holes have hair" would have sounded like a double entendre on the order of Belinda's "Hairs less in sight."[78] Today it implicates a dynamic figure of speech in an emergent understanding of the foundation, persistence, vulnerability, and destiny of bodily form. "Hair" in the quantum sense is any corona of information that appears around any physical body. Black holes have long been believed to destroy all information that falls into them, and physicists have often figured this idea in the observation that "black holes have no hair." Even black holes disappear in time, as the thermal radiation they emit results in steady energy loss. This has led physicists to imagine that any information they absorbed should be lost with them. Yet recent reconceptualizations of black holes' electromagnetic fields aided by new visualizing technologies create room to suppose that a vestige of fallen information clings to their radiant surfaces as "hair." It appears that hairs not seen can survive not only the demise of everything but that of nothing too.

CHAPTER SEVEN

Race and Ethnicity: Mortal Coils and Hair-Raising Revolutions

Styling "Race" in the Age of Enlightenment

HEATHER V. VERMEULEN

INTRODUCTION: "WITH THE BLACK TAIL BEHIND"

John Gay's "The Monkey who had Seen the World," from his collection *Fables* (1727), traces the journey of an anthropomorphized creature who, "to reform the times, / Resolv'd to visit foreign climes."[1] The monkey is captured, chained, and forced to entertain a lady at court (*Fab.*, lines 8–12) but eventually escapes to "his native woods" (*Fab.*, line 24), determined "To civilize the monkey weal" (*Fab.*, line 22). There, "The hairy sylvans" are "Astonish'd at his strut and dress," including "His dapper perriwig [...] / With the black tail behind" (*Fab.*, lines 29–30) and "His powder'd back" (*Fab.*, line 31). The monkey relates that he "come[s] to make a nation wise" (*Fab.*, line 36) and declares his fellows to be "The next in rank to human race" (*Fab.*, line 38).

The fable and accompanying illustration (Figure 7.1) indicate that foreignness—here, mockery of English taste for French fashion—might carry racial undertones. In other words, the (French) "foreign climes" and the threat that adopting French ways poses to the (potentially simian) young Englishman participates in emerging scientific debates regarding the place of apes in relation to humans. Often, this discourse represented persons from the African continent as a link between the two: "The next in rank to human race." To invoke the "foreign" French, in other words, was always already to raise the specter of *farther* "foreign climes" and their inhabitants. It is no coincidence that the fable's illustration likens the "French" ponytail to the monkey's tail hanging between his legs.

Throughout the eighteenth century and well into the nineteenth, hair was a focal point for natural historians and philosophers seeking to define the human species and its nonhuman relatives. Indeed, beginning with the tenth edition of his *Systema Naturae* (1758–1759), Carl Linnaeus foregrounded hair as a means to discriminate among various *Homo sapiens*.[2] For example, "the *Europaeus*" had "long, blond hair," while "the *Afer*"

FIGURE 7.1: *The Monkey who had seen the World*, Fable XIV, illustration from John Gay's *Fables* (1727). Beinecke Rare Book and Manuscript Library, Yale University.

(African) had "'frizzled' black hair."[3] In Linnaeus's ranking of various *Mammalia*, each species became less hairy as it approached *Homo sapiens*. Such classification and ordering of humans and other animals, in turn, aided emerging conceptions of "race" designed to exclude persons from the African continent from Enlightenment notions of "universal" equality and freedom. According to popular scientific theories, "hair" was the purview of white Europeans, whereas "wool" was the proper designation for the hair of African persons, whom those theories sought to animalize and distinguish from the "human."[4] Of course, black hair as "wool" was a very long-standing trope, dating back at least as far as the fifth century BCE, in which Herodotus linked "black skins" to "woolly hair."[5] However, in 1849, speaking before the American Ethnological Society, Peter A. Browne still insisted upon a "hair" versus "wool" distinction, which led him to conclude that whites and blacks "belong[ed] to two distinct species."[6]

European nations and their imperial forces used Africans' "non-humanness" to rationalize their enslavement in the colonies and at home.[7] If, by the time of the French Revolution, as Darcy Grigsby argues, "racism was formulated as a pragmatic, ideological means of control, untrue yet necessary to maintaining colonial dominance," then it was as potentially mutable and dissembling—thus, as unstable and "untrue"—as hair.[8] Put differently, *hair*—racially charged yet constantly (re)styled—might serve to index the inability to "control" revolution and its potential subjects.

As Margaret K. Powell and Joseph Roach have explained, the rise of big hair in England had French origins, like many other English fashions. In the seventeenth century, Charles II sought to emulate hairstyles made popular by Louis XIV, and such styles maintained currency among both women and men in England throughout the eighteenth century. However, drawing on Alexander Pope's *The Rape of the Lock* (1712), the authors also remark upon "the widespread belief that daemons as well as gods inhabit the hair, a presence which makes it magical—the outward display of invisible powers."[9] What this suggests, and what I will explore here, is the way in which hair not only "mark[ed] different social roles, occupations, and conditions," but also indicated fears over the blurring of such boundaries, including racial demarcations.[10] In particular, how did seventeenth- and eighteenth-century depictions of hair raise and register Europeans' fears about its "others" and, eventually, about the French (1789–1799) and Haitian Revolutions (1791–1804)? Did contemporaneous cultural production merely reinforce pseudoscientific categorizations? Or did such media—whether satirical prints, literature, or theater performances—potentially call into question the intractability of hierarchical distinctions?

As Catherine Molineux argues, "Expanding the term 'encounter' to include fantasies of racial others reveals the growing centrality of people of color to the construction of imperial identities."[11] The potential unruliness of hair, as well as the tactics by which it might be styled otherwise, parallel threats that lurked beneath styled exteriors in the European Enlightenment imaginary. Hair was both *close to* (sprouting from) the body and *external to* the body—even, at times, derived from *other* bodies. Styled hair also implies the potential—indeed, the likelihood—of reversion to its original state. These characteristics rendered hair's potential to blur boundaries a powerful metaphor for Enlightenment-era theories regarding "racial" differences and the potential malleability and diversity of the human.[12]

Eighteenth- and nineteenth-century elaborate white European hairstyles—both wigs and sculpted masses (which required copious amounts of other people's hair, woven into one's own)—carried the tinge of the "unnatural" or "foreign." When satirists depicted the production of these "foreign" hairstyles as requiring the intimate attention of "foreign" enslaved black servants, they raised the possibility that one might be made "foreign" through proximity to or the desire for "other" hair. For example, the enormous up-dos and wigs favored by white Englishwomen and men were "frizzed"—transformed "into a mass of small, crisp curls."[13] At the same time, contemporaries often described black hair, such as that of the enslaved servants who attended these individuals' toilettes, as "frizzy." Indeed, as Felicity Nussbaum has pointed out, British author and patron of the arts Elizabeth Montagu once scoffed that the "friseur" employed to curl white women's hair "ma[d]e a young Lady look like a virgin Hottentot or Squaw."[14] What such a pronouncement suggests, is that attending to white British persons' adoption of French hairstyles reveals how such participation in "foreign" fashion might call into question one's own identity, including one's race. In particular, the genre of satire, unlike portraiture, suggests that the black enslaved servants who attend white persons in the prints discussed below are not mere "accoutrements," indicating white Europeans' wealth and capacity to control their "others."[15] Rather, these artists utilize "foreign" hair in conjunction with "foreign" bodies to hint at, but partially sublimate, latent fears of racial "contamination" by proximity.

THE "RACE" FOR STYLE

William Hogarth's six-part painting and print series *Marriage a-la-Mode* (1743–1745) takes as its subject the development and demise of a financially motivated—and (French) fashion-infused—marriage between two upper-class white English people.[16] The series' fourth scene, *The Toilette* (ca. 1743) (Figure 7.2), places in dyadic relation the black male servant who offers a white female guest a cup of sugared chocolate—a colonial product— and the white French hairdresser who attends to the countess's locks with curling paper. The caricatured black servant's tight curls are pronounced in the painting and even more so in the engraved version shown here, suggesting a comparison between his "foreign" curly hair and the "foreign" curly hairstyle that the hairdresser creates for his client.[17] Meanwhile, Hogarth has endowed the hairdresser with what appears to be a long black (pony-)tail. Largely out of sight, it reaches down his back to reappear in the space between his lower torso and that of the enslaved servant. Pointing toward the latter, the tail recalls the simian "tails" in images such as the illustration to Gay's "The Monkey who had seen the World."[18] What is additionally curious about the painting is that, in creating a shadow along the hairdresser's neck and lower jaw, Hogarth has browned his skin; he generates a color that appears nowhere else in the painting's shadowed *white* flesh. Instead, it almost precisely matches the skin tone of the turbaned black boy who plays

FIGURE 7.2: *The Toilette* from William Hogarth, *Marriage a-la-Mode*, Plate IV (1745). Courtesy of The Lewis Walpole Library, Yale University.

with "foreign" auction items in the foreground. The mouths of both black male servant and white French hairdresser are slightly agape as they concentrate on their respective labors; "imitation" goes both ways.[19]

Indeed, two years later, in his 1774 *History of Jamaica*, the racist planter-historian Edward Long makes remarks regarding hairstyles that suggest a linkage between the "wool" believed by people like Long to cover Africans' heads and the "cushions," some made of (animal) wool, upon which Englishwomen in particular piled their hair to achieve their desired coiffures.[20] "Fashion and custom," Long writes, "enslave the greater part of mankind, though often in opposition both to reason and convenience."[21] He mocks the "English belles in Jamaica," who follow "the late preposterous mode of dressing female hair in London, half a yard perpendicular height, fastened with some score of heavy iron pins, on a bundle of wool large enough to stuff a chair bottom, together with pounds of powder and pomatum." This fashion, Long asserts, "literally might be affirmed, *to turn all their heads*; for it was morally impossible to avoid stooping, and tottering, under so enormous a mass [emphasis in original]" (*HJ*, 522).

Earlier on in volume two of the *History*, Long uses "wool" to describe and animalize the hair of Africans and their descendants, referring to their "covering of wool, like the bestial fleece, instead of hair" (*HJ*, 352). Indeed, hair becomes a boundary marker in the Chain of Being that Long musters in defense of "discriminating" persons from the African continent "from the rest of men, not in terms of *kind*, but in *species* [emphasis in original]" (*HJ*, 375). He concludes his rhetorical "tour" of the African continent with the assertion "As we recede from Negro-land, this blackness gradually decreases, and the wool as gradually changes to lank hair." He adds, "We observe like gradations of the intellectual faculty from the first rudiments perceived in the monkey kind, to [...] the Guiney Negro; and ascending from the varieties of this class to the lighter casts, until we mark its utmost limit of perfection in the pure White" (*HJ*, 374–5).[22] Regarding the impact of climate, hair also serves as a limit case. For example, Long wonders if English persons relocated to China might, "in the course of a few generations, [...] acquire somewhat of the Chinese cast of countenance and person." And yet he qualifies, "I do not indeed suppose, that, by living in Guiney, they would exchange their hair for wool, or a white cuticle for a black" (*HJ*, 262). While "countenance and person" might change with climate, hair is a constant indicator of difference and, as a result, a potential justifier of Africans' enslavement.

However, Long's disdainful account of Englishwomen piling their hair upon "wool" prompts recollection of this other "wool"—his designation for the hair of African persons. That which creeps into Long's account—and, perhaps, into pictorial representations of women with "big hair"—is a sense of (racialized) contamination. Indeed, that Long deploys the phrase "*morally* impossible to avoid stooping" suggests not only a literal stooping of the women's bodies on account of their up-dos' weight and height, but also a figurative stooping of *morals* that might accompany their adoption of fashionably huge hair. After all, there is nothing that Long finds more amoral than intimate relationships between whites and blacks. For example, he rails against white female colonists' "constant intercourse from their birth with Negroe domestics, whose drawling, dissonant gibberish they insensibly adopt, and with it no small tincture of their awkward carriage and vulgar manners" (*HJ*, 278). He similarly disdains white male colonists "who would much rather riot in [black women's] goatish embraces"—another hairy, animalistic metaphor—than marry white women (*HJ*, 328). British-Dutch soldier John Gabriel Stedman's *Narrative, of a Five Years' Expedition; against the Revolted Negroes of Surinam* (1796) includes a scene that reflects similar anxieties over hair as boundary marker. On a visit to a friend's home, Stedman witnesses the man's young son "g[ive] a slap in the face to a grey-headed black woman, who by accident touched his powdered hair, as she was serving in a dish of kerry."²³

Philip Dawe's mezzotint *Can you forbear Laughing* (June 14, 1776) (Figure 7.3) explicitly associates the white Englishwoman's extravagant, feather-topped mountain of frizzed hair with the body of the turbaned black boy who assists her toilette. The woman reaches her right hand down to take a feather—the hombre coloring of which finds its match in her sculpted hair—from the bouquet he presents to her. The feather's quill reaches toward the boy's crotch and the woman's fingers seem to stroke its phallic shaft, while his hand (and that of the right-most white female servant) bisects her genital region.

FIGURE 7.3: Philip Dawe, *Can you forbear Laughing* (1776). Courtesy of The Lewis Walpole Library, Yale University.

Meanwhile, the folds of his turban evoke the lines of her hair, and his skin and dress mimic the colors of the feathers that top her coiffure. The peacock feathers in particular seem to emanate from the boy's back- or tail-side, as though the white maidservant plucks them not from the pinned-down bird but from his posterior.

If "French" already equaled "foreign," then it was an easy step to associate (black) "foreign" bodies with France and its emerging revolutionary politics, as I argue in the following section. The British came to associate France's violently enacted philosophies with potentially destructive implications for the institution of slavery upon which not only the French but also the British Empire relied. For British citizens, haunting the French Revolution was the Haitian Revolution, together with actual and imagined revolts among enslaved persons in the British West Indies. Hair was one of the mediating forms for British anxieties over these (black) revolutionary ideas and events.

FRIGHTFUL HAIR AND (UN)NATURAL LIBERTY

In book two of French Huguenot Charles de Rochefort's 1658 *The History of the Caribby-Islands*, translated into English by John Davies in 1666, the author writes of the "Negroes" enslaved on Caribbean islands that "the hair of their heads is all frizled, so that they can hardly make use of Combs" and that "they are very strong and hardy, but withal so fearful and unwieldy in the handling of Arms, that they are easily reduc'd under subjection."[24] He thereby distinguishes Africans from "the *Caribbians* [who] are very careful in combing themselves" and who, in styling their hair, "leave locks hanging down like so many Mustachioes, according to natural liberty [emphasis in original] (*HCI*, 252). Rochefort deploys hair and weapons (mis)management to encode and justify Africans' "subjection"—rendering it "easily" accomplished—on the one hand, and to index indigenous persons' "natural liberty," on the other.

British author Aphra Behn's 1688 novella *Oroonoko*—published, not coincidentally, in the year of the Glorious Revolution—similarly invests hair with metaphorical weight.[25] From the outset of the text, which relates the story of a captured and enslaved African prince named Oroonoko, Behn explores themes of "racial" mutability, reversion, and lurking revolt. To differentiate Oroonoko from other Africans, Behn draws on classical aesthetics:

> His face was not of that brown rusty black which most of that nation are, but a perfect ebony or polished jet […] His nose was rising and Roman instead of African and flat. His mouth, the finest shape that could be seen, far from those great turned lips which are so natural to the rest of the Negroes.

Following these remarks, Behn is at pains to straighten Oroonoko's hair: "His hair came down to his shoulders by the aids of art, which was, by pulling it out with a quill and keeping it combed, of which he took particular care." The quill presumably stretched his curls—though it also hints at potential (self-)authorship—and the combing helped maintain their length and straightness. Immediately following this approving description of Oroonoko's hair, Behn remarks upon "the perfections of his mind."[26]

Oroonoko is the character who, subsequently, leads enslaved persons on a Surinam plantation in a revolt against the white population. Rousing his comrades, Oroonoko declares that they "*are bought and sold like apes or monkeys*" and asks, "*Shall we render obedience to such a degenerate race, who have no one human virtue left to distinguish them from the vilest creatures?* [emphasis in original]" (*Oro.*, 64). It is as though his carefully elongated curls—signifiers of a man "who was more civilized, according to the European mode, than any other had been, and took more delight in the white nations, and, above all, men of parts and wit" (*Oro.*, 36)—spring back toward his head like an over-strained coil. A "Fury" emerges, hell bent on revenge (*Oro.*, 67).

A scene in Daniel Defoe's *Robinson Crusoe*, first published three decades later in 1719, similarly constructs an iconography of hairs-on-end or run amuck as an analogy for racial concerns. When the "marooned" Robinson Crusoe enters a dark cave on the island, he discerns "two broad shining Eyes of some Creature, whether Devil or Man [he] kn[ows] not," and flees.[27] After gathering his courage and venturing farther into the cave, Crusoe hears human-sounding noises that set his hair on end: "I stepp'd back, and was indeed struck with such a Surprize, that [...] *if I had had a Hat on my Head, I will not answer for it, that my Hair might not have lifted it off* [emphasis added]" (*RC*, 129).

Critically, Crusoe compares and then contrasts this hair-raising cave "Creature"—which turns out to be a dying goat (*RC*, 129)—with the indigenous man he will come to rename "Friday." When the man escapes from the "Savages" who wish to kill him and runs in Crusoe's direction, the latter is "dreadfully frightened" (*RC*, 146), just as he was upon perceiving the (goat's) glinting eyes. However, Crusoe relates further, "It came now very warmly upon my Thoughts, and indeed irresistibly, that now was my Time to get me a Servant, and perhaps a Companion, or Assistant; and that I was call'd plainly by Providence to save this poor *Creature's* Life [emphasis added]" (*RC*, 146). In return for driving off the man's pursuers, Crusoe receives various "token[s] of acknowledgment," which encourage him to claim possession of the man, referring to Friday as "[his] Savage" (*RC*, 147). However, it is not only Friday's actions that render him safe to Crusoe's person. Recalling Behn's description of Oroonoko, Defoe also codes Friday's nonthreatening presence through descriptions of his physical appearance, including his "*European* [...] Countenance," his "Hair [that] was long and black, not curl'd like Wool," and "his Nose [that was] small, not flat like the Negroes [emphasis in original]" (*RC*, 148–9). The very description of the indigenous man's hair as "long and black, not curl'd like Wool" presents him as relaxed, safe.

A frightened Crusoe's hair standing on end is the very sort of involuntary or "natural" response that, some five decades later, the actor David Garrick would seek to orchestrate when performing the role of Hamlet in the early 1770s, through the introduction of a "fright wig."[28] As Joseph Roach explains, Garrick enlisted a hairdresser to create "a mechanical wig to simulate the precise physiognomy of mortal dread" when Hamlet first encountered his father's ghost.[29] Roach concludes that, by activating the fright wig, Garrick sought to conjure Hamlet's "inner ghost or spirit" that "directed the performance of the corporeal machine [...] as invisible forces pushed bodies into action."[30] These psychosomatic mechanics invite a consideration of other fearful forces ghosting the eighteenth and nineteenth centuries that might have set British bodies—and hair—into motion. After all, it was the age of the American Revolution, the French Revolution, and the Haitian Revolution, attended by debates over the abolition of the slave trade and slavery itself. Analyses of colonial imaginaries in British theater often focus on plays with nonwhite central characters, such as Shakespeare's *Othello* or Thomas Southerne's 1695 adaptation of Behn's *Oroonoko*. Both were performed throughout the eighteenth and nineteenth centuries. However, it is entirely possible that theatergoers, familiar with these plays' explicit treatment of slavery and "foreign" threats, would have associated Hamlet's evocations of liberty and unfreedom with those "other" narratives sharing the London stage, as well as their "woolly-wigged" actors in blackface.[31]

Garrick made and starred in his own adaptation of *Hamlet*, which debuted at Drury Lane on December 18, 1772. The play contains multiple references to fright and to hair standing on end. When his father's ghost first speaks to Hamlet, the former declares that "the secrets of [his] prison house," could he share them, would cause his son's "knotted and combined locks to part, / And each particular hair to stand on end / Like quills upon the fretful porcupine."³² When the ghost appears to Hamlet in the Queen's closet, his mother is perplexed at her son, who "bend[s] [his] eye on vacancy" and whose "hair starts up and stands on end" (*Ham.*, 4.1.720, 724). That only Hamlet perceives the ghost in this scene underscores the ghost's potential fungibility in eighteenth-century print culture. The ghost might be anything, anywhere, shape-shifting with the times, apprehended by some and not by others—to their peril.

Further, references to slavery, liberty, and temptation pepper the play. In response to Hamlet's resolve to pursue his father's ghost, Horatio cautions that the ghost might "assume some other horrible form / Which might deprive [Hamlet's] sovereignty of reason / And draw [him] into madness" (*Ham.*, 2.2.54–6). That Garrick added the line "Which might deprive your sovereignty of reason" in this 1772 adaptation seems particularly relevant to a time in which "sovereignty"—particularly that of the British colonies in the Americas—was under debate and "revolution" occupied an uncertain relationship to Enlightenment "reason." Indeed, as E.H. Gombrich has remarked, "The grotesque ghost is a child of the Enlightenment."³³

Likewise, it is important to consider how Hamlet's "To be or not to be" soliloquy might have resonated differently at the height of plantation slavery in the British West Indies and as the British colonists in North America sought their independence. London audiences might have heard echoes of colonists' cries when Hamlet pondered,

> Whether 'tis nobler in the mind to suffer
> The slings and arrows of outrageous fortune
> Or to take arms against a sea of troubles,
> And by opposing end them. (*Ham.*, 4.1.63–6)

They might have shared the prince's concern that "in that sleep of death what dreams may come / When we have shuffled off this mortal coil, / Must give us pause" (*Ham.*, 4.1.72–4). Their thoughts might have wandered to enslaved persons in both the colonies and metropole at the lines

> For who would bear the whips and scorns of time,
> The oppressor's wrong, the proud man's contumely,
> [...]
> When he himself might his *quietus* make
> With a bare bodkin? (*Ham.*, 4.1.76–7, emphasis in original, 81–2)

What if the bearers of whips, scorns, and wrongs—those other ghosts haunting the Enlightenment subject—chose to turn the bare bodkin not against *themselves* but against their enslavers? As the nervous King declares to his advisor regarding the threat that Hamlet poses, "We will fetters put about this fear, / Which now goes free-footed" (*Ham.*, 4.1.527–8). In lines that Garrick also added to the play, the King asserts to the Queen, "His [Hamlet's] liberty is full of threats to all, / To you yourself, to us, to every one" (*Ham.*, 5.1.15–16). Whose "liberty" might a white British audience have considered hair-raisingly "full of threats" during this period?³⁴

In contemporaneous print culture, hair provided a means by which to register these "ghosts" of revolution, revolt, and developing Enlightenment concepts of "Man" and "race." Permeating these images and texts is a concern over foreignness and contamination, of both ideas and bodies—together with the possibility of ideas activating bodies, hair included.

BLACK MORTAL COILS AND FRIZZED BRITISH MEN

During the French Revolution, frightful imagery experiences a decided resurgence in British print culture, with resurrected Garrick-like frightful hair being an index of various emerging "ghosts." Both the British and the French, including colonists, had long resorted to metaphors of "slavery" to describe their plights. However, that which Darcy Grigsby terms "an amnesiac double talk" was unsustainable: "While actual slaves were [...] (temporarily) relegated to the shadows of French rhetoric, the trope of slavery recklessly linked a classical abstraction to a real condition. It also uncomfortably tethered the bodies of French citizens to their vilified and repressed other: the black slave."[35] If, as John Brewer explains, "revolutionary politics had its own [...] forms of deportment and costume—including hairstyles," then researchers also must attend to the racial coding of (revolutionary) hair.[36] Foreign "contaminations" were not only "French" but also "black"; frightful hair was produced not only by the ghost of French Revolutionaries but also by the mortal coils of enslaved Revolutionaries.

William Dent's satirical print *Abolition of the Slave Trade, or the Man the Master* (May 26, 1789) (Figure 7.4), published nearly eighteen years before the actual British

FIGURE 7.4: William Dent, *Abolition of the Slave Trade, or the Man the Master* (1789). © The Trustees of the British Museum.

abolition of the slave trade in March 1807, but on the precipice of the French Revolution, implies that the upturning of power hierarchies in forms of governance might impact racial hierarchies, and vice versa. Once more, unruly hair signifies unruly politics and their threat. In a reversal of the widely circulated abolitionist "Am I Not a Man and a Brother?" iconography that depicted a kneeling enslaved black man, here, a white Englishman in a green loincloth, mouth open in supplication, kneels before a black man.[37] The latter, sporting close-cropped, curly hair, a mustache, and fancy "white" garments, prepares to bring a sugarcane stalk down upon the prostrate figure. He utters the words, "Now Massa, me lick a you, and make you worky while me be Gentleman." The most immediate conceit of the print is that the British abolition of the slave trade—advocated by men such as William Wilberforce, Granville Sharp, and Olaudah Equiano—would place the British in the position of "slaves" to other European nations (here, France and Spain). But it also insinuates that the weakened British might lose control over the enslaved populations already in their colonies.

The kneeling "enslaved" Englishman's wiry black hair stands in contrast to the white wigs of his countrymen at home, as though altered by a particularly "black" terror. Appearing the same year as *The Interesting Narrative of the Life of Olaudah Equiano, Or Gustavus Vassa, The African*, Dent's print also forecasts British responses to the imagined and actual terrors of the French and Haitian Revolutions.[38] Indeed, the artist's print *Hell broke loose, or, The murder of Louis* (January 25, 1793), published four days after Louis XVI's execution, makes it clear that Dent associates the terrors of the French Revolution with dark and devilish skin.[39] Three blackened devils have traded their wings for white wigs as they preside over the monarch's death by guillotine. Part of rendering the (black) man the "master" is the donning of powerful (white) hair.

In November 1790, Irish politician and philosopher Edmund Burke had published *Reflections on the Revolution in France*, which contained his notorious and disapproving assertion that the revolution's proponents "ha[d] been content to be represented as a gang of Maroon slaves, suddenly broke loose from the house of bondage, and therefore to be pardoned for [their] abuse of the liberty to which [they] were not accustomed and ill fitted."[40] The specter of the maroons—people of African descent who escaped slavery in the West Indian colonies and formed militarized communities, at times attacking colonists—enabled Burke to blacken the terrors that he perceived in the French Revolution. The author wrote in a moment when the humanity of persons from the African continent and their descendants—and, by extension, their candidacy for "freedom" and "equality"—was under fierce debate. Thus, it is not only white working-class Frenchmen whom Burke has in mind. And it is of no small significance that he singles out "the occupation of a hair-dresser"—that vector of the "foreign"—as among the professions that "cannot be a matter of honour to any person."[41]

David Bindman observes that, although "Burke's *Reflections* [...] was much ridiculed at first," Britain's "main fear"—largely in line with Burke's—"was that the 'levelling' tendencies of the Revolution might spread to Britain, as it became clear that the British constitutional model was not going to prevail in France." However, when Bindman argues that "to a large extent, then, the story of the British response to the French Revolution is about British rather than French politics," his concern stops short of addressing the threat that revolution posed in both the French and the British colonies.[42] The British feared the implications of revolutionary thought and republican politics for the enslaved population upon whom their economy depended.

Such terrors permeate James Sayers's satirical print *Mr. Burke's Pair of Spectacles for short sighted Politicians* (May 12, 1791) (Figure 7.5). Published the following year, it conjures Burke's worst-case scenario, dark-skinned demonic creatures and all. Sayers even introduces a Medusa-like figure: one demon, seated lower right, wears a tricorn hat bearing the slogan "Vive la Nation" and has serpents for hair. He rests his left elbow on Thomas Paine's *Rights of Man* (1791–1792) and points to a document titled, "A Plan of the new Constitution of France, the Perfection of human Wisdom recommended as a Model for Canada by the R^t [Right]." The full title (the Right Honorable Charles James Fox) is cut off, which presents the authority behind French-inspired plans of governance as open for interpretation and seizure. Indeed, that a black "demon" holds the document—while three other black "demons" assist in demolishing England—hints at the very fears of black revolt against slavery that terrified Burke and, here, the Duke of Portland (seated left).

Hair plays a role as well. In fact, there is a precedent for associating black hair with Medusa's writhing snakes. In his *Histoire Générale des Antilles Habitées par les François* (1667), volume two, the Dominican Father Jean-Baptiste Du Tertre not only deemed Africans' hair "frizzy" or "crispy" ("cheveux crêpus") but also claimed that the style they

FIGURE 7.5: James Sayers, *Mr. Burke's Pair of Spectacles for short sighted Politicians* (1791). Courtesy of The Lewis Walpole Library, Yale University.

achieved by wrapping their hair with strips of cotton to elongate it ("les attachment à des filets de coton pour les render plus longs") made them look like artistic renditions of the Medusa ("Meduse").⁴³ Unlike Behn's Oroonoko, whose elongated hair rendered him semi-European, Du Tertre's "Négres" appear all the more monstrous when they attempt a similar style. Implied, is that they carry the potential to petrify the (white) colonizing and enslaving beholder. Further, in Sayers's print, the demon's snaky hair finds its formal echo in the long, wavy locks of Whig opposition leader and Republican sympathizer Charles James Fox. Standing to the left of the central tree representing England, Fox wields an axe labeled, "Rights of Man," and a hat labeled, like the demon's, "Vive la Nation." His five o'clock shadow, a common feature of satirical Fox depictions, discussed below, also serves to darken Fox's skin, juxtaposing it to that of the white and fearful Duke. Both hair and beard work in tandem to associate Fox with the (black) demonic figure of revolution gone too far.

Additionally, there was a precedent for associating Fox with the Medusa figure, in relation to another "foreign" place—the East Indies. *Gorgon* (1784), an anonymous satirical print published seven years earlier by Edward Hedges (Figure 7.6), mocks Fox's East India Bill, rejected the previous year. The artist darkens the politician's skin and depicts various political leaders, including the Duke of Portland (lower left) facing Burke (lower right), as snakes emerge from Fox's head.

FIGURE 7.6: *Gorgon* (Published by E. Hedges, 1784). Courtesy of The Lewis Walpole Library, Yale University.

Two months after Sayers's publication of *Mr. Burke's Pair of Spectacles*, James Gillray, extending the black Medusa theme further, produced *ALECTO and her Train, at the Gate of Pandæmonium:—or—The Recruiting Sarjeant enlisting JOHN BULL into the Revolution Service* (July 4, 1791) (Figure 7.7). Katherine Hart has argued persuasively that one cannot consider this print, bearing a caricatured, brown-skinned rendition of the fury Alecto, a frightful figure from Greek mythology, solely in light of fears over the (white) French Revolution. The imagery carries decided racial undertones.[44] Here, I want to draw attention to the way in which hair—in this case, serpents for hair—adds to the terror (and racialization) of the scene.

Hesiod's *Theogony* relates that the Furies were born when Kronos, son of Gaia and Ouranos, castrated his father at Gaia's request (Ouranos had been destroying Gaia's children), and Ouranos's blood fell upon Gaia.[45] Aeschylus's play *The Eumenides* additionally described the Furies as "black" and "repulsive."[46] Their leader demands from Orestes "blood for blood."[47] In the eighteenth century, in other words, a brown-skinned Fury—evoking the retribution that proslavery individuals feared enslaved persons might seek—would have been terrifying indeed. Merging Medusa with the figure of the Fury, Gillray produces a powerful, terrible signifier of raced and gendered revolution, even bloody revenge—"Am I Not a Man and a Brother?" gone awry.[48]

FIGURE 7.7: James Gillray, *ALECTO and her Train, at the Gate of Pandæmonium:—or—The Recruiting Sarjeant enlisting JOHN BULL, into the Revolution Service* (1791). Beinecke Rare Book and Manuscript Library, Yale University.

Gillray published *ALECTO and her Train* less than three months after Fox delivered a speech to Parliament opposing the slave trade.[49] The print, Hart concludes, "illuminates the deep underlying unease over slavery that colored the English reaction to the early progress of the French Revolution and the earlier success of the American"; it "touches upon the anxiety around the ever-present discourse on civil liberties and abolition in a society so fundamentally tied to the systematic enslavement of thousands of individuals for economic gain."[50] Gillray's print is one of numerous depictions that link Fox to French revolutionary rhetoric threatening to seduce Britain's politicians and populace.[51]

Alecto emerges from the Crown & Anchor Tavern in the Strand, at which the Revolution Society had hosted pro-Republic events.[52] This setting suggests that French Republican politics, grown from Enlightenment notions of *Liberté, égalité, fraternité*, have produced a "monster" in the form of a black Fury who has seized upon those doctrines. The snakes in Alecto/Medusa's hair writhe with tongues outstretched in the direction of "John Bull," signifier of Britain. Gillray caricatures the latter as a working-class tenant concerned over leaving the service of "Varmer- [Farmer] George" (King George III), who "has been a rare good Measter [Master]." Bull, however, is tempted by revolutionary ideas: he admits, "I is half in love with the sound of your drum"—Fox beats a drum bearing an image of Medusa's head—"& wishes to leave off Ploughing & dunging, and wear one of your vine [fine] cockades, & be a French Gentleman." It is impossible not to discern other laboring bodies behind this statement and its stereotypical "dialect": enslaved persons in the British (and French) colonies.[53] In turn, the brown-skinned Alecto, promising to "make [Bull] one of the Masters of England," evokes not only "a perversion of the allegorical figure of liberty" but also the enslaved person who might seize liberty under similar rhetoric or as a direct result of French foreign policy.[54] The Earl of Stanhope (far right) even dubs Alecto the "Black Sarjeant."

While hand-colorings of *ALECTO and her Train* vary, they create sartorial links between Alecto and Fox—the colors of their jackets match—and Alecto's brown skin finds its counterpart in Fox's brown curly hair, bushy eyebrows, and five o'clock shadow. Fox's beard is so pronounced in certain renditions that his *skin* appears brown—as though half of his face is "white" and the other half "black." In satirical portrayals of Fox as a "sans-culotte," artists often give the politician this "hairier" and "darker" aspect. Following racist taxonomies like Edward Long's, Fox's hairiness also might imply greater proximity to "Africans." Hair, therefore, serves as a conduit for linking the white politician with the black persons whose position vis-à-vis Republican politics was under deliberation.[55]

Earlier in 1791, enslaved persons had rebelled in British Dominica; French Saint-Domingue saw a rebellion the previous year.[56] On August 22, 1791, the month after Gillray produced *ALECTO and her Train*, enslaved persons in the northern region of Saint-Domingue launched a massive, highly orchestrated revolt that undeniably inaugurated what would come to be known as the Haitian Revolution.[57] The revolutionaries burned plantation structures and killed white colonists, terrifying the inhabitants. By one white colonist's account, a recaptured enslaved man had in his pockets "pamphlets printed in France [claiming] the Rights of Man."[58] Whether true or invented, this accusation is instructive: white colonists feared that Enlightenment ideas carried the potential to disrupt the racial hierarchies upon which their wealth depended. Thus, when one sees a caricatured white politician, hair standing on end in fright, one cannot solely consider his terror in relation to the (white) French.

For example, in Gillray's *The Dagger Scene: or The Plot discover'd* (December 30, 1792) (Figure 7.8), published three months after the declaration of the French Republic,

FIGURE 7.8: James Gillray, *The Dagger Scene: _or_ The Plot discover'd* (1792). Courtesy of The Lewis Walpole Library, Yale University.

William Pitt's terrified posture and wild hair mimics the psychosomatic response of Garrick's Hamlet to seeing his father's ghost. The reference for the print is a debate that took place two days earlier in the House of Commons regarding the "Alien Bill" that would register foreigners.[59] An infuriated Burke (far right) throws down a dagger before the gathered politicians and declares,

> There! that is what you are to gain by an alliance with France!—such are the Instruments with which they have determined the destruction of the Human race!— Three Thousand such Daggers are now manufacturing for this Country! for where French principles are introduced, you must prepare your hearts for French Daggers!

In response, Fox shrinks back and whispers to fellow Parliamentarian and playwright Richard Brinsley Sheridan, "Confusion!—one of Our daggers, by all thats bloody! how the devil did he come by that?" Echoing fears over the "leveling" potential of French Revolutionary politics, Sheridan cries out to Fox, "O Charley, Charley!—farewell to all our hopes of Levelling Monarchs!" Tellingly, Fox's brown curls and five o'clock shadow stand in striking contrast to Pitt's electrified white hair.

Gillray's *The Dagger Scene* subtly introduces another valence of "the Human race" whose imminent and French-mediated destruction Burke predicts therein. Signified in part through not only skin color but also hair are British fears over the implications of

French revolutionary politics for enslaved persons. Pitt has seen the ghost of the Republic; Fox—hair curled, perhaps even "wooly," and skin darkened—has become tainted by its potential implications.

Isaac Cruikshank's *A Right Honorable alias a Sans Culotte* (Figure 7.9) goes so far as to split Fox in half, giving the white politician a "browner" and hairier alter-ego. Fox's left—and whiter—side sports a white wig, grasps a roll of parchment titled, "Association against Levellers," and declares, "God Save Great-George our King." His right—and browner—side wears tattered clothes associated with satirical depictions of the sans-culottes. Crying out "Ca Ira, Ca Ira, Ca Ira," referencing the French Revolutionary song "Ça ira" (It'll be fine), Fox wields a club and sports a pistol in his belt. Here, his shadow beard has grown so thick as to render the bottom half of his face dark brown and the top half of his face is likewise of a browner hue. His hair, dark in color and curly, compounds Fox's (racial) "foreignness." In turn, the water separating the two landmasses that he straddles might not represent solely the English Channel, but also the Atlantic Ocean. Perhaps he has one foot in England, and one in Saint-Domingue, or even Dominica.

By the time of Gillray's *Doublûres of Characters; or striking Resemblances in Phisiognomy* (November 1, 1798) (Figure 7.10), Satan or "The Arch-Fiend," complete

FIGURE 7.9: Isaac Cruikshank, *A Right Honorable alias a Sans Culotte* (1792). Courtesy of The Lewis Walpole Library, Yale University.

FIGURE 7.10: James Gillray, *Doublûres of Characters; __ or __ striking Resemblances in Phisiognomy* (1798). Courtesy of The Lewis Walpole Library, Yale University.

with a snake coiled about his neck, shadows Fox, mockingly dubbed "The Patron of Liberty." Hellish flames serve as their backdrop and mortal coils have replaced Fox's wavy locks; stubble browns his skin. The most prominent indication of a racialized reading of the political implications of the French Revolution, however, comes in the depiction of Lord Derby or "Strong Sense," whom Gillray pairs with "A Baboon." The latter wears a Phrygian cap—to which the artist adds a "fool's bell"—covering what might be an entirely bald head.[60] The individual's caricatured simian features suggest a comparison with the caricatured depictions of black persons also widely circulated at this time. Perhaps more "hair-raising" for the British would be the individual's possible albinism.[61] With "telltale" hair removed or obscured through "French" revolutionary fashion, albinism, in turn, masks the other chief marker of racial difference: skin color.

HAIR AS "CONTACT ZONE"

One year before Gillray's *Doublûres of Characters*, the French painter Anne-Louis Girodet produces another "doubling," or opposition, of character in his portrait *C[itizen] Jean-Baptiste Belley, Ex-Representative of the Colonies* (1797) (Figure 7.11).[62] Belley was enslaved in Saint-Domingue until he obtained "freedom" through French colonial military service, which additionally provided him with power over lower-ranking white soldiers. He later became the representative of black Saint-Domingue's equal claims to the ideals of Revolutionary France at Paris's 1794 National Convention.[63] Grigsby proposes that Girodet's painting of Belley constitutes "France's most ambitious painted response to the pressures exerted upon Revolutionary politics and art by the 'colonial battalion.'"[64]

FIGURE 7.11: Anne-Louis Girodet-Trioson, *C[itizen] Jean-Baptiste Belley, Ex-Representative of the Colonies* (1797). Musée National des Châteaux de Versailles et de Trianon, Versailles, France. Photo by Leemage/Corbis. Getty Images.

Girodet's composition depicts Belley leaning on a white marble bust of Guillaume-Thomas Raynal, author of the *Histoire des deux Indes*. As Grigsby points out, the second and third editions of Raynal's widely read *Histoire*, published in 1774 and 1780, respectively, "justified violent slave uprising and linked it prophetically both to 'revolution' and to 'the sacred standard of liberty.'"[65] In the painting, Belley might be said to turn his back on Raynal as much as "lean on" him—and, metaphorically, on his ideas. Raynal's bright white and stony bald head contrasts not only with Belley's dark skin but also with his black, but graying, hair. Girodet depicts Belley's hair combed back but with discernable "frizz." By contrast, the artist figures Raynal, who died the previous year, with neither hair nor body. His blank eyes deny an exchange of gazes, his head seems to rest in the clouds. The image evokes a quasi-"universal" aspect, a disembodied intellect engraved into history. Belley's graying hair and contemplative gaze, meanwhile, intimate his mortality as much as his potential legacy. At the same time, his hair might be read as reflecting the bright white of Raynal's bust, enlightened by the philosopher's prophecy. However, that Belley rests casually against the statue and looks away from it equally suggests that Raynal might be "in the back of his mind," as it were, but hardly the sole source of his vision. Simultaneously, Belley's blackness shadows the left side of Raynal's hairless head. Put differently, Girodet creates, in part through hair, an ambiguous point of connection and distinction between the two men. Raynal later rethought his support of revolution and his anti-slavery sentiments.[66] Thus, Raynal might be a ghost of Belley's revolution, as much as Belley might be a ghost of his.

Girodet's portrait of Belley and the texts discussed in this chapter suggest that hair itself is a "contact zone."[67] It is a dynamic racialized, gendered, sexualized, and classed site of mimicry, rejection, and self-styling, a repository of anxieties and aspirations. Hair functions as a mediating matter that is sprung, frizzed, straightened, raised, and revolutionized by all who navigate this mortal coil.

CHAPTER EIGHT

Class and Social Status: Hair and Social Boundaries

MANUSHAG N. POWELL

The complex and often barbed relationship between hair and socio-legal identity, currently an all-too common topic within recent political discourse, has of course long been obvious to eighteenth-century readers. In one powerful indication of how hair can suggest power and class status, the *Oxford English Dictionary*'s first recorded use of "bigwig" to describe an important person is in 1703, from the periodical *The London Spy*. Or perhaps the clearest evidence of what hair means to the period's cultural categories is the fact that actors, people whose job it was to personate many different identities on the stage, came to see hairstyle, both for the head and face, as an indispensable part of their task. Early in the period, actors favored large, formal wigs for most roles, but according to the curious compendium called *Plocacosmos: Or, The Whole Art of Hair Dressing* (1782), the great actor David Garrick's "active genius" in his eager pursuit of improvements to theatrical practices "attacked the mode of dress, and no part more than that of the head and hair. The consequence of this was, that a capital player's wardrobe" soon required large assortments of "what they call, natural heads of hair: there is the comedy head of hair, and the tragedy ditto; the silver locks, and the common gray; the carroty poll, and yellow caxon; the savage black, and the Italian brown, and Shylock's and Falstaff's very different heads of hair, and very different beards."[1] That hair can indicate whether a character is rich or poor, old or young, is no surprise, but *Plocacosmos* describes a far more varied set of gradations than this: styles and colors correspond evidently to economic security (silver locks vs. common gray), ethnic affinity, and Shakespearean favorites—as well as to genre itself. Actors occupied an unusual social stratum, in that as they were public laborers theirs was not an especially honorable profession, yet the celebrity superstars among them could compete with royalty for influence and social attention. Acting also frightened religious conservatives who nursed the suspicion that such public pretending was licentious and libertine. As professional boundary-breakers, then, it is telling that such men and women as professional actors depended on hair both to establish social and performative categories, and to move between them at will. For, much as hair has great power to reinforce and make visible identity categories, it has equal power to signal the rejection of the same.

A focal point of this chapter will be a handful of famous criminals, both real and fictional, whose specialty was the violation of the boundaries between ordinary categories of identity, and who made, not coincidentally, odd tonsorial choices. One such person, Jack Sheppard (1702–1724), was also particularly good at violating the boundaries of his cell walls. An infamous escape artist and, crucially for our purposes, a popular subject for portraiture while he faced execution in 1724, Sheppard was a handsome man, a skilled carpenter, an incompetent thief, and a phenomenal jail-breaker. In his final year of life, he was arrested five times and escaped the first four, becoming in the process a quondam celebrity and something like a folk hero to the poorer classes, who were thrilled by his unflappable ingenuity in the face of imprisonment (his last escape was from a Newgate strong room while both chained to the floor and handcuffed). The most famous portrait of Sheppard is presented here as Figure 8.1, and shows his curly dark hair cropped close around his head.[2] The short hair evokes in the modern viewer an air of the criminal—has it been shaved in the penitentiary in preparation for his execution?—but for contemporary audiences, it may be a nod to Sheppard's state at capture. Sheppard was taken after having burgled a pawnbroker's, and while he was reportedly quite drunk, he was also according to the newspapers dressed elegantly, "in a handsome Suit of Black, with a Diamond Ring and a Cornelian ring on his Finger, and a fine Light Tye Peruke."[3] The fine peruke underscores at least as much as the rich clothes the disparity between his criminal behavior and the genteel figure he parodies as he turns London's law and order topsy-turvy.

FIGURE 8.1: William Thornhill, *John Sheppard* (1724). © National Portrait Gallery, London.

But in Thornhill's portrait, he has no wig. As Marcia Pointon nicely puts it, while women might wear or might not wear false hair, British men who appear publicly *sans* wig "are defined by that absence."[4] And while lack of a wig is fraught with meaning, decoding its lack is not so simple as to associate a wig with rank and "natural" hair with its opposite. The status of a well-dressed servant who is un-bewigged in a room full of powder and curls is marked out in large part through his plain hair (though livery often included wigs); at the same time, however, a higher-ranked man, such as the successful artists Pope or Hogarth, could be painted without a wig in part as an indication of his status security, the marks of profession (books, a palette) showing that a wig is, for him, a choice.[5] It was also not uncommon for genteel men to be painted in wigs that were more generic than their real ones, or even in turbans or skullcaps, so as not to date their images, because wigs were as subject as suits to fashionable whims. In such cases the shorn hair stands in for the absent wig as a signifier of status. Sheppard's shaved head, then, evokes the missing wig that would have been confiscated after his arrest, and in doing so emphasizes just how hard ordinary social boundaries, including legal ones, found it to contain him. By way of contrast, consider William Hogarth's famous depiction of the Newgate scene in John Gay's 1728 musical smash hit, *The Beggar's Opera* (Figure 8.2), in which the antihero Macheath, a highwayman whose appeal and exploits were in large part based on Sheppard's legend, appears in a full powdered wig. Alternative images of

FIGURE 8.2: William Blake after William Hogarth, *Beggar's Opera*, Act III (1790). Courtesy of The Lewis Walpole Library, Yale University.

Sheppard (Figure 8.3), showing him just before escape number four, depict him in finery similar to that of his final capture: hat, wig, large decorative shoe buckles—or, in the receding image that covers, Shawshank-like, the chimney through which he escaped, in a plain cap. The Thornhill portrait shown in Figure 8.1 is apparently the most lifelike we have of Sheppard and was praised at the time for its accuracy; other images appear to be more interested in conveying a set of popular icons gathered about Sheppard: the site of his escape, his imprisonment, his poverty, his insouciance, and his headgear.

As Margaret K. Powell and Joseph Roach have argued, in the eighteenth century, "At work and at play, big hair became one of the most visible ways of marking different

FIGURE 8.3: *Jack Shepherd Drawn from the Life* (Published by John Bowles, 1724). © The Trustees of the British Museum.

social roles, occupations, aspirations, and conditions."[6] What is true of big hair is equally true of wig hair. Macheath and Sheppard were intensely interesting to the higher classes but also worrisome, because of the power of their appeal to the lower ones. Macheath was a fantasy of gentleman-highwayman whose fan appeal muddied the clarity of John Gay's harshly satiric barbs about widespread social corruption; Sheppard was a real, if highly improbable, man who made defiance itself popular. When visited in prison by such crowds that his jailers were rumored to hit a major payday, he was remarkable for the cheerful, polite, and witty disposition he displayed to all comers.[7] By the nineteenth century, Sheppard's legend had become so popular (and apparently this popularity was so disturbing) that for forty years the Lord Chamberlain's Office refused to license new entertainments about him. Macheath's and Sheppard's legends run parallel to their hair: the wig of each man (or the shadow of its lack, in Sheppard's case) underscores the transgressive potential of what became, throughout most of the eighteenth century, an indispensable part of most men's public identities. Lynn Festa argues emphatically that a major source of anxiety around the wig is how easily it—and the parts of identity it signifies—can be assumed, removed, and exchanged.[8] Hair indicates status, profession, personality—but not in any fixed way; wigs exacerbated the potential and problem of hair's mutable significations.

One obvious way for hair to connect to social class is through the ornateness of its style, and there is no discussing hairstyle in the eighteenth century without also discussing false hair. Wigs became popular in Europe first in the French courts of (the balding) Louis XIII and XIV; they were soon adopted as an indicator of aristocracy and later popularized in England by Charles II. In the diary of Samuel Pepys we find a telling remark: "I heard the Duke say that he was going to wear a perriwigg; and they say the King also will. I never till this day observed that the King is mighty gray" (November 2, 1663).[9] Pepys, avid theater-goer and diarist as well as a tailor's son who became Chief Secretary to the Admiralty and an MP, is well known today as an example of spectacular upward social mobility suddenly made possible in the seventeenth and eighteenth centuries. He had just ordered his first wig when he noted the circumstance that had driven Charles II to the same decision, and Pepys was clearly still not quite certain how to feel about the affectation. The next day (November 3, 1663) he commits to the style, but not without some real pangs, both for his hair and for his money, calling upon his female serving staff for reassurance:

> By and by comes Chapman, the periwigg-maker, and upon my liking it, without more ado I went up, and there he cut off my haire, which went a little to my heart at present to part with it; but, it being over, and my periwigg on, I paid him 3l. for it; and away went he with my owne haire to make up another of,[10] and I by and by, after I had caused all my mayds to look upon it; and they conclude it do become me; though Jane was mightily troubled for my parting of my own haire, and so was Besse.

Pepys ultimately decided, "I perceive after a day or two it will be no great matter," though he continues to track the wig's appearances in his wider social circle closely for the next weeks: "I found that my coming in a perriwigg did not prove so strange to the world as I was afear'd it would, for I thought that all the church would presently have cast their eyes all upon me, but I found no such thing" (November 8, 1663). Still wavering, Pepys later returned to wearing his own hair but found (as did many men in an era without leave-in conditioners or hot running water) that he'd become addicted to the convenience of his wigs: "after I had suffered my owne hayre to grow long, in order to wearing it, I find the convenience of periwiggs is so great, that I have cut off all short again, and will keep to periwigs" (May 5, 1665).[11] Pepys, then, is an almost crystallized rendition of wigs making the jump from aristocracy to more populated ranks in England.

By the middle of the eighteenth century, complaints that the affectation of wigs had spread too far down the social ladder were widespread.[12] (One way to help delineate social distinctions as the wig became all but universal was to use hair powder: wigs and extensions might be widely worn throughout society, but the added expense of powder—which might cost up to two pounds per head—was more restricted to elites.[13]) Wigs were popular partly due to emulation but also, as Pepys found, because of convenience and as a matter of custom. Shaving the head and wearing a wig freed men from the daily labor and pains of hair care and let them cover gray or thinning locks with some degree of comfort, especially as wigs became shorter and lighter.[14] Yet, as wigs came to be sleeker and better made, more natural and "authentic" looking, "the wig came to be considered as much a prosthesis as an article of fashion."[15] In the case of men, "the wig is an immediately legible sign of rank and occupation," for each rank, and even many professions, had codes and commonalities in wig cuts and stylings.[16]

Loosely speaking there is something of a natural/unnatural hierarchy regarding wigs, hair, and social status in the eighteenth century: the higher the social rank, the larger the wig and the less hair beneath it; and vice versa lower on down. Wigs themselves, then, could replicate social hierarchies, with an aristocrat's large wig requiring the heads of several lesser men or women to maintain it.[17] Not all wigs were made of human hair, of course (goats and horses, not the most fragrant of hirsute mammals, were common substitutes), but of those that were, usually the donors were not of the highest classes. Nearly all high fashion relies to some extent on the poorly remunerated labor of other creatures, but in the case of false hair there does seem to be something eerily intimate about the boundary violation. Pointon has teased out "the elision of class and gender boundaries implied by the manufacture of wigs from the hair of poor country girls for the heads of city gentlemen" and the related "fear that one might be wearing a wig made from the hair of harlots, cadavers, or plague victims" (121). Wigs, then, physically dissolve the very divisions they make visible. Similarly freighted is the necessary intimacy between the lower-status men and women who dressed hair, and the higher-status people who paid them to do it. Suspicion of the relationship between women and male stylists was a perpetual source of satire, for example (Figure 8.4). While it was commonly joked about that ladies might be having more than their hair done by the male dressers they employed, contemporary manuals describing such labor make this seem unlikely. "Professional scruple, class hierarchy, and personal honor or orientation aside, the size and complexity of the job left no time for anything else."[18] Setting their potential sexual innocence aside, Don Herzog tracks a status change for both hairdressers and barbers across the eighteenth century, associating their drop in status with the social anxieties stirred up by the French Revolution.[19]

Professional independent hairdressers were mostly men, but servants of both sexes in wealthy households were expected to be able to care for and style their employers' hair. Guides like *Plocacosmos* explaining how to do so abounded and could be both elaborate and emphatic about the importance of the tonsorial tasks they taught. *The Duties of a Lady's Maid* (1825), for example, which is about equal parts fashion history, practical how-to manual, and tiresome middle-class moral admonishments, tells the story of Zephirina, a woman who appeared at a masquerade to breathtaking advantage in a shepherdess's straw hat with her hair "gracefully flowing"—but in everyday life, "Under

FIGURE 8.4: Philip Dawe, *A Hint to the Husbands, or the Dresser, properly Dressed* (1777). © The Trustees of the British Museum.

the contour of a deep hat," and without "the waving ringlets of her flowing hair," her beauty was not merely diminished but "totally extinguished."[20] But the same manual that waxes rhapsodic about proper lighting is also alarmingly clear-sighted as to the price paid by both servant and mistress for adhering to the dictates of hair fashion. It warns that most commercial hair dyes, which ladies will want to use once they begin to gray, "are all nothing more than several ways of disguising the nitrate of silver, or lunar caustic," which will certainly produce a reliable black color, but the hair-dressing maid "must take care [...] not to burn [herself] with it, as it will eat through [her] skin like a piece of red hot iron."[21] The savvy lady's maid is therefore urged for safety's sake to manufacture her own cheaper and less horrifying concoctions, recipes for which the manual provides.

Though they had caustic dyes to contend with, women in the eighteenth century at least were not subject to the rigors of hot wax. For men of all ranks, though, shaving was big business, for beards were out of fashion and shaving had seen a major technological and manufacturing advance. The invention of the strop razor and the unprecedented advertising campaign that came along with it were prominent in the era's periodicals and popular media.[22] Shaving—as now—became a major issue in the teenaged male's life, particularly for the college-bound. Formal hair (or wig) dressing before dinner, complete with curls and powder, was both the enforced norm and a heavy burden for the hungry boys and young men at Oxford, who could not properly appear in the dining hall uncoiffed; the collegiate dress code was, therefore, a boon to local barbers.[23] Hairdressing also helped preserve status distinctions among the black-clad students. George Whitefield, before he became one of the founders of Methodism, was an innkeeper's son admitted to Pembroke College in the position of servitor (i.e. a commoner who received board and tuition remission in exchange for serving the better moneyed students). Servitors were instantly recognizable due to their cheaper clothes, plain black stuff gowns, and, as Whitefield remembered, "unpowdered hair" beneath the plain round cap of low rank that was mandatory for them until the 1770s.[24] Wearing one's hair "naturally," then, or in a plain, unadorned style, marked out a person as possessing less power, social acceptance, or even manliness than did wearing a wig. Wigs were rarely seen on English children (apart from on pages or footboys, interestingly), but by age eighteen most young gentlemen would be wearing them.[25] And so for men and women, young and old, rich and poor, the labor that went into hairstyling (and who performed that labor) was a major demarcation of privilege.

But this hierarchy was by no means stable or certain. Bob wigs—which were short and, therefore, cheaper and practical—were initially popular among the lower ranks, but by mid-century their more ornate forms could be found throughout society.[26] As this suggests, length wasn't everything; style also spoke volumes. Physicians wore their wig hair frizzled, for example; clergymen liked their bobs poufy and sometimes with feather tops. And of course, wearing one's own hair was never not some sort of identity statement. This was particularly true in the military and at sea. In the army and navy, at least until early in the nineteenth century, officers wore queue wigs; those lower down had to grow their own queues naturally; length of pigtail could indicate length of service.[27] Sailors who wore wigs favored woolen ones, which "stayed longer in curl" while at sea, where sophisticated hairdressing could be harder to come by.[28] And (as everyone knows) sailors sometimes tarred their pigtails.[29] While hair and wig stylings enacted, to borrow a phrase from Powell and Roach, a highly visible "performance" that "happens at the boundary of self-expression and social identity," they could do more than delineate identity categories such as sex, class, and profession: as the crop-haired Jack Sheppard suggests, hair choices metonymically invoke not only social class but also the identity trespass of criminality.[30] It makes good sense, then, that hair turns out to be intimately linked to property crimes: theft of hair or a wig (both were common) was the theft of a fungible good but also the theft of a status symbol. Hair could cause the forcible reallocation of wealth by being stolen—or by enabling theft.

By far the most common reason for hair to come up in criminal proceedings is because someone is dealing in it or has stolen some of it, but it appears in more active roles as well. In April 1745, a teenaged servant girl was convicted of stealing silver and a key from her master, which she had tried to conceal "all tied up in her hair."[31] This improvised means of concealment was not uncommon. The *Proceedings of the Old Bailey* lists a number of seventeenth- and eighteenth-century cases of maidservants being apprehended with their masters' money in their hair, as, for example, "whilst the Family was abroad, [the serving woman] took the Key out of his Breeches and unlockt a Trunk and took the money out, and was going away with it, but was happily stopt by the Neighbors, and the money found in her Hair" (June 29, 1692).[32] One Mary Wiltshire was apprehended similarly: "tho' she afterwards denied receiving a Guinea on such Account, yet they found the Guineas upon her in her Hair" (August 28, 1728).[33] In other cases, the state of an accused criminal's hair is treated as key evidence: a very common question asked of witnesses in trials for robberies by men was whether the robber wore a wig or "his own hair." Wearing one's own hair seems to be remarkable enough (particularly for redheads, who were already likely to be mistrusted) that the stylistic choice is frequently offered in physical descriptions of suspects.[34] But at the same time, from the number of witnesses who have difficulty answering the question of whether their attackers wore a wig or not, it seems not to have been especially scandalous for a lower-class man to appear either wearing, or without, a wig (wearing one's own hair becomes noticeably more common in mid-century decades, but this category for describing a suspect remains important).

It is also clear that some robbers tucked their hair under their hats, or so it was commonly suspected, in order to prevent being identified later by their haircut and color, or employed other tonsorial maneuvers to confuse matters. Testifying against a gang of alleged highwaymen, one witness stumbled in identifying some of the perpetrators: "He swore positive to Howel and Grimes, but could not be positive to the other three, they having disguised themselves, and had the Hair of their Periwigs in their Mouths" (April 22, 1691).[35] In the trial of a man suspected of murder, it is recorded that "There was a Barber that swore positively that [...] the Prisoner came the next evening to the Barber's Shop (but he did not mistrust him) and bought a Peruke, and cut off his hair for fear of being discovered. The Prisoner denied the Fact, but said that he cut off his hair to fight a man" (February 27, 1696).[36] Cutting off one's hair prior to a boxing match was prudent, as otherwise an opponent might easily use a pigtail to pinion or jerk the head about, but advancing such an excuse also tells us that the accused man is below the social ranks that would have required dueling to settle affairs of honor, since a proper military queue wig was no hindrance in a sword or pistol fight, and a man used to wearing a more ornate wig could remove it. In the British Americas, hairstyling was one of the very few avenues open to convicts and indentures for self-expression, in part because wigs were very rare in the transported population; hair color and favorite hairstyles were all the more important as identifying marks to the marginalized colonial population.[37] Even among the transported, though, beards were uncommon enough that possessing one, particularly a big black beard, was noteworthy in advertisements for runaway servants.[38]

Beards, be they black or carroty, were significant enough as a mark of outsiderliness to be remarked upon in a variety of criminal depositions. Allan Peterkin explains the oddity of beards as he detects an inverse correspondence between the glory of the wig and the presence of facial hair: "As wigs grew larger and more elaborate through the seventeenth century, the mustache became smaller," eventually dropping off the fashionable face altogether except in the military. Worse, for pogonophiles, "the eighteenth century seemed to shun beards altogether. They were worn only in isolated cases by the old, mad, or clueless," though soldiers kept their mustaches.[39] Conversely, as wigs vanished at the end of the eighteenth century, beards returned.[40] In addition to status, hair was certainly implicated in "registering ethnic divides," in which the well-kept, moderately hirsute European coiffure was to be preferred to supposedly savage or over-sleek alternatives from other continents.[41]

Worst of all was to branch out of the beard into new territories of face and body hair: in 1802 Henry Fuseli was appalled to see French soldiers with short, unpowdered hair, and, italics his, "the *Chin shaved & the throat unshaved*, which is a beastly custom making a Man like an Animal."[42] For Linnaean followers, "the growth of the beard was thought to be particularly meaningful in that it linked ethnicity and gender directly" even though the majority of eighteenth-century European Christian men did not wear beards.[43]

Much of the second half of this chapter's energy is devoted to facial hair in the Enlightenment, which it will read backwards against the preexisting strong scholarship on wigs. Viewing the wig and beard together offers an interesting mirror reversal: wigs are, so to speak, "unnatural," and go backwards from the head, while beards are "natural" and grow outwards from the face. Beards are comparatively quite rare in our period, while wigs are, during much of the century, nearly universal. My suspicion is that beards work as a test of the limits of the well-known power of wigs to signify identity categories. The ability to grow a beard is for most European cultures a traditionally positive sign of masculinity, maturity, and strength—but actually wearing a beard is a far less stable signifier.[44]

To summarize a complicated issue, the European ideal was that one *could* grow a beard if one liked but that a man also would have the wherewithal to keep it shorn: groups deemed either excessively hirsute *or* depilous were regarded as inferior. The beard, argues Londa Schiebinger, "took on special significance" in mid-eighteenth-century attempts to delineate race: "Women, black men (to a certain extent), and especially men of the Americas simply lacked that masculine 'badge of honor'—the philosopher's beard."[45] (To neoclassical naturalists, a leading theory was that beards grew because of men's superior body heat and as an outlet for "reabsorbed semen."[46]) So for reasons of social status, ethnic identity, profession, and fashion, in the eighteenth century facial hair was not very common throughout Europe, with the exception of some of the higher-status men in Central Europe, who borrowed from the Ottomans a preference for large mustaches, a trend that other Europeans interpreted as fierce-looking and exotic.[47] Peter the Great infamously forced Russian men to shave or pay a fine in an attempt to modernize his society's pan-European social standing.[48] (Some peasants who could not afford the luxury tax shaved their beards but, according to John Perry, kept them to be buried with in the due course of time.[49]) And even within Britain's own borders, Jews' beards are commonly called out as one of their markers of otherness.

But hair indicated far more nuanced categories than ethnicity, religion, or nationality, and hairstyles were so specific that they could be tied to particular trades as well as social ranks taken more broadly. The full-bottom wig was (and is) a constant among the judiciary, even when it had fallen out of fashion elsewhere in favor of the queue wig.[50] According to John Woodforde, in the early eighteenth century lawyers found robust beards so unprofessional that "an order was issued by the Inner Temple that no member 'should wear his beard above three weeks' growth" or face a fine of 20s.[51] Hair and wigs, then, delineated multifarious categories of cultural identities, but beards indicated a disregard for social standards entirely: wearing a slightly outré but removable wig is nothing to cultivating a fashionable violation of one's very bodily growth. The most extreme (but tellingly so) indicator we have inherited of the eighteenth-century reading of beards as anarchistic is the legend of the dread bearded pirate: Blackbeard.

Pirates, we need to stipulate here, are the ultimate criminals, at least symbolically speaking, in that they abjure social and professional hierarchies and national identity. As they have entered the popular imaginary, there are two main archetypes of pirates: the swashbuckler with pretensions to genteel attractions (see Figure 8.5, depicting Captain

FIGURE 8.5: B. Cole, *Captain Bartho. Roberts with two Ships, Viz. the* Royal Fortune *and* Ranger, *takes 11 Sail*, illustration from *A General History of the Pyrates* (1724). Beinecke Rare Book and Manuscript Library, Yale University.

Bartho. Roberts) and the nihilistic devil destroyer (see Figure 8.6, Blackbeard). Roberts is the pattern for such suave villains as Captain Hook.; he went into his final battle bejeweled and dressed to the nines, and his portrait in the *General History of the Pyrates* shows him wearing a neat wig befitting a captain's rank. Blackbeard, meanwhile, is clearly wearing his own hair, both above and below the eyes. The perhaps obvious but still important point here is that it is no coincidence the visual division between these men is made of hair and starts with a wig's absence and facial hair's presence. As the saga of Edward Thatch or Teach, alias Blackbeard, heads towards its conclusion in the 1724 *General History of the Pyrates*, which remains the chief source for his legend, the narrator shifts gears towards what the reader has presumably been waiting for:

> Now that we have given some Account of Teach's Life and Actions, it will not be amiss, that we speak of his Beard, since it did not a little contribute towards making his Name so terrible in those Parts.
>
> Plutarch, and other grave Historians have taken Notice, that several great Men amongst the Romans, took their Sir-Names from certain odd Marks in their Countenances; as Cicero, from a Mark or Vetch on his Nose; so our Heroe, Captain Teach, assumed the Cognomen of Black-beard, from that large Quantity of Hair, which, like a frightful Meteor, covered his whole Face, and frightened America more than any Comet that has appeared there a long Time.
>
> This Beard was black, which he suffered to grow of an extravagant Length; as to Breadth, it came up to his Eyes; he was accustomed to twist it with Ribbons, in small

FIGURE. 8.6: B. Cole, *Blackbeard the Pirate*, illustration from *A General History of the Pyrates* (1724). Beinecke Rare Book and Manuscript Library, Yale University.

Tails, after the Manner of our Ramilies Wiggs,⁵² and turn them about his Ears: In Time of Action, he […] stuck lighted Matches under his Hat, which appearing on each Side of his Face, his Eyes naturally looking fierce and wild, made him altogether such a Figure, that Imagination cannot form an Idea of a Fury, from Hell, to look more frightful.⁵³

Because of this tendency to double bits of his beard up like so many tiny queue wigs, it is easy, in looking at the illustrations, to mistake the lighted matches sticking over his ears for his own hair; in time this has come to be a common misremembering of the legend: Blackbeard is now not atypically depicted with his beard actually on fire, literally glowing with malice.⁵⁴

Teach is quite simply excessively hairy, even "extravagantly" so, treating his alienating facial hair with the care he is supposed to be giving to his nonexistent captainly wig. He is also excessively evil, even towards his own men.

> One Night drinking in his Cabin with Hands, the Pilot, and another Man; Black-beard without any Provocation privately draws out a small Pair of Pistols, and cocks them under the Table, which being perceived by the Man, he withdrew and went upon Deck, leaving Hands, the Pilot, and the Captain together. When the Pistols were ready, he blew out the Candle, and crossing his Hands, discharged them at his Company; Hands, the Master, was shot thro' the Knee, and lam'd for Life; the other Pistol did no Execution.—Being asked the meaning of this, he only answered, by damning them, that if he did not now and then kill one of them, they would forget who he was.[55]

A man rumored to be more violent, unpredictable, and savage than most of the other Caribbean pirates of his day, Teach's deliberately prominent beard becomes representative of the rest of his vicious lunacy; it also clearly codes him as un-European, uncivilized.

In seventeenth- and eighteenth-century maritime law, pirates were *Hostis humani generis*: enemies to all and belonging to none, they were understood as men of no nation, beyond the reach of moral reproach, conventional class status, or civilization. Yet even among such a desperate group, beards were not particularly common, certainly not as a matter of cultivation. What Blackbeard's case displays, then, is *not* that pirates all have beards: it is that beards are so odd and even redolent of evil that only the worst of the worst pirates would dare—or want—to brandish one so boldly as he. It is from his example that the association between beardedness and piracy springs, not the other way around. The sixteenth-century corsairing admiral brothers Barbarossa (really Oruç and Hayreddin) are only known as "Redbeard" in European traditions.[56] Graham Chapman's memorable 1983 creation of the vilest pirate ever to sail was called Yellowbeard. And there are at the moment of this writing not one but two lines of men's facial-care products named for Bluebeard: *Bluebeards Original* and *The Bluebeard's Revenge*, both emblazoned liberally with jolly rogers. The fact that Bluebeard, a French fairy-tale aristocratic wife murderer, was never a pirate to begin with but is now commonly recalled as one, shows how strongly a beard has come to mean not just any pirate but a stand-out, truly infamous pirate, the manly transgressor of all decorous bounds and behaviors.

Yet curiously, as the earlier examples of female thieves stashing coins in their coifs reminds us, not all transgressive hair is manly or masculine. "Like the division of labor that men's wigs symbolized, women's hairdos assigned them to specific tasks in the performance of everyday life": the twist for the case of women is that the looser and more relaxed their hair, the closer it came to signifying something negative about the lady to whom it was attached.[57] In the seventeenth century, Puritans had objected to wigs in part because long hair seemed the province of women; wigs confounded gender markings both by making long hair available to anyone and by being detachable.[58] There were similar anxieties in the same period that wearing male garb would embolden and masculinize a woman.[59] At least one historian has argued that in the seventeenth century, given the elaborateness of men's full and flowing wigs and the fashions for women in the upper crusts, "conventions about one style being feminine and another masculine barely existed"; indeed, some sporting women even wore masculine wigs while riding.[60] Still, most women did not wear wigs, but for formal up-dos, their hair was, to quote Festa, "supplemented by prosthetic tresses," though this practice opened the wearer to satire and critique, since it implied something inadequate about the woman's natural head.[61]

Pepys, our Restoration wig purchaser from earlier, did not allow his beautiful young wife to wear false hair. Men laid claim to their place in (or rejection of) society by shaving their faces and heads and picking the right wigs to place atop them, but they also enforced social boundaries by controlling women's access to the conveniences they enjoyed from the use of artificial locks. Much later in the period from Pepys's days, we encounter a classic moment in Frances Burney's *Evelina* (1778) where her awful grandmother, the victim of a practical joke, loudly laments the loss of her false hairpieces:

> Her anger now subsiding into grief, she began most sorrowfully to lament her case. "I believe," she cried, "never nobody was so unlucky as I am! [...] that puppy has made me lose my curls!—Why, I can't see nobody without them:—only look at me,—I was never so bad off in my life before. Pardi, if I'd know'd as much, I'd have brought two or three sets with me: but I'd never a thought of such a thing as this."[62]

The heroine's mortification is twofold: that her grandmother should wear false curls and, worse, that she should be so crass as loudly to admit to it. Evelina's claims to a genteel status are already precarious; for her to be associated with this woman who has violated all norms of both manners and hair compromises them still further, to her dread and embarrassment.

The paradox of women's hair norms is that most often, hair is expected to be long—"'naturally' long," as Penny Howell Jolly points out—but also, at least among the English, neatly controlled.[63] (This was true to some degree for men as well, particularly as a racial marker: the Afro-Briton Olaudah Equiano—who would later become a skilled hairdresser—twice remarked on how frightening to him was the appearance of European slavers the first time he saw them, a major factor of which was their "long" and "loose hair." But the slavers themselves did not find their hair appalling, unlike in Burney, where women help police other women with uncontrolled hair.) In a neat piece of symmetry, a woman indicted for, but not convicted of, stealing a man's wig was described in the 1720s as a "Lunatick, us'd to run about the Streets with her Hair loose" (January 12, 1722).[64] Her unconfined hair seems to be her alibi or a mitigation of the purported crime, which was essentially disturbing a man's public tonsorial integrity. Worse than an old woman in a wig is a young one with her hair unbound and, as the saying goes, all down about her ears. For a woman to have her hair loose in public is generally shorthand for the kind of extreme distress that can only be the result of major transgression or loss.

So in complement to the bearded man stands the loose-haired woman, since women typically do not grow beards, at least not by choice. If there is no perfect female analog to Blackbeard, there is at least an instructive example of she-pirates we might turn to. In the earliest known image of the female pirates Anne Bonny and Mary Read (Figure 8.7), the women are wearing sailors' slops: loose, practical shipboard clothing that does little to mark their biological sex. What tells the viewer what he or she is looking at is their long, unbound hair. (Recall here that long hair was common enough among sailors even after it had ceased to be fashionable on land—but sailors usually wore pigtails.) Read and Bonny's long hair, draped in small kerchiefs almost as an afterthought, marks them as feminine because they are not male sailors with neat queues, or captains in wigs and hats—but it also marks them as improperly feminine.[65] Their locks' looseness stands for transgression just as much as the naked blades in their hands (the latter, but importantly not the former, being a common icon for male pirates as well). To get a sense of just how out of bounds Bonny and Read are, compare them to the portraits of Elizabeth Canning and Mary Squires (Figure 8.8), who were, in their way, equally infamous criminals, subjects of one

CLASS AND SOCIAL STATUS 169

FIGURE 8.7: B. Cole, *Ann Bonny and Mary Read convicted of Piracy*, illustration from *A General History of the Pyrates* (1724). Beinecke Rare Book and Manuscript Library, Yale University.

FIGURE 8.8: Double Portrait of Elizabeth Canning and Mary Squires the Gypsy (*The London Magazine*, May 1754). Courtesy of The Lewis Walpole Library, Yale University.

of the century's most notorious unsolved mysteries. In 1753, the maidservant Elizabeth Canning disappeared for a month, claiming upon her return that women named Susannah Wells and Mary Squires had held her captive and attempted to force her into prostitution. They were tried and found guilty (Squires of the theft of Canning's stays, a capital crime), but Canning was later tried and convicted of perjury and Squires was pardoned. Despite their infamy and low social status, which in the case of Squires also includes some racial othering, both have hats, their hair carefully covered, bounded, controlled.

Boundary-flaunting hair, then, is not merely about communicating the delinquent subject's economic, social, or moral poverty—far from it; in fact, sometimes quite the opposite is true. Whether displaying a soldier's length of military experience or a pirate's precise degree of transgressions, that there was a common language of locks was readily apparent on sea and land, Caribbean and London, even when no language of law could make the same claim. Wigs demand their own code of manners and behaviors: to disturb a wig, either through vigorous physical activity or because of discomfort—even to hear better or wear glasses properly—was to be avoided in formal arenas, particularly in professional, or mixed-sex surroundings.[66] (And professional circumstances encompass a wider variety of arenas than one might think: even laborers or farm hands might wear wigs to stay warm outdoors.[67]) Yet wigs could be removed temporarily to scratch or for comfort during some activities; even during formal occasions wigs might come off among male intimates.[68] Still, there is a considerable and important difference between having a wig but removing it and appearing without a wig altogether. By the 1760s, men were starting to wear their own hair more often, and though wigs came back in fashion a decade later, the end was near.[69] The nail was driven into their coffin by the 1795 tax on hair powder.[70] By the turn of the nineteenth century, gentlemen wore their hair cropped short and neat—but footmen in livery were still required to wear wigs, as did doctors, lawyers, and the clergy—and sailors still had their pigtails. Hair, in other words, preserved those distinctions that remained fixed even as social mobility was on the increase.

Criminal hair conveys a threat because it refuses, in its presence, its lack, its wildness or demure style, to line up with other key traits of its wearers. Pickpockets and pirates can all be made subject to the law, but in some truly notorious cases the intersection of biology and fashion that we call hairstyle represents a powerful rejection of convention. The comic ballad *The Flying Dragon and the Man of Heaton* (1775) tells the tale of a Lancashire man who sees in London the French fashion for "large Pig-tails and Ear-locks," i.e. a Ramillies wig, but loses the false hair to a stiff wind. The poem sees the wig as absurd, an urban affectation out of place in the true English countryside: "With Powder dusted; smooth'd by Tonsure / He look'd as grand as Monkey Monsure!"[71] A "Country man" of Heaton sees the hair and thinks it a dragon, and does battle with the "long, black, thing; with Wings and tail / The Wings quick moving with the wind."[72] Eventually a parson convinces him of his error, but if the country man is shown to be thoroughly simple, the wig is certainly never rehabilitated: it is at once monstrous, French, and a sad, silly thing. This ballad is about social status in its reliance on the better-educated parson to settle things, but it's also about national identity in a fairly complicated way: both the wig and the Man of Heaton are butts of the joke, and the implication is that though they must not indulge in Gallic excessive versions or worship of them, still it is incumbent upon Englishmen great and small at least to understand and decode a wig when they see one. And, it actually goes without saying, to shave their beards.

CHAPTER NINE

Cultural Representations: Hairstory

CRYSTAL B. LAKE

"From observing the growth of a hair, can we learn any thing concerning the generation of a man?"[1] Such is the hair-raising inquiry of Philo, David Hume's foil in his *Dialogues Concerning Natural Religion* (1779). In what follows, I linger with Philo's glib incredulity and the proposition that provokes it: that we can indeed learn a lot by observing hair. I begin by considering how Philo's invocation of hair is more substantial than it at first appears; it reveals the ways in which questions about materiality and temporality—and scale and causality—shaped the *Dialogues*' overarching concerns with the relationships between body and spirit. Philo's clever quip, therefore, stands as a representative example of some of Enlightenment philosophy's most famous preoccupations, but Hume's hair-splitting hardly settled the problem of matter or of hair. Hume's posthumous reputation continued to be entangled with hair, even his own, in works such as Edward Bulwer-Lytton's supernatural romance *A Strange Story* (1862). Using Bulwer-Lytton's insights about the philosophy, science, and literature of the century that preceded his novel, I argue that the cultural representations of hair throughout the Enlightenment unexpectedly anticipated recent thinking on materiality exemplified by works like Samantha's Frost's *Biocultural Creatures* (2016).

Traditionally, the study of hair has focused predominantly on the performative role it plays in anthropological and psychoanalytical contexts. Consequently, Joseph Roach and Margaret K. Powell have argued convincingly that hair in the eighteenth century—coiffed, stacked, and bewigged—was not only big (and big to do) but also a big deal. Poised between the private and the public, "big hair" was "one of the most visible means," Roach and Powell write, "of marking different social roles, occupations, aspirations, and conditions."[2] Roach and Powell find that hair enthusiasts in the 1700s—ranging from fashionable celebrities to laboring maids—also reflected the transhistorical nature of hair's cultural functions. We can glimpse in a variety of documents the period's forays into what Roach and Powell call "hair theory": the recognition that hair is "sacred," styled and cut with purpose, and as important in myth as it is in daily practice.[3] All of this is right, but Hume's hair-raising suggests that hair theory must also take into account hair's curiously invisible, seemingly impossible performances: its unwilled acts that precede, produce, and "raise," rather than reflect, meaning.

I suggest, therefore, that "hairstory" should be seen as a crucial piece of hair theory. "Hairstory" is the term I use to name the cultural representations of hair that alight on its tendrils, strands, and microscopic properties in order to reconsider the nature of hair's materiality: its mysterious thingly power not only to perform culture but also to shape and make culture. Whereas theory remains important for my readings of hair, the word "story", I argue, captures hair's unique aesthetic affordances. Inspired by the work of Caroline Levine and Walter Benjamin, "hairstory" denotes hair's propensity for generating narratives that are preoccupied with objects, scale, time, and causality. After teasing out the implications of Philo's reference to hair, therefore, I next turn to consider representations of Hume's own hair; Bulwer-Lytton bound Hume's hair up in a history of Enlightenment philosophy, science, and art, illustrating the ways in which the Enlightenment vested hair with agency, despite claims like Philo's that might suggest otherwise.

With both Frost's concept of the biocultural as well as Bulwer-Lytton's interest in "supernatural agency" in mind, I swing back to the eighteenth century in order to explore how iconological representations of concepts such as curiosity reflected a sensibility shared by medical and scientific treatises: that hair was a liminal entity located "betwixt and between" (in Victor Turner's famous phrasing) the human and the nonhuman, the interior and the exterior, the present, the past, and the future. Robert Hooke's microscopic observations and depictions of hair provide a representative example of how hair's biocultural, liminal qualities afforded a range of narrative styles and organizations that complicate traditional accounts of how the Enlightenment ordered its ideas about objects as well as causalities. Hooke's influence on the Royal Society also leads me to examine how members of its sister organization, the Society of Antiquaries, collected historical specimens of hair. Antiquarian interest in the hair of monarchs like Charles I add volume to the hairstory told by Hooke's *Micrographia* by illustrating how hair afforded narratives about history in which disparate times and distant spaces were enfolded together. In this way, I find that hair is the kind of storyteller explicated by Benjamin. The period's hairstories, then, give us an unusual peak under the wig, as it were, of the Enlightenment. Hairstories preserve modes of enchantment in which a mere hair's breadth measured the distinctions between self, matter, and spirit as well as between the past and the present.

Philo's insistence aslant that the growth of a hair cannot explain the generation of a man voices Hume's notorious skepticism about Christian doctrine that would buttress the *Dialogues*' claims for faith on reason. Hume's *Dialogues* features two speakers in addition to Philo: the church apologist, Demea, and Cleanthes, whose religious convictions are based on his argument for and from design. The *Dialogues* lops Demea off handily; he stomps out even before the argument is settled. Cleanthes, however, is a trickier adversary, arguing eloquently that faith can be arrived at through reason rather than revelation. Cleanthes is Philo's most persuasive philosophical opponent and the one Philo claims would hang too much on a strand of hair.

Cleanthes's argument is worth quoting at length because it reveals the stakes behind Philo's hair-raising provocation. Cleanthes invites Philo to "Look around the World: Contemplate the Whole and every Part of it."[4] Philo, Cleanthes believes, will soon find the world to be a

> great Machine, subdivided into an infinite Number of lesser Machines, which again admit of Subdivisions, to a degree beyond what human Senses and Faculties can trace and explain. All these various Machines, and even their most minute Parts, are adjusted to each other with an Accuracy, which ravishes into Admiration all Men, who have ever contemplated them. The curious adapting of Means to Ends, throughout all Nature, resembles exactly, tho it much exceeds, the Productions of human Contrivance; of

human Design, Thought, Wisdom, and Intelligence. Since therefore the Effects resemble each other, we are left to infer, by all the Rules of Analogy, that the Causes also resemble; and that the Author of Nature is somewhat similar to the Mind of Man; tho' possessed of much Larger Faculties, proportion'd to the Grandeur of the Work, which he has executed. By this Argument *a posteriori*, and by this Argument alone, do we prove at once the Existence of a Deity, and his Similarity to human Mind and Intelligence.[5]

Philo will eventually agree with Cleanthes's claim that the world does, indeed, appear to be ordered reasonably, designed like an infinitely complex piece of clockwork. As Alexander Pope would write, "All are but parts of one stupendous whole" in which a spirit breathes "as full, as perfect, in a hair as heart."[6] Philo will maintain, however, that revelation rather than reason must inspire this faithful conviction. Such is Philo's unexpected celebration of fideism, but one controversially made in the absence of Demea's orthodox oversight.

Philo's suggestion that Cleanthes's ideas are harebrained occurs before he is convinced, however, and it exemplifies his attack on both Cleanthes's philosophical method and his rhetorical style. We can see in Cleanthes's description of the universe as "one great machine" the roots of Philo's discomfort with Cleanthes's twisted reasoning. Philo seizes on Cleanthes's admission that his argument depends upon an analogy and is *a posteriori*. Cleanthes bases his generalizations on particulars. Since the whole is unavailable for comprehension, Cleanthes inductively draws big conclusions from his observations of small things: "lesser Machines" that are subdivided into the "most minute Parts." Philo, therefore, charges Cleanthes with basing his argument on an observational method built from the ground up while concluding that such observations prove that the whole is designed from the top down. Moreover, this inverted relationship in which the category of qualitatively tiny things produces the quantitatively vast idea further coincides with a temporal confusion in Cleanthes's argument. For Philo, the cause is revealed as such only after the fact of its purported effect.

Philo suggests that Cleanthes's argument is, therefore, not only paradoxical but also mythological, springing humans from hairs as if from the brow of Zeus. Philo's use of hair to prove his point is not accidental; it indicates that he is troubled by the ways Cleanthes would invest bodies with untimely enchantments. Because the body and the mind loom large at the analogical center of Cleanthes's argument for design, Philo recognizes that those who would follow along with Cleanthes as he makes his case are invited to think about their own bodies, even though Cleanthes never directly mentions the body in this particular passage. For example, the imaginative tracing Cleanthes encourages draws attention to sensual perception and invites a metacognitive awareness of sensation: what the "human Senses and Faculties *can* trace and explain [emphasis added]." One might begin, therefore, as philosophers so often do, by thinking about what it feels like when our extremities make contact with external objects: a fiery coal at hand, a billowy bed steps away. From considerations of sensory thresholds—those borders of tactility where our bodies first feel the things they touch and register pain or pleasure—Cleanthes encourages an awareness of the will: the mind that wisely pulls the hand away from the hot coal or directs the feet to the soft bedside.

Cleanthes's argument develops outwards from these intimations of tactility and intention, but his rhetoric does not. Despite invoking what the "human Senses and Faculties *can* trace and explain," Cleanthes draws conclusions about "a degree beyond" the observable body and the rational will: the hand that jerks before we cogitate, the dream we do not plot. For Cleanthes, bodies and intentions entail a quickness of speed and a minuteness of parts that, counterintuitively for Philo, construct a predetermining history and an invisible, but no less quantitatively vast, object of design. The deity Cleanthes imagines is notably "possessed of much *Larger* Faculties, porportion'd to the *Grandeur* of the Work, which he has executed [emphasis added]," phrasing that indicates how easily Cleanthes slips between size and quantity and how quickly he collapses time and expands duration. Philo fundamentally disagrees with Cleanthes's analogical skips: a body is not the same as an idea, an idea is not the same as an intent, intent is not the same as design. Bodies, ideas, intent, and design differ in substance and in form, for Philo, and to conflate them is to time-warp the order of things.

This is why Philo's turn to the question of hair makes so much sense out of nonsense. Visibly but precariously rooted in the shallows of corporeal extremity, hair itself offers an analogical way of imagining the circuitry of the body's interior: its tangled nerves and veins. Yet hair does not feel and is not subject to willed motion. Cleanthes would insist that, nevertheless, it is as minutely wrought as the nerves and veins, infused with the same mechanisms of motion that pump and thoughts that will. Even a split end, therefore, would be "curious[ly] adapt[ed]" to some rational "means"; even a thread of hair would "ravish" us into "admiration" and shine with "thought, wisdom, and intelligence" in Cleanthes's schema. Here is where Philo as Hume's proxy will strike; although he will agree that the whole appears intricately rational and ravishing, he will disavow that minute parts—like an unfeeling, unwilling filament of hair—are capable of confirming such truths. Moreover, philosophical schemas that resort to observations of particulars make particulars themselves causally responsible for generating the rational whole and, subsequently by extension, the whole becomes a mere effect of its particulars: a teasing conundrum, a sheer impossibility to Hume's mind. In other words, Cleanthes's worldview and philosophical method tangle, for Hume, parts with wholes, bodies with spirits, material things with ineffable ideas, and causes with effects.

Philo was wrong about hair. Philo's appeal to the hair that generates a man makes the same error of analogy that he accuses Cleanthes of making. That is to say, Philo's argument itself hangs on a tendril; if for Philo hair was incapable of producing a body or a mind or a world, it remained capable of exemplifying a concept and a counterpoint. Hair proved uncannily generative of a philosophical premise, even for Philo. Philo's clip about hair notably occurs within the larger context of his ongoing interrogation into the existence of spirit, soul, and deity, and so Philo well knew that one could learn a great deal about death from hair, too. Hume's hair, at least, could mark the degeneration of a man. Describing his visit to Hume's deathbed in 1776, James Boswell reported that Hume was "lean, ghastly, and quite of an earthly appearance."[7] Reading his copy of Campbell's *Philosophy of Rhetoric* and wearing a simple gray suit, Hume peaked out, "placid and cheerful," from under "a kind of scratch wig."[8] Donned in his informal, partial hairpiece, Hume prepared to die, declaring to Boswell with cheerful resignation that "he was just approaching to his end."[9]

Boswell "contrived to get the subject of immortality introduced": did the promise of a future state now, perhaps, dance before Hume's dying eyes? Immortality was possible, Hume conceded, in the same way that it was possible that "a piece of coal put upon the fire would not burn." Possible, but highly unlikely. And in any regard, what was so appealing about immortality, Hume mused, if it meant that the "trash of every age must be preserved?"[10] Boswell was unsettled, and he "felt a degree of horror" that set his mind traipsing in a "sort of wild, hurrying recollection" of his "excellent mother's pious instructions, Dr. Johnson's noble lessons, and of [Boswell's own] religious sentiments and affections during the course of [his] life."[11] He tried another tack with Hume: wouldn't he "regret annihilation" because he had "written such an admirable history"; wouldn't he "be sorry to leave" that history forever? It really was no matter to Hume. "I shall leave that history," he said, "as perfect as I can"; its past was past, for Hume, and he was no more bothered by the idea that no future state awaited him as he was by the "thought that he had not been" to begin with, "as Lucretius observes." Hume had no "wish to be immortal," he was convinced that greatness and accomplishments were only measurable in proportion to the present in which they occurred, and he was doubtful that futures were better than their pasts. They might easily be worse. A scratch wig philosophy, if there ever was one.

Boswell was "disturbed for some time," troubled by the idea that Hume, renowned philosopher and historian, would simply "[waste] away" and cease to exist. Touched by Boswell's unease—his sense of despair at the idea of the historian erased, the philosopher lost—I wondered: what of Hume's hair? Boswell's attention to Hume's dress and his wig presages his deep distress over Hume's casual willingness to let the soul slip away with the body into nothingness. If neither Hume nor Philo would accept the premise that a hair could generate a man, might they have at least acknowledged that hair could prove or preserve a man's existence? Boswell was not unaccustomed to requesting locks of hair.[12] And even if Boswell didn't venture to acquire this part of Hume's bodily history, the practice of saving locks of hair was common enough: might someone else have preserved Hume's hair? Or could someone have stolen it, insistent that Hume did, in spite of himself, materially exist and would continue to do so in a future state he himself defiantly refused to believe in until even the bitter end?

I've looked everywhere I can think of to find a lock of Hume's hair.[13] Although I've turned up locks from his friends, associates, and contemporaries, no hair of Hume's seems to have been kept or to have survived; Hume, at least in this regard, appears to have enjoyed the courage of his convictions. His hair, however, lived on in its way. We might recognize Boswell's brief and arguably unnecessary mention of Hume's scratch wig as one form of preservation; but Hume's hair would also go on to make a surprise appearance in a nineteenth-century Gothic novel about encounters with the hair-raising dead: *A Strange Story* (1862) by Edward Bulwer-Lytton, who coined the phrase "It was a dark and stormy night." Bulwer-Lytton included a dialogue at the end of *A Strange Story* in which various characters debate the nature of narratives like the one they have just read; the preceding century's philosophical and scientific works guide their reading. Hume's work, in particular, haunts *A Strange Story*.

A Strange Story is a supernatural romance replete with a clairvoyant who grips a lock of hair in a spooky séance.[14] The serial novel is peppered, however, with the quintessential realisms proffered by philosophical science and scientific philosophies; its main character, Allen Fenwick, stages the "progress" of the larger history of "metaphysical science" as it had "moved through the brain of Europe" in the preceding century.[15] From a "blind faith in reason" to an expanding appreciation for the wonder of the "perplexities of nature," Fenwick—for whom Hume, especially, was an early "favourite"—finally comes to believe, despite his initial skepticism, in ghosts.[16] Fenwick will ultimately concede that the kind of reasoning exemplified by Hume strips the world not only of its miracles and spirit, but of its matter and body itself, producing—in the end—a philosophical paradox in which all the world is, in its way, the very same type of ineffable chimera that Hume disavowed.[17]

Taking Hume's philosophy to its limits, in other words, Fenwick confronts its contradictions, discovering something very similar in structure to my own claim about the way in which Philo's dismissal of hair is accidental proof of its mysterious capacity for generation. Fenwick finds that Hume's "metaphysical crotchets" produce a "miracle greater than any" he tried to dismiss. Despite "being then alive and in the act of writing," Hume "gets rid of himself altogether."[18] For Fenwick, musing on the philosopher three quarters of a century after Boswell visited Hume's deathbed, Hume remains perplexingly alluring and inescapable. And so—by the end of the novel—Fenwick will become one of those "dreamers of 'bright fancies'" that Hume condemned, preferring "to believe all the ghost stories upon record than believe that [he is] not even a ghost."[19] In other words, although Hume decides that his own selfhood, even in the lively act of writing, remains "nothing but a heap or collection of different perceptions or objects," Fenwick will experience Hume as something otherwise, having encountered and been profoundly influenced seemingly by the ghost of Hume in the course of reading his works. This kind of philosophical knot will lead Fenwick to feel that "still something [was] want[ing]" even in Hume's philosophy: "some key to the marvels" of the world that could explain, not least of all, his inexplicable connection with Hume's ghost.[20]

A Strange Story addresses Hume and his philosophy directly throughout, while the imagined dialogue between the cast of characters who have just read the novel and proceed to debate its merits and purpose offers a structural homage to Hume and his *Dialogues Concerning Natural Religion*. As Philo is to Hume in the *Dialogues*, so the delightfully named Professor ***** is to Bulwer-Lytton in *A Strange Story*'s metacommentary. Although intrigued by Hume, Professor ***** nevertheless finds, like Fenwick, that his skepticism fails to explain the miracles and "marvelous agencies" of works of art such as *A Strange Story*. For example, the characters in the dialogue that follows *A Strange Story* begin by considering the relationships between the straight facts preferred by empiricist scientists and historians, the skepticisms tendered by philosophers, and the alluring curls of the imagination coaxed by works like *A Strange Story*. Professor ***** dismisses the other speakers' interest in interrogating *A Strange Story* as a tale based on purported facts or histories as "idle inquir[ies]"; they'd heard local gossip about people and events that suggested some of the novel may have been drawn from these real-life folks sources.[21] "Whether or not the author of the story took any sketches of character from life, or any incident in his narrative from real occurrences," doesn't matter for Professor *****. What matters is that "the author and reader must both abide by the laws to which Art subjects works of imagination. The beings introduced in the work are real or not, according as they seem real in their own world, not according as they may or may not have lived in ours."[22]

As Professor ***** recognizes, *A Strange Story* makes occasional hints that not only might its fictions be based on historical facts but also its "supernatural effects" might also be the reasonable, predictable consequences of "natural causes"; Professor ***** finds, however, that the novel's invocations of philosophy and science are aslant. Rather than comb out the novel's mysteries, appeals to reason exemplified by the novel's references to philosophy and science plump body and volume into *A Strange Story*; the experience of the unbelievable and impossible is heightened by virtue of its juxtaposition to the believable and the possible. Such juxtapositioning not only makes the fiction more powerful, it also exposes the "imaginative side" of a scientific or philosophical mindset. Even the most strident skeptic, Professor ***** is convinced, begins with the desire to speak with the dead.[23]

A Strange Story's interest in stories of strangeness is part and parcel, therefore, of its interest in the reverse: the strangeness of stories. This makes the novel especially aesthetically accomplished, according to Professor *****. Depictions of "supernatural agency," he observes, constitute the "loftiest province of poetic art" and the "highest forms of imaginative narrative"; works written by the best authors, from Homer to Shakespeare, are notably preoccupied with this "supernatural agency."[24] Consequently, Professor *****'s commentary on *A Strange Story* conveniently declares Bulwer-Lytton's novel an aesthetic success, but he doesn't stop there. He insists that the novel's aesthetic form and interests are generative: "some of [the] most severe and searching philosophical treatises" are thinly veiled "attempts to discover the most hidden secrets of art, and the art of fiction more especially"; the "fancies of poets" are, therefore, more often than not the secret sources for the "physiologist" and the "metaphysician."[25]

Moreover, because these fictional worlds inspirationally precede philosophical and scientific investigation, the representations taken up by works such as *A Strange Story* are, in a way, more real because they antedate the ones that the dry and dusty works of philosophers and scientists would explain. Aesthetic productions contain multitudes, preserving the miraculous, the wonderful, and the dead. Therein live our collective histories and mysteries: as—perhaps even more—material than the stuff that scientists and philosophers pick apart. Professor ***** turns here to the minds of children for proof positive: their imaginations, overflowing with fictions, engender states of enchantment that are more real than the wonderful things supposedly explained by reason. Referring to the rather unexpectedly common nineteenth-century practice of encouraging children to attend séances and "meet the dead in a soiree," Professor ***** draws attention to the séance's rituals, especially the repeated "assur[ances]" offered to children around the table that "nothing therein concerned can frighten, much less harm them."[26] These assurances and their related appeals to reason can turn even a child's séance with the dead into a "comfortable and pleasant" experience.[27] If, however, left to the devices of their own imaginations tripping through the pages of a supernatural romance and primed to doubt the reliability of their quotidian experiences, children all "share in feats of necromancy" that would make even "David Hume's hair stand on end."[28]

These two related examples of Hume's hair-raising—Philo's glib quip about hair that generates a man and Professor *****'s conviction that a child's imagination could make even Hume's hair stand on its end—indicate the ubiquitous appearance hair cut in philosophical discourses that interrogated the distinctions and relationships between matter and spirit, the body and ideas; in turn, these discourses gesture to the surprising prominence of place hair enjoyed in the related early practices of science undertaken by members affiliated with the Royal Society. Cultural representations of hair reflected these questions and practices, so much so that to talk of hair as a cultural representation is to miss an important part of its story in the long eighteenth century: as a hybrid actant, the material qualities of which made it a site for both the representation and also the generation of culture. To borrow Philo's suggestion: hair is not simply the pure effect of culture's preexisting conditions but part of its causes. To borrow Bulwer-Lytton's argument: hair is, moreover, particularly pertinent to aesthetic productions, and this pertinence may—counterintuitively—be most recognizable in scientific and philosophical engagements with hair. In registering aesthetic force and efficacy, hair provokes an enchanting reassessment of the nature of materiality. Hair's singular nature insists that we reevaluate our perceptions of the boundaries between the physical and the ineffable, the organic and the inorganic, our selves and our environments; in so doing, it also invites a wholescale reevaluation of our ideas about matter and time, the order and ordering of things. Hair, in other words, stands a lot on its end.

As Frost explains in her *Biocultural Creatures*, the recent surge of renewed interest in materialism invites us to reassess what we mean by the term "human." Inspired by the work of Enlightenment thinkers, conventional accounts of the human understand it as a universal category defined by a moral imperative; humans, in contrast not only to animals but also to objects, are therefore presumed to be uniquely in possession of consciousness and will. Frost's *Biocultural Creatures* proposes that we undertake an "experimental rebuilding" in which we reconceive the "human" as a "biocultural creature."[29] For Frost, biocultural creatures are defined by porosity. The boundaries between the body and the world are always permeable, and "the 'inside' and the 'outside'" do not "mark different substances but different zones of activity."[30] A biocultural creature is suspended in a whirling microscopic universe of molecular processes characterized by their energetic encounters and exchanges. Frost attempts, in other words, to "figure humans in a way that does not exclude materiality, 'objectness,' animality, or embeddedness in habitats."[31] The body of the biocultural creature is neither purely conditioned by its relationship to culture nor determined precisely by its nature; instead, the relationships between form and matter, which operate at startling ranges of scale that challenge our perceptions of time and space as well as cause and effect, figure and are figured by the biocultural creature.

Eighteenth-century hairstories offer an unexpected prehistory of this way of thinking: they suggest that many in the Enlightenment, including even David Hume, entertained the concept of the biocultural creature. Philo's proposition—although it is set aside by the *Dialogues*—is, nevertheless, one of many examples of this prehistory. Importantly, eighteenth-century hairstories also illustrate aspects of biocultural creatureliness that have not yet received full consideration. For writers such as Frost, work done in the sciences tends to serve as an inspirational starting point; scientific insights into the microscopic, cellular, and subatomic accordingly provoke supposedly new ways of thinking about humanist subjects. Eighteenth-century hairstories, however, not only took similar cues from scientific findings, they also recognized that science had much to offer art and just as importantly, as Bulwer-Lytton knew, that art had much to offer science.

Several aspects of hairstories can be glimpsed in Cesare Ripa's *Iconologia: or Moral Emblems* (1709). Representative of emblem books, the *Iconologia* is a set of allegorical images that personify abstractions; a brief textual explication accompanies each illustration. The *Iconologia*'s personifications are biocultural creatures in their way: its humans are promiscuous assemblages of animals and objects in strange habitats, and the nonhuman elements carry the bulk of the allegorical weight. What adorns each figure's head is especially significant. Some hair is loose and some styled. Many figures have laurels and helmets of varying meanings, and birds of different stripes alight accordingly. Flames and serpents are not uncommon. Some figures, however, are decked out in headdresses that are notably surreal: an allegorical anticipation, perhaps, of the craze for hair accessories famously satirized in the second half of the century. For example, a "pair of compasses" sits atop Theory's head, and Horography wears an hourglass for a hat.

The figure of Curiosity is the only figure, however, whose natural hair twists into a shape that might be easily confused for an object, so unnatural does it at first appear even in a work where figures wear objects as hats and on a specific figure, no less, who wears a robe stitched with frogs and dismembered ears (Figure 9.1). As Ripa explains, the depiction of Curiosity is designed to illustrate "the *Itch* of knowing more."[32] The frogs'

CULTURAL REPRESENTATIONS 179

FIGURE 9.1: The figure of Curiosity from Isaac Fuller's English edition of Cesare Ripa's *Iconologia* (London, 1709). Wellcome Library, London.

"goggle-Eyes" represent Curiosity's "*Inquisitiveness*," making manifest her desire to look. The ears symbolize her readiness to hear gossip and "news." Both capture, in their way, her propensity for story. And her hair, of course, "stands up on end."[33] Curiosity's electric hair mediates between her body, grounded by a surreal re-centering of its capacity for the sensory experiences of sight and sound, and the ineffable and unknown that Curiosity seeks to locate somewhere between the landscape and the sky. Curiosity wears wings on her shoulders, too; they are never explained by Ripa, but they associate her with other noteworthy personifications. "Poetical Fury" and "Poetry" both have wings for hair, signifying their propensity for "quickness," while Invention, Mathematics, and—finally—Science all have winged hair that represents the "*Elevation*" of "Intellect," "high Contemplation," and the "Spirit to the Things that are to be learnt," respectively.

Eighteenth-century hairstories coil—like Curiosity's hair—the categories of the material and the immaterial together, and hair rises with a kind of electric agency of its own; rather than purify the productions of nature and culture, hairstories represented those productions as mutually, productively constitutive. This, then, is why hair should be understood as story as well as theory, for the term "story" captures hair's aesthetic affordances: how its physical properties—which included its shape, location, and duration—brimmed with "potential uses or actions."[34] The "latent" potentiality that inhered in hair's "materials" meant that it authored hairstories notable for their affinity to the stories Walter Benjamin describes as the creations of the storyteller. The storyteller brings distant pasts and geographical hinterlands into an uncanny intimacy in the present moment between the body of the storyteller and her interlocutor. In this moment, the "most extraordinary things, marvelous things, are related with the greatest accuracy, but the psychological connection of the events is not forced on the reader"; the storyteller's story becomes a piece of personal and collective memory.[35] Such was the case with the hairstories that proliferated around the work conducted by members of the Royal Society who, in their way, were the real-life versions of the abstractions Ripa personified: the winged creatures of the sciences driven by wild-haired Curiosity. Their hairstories offered unusually intimate depictions of biocultural creatures, and they were remarkable for their formal experimentations in representing objects, scale, time, and causality.

Much of the eighteenth-century science of hair that piqued the curiosity of members of the Royal Society took as its starting point Aristotle's "Problems," a work first published in the sixteenth century that, like the sexually charged *Aristotle's Masterpiece*, remains questionably attributable to Aristotle himself. Nevertheless, the "Problems" was a frequently referenced and reprinted work well into the 1700s. Presented as a series of questions and answers, the "Problems" attempts to explain the unexplainable body. In most editions of the work, the problem of hair appeared second only to the problem of why human faces look towards the sky, given that animals' faces are oriented in the opposite direction: towards the ground. The question of tilting countenance was answered by an appeal to the will and sagacity of a divine judgment that implores humans, specifically, to look up. The question of "Why is the head of beasts hairy" follows; despite the question's phrasing, the answer focuses extensively on the nature of human hair. In contrast to the first question, this question is answered by an inverse appeal to the generative capacity of the earthy body: an unwilled swelling of matter rather than an invitation of spirit produces hair. To put it less delicately, the "Problems" understands hair as excrement: the means by which the "brain [was] purged and evacuated of gross humours."[36] Where the eyes cry out the body's excess water, the ears unstop its melancholy, and the nose breathes out its choler, hair disposes of the body's and the brain's "phlegm."[37]

All manner of hair's varying properties could seemingly be explained, consequently, by the wet, humoral interior. For instance, human hair is supposedly longer than animal hair for two reasons: because the human brain is the "moistest brain of all" and the "humours of man are fat, and do not become dry easily."[38] The process of excreting the brain's excess moisture, therefore, was a matter of time measured, literally, in length and in the processes of thought made manifest. Women's hair is longer not only because they have no beard to help purge their phlegm but also because they "are moister than men."[39] Heat produces thick, curly hair; coldness grows hair that is soft and smooth. Women have less chest hair and no beards but more pubic hair than men because their bodies are colder, while their moisture settles near their wombs. Hair grays when the heat of the heart and the coolness of the brain no longer place a temperature cap on the stomach and the vapors of digestion are left to rise freely and putrefy out the head—a theory thought to be evidenced by the grayness of wolves, "devouring beasts," whose grisly gluttony means that they eat without chewing and, consequently, that the meat whitens their fur as it rots in their bellies.[40]

In the "Problems" and the physiological works that followed suit, hair was—we might say—biocultural, poised between the human and the animal, the exterior and interior of the body, the living and the dead. The "Problems" also indicates the ways in which hair was encountered, in the anthropologist Victor Turner's terminology, as a type of "liminal entity," eliding conventional distinctions between well-worn dichotomies. Drawing from Arnold van Gennep's study of the "liminal phase" that occurs in the midst of *rites de passage*, Turner argues that liminal entities exist "betwixt and between" time and space as "ambiguous" and "indeterminate" expressions that are not readily assignable to the category of either nature or culture. Turner indisputably identifies liminal entities in terms that prioritize the human (one synonym Turner uses for liminal entity is "threshold personae"), and he concludes that liminal entities ultimately express "communitas"— "what David Hume has called 'the sentiment for humanity'"—within structured societies.[41] Yet Turner is also careful to acknowledge the materiality that inheres in liminality, from the objects used in rituals to the insistence on the threshold personae as "clay or dust, mere matter."[42] Liminality itself, according to Turner, entails "periodical reclassifications of reality" and remains a crucial state for the "generation" of "myths, symbols, rituals, philosophical systems, and works of art."[43]

When Thomas Gibson, in his *The Anatomy of Humane Bodies Epitomized* (1703), explained hair, much of his explanation drew on the "Problems," but he also relied on a set of new metaphors that continued to explore hair's unusual propensity for shape-shifting liminality. Gibson continued to represent hair as excrement: hair is *"bred"* and *"nourished,"* he writes, by a "moist, fuliginous, crass, earthy, and somewhat viscid excrement."[44] Gibson here is largely in agreement with the "Problems" that the moist source of hair's growth is phlegm, but he includes a dissenting voice that suggests instead that hair draws on the body's blood supply; the feathers of birds after all, when plucked, have bloody ends.[45] Gibson, however, takes recourse in an additional analogy than that offered by the animal kingdom; the "white roots of the hairs" attract either phlegm or blood, "just as Plants receive nourishment out of the Earth by their Roots."[46]

Gibson returns again and again to plants in order to explain by recourse to analogy the nature of hair. For instance, the fact that hair continues to grow after death is an especially vexing phenomenon to elucidate. The "Problems" includes the following query: "Why doth the hair grow in them that are hanged?"[47] The answer: "Because their bodies are exposed to the sun which through its heat does dissolve all the moisture into a fume or vapour, of which the hair doth grow and increase."[48] Gibson, though, has a different explanation. The hair is like "Polypody"—a type of fern—that "grow[s] upon an old Tree, [and] which continue[s] to grow after the tree is dead as [it] did before, because [the polypody] [has] a proper life distinct from the form or *anima* of the Tree."[49] Here, Gibson's use of the phrase, "a proper life distinct from the form or *anima* of the Tree," illustrates his conviction that hair has its own kind of agency but one notably distinct from the kind of free will we associate with the category of the human or even the instinct we associate with animals. Hair, for Gibson, remains "no parts of the body" because it is bereft of *"Animal* life." Instead, hair is replete with a *"Vegetative* life" unique unto itself. How, then, to explain the purpose of hair? Gibson decides that it has "three *Uses:"* "Defence," to "Shew the temperature of the whole Body and Skin" (which explains variations in hair color and texture), and "for Beauty."[50]

In 1665, the ever-curious Robert Hooke plucked some of his own hairs and placed them under his new microscope. There, they loomed large beside the bristles of a hog, some strands of horse hair, the fur from an "Indian deer," and the "Mustacheos of a Cat."[51] Schema V, the illustration that Hooke created to represent his observations, offers another startling example of the ways in which hair's bioculturalness afforded states of liminality (Figure 9.2). Not only did hair's bioculturalness mean that it readily straddled

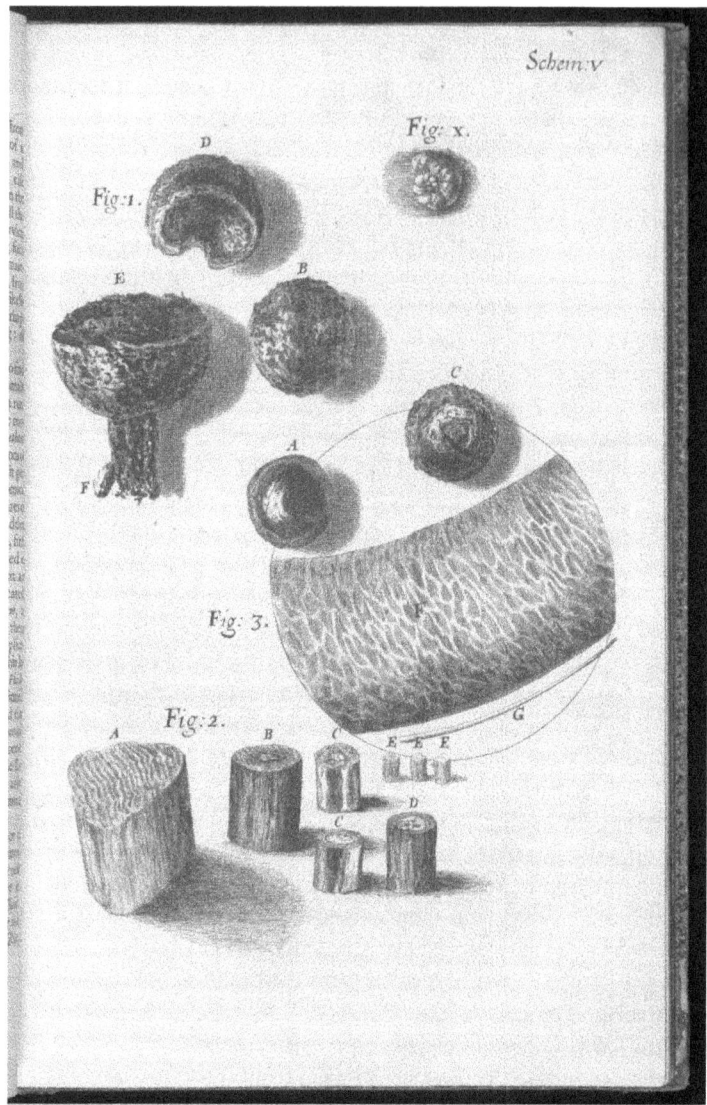

FIGURE 9.2: "Schema V" from Robert Hooke's *Micrographia* (1665). Wellcome Library, London.

distinctions between the categories of the animal and the human (and notably also between the public and the private, the wild and the tame, the domestic and the foreign), but it also suggested that what Gibson describes as a "vegetative life" was far more lively than we might otherwise assume. Hooke's "Schema V," which depicts the hairs, highlights the ways in which "vegetative life" was no mere state of stasis; rather, it entailed a degree of what Bulwer-Lytton would later characterize as "supernatural agency."

Hooke's illustration, though a characteristic representation of the Enlightenment's enthusiasm for science and empirical philosophy, also indicates that out of all of the "uses" of hair that Gibson identifies, its "use" "for beauty" was its most beguiling—

but not, perhaps, in the ways we might expect. Hooke's image shows that hair's beauty need not be encountered strictly as style defined and enacted within the category of the human or in the terms defined by human perceptions. The *Micrographia* represents hair as something more and other than an artful artifice designed by ideas, shaped with intent, and perceived with purpose. Hooke's findings imply that the "vegetative life" that inhered in hair's intricate and intimate substrates vested hair with the power to form assemblages based on shape and texture. In Hooke's *Micrographia*, the assemblages that result from the aesthetic qualities that inhered in hair's materiality create narratives that are remarkably imaginative, even fanciful, in their evocations of scale and time. Hooke's specimens of hair are simultaneously gigantic and microscopic, and they are also timeless and timely. As a result, hair "reclassifi[es] reality" by upending causal explanations that would insist that a rational similitude and strict chronology inhere in the relationships between causes and their effects.

Hooke's Schema V depicts the *Micrographia*'s Observation XXXII: "Of the Figure of Several Sorts of Hair, and of the texture of Skin." Observation XXXII sets out in particular to settle the question of hair strands' basic physical shape and texture, with particular attention to Hooke's own hair, which he finds to be more cylindrical than prismatic, transparent but "not very cleer," smoother rather than rough, more solid than porous, lacking in "pith" and "rind," and—at the end—split "like the end of a a stick" and "beaten till it be all flitter'd."[52] However, unlike other illustrations in the *Micrographia*, such as the iconic Schema XXXIV which features a pull-out image of the flea impossibly precise and gargantuan (see Introduction, Figure I.2), Schema V represents objects from not one but three "observational experiments." All of the hairs appear, therefore, alongside illustrations based on Observation VIII ("Of the Fiery Sparks struck from a Flint or Steel") and Observation XI ("Of Figures Observ'd in Small Sand"). Schema V is one of the few illustrations in the *Micrographia*, in other words, that represents findings from more than one observational experiment. The relationships among the hairs, fiery sparks, and sand represented in Schema V are also less immediately clear than in the other cases where a single plate records more than one observation.[53] In fact, Schema V appears to be the most inexplicable grouping in the *Micrographia*, pulling images from three noncontiguous observations that, at first glance, look fundamentally unrelated.

It seems unlikely, however, that Hooke included one illustration that lacked a logic the other thirty-seven illustrations apparently share. Fiery sparks, sand, and the hairs of both humans and animals have more in common for Hooke than just their microscopic interest. Schema V suggests that Hooke was aware of, even charmed by, hair's shapely mediations between the earthy and the ethereal: mediations that, moreover, indicated that hair enjoyed a vegetative life and supernatural agency that would make Hume's hair stand on end. Schema V features sixteen objects divided into the three observational experiments (Figure 9.2). Three rough, vaguely spherical shapes sit in the upper left quadrant, marked as "Fig: 1." A tiny shell-shaped coil of sand rests in the upper right-hand corner, marked as "Fig: x." In the right center of the image and encircled as if in the lens of the microscope, is "Fig: 3," the largest image of all, representing a thick strand of hair. A much smaller strand of hair glides below it, while two more circular shapes, like those in Fig: 1, hover above it, slipping outside of the lens's delicate frame. In the bottom left quadrant of the image is "Fig: 2," with eight strands of hair chopped and set up like miniature stone henges. Three of these henges are Hooke's own hairs, and they are the smallest figures on the plate. As he reports with clever phonetic indulgence: their roots are shaped like a parsnip.

In the three textual explanations that accompany the plate, Hooke consistently attends to the aesthetic qualities of these figures, describing their shapes and textures. Within the local context of the plate itself, the explanations provided for the shell-shaped coil of sand and the specimens of hair have the most in common. Both explanations, for example, spare a thought for beauty and for nature. Hooke explains how the various shapes of sand are like those found in stones, implicitly drawing our attention back to the monumental shapes the hair-henges assume, standing on their ends. In his description of the shell-shaped coil of sand, Hooke also notes that it offers a delightful "instance of the curiosity of Nature" that includes objects "by reason of their minuteness" that are "beyond the reach of our eyes."[54] Hooke immediately mentions here those "several sorts of Insects" that we cannot see, but that he promises to reveal in later Schemas. The louse that defiantly grips a strand of hair in Schema XXXV is implicitly, therefore, folded into Schema V. Hooke is also attuned to the microscopic life of plants like rosemary in his entry on sand, a theme to which he will also return in his observations on hair.

The description of the fiery sparks' detritus—the rough, round spots on the plate—does not, however, spare a thought for beauty or reminisce on the curious microscopic lives of plants and animals. Yet in Schema V the fiery sparks are visually closer to the hair than to the sand, and they are connected more explicitly to the hair by virtue of the outline of the lens that encompasses two bits of spark and two bits of hair. The sparks, in other words, offer a gloss on how Hooke perceived the nature of hair that is as significant as that suggested in the textual explanations of the sand. Hooke explains in Observation VIII, which is the first experiment depicted on the plate, that his investigation into flint and steel was inspired, specifically, by René Descartes. Hooke concludes that flint and steel spark because their friction generates heat, and a fire results when a hot piece of either flint or steel alights on proximate, combustible matter. Hooke tacitly questions Descartes's dualism, in other words, while he specifically rejects two previous theories of fire: the first that claimed it moved mysteriously through the ether to the sparky object, "like Vultures or Eagles to a putrifying Carcass,"[55] and the second that claimed fire was a discreet element that remained trapped inside physical bodies until it was released. Instead, fiery sparks originate in the flint and in the steel. Observations such as this one lead Hooke to a conclusion he asserts again and again throughout the *Micrographia*: that the world is, in fact, intricately designed in the way Cleanthes would assert. As Hooke puts it in his Observation XXXII on the several sorts of hair: the "*Schematism* or structure" is "altogether *mechanical*."[56]

This mechanical schematism, however, is far more lively than the term "mechanical" connotes. Schema V's hairstory arcs electrically around the plate and throughout the *Micrographia*. Its mechanical schamatism entails dynamic assemblages with "every Tribe of *Animals*, [and] *Vegetables*"—insects and plants, especially—that Hooke examined. The *Micrographia*'s hairstory also comingles with the less obviously organic and seemingly more inanimate category of objects Hooke classes as "*Minerals*." In other words, Schema V emphasizes hair's shape and texture and depicts hair as a porous "zone of activity," in Frost's phrasing, and as a liminal entity between that which appears to be living and that which appears to be dead. The positioning of the hair on the plate is also significant in this regard. The hair occupies the center of the plate, placed between the opposing vertical categories represented by the sparks that were launched with motion and force into the air and the sand that was discovered resting underfoot.

The whole image also challenges our sense of scale, as we might expect: the hairs vary widely in terms of their size, comprising the plate's largest as well as its smallest items.

The sparks and the sand seem impossibly large and minuscule by comparison. The image, however, also challenges our sense of the order of things. The hairs are the only objects situated both horizontally and vertically. The central image of hair curves upwards to the sand that coils inward, while it also sweeps leftwards—as if gesturing towards the linear filament that one sparky detritus possesses, which, in turn, points directly downwards to the first, ostentatious specimen in the line of hair henges. Such an ordering draws our attention back to the fact that the image has positioned hair both at its center and also at its base; from both locations, the hair seems simultaneously to mediate and to generate, respectively, the plate's fire and its grit.

From such an ordering, it is difficult to resist imagining the ways in which Schema V may also be in dialogue with Schema II, which depicts a full stop, a pin, and a razor's edge. The link between the hair and the razor is associative but intuitive, and Hooke describes how he poked and prodded the shell-shaped coil of sand with a pin. The sparks and the full stop notably bear a shapely affinity, and Hooke explains that he preserved the sparky detritus for microscopic examination by capturing it on paper. The full stop in particular invites a flight of textual fancy. The shell-shaped coil of sand, on close inspection, contains tiny letters embedded within the object itself that mark the progression of its spiral shape ever inward into invisibility; for each of the fiery sparks, in contrast, the letter hovers outside of the object. In the local context established by Schema V, the hair specimens alone feature letters in both locations: embedded in their surface and free floating in their periphery.

Such arrangements of texts and objects are common enough throughout the *Micrographia*, but in Schema V the arrangement speaks to hair's capacity for challenging our sense of temporality and causality. The hair is the only object that appears simultaneously commensurate with text and productive of text, and the illustration thus implicitly foregrounds hair's affinities with stories, narratives, and fictions. Hooke was not the only person potentially to grasp in hair a particular affinity between it and writing. In 1711, Joseph Addison described a legendary portrait of Charles I as one example, alongside George Herbert's famous object poems, of the delight the previous century instigated in "false wit."[57] The "famous Picture of King Charles the First," which represents Charles I as a martyr, has the "whole Book of Psalms written in Lines of the Face and the Hair of the Head" (Figure 9.3).[58] Addison tried to "peruse" "the Whiskers," but was forced to the side by the clamber of a crowd eager to read for themselves the martyrdom of Charles I written in and by his hair.[59] Addison admits that he has "since heard, that there is now an eminent Writing-Master in Town, who has transcribed all the *Old Testament* in a full-bottomed periwig."[60] "Locks" that contained "all the *Apocrypha*" were sure to follow, Addison chuckles.[61] Addison, we now know, was looking at a drawing in brown ink and metalpoint copied from a print; digital photography has since confirmed that some of the psalms in the portrait do indeed appear in Charles I's hair, although the whole image has yet fully to be read. Micrography, the minute writing that makes up the lineaments of the portrait, was an art largely lost to the age of print; therefore, Charles I's hair psalms testify, in their way, to hair's powers of preservation. And appropriately enough, the portrait inspired poetic rhapsody; Jeremiah Wells rhapsodized that the portrait inspired a "double reverence": a phrase he used to represent his celebration of its artistry as both a "picture and a book" and its representation of Charles I as a king and as a saint.[62] Wells maintains that to recognize the strange "lustre" represented and generated by the portrait's contrivances is not necessarily to succumb to "Superstition," but he, nevertheless, imagines how the hair as text and the text as hair—which circle

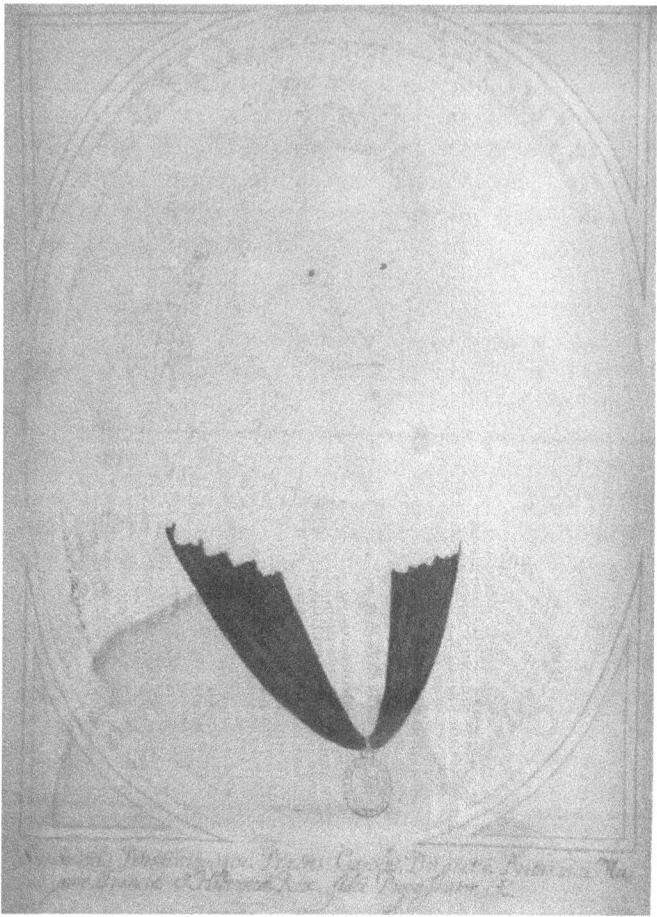

FIGURE 9.3: Portrait of Charles I in which his hair was thought to include copies of the psalms. Reproduced by permission of the President and Fellows of St John's College, Oxford.

and "spread" like a halo around Charles I's head—make the portrait seem miraculously capable of speaking in ways that defy the senses.[63]

Schema V's organization of hair and letters similarly exemplifies how difficult it can be to determine which comes first, the hair or the text. This kind of temporal confusion is mirrored by the plate itself. The fiery sparks rest unusually heavy on the page, despite the transient quickness of their effects. The shell-shaped coil of sand is rendered with exquisite delicacy, despite the fact that Hooke speculates it has been subject to the slow, deep time of petrification. The hairs float above, lie between, and stand below these temporal moments of immediacy and permanence, the enduring past and the fleeting present. The hairs at the bottom of the plate are like roots out of which the rest of the objects seem mysteriously to grow, while they are also the last, monumental objects the reader of the plate encounters were she to read the plate like prose on a page. All the while, the other specimens of hair persist at the plate's center, mediating betwixt and between the plate's other objects and their temporalities.

Hooke's depiction of hair, therefore, anticipates both Cleanthes's ravished admiration of a world impossibly vast in its intricacy and also Philo's claim that Cleanthes's argument—despite the agency it will settle on a deity—invests objects like hair with strange powers. Schema V, in other words, places hair in the categories of the micro as well as the mega and figures hair as both cause and effect, depicting it as a site for playful and productive analogical thinking about the mysteries of objects, time, and agency. That Hume had Hooke's work on hair specifically in mind may be likely given that even Samuel Johnson defined hair by its microscopic qualities and glossed his definition, in a moment of delightful if accidental cheekiness, with a quotation from John Locke.[64] Locke's words are, perhaps not coincidentally, drawn from his discussion of language in the *Essays* and exemplify Locke's conviction that the external appearances of things do not necessarily correlate with their "internal constitution."[65] This sense that the hairstories were curiously and compellingly out of order and outsized also explains some of the work of the antiquaries who were affiliated with the Royal Society. Although incorporated later than the Royal Society—largely due to suspicions over antiquaries' political motivations—the Society of Antiquaries shared with the Royal Society a penchant for collecting. Nehemia Grew's 1685 catalogue of the Royal Society's museum shows that Hooke, armed with his microscope, was not the Society's only member to be intrigued by specimens of hair culled from a range of bodies. Under the category "Humane Rarities," for example, the museum featured two donated specimens of "hair taken out of the Ovary of Woman."[66]

Observations on hair or hair-like features also feature in many of the entries describing other items in the society's collection, especially its insects, plants, and minerals—as we might expect from the descriptions contained in Hooke's *Micrographia*. The Society of Antiquaries capitalized on the acquiring impulse of the Royal Society, which filtered throughout the popular collections housed in public museums. Don Saltero's coffeehouse museum, for example, featured among its first rarities "balls of Hair taken out of the Maws of Oxen and Calves."[67] Later editions of the catalogue show that Saltero continued to grow his collection of hair objects; by 1795, visitors to the museum could also examine a "piece of crystal with hair in it," "lace made of human hair, very curious," a "curious lock of a China man's hair," and the "lock of hair off the Goa goat."[68] At Don Saltero's competitor site, Adam's, visitors could also see balls of hair found in a cow's maws,[69] take in sumptuous samples of long hair cut by the proprietor,[70] view the hair of a camel,[71] and marvel at the Jacobite Simon Fraser's physiognomic profile done with such detail, it was described as "to a Hair."[72]

The natural curiosities and items of curious workmanship in museums such as Don Saltero's and Adam's sat inside their glass cases and on their shelves alongside historical artifacts. Like members of the Royal Society, therefore, antiquaries also collected specimens of hair and paid careful attention to hairstyles that appeared in a variety of other artifacts they collected, such as historical portraits, medals, and coins. However, because members of the Society of Antiquaries were frequently suspected of harboring Jacobite and Catholic sensibilities throughout the eighteenth century, it is tempting to read their acquisitions of objects like hair as indicative of their sentimental nostalgia for the past and its reliquaries—a sentimentalism that would go on to shape the secular popularity of Victorian hairwork as an intimate *memento mori*. Hair relics did, in fact, attract the notice of antiquaries, even when they were no longer thought to exist—a Humean problem if there ever was one. The Jacobite and noncomformist antiquary Thomas Hearne, for instance, remarked that "some of the Lord's Hair" was known to have been preserved at the abbey, which had been in ruins since the sixteenth century, along with a thorn from Christ's crown, shards from his cross and tomb, and milk from the Virgin Mary.[73]

Relatedly, Charles I's hair also proved enduringly fascinating for antiquaries. As the portrait of Charles I that intrigued Addison at Oxford illustrates, Charles I's hair told an especially poignant hairstory; descriptions of his execution included as a touching testimony to his gentle character the anecdotal report that he asked the executioner, "Does my Hair trouble you?"[74] Concerned for the ease of the executioner's difficult task, Charles I reportedly gathered all of his hair into his cap, asking again—"Is my Hair well?"—before he "laid his Neck upon the Block."[75] Even Hume noted that Charles I had let his hair go in the midst of the civil wars; his beard and his locks were "allowed […] to grow, and to hang disheveled and neglected," and Charles memorialized his "grey and discrowned head" in verse.[76] A wide variety of relics from Charles I and the execution, many of questionable authenticity, also populated collections of antiquities throughout England. These included the cap as well as locks of Charles I's hair, snatched after the execution. Determining the authenticity of these locks and where they ended up is difficult; the histories of a single strand's hairstory tend to oscillate between the intricate and the invisible, the factual and the fictional. When members of the Society of Antiquaries discovered and exhumed Charles I's grave in 1813, they themselves seemed aware of this feature of hairstories; they confirmed that Charles I's hair had been ravaged, although they left the question as to whether the ravaging was the work of the executioner or the mob unanswered. The antiquaries at the exhumation themselves snipped some locks from the corpse's beard and right temple, although they never did explain why.[77]

Eighteenth-century antiquaries' interest in hair as relic does not, however, quite tell the whole story of hair's history. Neither nostalgic partisanship nor naïve superstition can fully explain the locks of hair that intrigued antiquaries; when given the opportunity, antiquaries, for example, snipped a lock from the head of Edward IV when they exhumed the body in 1774 (Figure 9.4), alongside a vial of the liquid that had pooled at the bottom

FIGURE 9.4: A lock of Edward IV's hair, recovered by members of the Society of Antiquaries in 1774. By kind permission of the Society of Antiquaries of London.

of the tomb; the latter was subsequently subjected to a variety of scientific experiments that flirted with the scandalously sacrilegious.[78] In 1785, Lady Moira sent the society samples of plaited hair she had recovered from a bog body.[79] And descriptions of archeological discoveries of Roman urns dug up throughout England frequently remarked on the grave goods they contained, which often included locks of hair.[80]

The public and private collections in which hair featured suggest that it readily assembled with disparate objects in a manner similar to that captured by Hooke's *Micrographia*, testifying to a variety of competing ideologies and practices. As a liminal entity, the material properties of which afforded assemblages with a wide range of objects both organic and inorganic, hair exposed history itself as something biocultural and creaturely. Antiquaries' interest in hair also indicates how its temporal play with the relationships between the past and the present, the dead and the living, proved as wondrous and compelling as the assemblages it afforded between the categories of the artificial and the natural, the big and the small, the singular and the many (Figure 9.5). For antiquaries, the past continued to live on in the present through its objects—indeed, it lived on as an effect of artifacts' causal materiality—and few objects were or are as capable of exemplifying this secular, supernatural haunting than hair which continues to grow even after we die.

As Benjamin explains in his description of the type of story told by the storyteller: "story […] does not expend itself. It preserves and concentrates its energy and is capable of releasing it even after a long time."[81] Thus, Benjamin finds that the storyteller "borrow[s] […] authority from death," and death is "the sanction for everything that the storyteller can tell."[82] The story, however, is hardly morbid. Rather, death operates simultaneously as origin and telos, and the story itself capitalizes on a "revolving procession of creatures" that makes it more akin to natural history than to chronicle or fiction. Storytellers craft narratives that are epic and poetic, reliant simultaneously on the memories of specific

FIGURE 9.5: Example of Victorian hairwork. Wellcome Library, London.

events and the cyclical, ritualized revolutions of nature. Like hair, stories are betwixt and between, "keep[ing] faith" with both the "history of the world" and "naïve poetry."[83] Stories "[reach] down into the abyss of the inanimate by many gradations," and in the "depths of inanimate nature" stories transform the "lowest stratum of created things" into the "highest," and the most "mystical."[84] These features of the stories told by storytellers mean that they are secular but remain inextricably tied to the sacred. With real difficulty, therefore, do we try and determine whether the "web" in which the storyteller's stories exist is "the golden fabric of a religious view of the course of things, or the multicolored fabric of a worldly view" of things themselves.[85] Such is the case with hairstories, and we might now respond to Philo's quip, "From observing the growth of a hair, can we learn any thing concerning the generation of a man," with Pope's declaration in *The Rape of the Lock*: "Mighty Contests" do, indeed, "rise" from seemingly "trivial Things."[86]

NOTES

Introduction

1. Alexander Pope, *The Twickenham Edition of the Poems of Alexander Pope*, Volume II, *The Rape of the Lock and Other Poems*, ed. Geoffrey Tillotson, 2nd ed. rev. (London: Methuen, 1954), 144.
2. For recent perspectives, see Sarah Cheang and Geraldine Biddle-Perry, *Hair: Styling, Culture, and Fashion* (Oxford: Berg, 2008); for the eighteenth-century context, see Angela Rosenthal, ed., *Hair*, a special issue of *Eighteenth-Century Studies* 38, no. 1 (2004), *passim*. For an authoritative account of the remarkable importance of hair in the realm of politics by the close of the eighteenth century, see John Barrell, "Hair Powder," in *The Spirit of Despotism: Invasions of Privacy in the 1790s* (Oxford: Oxford University Press, 2006), chap. 4.
3. James Stewart, *Plocacosmos, or, The Whole Art of Hair Dressing* (London: Printed for the Author, 1782), 175.

Chapter 1

1. Charles Taylor, *Sources of the Self: The Making of Modern Identity* (Cambridge, MA: Harvard University Press, 1989), 160–1.
2. Matthew Crawford, *The World beyond Your Head: On Becoming an Individual in an Age of Distraction* (New York: Farrar, Strauss, and Giroux, 2015). Crawford argues that, in late capitalism, consumer choice masquerades *as* freedom and displaces other experiences of agency. See also Frederic Jameson, *Postmodernism: or, the Cultural Logic of Late Capitalism* (Durham, NC: Duke University Press, 1991), 15.
3. Joseph Roach, "It," *Theatre Journal* 56, no.4 (2004): 555.
4. Blair Worden, *The English Civil Wars, 1640–1660* (London: Penguin, 2009), 2.
5. Janet Arnold, *Perukes and Periwigs* (London: Her Majesty's Stationery Office [National Portrait Gallery], 1970), 28.
6. Thomas Hall, *Comarum Akosmia. The Loathsomnesse of Long Haire …* (London: printed by J.G. for Nathanael Webb and William Grantham, 1654), 13.
7. Stephen Dobranski, "Clustering and Curling Locks: The Matter of Hair in *Paradise Lost*," *PMLA* 125, no. 2 (March 2010): 340.
8. John Milton, *Paradise Lost* (Oxford: Oxford World's Classics, 2008), 4:300–11.
9. John Rogers, "Transported Touch: The Fruit of Marriage in *Paradise Lost*," in *Milton and Gender*, ed. Catherine Gimelli Martin (Cambridge: Cambridge University Press, 2004), 128.
10. Catherine Belsey, *John Milton: Language, Gender, Power* (Oxford: Blackwell, 1988), 6.
11. *The Diary of Samuel Pepys*, introduction and notes by G. Gregory Smith (The Globe Edition, London: MacMillan, 1905), 193. The entry date is May 9, 1663.

12. Jenny Uglow, *A Gambling Man: Charles II's Restoration Game* (New York: Farrar, Strauss, and Giroux, 2009), 452.
13. George Whitefield, *A Short Account of God's Dealings with the Reverend Mr. George Whitefield* (London: W. Strahan, 1740), 39.
14. Christopher Anstey, *The New Bath Guide: Or, Memoirs of the B-r-d family. In a Series of Poetical Epistles* (London: J. Dodsley, 1767), 128.
15. John Cleland, *Memoirs of a Woman of Pleasure*, ed. Peter Sabor (Oxford: Oxford University Press, 1985), 182.
16. Quoted in Phyllis Mack, *Heart Religion in the British Enlightenment: Gender and Emotion in Early Methodism* (Cambridge: Cambridge University Press, 2008), 134 (emphasis in the original).
17. John Wesley, "An Account of his Residence at Oxford," reprinted in *The Life and Journal of the Rev. John Wesley, A.M.*, vol. 1, ed. Joseph Benson (New York: Harper, 1827), 81.
18. Henry Abelove, *The Evangelist of Desire: John Wesley and the Methodists* (Stanford, CA: Stanford University Press, 1990), 8.
19. John Nelson, *An Extract from John Nelson's Journal* (London, 1782), 13.
20. Ibid., 14.
21. Horace Walpole, *The Yale Edition of the Correspondence of Horace Walpole*, ed. W.S. Lewis (New Haven, CT: Yale University Press, 1937–1983), 35:119.
22. Joseph Roach, *It* (Ann Arbor: University of Michigan Press, 2007), 8.
23. Robert Southey, *The Life of Wesley, and the Rise and Progress of Methodism* (London: Longman, Brown, Green, and Longmans, 1846), 2:297.
24. Quoted in Abelove, *The Evangelist of Desire*, 8. See Nehemiah Curnock, ed., *The Journal of the Rev. John Wesley, A.M.* (London: R. Culy, 1909–1916), 5:189 and 6:413.
25. John Wesley, *Minutes of Several Conversations between the Rev. John Wesley, A.M. and the Preachers in Connection with Him* (London: G. Whitfield, 1779 [1797]), 35.
26. John Wesley, *The Journal of the Rev. John Wesley* (London: J. Dent, 1906), 2:318. The entry is dated January 27, 1756.
27. [John Wesley], *The Arminian Magazine* 19 (April 1796): 205.
28. Daniel O'Quinn, "Bread: The Eruption and Interruption of Politics in Elizabeth Inchbald's *Every One Has His Fault*," *European Romantic Review* 18, no. 2 (2007): 153.
29. *The Arminian Magazine* 19 (April 1796): 203.
30. John Cennick, *An Account of a Late Riot at Exeter* (London: J. Harte, 1745), 10.
31. John Wesley, *The Journal of the Rev. John Wesley, AM*, ed. Nehemiah Curnock (London: R. Culy, 1909–1916), 3:371.
32. Ibid., 1:440.
33. Ibid., 1:442.
34. Abelove, *The Evangelist of Desire*, 15. Abelove's primary source for these quotations is *Diary of the Rev'd William Jones, 1777–1821*, ed. O.F. Christie (London, 1929), 75–6.
35. "The Methodist" (London: Printed for the Author [Evan Lloyd?], 1766), n.p.
36. George Alexander Stevens, *The Celebrated Lecture on Heads* (London: Bond, 1765), 20.
37. Richard Graves, *The Spiritual Quixote, or, the Summer's Ramble of Mr. Geoffry Wildgoose*, ed. Clarence Tracy (London: Oxford, 1967), 41.
38. Ibid., 40.
39. Ibid., 41.
40. Ibid., 70.
41. Ibid., 100, 102.
42. Ibid., 103.

Chapter 2

1. Mark Rose, *Authors and Owners: The Invention of Copyright* (Cambridge, MA: Harvard University Press, 1995); Jody Greene, *The Trouble with Ownership: Literary Property and Authorial Liability in England, 1660–1730* (Philadelphia: University of Pennsylvania Press, 2005); and Helen Deutsch, *Resemblance and Disgrace: Alexander Pope and the Deformation of Culture* (Cambridge, MA: Harvard University Press, 1996) have all written about this topic in fascinating and illuminating ways.
2. Margaret K. Powell and Joseph R. Roach's article "Big Hair," *Eighteenth-Century Studies* 38, no. 1 (2004): 79–99, goes into more detail about the connections between the wig as health precaution and the wig as cultural symbol.
3. James Boswell, *Life of Johnson*, rev. ed., ed. R.W. Chapman (Oxford: Oxford University Press, 1985), 280.
4. Lynn Festa, "Personal Effects: Wigs and Possessive Individualism in the Long Eighteenth Century," *Eighteenth-Century Life* 29, no. 2 (2005): 83. See also Marcia Pointon, *Hanging the Head: Portraiture and Social Formation in Eighteenth-Century England* (New Haven, CT: Yale University Press, 1993).
5. The most influential of these critiques include Nancy Fraser, "Rethinking the Public Sphere: A Contribution to the Critique of Actually Existing Democracy," *Social Text* 25–26 (1990): 56–80, and Joan Landes, *Women and the Public Sphere in the Age of the French Revolution* (Ithaca, NY: Cornell University Press, 1988). See also Joan Landes, ed., *Feminism, the Public, and the Private* (New York: Oxford University Press, 1998); Michael McKeon, *The Secret History of Domesticity: Public, Private, and the Division of Knowledge* (Baltimore, MD: Johns Hopkins University Press, 2006); Michael Warner, *Publics and Counterpublics* (Brooklyn, NY: Zone Books, 2002); *Habermas and the Public Sphere*, ed. Craig Calhoun (Cambridge, MA: MIT Press, 1993); Angela Vanhaelen and Joseph P. Ward, eds., *Making Space Public in Early Modern Europe: Performance, Geography, Privacy* (New York: Routledge, 2013); and Bronwen Wilson and Paul Yachnin, eds., *Making Publics in Early Modern Europe: People, Things, Forms of Knowledge* (New York: Routledge, 2010).
6. See Amy Louise Erickson, *Women and Property in Early Modern England* (London: Routledge, 1993); and Susan Staves, *Married Women's Separate Property in England, 1660–1833* (Cambridge, MA: Harvard University Press, 1990).
7. For a more detailed history of English laws on rape than I can offer in this chapter, see Nazife Bashar, "Rape in England between 1550 and 1700," in *The Sexual Dynamics of History: Men's Power, Women's Resistance*, ed. London Feminist History Group (London: Pluto, 1983); and Julia Rudolph, "Rape and Resistance: Women and Consent in Seventeenth-Century English Legal and Political Thought," *Journal of British Studies* 39, no. 2 (April 2000): 157–84.
8. Tim Stretton, *Women Waging Law in Elizabethan England* (Cambridge: Cambridge University Press, 2005). See also Susan Dwyer Amussen, *An Ordered Society: Gender and Class in Early Modern England* (New York: Columbia University Press, 1993) and Laura Gowing, *Domestic Dangers: Women, Words, and Sex in Early Modern London* (Oxford: Clarendon, 1996).
9. Sir Matthew Hale, *Historia Placitorum Coronae. The History of the Pleas of the Crown. By Sir Matthew Hale … Published from the Original Manuscripts by Sollom Emlyn. A New ed.: Carefully rev. and cor.; with Additional Notes and References to Modern Cases Concerning the Pleas of the Crown. Together with an Abridgement of the Statutes Concerning Felonies Which Have Been Enacted since the First Publication of this Work. By George Wilson* (London: T. Payne, 1778), 1:633.

10. See Laura J. Rosenthal, *Playwrights and Plagiarists in Early Modern Drama: Gender, Authorship, Literature, Property* (Ithaca, NY: Cornell University Press, 1996); and Misty Anderson, *Female Playwrights and Eighteenth-Century Comedy: Negotiating Marriage on the London Stage* (New York: Palgrave, 2002).
11. The links between eighteenth-century actresses and prostitutes have been explored extensively; see, in particular, Kristina Straub, *Sexual Suspects: Eighteenth-Century Players and Sexual Ideology* (Princeton, NJ: Princeton University Press, 1992); Jacqueline Pearson, *The Prostituted Muse: Images of Women and Women Dramatists, 1642–1737* (New York: St. Martin's, 1998); and Gilli Bush-Bailey, *Treading the Bawds: Actresses and Playwrights on the Late Stuart Stage* (Manchester: Manchester University Press, 2006).
12. Felicity Nussbaum, *Rival Queens: Actresses, Performance, and the Eighteenth-Century British Theater* (Philadelphia: University of Pennsylvania Press, 2010). See also Deborah C. Payne, "Reified Object or Emergent Professional? Retheorizing the Restoration Actress," in *Cultural Readings of Restoration and Eighteenth-Century English Theater*, ed. J. Douglas Canfield and Deborah C. Payne (Athens: University of Georgia Press, 1995), 13–38.
13. I have written about the wigs of both Charke and Bellamy at some length (and in a different context) in *Spectacular Disappearances: Celebrity and Privacy, 1696-1801* (Univ. of Michigan Press, 2016).
14. Colley Cibber, *An Apology for the Life of Colley Cibber: With an Historical View of the Stage During His Own Time*, ed. B.R.S. Fone (Ann Arbor: University of Michigan Press, 1968), 201–2.
15. *The Laureat; or, the Right Side of Colley Cibber, Esq.* (London: J. Roberts, 1740), 7, 15.
16. Thomas A. King, *The Gendering of Men, 1600–1750* (Madison: University of Wisconsin Press, 2004), 1:250–3. See also Straub's discussion of Cibber in chaps. 2, 3, and 4 of *Sexual Suspects*. Elaine McGirr's *Partial Histories: A Reappraisal of Colley Cibber* (London: Palgrave Macmillan, 2016) challenges many of these interpretations of Cibber's character.
17. Charlotte Charke, *A Narrative of the Life of Mrs. Charlotte Charke* (London: Printed for W. Reeve, A. Dodd, and E. Cook, 1755), 18.
18. Ibid., 18–19.
19. John Nichols, "Some Account of the Life of Mrs. Charlotte Charke, youngest daughter of Colley Cibber, Esq.," *The Gentleman's Magazine and Historical Review* 25 (October 1755): 456. https://babel.hathitrust.org/cgi/pt?id=hvd.hw2932;view=1up;seq=498 (accessed September 5, 2016).
20. Terry Castle, ed., The *Literature of Lesbianism: A Historical Anthology from Ariosto to Stonewall* (New York: Columbia University Press, 2003).
21. For readings of Charke as a pioneer of feminist autobiography, see Cheryl Wanko's *Roles of Authority: Thespian Biography and Celebrity in Eighteenth-Century Britain* (Lubbock: Texas Tech University Press, 2003), esp. 71–89; Straub's *Sexual Suspects*, esp. 138–42; and Patricia Meyer Spacks's *Imagining a Self: Autobiography and Novel in Eighteenth-Century England* (Cambridge, MA: Harvard University Press, 1976), esp. 57–91. Erin Mackie ("Desperate Measures: The Narratives of the Life of Mrs. Charlotte Charke," *ELH* 58 [1991]: 841–65) and Sidonie Smith (*A Poetics of Women's Autobiography: Marginality and the Fictions of Self-Representation* [Bloomington: Indiana University Press, 1987]) read Charke's cross-dressing as an attempt to win her estranged father's affections by becoming the son he wanted. The debate about whether Charke's gender performances are expressions of her psychology seems to have come full circle, with her earliest twentieth-century critics (Sally Minter Strange, "Charlotte Charke: Transvestite or Conjuror?" *Restoration and Eighteenth-Century Theatre Research* 15, no. 2 [1976]: 54–9; Charles D. Peavy, "The Chimerical Career of Charlotte Charke," *Restoration and Eighteenth-Century Theatre Research* 8, no. 1 [1969]: 1–12; and

Fidelis Morgan, *The Well-Known Troublemaker: A Life of Charlotte Charke* [London: Faber and Faber, 1980]) arguing that her transvestitism is a ruse; her critics of the 1980s and 1990s (Felicity Nussbaum, *The Autobiographical Subject: Gender and Ideology in Eighteenth-Century England* [Baltimore: Johns Hopkins University Press, 1989]; and Robert Folkenflik, "Gender, Genre, and Theatricality in the Autobiography of Charlotte Charke," in *Representations of the Self from the Renaissance to Romanticism*, ed. Patrick Coleman, Jayne Lewis, and Jill Kowalik [Cambridge: Cambridge University Press, 2000], 97–116) arguing that it is a queer expression; and her most recent critics (Wanko and Straub, as well as Danielle Gissinger in "'The Oddity of My Appearance Soon Assembled a Croud': The Performative Bodies of Charlotte Charke and Cindy Sherman," in *The Public's Open to Us All: Essays on Women and Performance in Eighteenth-Century England*, ed. Laura Engel [Newcastle: Cambridge Scholars, 2009], 264–7) arguing that it is a performance designed to expose all gender as performative.

22. George Anne Bellamy, *An Apology for the Life of George Anne Bellamy*, 4th ed. (London: J. Bell, 1786), 5:42–3.
23. Ibid., 5:43–4.
24. Ibid., 5:44.
25. *Oxford English Dictionary Online* (2016), s.v. "Merkin."
26. Alexander Smith, *A Compleat History of the Lives and Robberies of the Most Notorious Highway-Men, Foot-Pads, House-Breakers, Shop-Lifts, and Cheats, Of both Sexes*, 5th ed. (London: Printed for Sam Briscoe, 1719), 2:5–6. Eighteenth-Century Collections Online (accessed September 5, 2016).
27. Ibid., 6–7.
28. Although Pope had published an initial, two-canto version of the poem in 1712, the one most often cited is the five-canto revised edition, which appeared in 1714.
29. Alexander Pope, *The Rape of the Lock* (1714), in *The Poems of Alexander Pope*, ed. John Butt (New Haven, CT: Yale University Press, 1974), V.103–4.
30. One of the best known examples is Laura Brown, *Alexander Pope* (Oxford: Basil Blackwell, 1985). See also Alex Eric Hernandez's reading of the Bible as a consumer item in "Commodity and Religion in Pope's *The Rape of the Lock*," *SEL Studies in English Literature, 1500–1900* 48, no. 3 (2008): 569–84; as well as Stewart Crehan's examination of the poem in terms of commodity fetishism in "*The Rape of the Lock* and the Economy of 'Trivial Things,'" *Eighteenth-Century Studies* 31, no. 1 (1997): 45–68. Richard Kroll, relatedly, links "the body politic and the body natural" in his essay, "Pope and Drugs: The Pharmacology of *The Rape of the Lock*," *ELH* 67, no. 1 (2000): 99.
31. Pope, *The Rape of the Lock* (1714), II.90, II.97, I.127, I.138.
32. Ibid., IV.176.
33. Ibid., III.174.
34. Ibid., V.127–8.
35. Ibid., V.141–50 (emphasis in the original).
36. Perhaps the most influential discussions of Belinda's objecthood in *The Rape of the Lock* are Laura Brown, *The Ends of Empire: Women and Ideology in Early Eighteenth-Century English Literature* (Ithaca, NY: Cornell University Press, 1993); Cleanth Brooks, *The Well-Wrought Urn: Studies in the Structure of Poetry* (San Diego, CA: Harcourt, Brace, and Company, 1975); Felicity Nussbaum, *The Brink of All We Hate: English Satires on Women, 1660–1750* (Bowling Green: University Press of Kentucky, 1984). See also Tita Chico, "The Arts of Beauty: Women's Cosmetics and Pope's Ekphrasis," *Eighteenth-Century Life* 26, no. 1 (2002): 1–23; Ellen Pollak, "Rereading *The Rape of the Lock*: Pope and the Paradox of Female Power," *Studies in Eighteenth-Century Culture* 10 (1981): 429–44; and Eugenia Zuroski Jenkins, "'Nature to Advantage

Drest': Chinoiserie, Aesthetic Form, and the Poetry of Subjectivity in Pope and Swift," *Eighteenth-Century Studies* 43, no. 1 (2009): 75–94.

Chapter 3

1. Richard Corson, *Fashions in Hair: The First Five Thousand Years* (London: Peter Owen, 1995), 261–396.
2. Margaret K. Powell and Joseph Roach, "Big Hair," *Eighteenth-Century Studies* 38, no. 1 (2004): 83.
3. David Ritchie, *Treatise on the Hair* (London: Printed for the Author, 1770), 91.
4. An English Periwig-Maker, *A Dissertation upon Head Dress* (London: Printed for J. Williams, 1767), 3.
5. Norbert Elias, *The History of Manners*, trans. Edmund Jephcott (New York: Pantheon Books, 1978).
6. Richard Graves, *The Spiritual Quixote: Or, the Summer's Ramble of Mr. Geoffry Wildgoose* (London: Printed for J. Dodsley, 1773), 1:187.
7. Walter Benjamin, *The Arcades Project*, trans. Howard Eiland (Cambridge: Belknap Press, 2002), 9.
8. Louisa Cross, "Fashionable Hair in the Eighteenth Century: Theatricality and Display," in *Hair: Styling, Culture and Fashion*, ed. Geraldine Biddle-Perry and Sarah Cheang (Oxford: Berg, 2008), 15.
9. Timothy Campbell, *Historical Style: Fashion and the New Mode of History, 1740–1830* (Philadelphia: University of Pennsylvania Press, 2016).
10. Mandeville, *Fable of the Bees: Or, Private Vices, Publick Benefits* (Indianapolis, IN: Liberty Fund, 1988), 1:25.
11. Haulman, *The Politics of Fashion in Eighteenth-Century America* (Chapel Hill: University of North Carolina Press, 2011), 4.
12. See Aileen Ribeiro, *Dress and Morality* (Oxford: Berg, 2003), 85–6.
13. John Bulwer, *Anthropometamorphosis, Man Transform'd: or, the Artificiall Changling* (London: William Hunt, 1653), 62 (emphasis in the original).
14. Corson, *Fashions in Hair*, 215.
15. Hall, *Comarum Akosmia: The Loathsomnesse of Long Haire* (London: J.G. for Nathanael Webb and William Grantham, 1654), 15, 15–16, 16.
16. *The Theological Works of the Reverend Charles Leslie* (Oxford: Oxford University Press, 1832), 5:466.
17. Thomas Wall, *Spiritual Armour to Defend the Head from the Superfluity of Naughtiness* (London: Printed for the Author, 1688), 39.
18. Haulman, *The Politics of Fashion in Eighteenth-Century America*, 59.
19. Corson, *Fashions in Hair*, 267.
20. Kalm, *Kalm's Account of his Visit to England on His Way to America in 1748*, trans. Joseph Lucas (London: Macmillan, 1892), 52 (emphasis in the original).
21. Marcia Pointon, *Hanging the Head: Portraiture and Social Formation in Eighteenth-Century England* (New Haven, CT: Yale University Press, 1993), 124–5.
22. Ibid., 112.
23. John Woodforde, *The Strange Story of False Hair* (London: Routledge, 1971), 16; Corson, *Fashions in Hair*, 223.
24. *Coma Berenices; or, the Hairy Comet* (London: Printed for Jonathan Robinson and John Hancock, 1676), 4.

25. Liza Picard, *Dr. Johnson's London* (London: Weidenfeld and Nicolson; New York: St. Martin's Press, 2000), 296. The need for wigs led to a thriving trade in human hair, which, in 1782 England, cost from 5s to £5 per ounce, and in mid-century France, from four francs to fifty écus per pound, depending on its quality. James Stewart, *Plocacosmos, or, The Whole Art of Hair Dressing* (London: Printed for the Author, 1782), 184; *Encyclopédie, ou dictionnaire raisonné des sciences, des arts et des métiers, etc.*, ed. Denis Diderot and Jean le Rond d'Alembert (Chicago: University of Chicago and ARTFL Encyclopédie Project, Spring 2016), s.v. "cheveux"; 3: 319.
26. Pointon, *Hanging the Head*, 128.
27. George Colman, "Prologue," in David Garrick, *Bon Ton; Or, High Life above Stairs* (Dublin: H. Camberlaine, 1785) (emphasis in the original).
28. Corson, *Fashions in Hair*, 261.
29. George Alexander Stevens, *The Celebrated Lecture on Heads* (London: Bond, 1765), 2.
30. Jacques-Antoine Dulaure, *Pogonologia, or a Philosophical and Historical Essay on Beards*, trans. Anon. (Exeter: R. Thorn, 1786), 9.
31. Goldsmith, *The Citizen of the World* (Dublin: Printed for J. Williams, 1769), 1:14.
32. R. Campbell, *The London Tradesman* (London: T. Gardner, 1747), 191.
33. Elizabeth Wilson, *Adorned in Dreams: Fashion and Modernity*, rev. ed. (New Brunswick, NJ: Rutgers University Press, 2003), 6.
34. "Miscellaneous Articles from the Papers. Monday 11," *The Gentleman's Magazine and Historical Chronicle* 35 (1765): 95.
35. Letter to Unwin, February 6, 1781, Cowper, *Letters and Prose Writings of William Cowper*: vol. 1, *1750–1781*, ed. James King and Charles Ryskamp (Oxford: Clarendon, 1979), 442.
36. J.C. Flügel, *The Psychology of Clothes* (London: Hogarth Press, 1930), 113.
37. "On the Education of the Fair-Sex. Essay X. Argument. Thoughts of a Persian Philosopher upon Fashions," *The Lady's Magazine* 4 (1773): 249–50.
38. John Barrell, *The Spirit of Despotism* (Oxford: Oxford University Press, 2006), 184.
39. Fawconer, *Essay on Modern Luxury* (London: Printed for James Fletcher and J. Robson, 1765), 18.
40. Corson, *Fashion in Hair*, 302.
41. Ritchie, *Treatise on the Hair*, 41.
42. Christopher Oldstone-Moore, *Of Beards and Men: The Revealing History of Facial Hair* (Chicago: University of Chicago Press, 2015), 134.
43. Will Fisher, "The Renaissance Beard: Masculinity in Early Modern England," *Renaissance Quarterly* 54, no. 1 (2001): 173–5.
44. Alun Withey, *Technology, Self-Fashioning and Politeness in Eighteenth-Century Britain: Refined Bodies* (Basingstoke: Palgrave Macmillan, 2016), vii–viii, 41–64.
45. On beardlessness see Roxann Wheeler, *The Complexion of Race: Categories of Difference in Eighteenth-Century British Culture* (Philadelphia: University of Pennsylvania Press, 2000), 69, 73, 79, 96–7.
46. Dulaure, *Pogonologia*, v.
47. *The Macaroni and Theatrical Magazine, or Monthly Register* (October 1772): 1.
48. "Character of a Macaroni," *The Town and Country Magazine* (1772): 243, quoted in Peter McNeil, "'That Doubtful Gender': Macaroni Dress and Male Sexuality," *Fashion Theory* 3, no. 4 (1999): 432.
49. Amelia Rauser, "Hair, Authenticity, and the Self-Made Macaroni," *Eighteenth-Century Studies* 38, no. 1 (2004): 104.

50. "The Macaroni; A New Song," *Macaroni and Theatrical Magazine* (October 1772): n.p.; also quoted in Rauser, "Hair, Authenticity," 106.
51. Ellis Pratt, *The Art of Dressing the Hair* (Bath: R. Cruttwell, 1770), 5, 6, lines 1–4, 265–8.
52. *The Tatler* 151 (March 28, 1710), in *The Tatler*, ed. Donald F. Bond (Oxford: Clarendon Press, 1987), 2:350.
53. Robert Hitchcock, *The Macaroni: A Comedy* (York: Printed by A. Ward, 1773), 3 [pagination is incorrect: actual p. 7].
54. See Powell and Roach, "Big Hair," 87.
55. McNeil, "'That Doubtful Gender'," 426.
56. Miles Ogborn, "Locating the Macaroni: Luxury, Sexuality, and Vision in Vauxhall Gardens," *Textual Practice* 11, no. 3 (1997): 456.
57. Amelia Rauser, "Sex and Sensibility: Hair in the Macaroni Caricatures of the 1770s," in *Hair: Untangling a Social History*, ed. Penny Howell Jolly (Saratoga Springs, NY: Skidmore College Art Gallery 2004), 33.
58. See Corson, *Fashions in Hair*, 327–96; Mary Trasko, *Daring Do's: A History of Extraordinary Hair* (Paris: Flammarion, 1994), 37–72.
59. Biddle-Perry, "Introduction," in Biddle-Perry and Cheang, eds., *Hair: Styling, Culture and Fashion*, 8. The some 500 women working as hairdressers in Paris in 1700 swelled in numbers to 2,000 by the end of the century, while some 1,200 male hairdressers were practicing in Paris in 1760. Jennifer Jones, *Sexing la Mode: Gender, Fashion and Commercial Culture in Old Regime France* (London: Bloomsbury Academic, 2004), 89, 79, 89.
60. Addison, *The Spectator* 45 (April 21, 1711), in *The Spectator*, ed. Donald F. Bond (Oxford: Clarendon Press, 1965), 1:192.
61. Addison, *The Spectator* 15 (March 17, 1711), in Bond, ed., *The Spectator*, 1:67, 1:69, 1:67, 1:67.
62. Peter Gilchrist, *Treatise on the Hair* (London, 1770), 9.
63. Caroline Weber, *Queen of Fashion: What Marie Antoinette Wore to the Revolution* (New York: Henry Holt, 2006), 104–7.
64. Diana Donald, *The Age of Caricature: Satirical Prints in the Age of George III* (New Haven, CT: Yale University Press, 1996), 88.
65. "The Friend to the Fair Sex. Chapter VI. On Dress," *The Lady's Magazine* 4 (December 1773): 637.
66. Henri Focillon, *The Life of Forms in Art*, trans. Charles Hogan and George Kubler (1948; Cambridge, MA: MIT Press, 1996), 85.
67. English Periwig-Maker, *Dissertation upon Head Dress*, 39.
68. Mary Frampton, *Journal of Mary Frampton from the Year 1779, until the Year 1846* (London: Sampson Low, 1885), 3.
69. Henriette-Lucie Dillon, marquise de la Tour du Pin Gouvernet, *Recollections of the Revolution and the Empire*, ed. and trans. Walter Geer (New York: Brentano's, 1920), 7.
70. Donald, *The Age of Caricature*, 86.
71. See Campbell, *Historical Style*, 146.
72. Trasko, *Daring Do's*, 68; see Weber, *Queen of Fashion*, 123.
73. English Periwig-Maker, *Dissertation upon Head Dress*, 5, 24, 27, 27.
74. William Barker, *Treatise on the Principles of Hair-dressing* (London: J. Rozea, ca. 1785); quotations drawn from excerpts reproduced in *Scots Magazine* 47 (February 1785): 76.
75. Nina Rattner Gelbart, "The Blonding of Charlotte Corday," *Eighteenth-Century Studies* 38, no. 1 (2004): 205.
76. Aileen Ribeiro, *Fashion in the French Revolution* (New York: Holmes and Meier, 1988), 117.

77. John Barrell, *The Spirit of Despotism* (Oxford: Oxford University Press, 2006), 145–209.
78. Wilson, *Adorned in Dreams*, 58.
79. Benjamin, *Arcades Project*, 8, 63.

Chapter 4

1. I follow the lead of studies such as Ursula Klein and Wolfgang Lefèvre's *Materials in Eighteenth-Century Science: A Historical Ontology* (Cambridge, MA: MIT Press, 2007), which offer history as the "interweav[ing]" of multiple "historical and philosophical themes [such as]: ontologies of materials, practices of making, identifying and classifying materials, and the science of materials" (2).
2. Thomas S. Kuhn, *The Structure of Scientific Revolutions* (Chicago: University of Chicago Press, 1962). Scholarship on the period from Boyle to Levoisier is magnificently canvassed by Victor D. Boantza, *Matter and Method in the Long Chemical Revolution: Laws of Another Order* (London: Routledge, 2016).
3. Jordan Goodman, *Tobacco in History: Cultures of Dependence* (London: Routledge, 1994), 88–198; Sidney Mintz, *Sweetness and Power: The Place of Sugar in Modern History* (New York: Viking-Penguin, 1985).
4. Philip D. Curtin, *The Rise and Fall of the Plantation Complex: Essays in Atlantic History* (Cambridge: Cambridge University Press, 1984); Mintz, *Sweetness and Power*.
5. See Michael Kwass, *Contraband: Louis Mandrin and the Making of a Global Underground* (Cambridge, MA: Harvard University Press, 2014); R.A. Austen and W.D. Smith, "Private Tooth Decay as Public Economic Virtue: The Slave-Sugar Triangle, Consumerism and European Industrialization," *Social Science History* 14, no. 1 (1990): 95–115. On cotton, Ann DuPont, "Captives of Colored Cloth: The Role of Cotton Trade Goods in the North Atlantic Slave Trade (1600–1808)," *Ars Textrina* 24 (1995): 177–83, and Colleen E. Kriger, "Guinea Cloth: Production and Consumption of Cotton Textiles in West Africa before and during the Atlantic Slave Trade," in *The Spinning World: A Global History of Cotton Textiles, 1200–1850*, ed. Giorgio Riello and Prasannan Parthasarathi (Oxford: Oxford University Press, 2011), 105–26; Giorgio Riello, "The Globalization of Cotton Textiles: Indian Cottons, Europe, and the Atlantic World, 1600–1850," in Riello, ed., *Spinning World*, 261–90.
6. Lorna Weatherill, *Consumer Behavior and Material Culture: 1660–1760* (London: Routledge, 1988); Michael Kwass, "Ordering the World of Goods: Consumer Revolution and the Classification of Objects in Eighteenth-Century France," *Representations* 82, no. 1 (2003): 87–116.
7. Charles Saumarez-Smith, *Eighteenth-Century Decoration Design and the Domestic Interior in England* (New York: Harry N. Abrams, 1993).
8. Jan de Vries, *The Industrious Revolution: Consumer Behavior and the Household Economy, 1650 to the Present* (Cambridge: Cambridge University Press, 2008).
9. See John Brewer, *The Pleasures of the Imagination: English Culture in the Eighteenth Century* (London: Routledge, 1997).
10. Neil McKendrick et al., *The Birth of a Consumer Society: The Commercialization of Eighteenth-Century England* (Bloomington: Indiana University Press, 1982); Maxine Berg, *Luxury and Pleasure in Eighteenth-Century Britain* (Oxford: Oxford University Press, 2005); Ina McCabe, *A History of Global Consumption: 1500–1800* (London: Routledge, 2014). On luxury, fashion, and fibers, see Beverley Lemire, *Fashion's Favourite: The Cotton Trade and the Consumer in Britain: 1660–1800* (Oxford: Oxford University Press, 1991).

11. Herbert S. Klein, *The Atlantic Slave Trade* (Cambridge: Cambridge University Press, 1999).
12. My discussion of the early modern woolen industry follows Kenneth G. Ponting, *The Wool Trade: Past and Present* (Manchester: Columbine, 1961); John Smail, *Merchants, Markets, and Manufacture: The English Wool Textile Industry in the Eighteenth Century* (Basingstoke: MacMillan, 1999); Herman van der Wee and John Munro, "The Western European Woollen Industries, 1500–1750" in *The Cambridge History of Western Textiles II*, ed. David Jenkins (Cambridge: Cambridge University Press, 2003), 397–472. It also incorporates details from John Smith's sourcebook, *Chronicon Rusticum-Commerciale, or Memoirs of Wool, Woolen Manufacture, and Trade*, 2 vols. (London, 1756–1757).
13. Richard Hakluyt, *The Principal Nauigations, Voiages, Traffiques and Discoueries of the English Nation* (London: George Bishop, Ralph Newberie, and Robert Barker, 1598–1600).
14. Lawrence Stone, "Elizabethan Overseas Trade," *Economic History Review* 2, no. 1 (1949): 39.
15. Thomas Johnson, *Discourse Consisting of Motives for the Enlargement and Freedome of Trade* (London: Richard Bishop for Stephen Rowtell, 1645), 3.
16. Arthur Young, *Political Essays Concerning the Present State of the British Empire* (London: Printed for W. Strahan and T. Cadell, 1772), 197. See Phyllis Deane, "Output of the British Woolen Industry in the Eighteenth Century," *Journal of Economic History* 17, no. 2 (1957): 207–23.
17. Daniel Defoe, *A Plan of the English Commerce* (London: Printed for Charles Rivington, 1730), 190. See Smith, *Memoirs of Wool*.
18. William III, 1698, "An Act to Prevent the Exportation of Wool out of the Kingdoms of Ireland ....," in *Statutes of the Realm*, vol. 7, 1695–1701, ed. John Raithby (London: Printed by George Eyre and Andrew Strahan, printers to the King, 1820), 524–8. See Pamela Clabburn, *Furnishing Textiles* (New York: Viking, 1988), 34–6.
19. R.L. Sickinger, "Regulation or Ruination: Parliament's Consistent Pattern of Mercantilist Regulation of the English Textile Trade, 1660–1800," *Parliamentary History* 19, no. 2 (2000): 211–32.
20. Smith, *Memoirs of Wool*, 1:157.
21. Derek Gregory, "The Woollen Industry and the English Space-Economy," in *Regional Transformation and Industrial Revolution: A Geography of the Yorkshire Woolen Industry* (Minneapolis: Univesity of Minnesota Press, 1982), 26–79, esp. 27.
22. See Jon Stobart's overview of these issues in the "Introduction" to *The First Industrial Region: North West England c. 1700–60* (Manchester: Manchester University Press, 2009), 1–9. Also see John Smail, "The Sources of Innovation in the Woollen and Worsted Industry of Eighteenth-Century Yorkshire," *Business History* 41, no. 1 (1999): 3; Pat Hudson, "Proto-Industrialization: The Case of the West Riding Wool Textile Industry in the 18th and Early 19th Centuries," *History Workshop Journal* 12 (1981): 34–61.
23. Pat Hudson and Steve King, "Two Textile Townships, c. 1660–1820: A Comparative Demographic Analysis," *Economic History Review* 53, no. 4 (2000): 706–41; Jonathan Healey, *The First Century of Welfare: Poverty and Poor Relief in Lancashire 1620–1730* (Woodbridge: Boydell, 2014), esp. 41–50; E.A. Wrigley, "Explaining the Rise in Marital Fertility in England in the 'Long' Eighteenth Century," *Economic History Review* 51, no. 3 (1998): 435–64; Stobart summarizes arguments about the relationship of urbanization to industrialization in *The First Industrial Region*, 16–27.
24. My discussion of woolens follows Roberts Beaumont, *Woollen and Worsted: The Theory and Technology of the Manufacture of Woollen, Worsted, and Union Yarns and Fabrics* (London: G. Bell, 1920); and John Styles, "Spinners and the Law: Regulating Yarn

Standards in the English Worsted Industry: 1550–1800," *Textile History* 44, no. 2 (2013): 145–70. The best discussion of everyday fabrics in eighteenth-century England is John Styles, *The Dress of the People: Everyday Fashion in Eighteenth-Century England* (New Haven, CT: Yale University Press, 2007).

25. One useful discussion of the history of fulling is Rupert Hall and N.C. Russell, "What about the Fulling-Mill?" *History of Technology* 6 (1981): 113–19. See also Beaumont, *Woollen and Worsted*, 624–7.
26. Smail, "Innovation." See also E.J.W. Barber's discussion of fiber properties, *Prehistoric Textiles* (Princeton, NJ: Princeton University Press, 1991), 216–18.
27. See, for instance, William Dermot Darby, *Wool: The World's Comforter* (New York: Dry Goods Economist, 1922), 25; Stephen Powers, *The American Merino: For Wool and for Mutton* (New York: Orange Judd, 1887), 27–39.
28. Geraint Jenkins, *The Wool Textile Industry in Great Britain* (London: Routledge, 1972). Short-staple wool generally has fiber lengths of roughly 2½–4 in.
29. Long-staple wool lengths might be 4–8 in. or 7–15 in., depending on the sheep breed.
30. Also parchment production. See, for instance, M.L. Ryder, *Sheep and Man* (London: Duckworth, 1983), 472–4.
31. Hudson, *West Riding Wool*, 110–13. See also Pat Hudson, "Limits of Wool and the Potential of Cotton in the Eighteenth and Early Nineteenth Centuries," in *The Spinning World*, 327–50; Ryder, *Sheep and Man*, 477–95.
32. See Kathleen H. Ochs, "The Royal Society of London's History of Trades Program: An Early Episode in Applied Science," *Notes and Records* 39, no. 2 (1985): 129–58.
33. Smail, "Innovation."
34. On Petty as craftsman and virtuoso, see Ted McCormick, *William Petty and the Ambitions of Political Arithmetic* (Oxford: Oxford University Press 2009), 14–83.
35. William Petty, "History of the Making of Cloth from Sheep's Wool," in *The History of the Royal Society of London*, ed. Thomas Birch (London: Millar, 1661), 1:58.
36. Ibid., 1:56–7.
37. Ibid., 1:5.
38. Ibid., 1:55.
39. It is worth pausing here to notice an absence. We might have expected Petty explicitly to compare wool threads to what we call the *threads* of the screw and nut, or at least to register that the analogy (from fibers to mechanical fasteners) depends on a silent echo. But the influence in fact runs the other way. We call the ridges on a screw its "threads" because William Petty noticed the resemblance; if Petty wasn't the first person to think that the mechanical force holding a screw to a nut might best be compared to the natural affordances of wool, he was at least the first person to register in print (less than a decade later) the unusual decision to call the ridges on a screw its "threads." This is a reminder that words, like concepts, do not emerge from nowhere; they emerge from particular cultural and material contexts.
40. Thomas Hobbes, *Elementorum Philosophiae: Sectio Prima, De Corpore* (London, 1655), III.xx. 180; Thomas Browne, *Pseudodoxia Epidemica* (London, 1646), 267.
41. Although "complicated" and "complex" have slightly different Latin roots, it is worth treating them as near synonyms, as a glance at their historical usage indicates that the difference was not always registered in seventeenth- and eighteenth-century thought.
42. On making as itself "textilic," see Tim Ingold, "The Textility of Making," *Cambridge Journal of Economics* 34, no. 1 (2010): 91–102.

43. Jaap Maat, *Philosophical Languages in the Seventeenth Century* (Dordrecht: Kluwer Academic, 2004), 185 (emphasis in the original).
44. John Wilkins, *An Essay Towards a Real Character and a Philosophical Language* (London, 1668), 295–6.
45. Robert Hooke, *Micrographia, or, Some Physiological Descriptions of Minute Bodies Made by Magnifying Glasses* (London: Jo. Martyn and Ja. Allestry, 1665), 8.
46. Ibid.
47. The atomism of Boyle's corpuscularianism has been much debated. One review of this debate appears in Anstey, *John Locke and Natural Philosophy*.
48. And vice versa—a point observed by Boyle and others—as, for instance, in Hooke's experiments with mettaline dyes (*Micrographia*, 67–79).
49. Boyle, in *Origin of Forms and Qualities*; Hooke, in *Micrographia*; Willis, in *Two Discourses Concerning the Soul of Brutes*, 70, etc. Boyle's corpuscularianism and its relationship to the much-later development of the periodic table of elements, has been the subject of much recent debate. The contours of this debate are usefully summarized by William R. Newman, "Robert Boyle, Transmutation, and the History of Chemistry before Lavoisier," *Osiris* 29, no. 1 (2014): 63–77. See also Marina Paola Banchetti-Robino, "The Ontological Function of First-Order and Second-Order Corpuscles in the Chemical Philosophy of Robert Boyle: The Redintegration of Potassium Nitrate," *Foundations of Chemistry* 14, no. 3 (2012): 221–34.
50. Hooke, *Micrographia*, 8–9 (emphasis in the original).
51. Ibid., 160 (emphasis in the original).
52. For a differing but sympathetic account, see Kirstin Girten, "Mingling with Matter; Tactile Microscopy and the Philosophic Mind in Brobdingnag and Beyond," *The Eighteenth Century: Theory and Interpretation* 54, no. 4 (2013): 503–4.
53. Hooke, *Micrographia*, 160.
54. Robert Hooke, "The Way of Making Felts" (Royal Society, GB 117 Classified Papers XX, 3), n.p.
55. Scholars of Robert Boyle's metaphysics and John Locke's epistemology are alike comfortable calling them "building-block" systems, because they are alike based on the aggregation of simple particles. For instance, Michael Ayers, *John Locke: Epistemology & Ontology*, 2 vols. (London: Routledge, 1991), 1:41; Peter Anstey, *John Locke and Natural Philosophy* (Oxford: Oxford University Press, 2011), 18.
56. John Locke, *Locke's Drafts for the "Essay Concerning Human Understanding,"* ed. P.H. Nidditch and G.A.J. Rogers (Oxford: Clarendon Press, 1990), 1–2.
57. Complexity is for instance among the concepts in the *Port-Royal Logic*, but they employ it in a fundamentally different way—as a name for the compounds made up of two simple forms: as the formal words "man" and "prudent" might together be welded into the single complex term: "prudent man." Pierre Nicole and Antoine Arnauld's *La Logique ou l'art de penser*—commonly known as the *Port-Royal Logic*. See Antoine Arnauld and Pierre Nicole, *Logic or the Art of Thinking*, ed. Jill Vance Buroker (Cambridge: Cambridge University Press, 1997), 44.
58. Klein and Lefévre, *Materials in Eighteenth-Century Science*.
59. On this point, see Mi Gyung Kim, "Stabilizing Chemical Reality: The Analytic-Synthetic Ideal of Chemical Species," *Hyle: International Journal for Philosophy of Chemistry* 20, no. 1 (2014): 117–39.

Chapter 5

1. Emily Cockayne, *Hubbub: Filth, Noise & Stench in England 1660–1770* (New Haven, CT: Yale University Press, 2007), chap. 3, "Itchy," 54–83.

2. "An Essay on the Hair, With the Most Proper Methods of Dressing and Preserving It," appended to *The New London Toilet* (London: Printed for Richardson and Urquhart, 1778), 99.
3. Peter Gilchrist, *A Treatise on the Hair* (London, 1770), 3.
4. James Stewart, *Plocacosmos, or, The Whole Art of Hair Dressing* (London: Printed for the Author, 1782), 172, 175.
5. Alexander Stewart, *The Natural Production of Hair* (London: Printed by the Author, 1795), 10.
6. Gilchrist, *Treatise on the Hair*, 38.
7. Stewart, *The Natural Production of Hair*, 9–11.
8. William Moore, *The Art of Hair-dressing* (Bath: J. Salmon, [1780?]), 8.
9. Jonathan Swift, "The Lady's Dressing-Room," in *The Essential Writings of Jonathan Swift*, ed. Claude Rawson and Ian Higgins (New York: Norton, 2010), 603.
10. Ibid., 603.
11. Moore, *The Art of Hair-dressing*, 3.
12. Tita Chico, *Designing Women: The Dressing Room in Eighteenth-Century English Literature and Culture* (Lewisburg, PA: Bucknell University Press, 2005), 149.
13. Jonathan Swift, "A Beautiful Young Nymph Going to Bed," in Rawson and Higgins, eds., *The Essential Writings*, 608.
14. Tobias Smollett, *The Adventures of Roderick Random*, ed. Paul-Gabriel Boucé (1748; Oxford: Oxford World Classics, 2008), 152.
15. "The Louse in Imitation of the Flea," in *A Collection of Miscellany Poems Never before Publish'd* (London: W. Warner, 1737).
16. Jon Wolcot, *The Works of Peter Pindar, Esq.* (London: J. Walker, 1812), 1:175.
17. Stewart, *The Natural Production of Hair*, 14.
18. Moore, *The Art of Hair-dressing*, 13–14.
19. *Notes by Lady Louisa Stuart on George Selwyn and His Contemporaries by John Heneage Jesse*, ed. W.S. Lewis (New York: Oxford University Press, 1928), 22–3.
20. Stewart, *Plocacosmos*, 278.
21. John Donaldson, *On the Use of Hair Powder*, 2nd ed. (London: T. Cadell and W. Davis, 1795), 11.
22. There is an example in the Louth Museum, Lincolnshire, which is 7 cm long, 1.5 cm wide; LOUTN: J453B; collections.louthmuseum.org.uk (Accessed August 14, 2016).
23. *The Diary of Samuel Pepys*, ed. Robert Latham and William Matthews (Berkeley: University of California Press, 1970–1983), 3:70 (hereafter in the text as *SP*).
24. Claire Tomalin, *Samuel Pepys: The Unequaled Self* (New York: Knopf, 2002), 118.
25. *The Workhouse Cruelty: Being a Full and True Account of one Mrs Whistle* (ca. 1731), quoted in Tim Hitchcock, *Down and Out in Eighteenth-Century London* (London: Hambledon and London, 2004), 106.
26. Ned Ward, *The History of the London Clubs: or, the Citizens Pastime* (London: Printed for J. Bagnall, 1709), 7.
27. Stewart, *The Natural Production of Hair*, 15.
28. Moore, *The Art of Hairdressing*, 11.
29. *The Complete Vermin-Killer*, 3rd ed. (London: Fielding and Walker, 1777), 6.
30. Ibid., 7.
31. William Barker, *A Treatise on the Principles of Hair-dressing* (London: J. Rozea, ca. 1785), 7.

Chapter 6

1. Robert Halsband, *The Rape of the Lock and Its Illustrations* (Oxford: Clarendon Press, 1980), 20.
2. John Gay, *Letters of John Gay*, ed. C.F. Burgess (Oxford: Clarendon Press, 1966), 11.
3. Charles Gildon, *A New Rehearsal, or Bays the Younger* (London, 1714), 43–4.
4. For a lively survey of feminist debates about *The Rape of the Lock* as its participants are or are not willing to contextualize Belinda within the gendered ideologies of her day, see Deborah C. Payne, "Pope and the War against Coquettes; or, Feminism and *The Rape of the Lock* Reconsidered—Yet Again," *The Eighteenth Century: Theory and Interpretation* 32 (1991): 3–24.
5. Alexander Pope, *The Rape of the Lock*, in *The Poems of Alexander Pope*, ed. John Butt (New Haven, CT: Yale University Press, 1974), 4.176 (hereafter in the text as *RL*).
6. Materialist interpretations of Belinda's hair and body dominate even the most recent and illuminating work on the poem. Three examples: Barbara Benedict, "Death and the Object: The Abuse of Things in *The Rape of the Lock*," in *Anniversary Essays on Alexander Pope's The Rape of the Lock*, ed. Donald W. Nichol (Toronto: University of Toronto Press, 2016), 131–49; and Sean Silver, *The Mind Is a Collection: Case Studies in Eighteenth-Century Thought* (Philadelphia: University of Pennsylvania Press, 2015), 248–54; Tita Chico deftly analyzes Belinda's hair as a "social form" made visible through microscopic poetics in "Couplets and Curls: A Theory of Form," *Philological Quarterly* 86:3 (2007): 251–68.
7. Eleazar Albin, *A Natural History of English Insects* (London: Printed for the Author, 1720), n.p.; Eleazar Albin, *A Natural History of Birds* (London: Printed for the Author, 1734), 130; Thomas Boreman, *A Description of a Great Variety of Animals and Vegetables* (London: John Tilly, 1736), 69.
8. Robert Hooke, *Micrographia, or, Some Physiological Descriptions of Some Minute Bodies made by Magnifying Glasses* (London: Jo. Martyn and Ja. Allestry, 1665), 146.
9. Ian Hacking, *Representing and Intervening: Introductory Topics in the Philosophy of Natural Science* (Cambridge: Cambridge University Press, 1983). For an extensive study of Hacking's theory in relation to the life of imperceptible particles in Enlightenment "Chymistry," see Helen Thompson, *Fictional Matter: Empiricism, Corpuscles, and the Novel* (Philadelphia: University of Pennsylvania Press, 2017).
10. *The Town and Country Magazine, or Universal Repository IV* (London: printed for A. Hamilton, 1772), 243. The topic is the Macaroni's coiffure: "two pounds of fictitious hair, formed into what is called a club." For general histories of false hair in the period see Janet Arnold, *Perukes and Periwigs* (London: Her Majesty's Stationery Office [National Portrait Gallery], 1970) and John Woodforde, *The Strange Story of False Hair* (London: Routledge, 1971). A careful exegesis of the Macaroni's false hair as a "potent and multivalent symbol of the selfmade man" (103)—albeit one that "blurred boundaries of class, gender, and nationality" (102)—may be found in Amelia Rauser, "Hair, Authenticity, and the Self-Made Macaroni," *Eighteenth-Century Studies* 38, no. 1 (2004): 101–17.
11. *The London Ladies Vindication of Top-knots* (London: Printed for P. Brooksey et al., [between 1688 and 1692]). Ballad sheet.
12. Joseph Addison, *Spectator* 98 (June 22, 1711), in *The Spectator*, ed. Donald F. Bond (Oxford: Clarendon Press, 1965), 1:413.
13. In an enlightening study of what might be at stake poetically in a "biology of crotches" (116), Raymond Stephanson examines Pope's "interest in [...] the sexual bodies of both men and women as they were distinguished and differentiated by their genitalia" (118).

"'Hairs Less in Sight': Pope, Biology and Culture," in Nichol, ed., *Anniversary Essays*, 113–30.
14. Locke of course maintains that "all Ideas come from Sensation or Reflection." See *An Essay concerning Humane Understanding* (London: Eliz. Holt, 1690), 2.1.2. Recent anatomies or skeptical considerations of the materialist grounds of Lockean ideation include Silver, *The Mind Is a Collection*; Thompson, *Fictional Matter*; and Brad Pasanek, *Metaphors of Mind: An Eighteenth-Century Dictionary* (Baltimore: Johns Hopkins University Press, 2015).
15. Marcia Pointon, *Hanging the Head: Portraiture and Social Formation in Eighteenth-Century England* (New Haven, CT: Yale University Press, 1993), 107–40; Lynn Festa, "Personal Effects: Wigs and Possessive Individualism in the Long Eighteenth Century," *Eighteenth-Century Life* 29, no. 2 (2005): 47–90. Other considerations of hair in relation to gender in the eighteenth-century context include Richard Corson, "'The Eighteenth Century: Men' and 'The Eighteenth Century: Women'," in *Fashions in Hair: The First Five Thousand Years*, rev. ed. (London: Peter Owen, 2001), 261–397; Georgine De Courtais, *Women's Headdress and Hairstyles in England from AD 600 to the Present Day* (London: Batsford, 1986).
16. Alexander Stewart, *The Natural Production of Hair* (London, 1795), 194.
17. Festa, "Personal Effects," 85.
18. Margaret K. Powell and Joseph Roach, "Big Hair," *Eighteenth-Century Studies* 38, no. 1 (2004): 79–99.
19. Londa Schiebinger, *Nature's Body: Gender in the Making of Modern Science* (New Brunswick, NJ: Rutgers University Press, 1993), 1–10; Thomas Laqueur, *Making Sex: Body and Gender from the Greeks to Freud* (Cambridge, MA: Harvard University Press, 1990); Dror Wahrman, *The Making of the Modern Self: Identity and Culture in Eighteenth-Century England* (New Haven, CT: Yale University Press, 2004), 46–82.
20. Charlotte Charke, *A Narrative of the Life of Mrs. Charlotte Charke*, ed. Robert Rehder (London: Pickering and Chatto, 1999), 10.
21. Judith Butler, *Gender Trouble: Feminism and the Subversion of Identity* (New York: Routledge, 1999).
22. J.C. Flügel, *The Psychology of Clothes* (London: Hogarth, 1930), 45–8. See also Aileen Ribeiro, *Dress and Morality* (London: Batsford, 1986); and Festa, "Personal Effects," which examines hair's affinity with the sartorial paradox of covering and exposure.
23. Sarah Cheang and Geraldine Biddle-Perry, "Introduction," in *Hair: Styling, Culture and Fashion*, ed. Sarah Cheang and Geraldine Biddle-Perry (New York: Berg, 2008), 5.
24. Glynis Ridley examines hair's place in what she interprets as an ultimately materialist history of mythic women in "Making the Perfect Woman: Female Automata from Pandora to Belinda," Nichols, ed., *Anniversary Essays*, 53–69.
25. On the hair of Milton's Adam and Eve as "the most spirituous and pure part of their bodies" (343) and thus part of a long-standing spiritual understanding of hair, see Stephen B. Dobranski, "Clustering and Curling Locks: The Matter of Hair in *Paradise Lost*," *PMLA* 125, no. 2 (2010): 337–53. On hair's place in various spiritual traditions more broadly, see Charles Berg, *The Unconscious Significance of Hair* (London: Allen & Unwin, 1951), and Edmund Leach, "Magical Hair," *Journal of the Royal Anthropological Institute* 88, no. 2 (1958): 147–64.
26. Ellen Pollak, *The Poetics of Sexual Myth: Gender and Ideology in the Verse of Swift and Pope* (Chicago: University of Chicago Press, 1985).

27. Thomas Hall, *Comarum Akosmia. The Loathsomnesse of Long Haire* (London, 1654), 15. See also William Prynne, *The Unlovelinesse of Love-locks* (London, 1628) and for a discussion of the contradictions built into Puritan conceptions of hair, Festa, "Personal Effects," 60–2, and Pointon, *Hanging the Head*, 124–5.
28. David Ritchie, *A Treatise on the Hair: Shewing its Generation, Means of its Preservation, Causes of its Decay. How to Recover it When Lost* (London, 1770), title page.
29. Charles De Zemler, *Once over Lightly: The Story of Man and His Hair* (New York, 1939), 20.
30. *An Extract of a Letter from Norimbergh [sic], dated April 1680*, in Royal Society, *Philosophical Collections*, ed. Robert Hooke (London, 1682), 2:10. This account fascinated British hair writers for centuries. In 1722 *The Philosophical Magazine* retooled the story for popular consumption, and the hairdresser James Stewart was still paraphrasing it in *Plocacosmos, or, The Whole Art of Hairdressing* (London: Printed for the Author, 1782), 183–4. See also Bela C. Perry, *The Human Hair and the Cutaneous Diseases Which Affect It* (New York: J. Miller, 1865), 36–9.
31. *Extract of a Letter*, 2:11.
32. John Lowthorp, ed., *The Philosophical Transactions and Collections to the End of the Year 1700, Abridged and Disposed under General Heads* (1740), 3:14 (emphasis in the original).
33. Ibid., 3:14 (emphasis in the original).
34. Ibid., 3:16; Henry Sampson, "Anatomical Observations on the Body of a Woman about Thirty years Old," *Philosophical Transactions* 12, no. 140 (1677): 133–42; James Yonge, "An Account of Balls of Hair taken from the Uterus and Ovaria of Several Women," *Philosophical Transactions* 25, no. 309 (1706–1707): 2387–92; Yonge, "An Extract of Another Letter upon the Same Subject," *Philosophical Transactions* 26, no. 323 (1708): 313–24; John Powell and Hans Sloane, "Concerning a Gentlewoman who Voided with her Urine, Hairy Crustaceous Substances," *Philosophical Transactions* 41, no. 460 (1739): 452–61.
35. Lowthorp, *The Philosophical Transactions and Collections*, 3:13.
36. Yonge, *An Account of Balls of Hair*, 2391.
37. Jane Bennett, *Vibrant Matter: A Political Ecology of Things* (Durham, NC: Duke University Press, 2010), x.
38. Karen Barad, *Meeting the Universe Halfway: Quantum Physics and the Entanglement of Matter and Meaning* (Durham, NC: Duke University Press, 2007), 72. For other examples of the new feminist materialism, see Diana Coole and Samantha Frost, eds., *New Materialisms: Ontology, Agency and Politics* (Durham, NC: Duke University Press, 2010), and Stacy Alaimo and Susan Hekman, eds., *Material Feminisms* (Bloomington: Indiana University Press, 2008).
39. Claire Colebrook, "On Not Becoming Man: The Materialist Politics of Unactualized Potential," in Alaimo and Hekman, eds., *Material Feminisms*, 56.
40. Barad, *Meeting the Universe Halfway*, 140.
41. Christiane Holm, "Sentimental Cuts: Eighteenth-Century Mourning Jewelry with Hair," *Eighteenth-Century Studies* 38, no. 1 (2004): 140. See also Kathleen M. Oliver, "'With My Hair in Crystal': Mourning Clarissa," *Eighteenth-Century Fiction* 23, no. 1 (2010): 35–60.
42. Jonathan Richardson, *Explanatory Notes and Remarks on Milton's Paradise Lost* (London, 1734), 156–8 (emphasis in the original).
43. Ritchie, *Treatise on the Hair*, 79.
44. Robert Boyle, *New Experiments, Physico-Mechanical, Touching the Spring of the Air* (1660), in *Works of the Honourable Robert Boyle*, ed. Thomas Birch (London, 1744), 1:8.
45. Boyle, *Of the Mechanical Origin of Electricity*, in *Works of the Honourable Robert Boyle*, 6.351.

46. George Adams, *An Essay on Electricity* (London, 1792), 498.
47. Erasmus Darwin, *The Botanic Garden: A Poem in Two Parts* (London, 1791), 1:24; 2:167; 2:34.
48. Stewart, *Natural Production of the Hair*, 11.
49. Ritchie, *Treatise on the Hair*, 9.
50. John Quincy, *Lexicon Physico-Medicum*, 5th ed. (London, 1736), 199.
51. Stewart, *Natural Production of the Hair*, 172.
52. William Hogarth, *The Analysis of Beauty*, ed. Ronald Paulson (New Haven, CT: Yale University Press, 1997), 34.
53. Stewart, *Plocacosmos*, 197, 175.
54. Oliver Goldsmith, *An History of the Earth, and Animated Nature*, 2nd ed. (London, 1779), 2:86–7. Georges Louis Leclerc, comte de Buffon, *The Natural History of Animals, Vegetables, and Minerals*, trans. W. Kenrick and J. Murdoch. (London, 1775–1776), 1:87.
55. Yonge, *An Account of Balls of Hair*, 2388.
56. Thomas Vicary, *The Englishemans Treasure, … with the True Anatomye of Mans Body* (1577; London, 1586), 12.
57. Daniel Sennert, *The Art of Chirurgery Explained in Six Parts* (London, 1663), 2613–14.
58. Samuel Johnson, *A Dictionary of the English Language* (London: W. Strahan, 1755), 1:956.
59. John Mather, *A Treatise on the Nature and Preservation of the Hair* (London, 1795), 10.
60. John Aitken, *Principles of Anatomy and Physiology* (London, 1786), 2:1–7, 8; Ritchie, *Treatise on the Hair*, 6.
61. Thomas Gibson, *The Anatomy of Humane Bodies Epitomized* (London, 1703), 365.
62. Stewart, *Plocacosmos*, 181.
63. Uvedale Price, *An Essay on the Picturesque* (London, 1794), 127.
64. William Roberts, ed. *Memoirs of the Life and Correspondence of Mrs. Hannah More* (London: R.B. Seeley and W. Burnside, 1834), 1:100.
65. Corson, *Fashions in Hair*, 352. See also "Female Head-gear. Later Eighteenth Century," *The Magazine of Art* 9 (1886): 428. The feminization of botany and cultural myths of women's deep affinity with the plant world are considered in Amy May King, *Bloom: The Botanical Vernacular in the English Novel* (New York: Oxford University Press, 2003) and Schiebinger, *Nature's Body*, 11–39.
66. An English Periwig-Maker, *A Dissertation upon Head Dress* (London: printed for J. Williams, 1767), 18. On the gender politics of hairscaping as Bakhtinian play "loosening a strict culture-nature dichotomy" (293), see Matthew Immergut, "Manscaping: The Tangle of Nature, Culture, and Male Body Hair," in *The Body Reader*, ed. Lisa Jean Moore and Mary Kosut (New York: New York University Press, 2010), 349–66.
67. William Barker, *Treatise on the Principles of Hair-dressing* (London: J. Rozea, ca. 1785), 318.
68. John Gay, "Iolaus Restor'd to Youth," in *Ovid's Metamorphoses*, 2nd ed., ed. Samuel Garth (London, 1720), 2:123.
69. An English Periwig-Maker, *A Dissertation upon Head Dress*, 36.
70. Horace Walpole to George Montague (July 30, 1752), in *The Yale Edition of Horace Walpole's Correspondence*, ed. W.S. Lewis (New Haven, CT: Yale University Press, 1937–83), 9:139.
71. Alan Bewell, "Erasmus Darwin's Cosmopolitan Nature," *ELH* 76, no. 1 (2009): 22.
72. Alexanna Speight, *The Lock of Hair: Its History, Ancient and Modern, Natural and Artistic* (London: A. Goubaud, 1871), 27–8.

73. Frances Burney, *Evelina; or, the History of a Young Lady's Entrance into the World*, ed. Edward Bloom, intro. Vivien Jones (Oxford: Oxford University Press, 2008), 28 (emphasis in the original).
74. Opinions on frizzing split, usually along lines of professional investment. Peruquiers held that hair is "abused and destroyed" by "perplex[ing]" (An English Periwig-Maker, *Dissertation upon Head Dress*, 36). The celebrity hairdresser Peter Gilchrist conceded that it "takes off the gloss, but this defect [...] is amply compensated by the advantage it gives in concurring [...] with the prevailing fashions." See Peter Gilchrist, *A Treatise on the Hair* (London, 1770), 13.
75. Burney, *Evelina*, 151.
76. Ibid., 168.
77. *A Dissertation upon Head-dress*, 31.
78. Stephen W. Hawking, Malcolm J. Perry, and Andrew Strominger, "Soft Hair on Black Holes," *Physical Review Letters* 116, no. 23 (June 10, 2016): 291301-1-281301-9.

Chapter 7

1. John Gay, "The Monkey who had Seen the World," in *Fables* (London: J. Tonson and J. Watts, 1727), 46–9 (lines 1–2) (hereafter cited in text as *Fab.*).
2. Linnaeus's *Systema Naturae* was first published in 1735.
3. Angela Rosenthal, "Raising Hair," *Eighteenth-Century Studies* 38, no. 1 (2004): 2.
4. For "wool" as an early modern designation for Africans' hair that implied their non-humanness and proximity to nonhuman animals, see Justin E.H. Smith, *Nature, Human Nature, and Human Difference: Race in Early Modern Philosophy* (Princeton, NJ and Oxford: Princeton University Press, 2015), 41–2.
5. Herodotus, *The Histories*, ed. John Marincola, trans. Aubrey De Sélincourt, rev. ed. (London: Penguin Classics, 2003), 134. In his introduction, Marincola cites the 450s–420s BCE as the period in which Herodotus likely researched and composed *The Histories* (xiii). I am grateful to Vanessa Lyon for suggesting this reference.
6. Peter A. Browne, *The Classification of Mankind, by the Hair and Wool of Their Heads: With an Answer to Dr. Prichard's Assertion, That "the Covering of the Head of the Negro Is Hair, Properly so Termed, and Not Wool": Read before the American Ethnological Society, November 3, 1849* (Philadelphia, PA: A. Hart, 1850), 20.
7. Cf. Londa Schiebinger, *Nature's Body: Gender and the Making of Modern Science* (New Brunswick, NJ: Rutgers University Press, 2004), 143–5. On "race" as a construction through which the French Revolutionaries sought to justify slavery, see Sue Peabody, *"There Are No Slaves in France": The Political Culture of Race and Slavery in the Ancien Régime* (Oxford: Oxford University Press, 1996); cited in Darcy Grimaldo Grigsby, *Extremities: Painting Empire in Post-Revolutionary France* (New Haven, CT: Yale University Press, 2002), 21.
8. Grigsby, *Extremities*, 20.
9. Margaret K. Powell and Joseph Roach, "Big Hair," *Eighteenth-Century Studies* 38, no. 1 (2004): 82.
10. Ibid., 80.
11. Catherine Molineux, *Faces of Perfect Ebony: Encountering Atlantic Slavery in Imperial Britain* (Cambridge, MA: Harvard University Press, 2012), 7.
12. Cf. Rosenthal, "Raising Hair," 1–2.
13. Roach and Powell, "Big Hair," 92; see *Oxford English Dictionary Online* (Oxford University Press), s.v. "Frizz, v.1." http://www.oed.com/view/Entry/74832 (accessed August 20, 2016).

14. Elizabeth Montagu in a letter to Elizabeth Carter, 1764 [November 25] [Bath] [Somerset], MO 3137, quoted in Felicity Nussbaum, *The Limits of the Human: Fictions of Anomaly, Race, and Gender in the Long Eighteenth Century* (Cambridge: Cambridge University Press, 2003), 141; cited in Rosenthal, "Raising Hair," 5.
15. For such an analysis of black pages in Renaissance painting, see Peter Erickson, "Representations of Blacks and Blackness in the Renaissance," *Criticism* 35, no. 4 (1993): 499–527. Molineux points out that "the black servant in livery" itself had "European origins" (*Faces of Perfect Ebony*, 23).
16. For a consideration of Hogarth's relation to the British and French nations, see Timothy Erwin, "William Hogarth and the Aesthetics of Nationalism," *Huntington Library Quarterly* 64, no. 3/4 (2001): 383–410.
17. This section's title plays upon Barbara Christian's essay "The Race for Theory," *Cultural Critique* no. 6 (Spring 1987): 51–63, in which the author places into conversation the "race" (fashion) for white Western theory in academia and the "race" (people of color) who have long theorized but in ways that academia traditionally dismisses. Ronald Paulson, somewhat differently, stresses "the contrast of art (or high culture) and nature, the dangerously close relationship between the two in the world of London, and the idea that art itself is merely a piece of property like the black slave [the seated child] who holds it up." *Hogarth: High Art and Low, 1732–1750* (New Brunswick, NJ: Rutgers University Press, 1992), 226–7.
18. Indeed, Hogarth's *Taste in High Life* or *Taste à la Mode* (1742), which Paulson identifies as "anticipating" the themes of works such as *Marriage a-la-Mode*, features a monkey in human clothes, reading from a menu written in French (*Hogarth*, 203–4). Behind the monkey, a fancily dressed man sports a long queue and black bow, which find their counterpart in the monkey's tail and the black bow that adorns it, on his posterior.
19. Paulson focuses on imitation in the series but does not consider the potentially reciprocal or mutually "contaminative" nature of imitation as it is presented here (*Hogarth*, 228). My reading would add to Molineux's discussion of Hogarth locating "the generation of blackness in deviant sexual behavior" (*Faces of Perfect Ebony*, 197).
20. For the use of the "cushion" in building women's towering hairstyles, see Powell and Roach, "Big Hair," 92.
21. Edward Long, *The History of Jamaica, Or, General Survey of the Antient and Modern State of That Island* ... (London: Printed for T. Lowndes, 1774), 2:520, emphasis in original (hereafter cited in the text as *HJ*).
22. Voltaire also linked Africans' "wool" to lower intelligence in his *Essai sur les moeurs et l'esprit des nations* (1756). See Smith, *Nature, Human Nature, and Human Difference*, 237.
23. John Gabriel Stedman, *Narrative, of a Five Years' Expedition; Against the Revolted Negroes of Surinam, in Guiana* ... (London: Printed for J. Johnson, 1796), 1:97.
24. Charles de Rochefort, *The History of the Caribby-Islands* ... *in Two* Books, trans. John Davies (1658; London: Printed by J.M. for Thomas Dring and John Starkey, 1666), bk II: *Moral History*, 201 (hereafter cited in the text as *HCI*). The Pseudo-Aristotelian *Physiognomics* (ca. 300 BCE) also made a link between the hair of "cowardice," which "stands up stiff," and "very wooly hair," which "also signifies cowardice, as may be seen in Ethiopians" (cited in Mireille M. Lee, *Body, Dress, and Identity in Ancient Greece* [New York: Cambridge University Press, 2015], 75).
25. As Janet Todd notes, Behn, who had supported James II, was concerned about negative repercussions of his potential—and realized—displacement ("Introduction," in Aphra

Behn, *Oroonoko*, ed. Janet Todd [London: Penguin Classics, 2004], xx). I am grateful to Jill Campbell for pointing me to Behn's *Oroonoko* and to Joseph Roach's essay on David Garrick's "fright wig," discussed below.

26. Behn, *Oroonoko*, 15 (hereafter cited in the text as *Oro.*).
27. Daniel Defoe, *Robinson Crusoe*, ed. Michael Shinagel, 2nd ed. (New York: W.W. Norton & Company, 1993), 128 (hereafter cited in the text as *RC*).
28. Following his visceral response upon seeing a shipwreck, which echoes the hair-raising cave incident, Crusoe summons the "Naturalists" to "explain these Things, and the Reason and Manner of them" (Ibid., 136). For the dating of the first appearance of Garrick's fright wig to the early 1770s—at least by 1773—see John Kleiner, "The Chairs—Hamlet and Stage Fright," *Literary Imagination* 17, no. 3 (November 20, 2015): 1.
29. Joseph R. Roach, "Garrick, the Ghost and the Machine," *Theatre Journal* 34, no. 4 (1982): 431.
30. Ibid., 438, 440.
31. As Felicity A. Nussbaum notes, prior to black actor Ira Aldridge's nineteenth-century performances, "eighteenth-century audiences [...] were accustomed only to the greasepaint, lampblack, smeared cork, pomatum, and woolly-wigged caricatures of blackness by white English actors who affected nativism" ("The Theatre of Empire: Racial Counterfeit, Racial Realism," chap. 3 in Kathleen Wilson, ed., *A New Imperial History: Culture, Identity, and Modernity in Britain and the Empire, 1660–1840* [New York: Cambridge University Press, 2004], 72). Nussbaum further points out that these plays might have black audience members, like author and critic Ignatius Sancho (71–2), who in fact wanted to perform in *Othello* and *Oroonoko*, but was prevented from doing so (78).
32. David Garrick, *Hamlet, Prince of Denmark: A Tragedy* (1772), Act II, scene II, ll. 91; 95–7, in *The Plays of David Garrick*, ed. Harry William Pedicord and Frederick Louis Bergman, vol. 4: *Garrick's Adaptations of Shakespeare, 1759–1773* (Carbondale: Southern Illinois University Press, 1981) (hereafter cited in the text as *Ham.*).
33. E.H. Gombrich, "Imagery and Art in the Romantic Period," *The Burlington Magazine* 91, no. 555 (1949): 157.
34. Intriguingly, Simon Gikandi highlights a letter dated July 23, 1751, that English slave captain (and subsequent clergyman and abolitionist) John Newton penned to his wife while aboard his vessel, in which Newton discusses David Garrick in the role of Hamlet. See Gikandi, *Slavery and the Culture of Taste* (Princeton, NJ: Princeton University Press, 2011), 81, on John Newton, *Journal of a Slave Trader, 1750–1754*, ed. Bernard Martin and Mark Sourrell (London: Epworth Press, 1962), 58. Additionally, twentieth-century commentators made associations between the issues discussed in *Hamlet* and transatlantic slavery. For example, American essayist John Jay Chapman compared Abraham Lincoln with the figure of Hamlet, aligning the "ghost of Hamlet's father, that spectre of impending retribution" with "the Slavery Question." He argued that the latter ghost "is always on the stage; and the drama of Lincoln's life consisted in this, that he could never frame a philosophy that would include the ghost" ("Lincoln and Hamlet," *The North American Review* 209, no. 760 [March 1919]: 371–9 [374]). David Scott has discussed at length the influence of the figure of Hamlet on Trinidadian author and historian C.L.R. James's narrative of the Haitian Revolution, *The Black Jacobins: Toussaint L'Ouverture and the San Domingo Revolution* (1938; rev. 1963). For Scott, James's Toussaint, riffing on Shakespeare's Hamlet, "inaugurates a new kind of individual, the modern colonial individual" (*Conscripts of Modernity: The Tragedy of Colonial Enlightenment* [Durham, NC: Duke University Press, 2004], 20).

35. Grigsby, *Extremities*, 18.
36. John Brewer, "'This Monstrous Tragi-comic Scene': British Reactions to the French Revolution," in *The Shadow of the Guillotine: Britain and the French Revolution*, ed. David Bindman with Aileen Dawson and Mark Jones (London: Published for the Trustees of the British Museum by British Museum Publications, 1989), 12.
37. Molineux also notes this reversal (*Faces of Perfect Ebony*, 244–5).
38. Dent already had responded to Sharp and Equiano's Sierra Leone resettlement plan for black people in Britain with *The Poor Blacks Going to Their Settlement* (January 12, 1787), which also mocks the fall of the Fox-North coalition government.
39. Katherine Hart notes the associations of devils with black men in eighteenth-century visual culture ("James Gillray, Charles James Fox, and the Abolition of the Slave Trade: Caricature and Displacement in the Debate over Reform," in *No Laughing Matter: Visual Humor in Ideas of Race, Nationality, and Ethnicity*, ed. Angela Rosenthal and David Bindman [Hanover: Dartmouth College Press, 2015], 90).
40. Edmund Burke, *Reflections on the Revolution in France*, 2nd ed. (London: Printed for J. Dodsley, 1790), 52.
41. Ibid., 72–3.
42. David Bindman, "Introduction," Bindman, ed., *The Shadow of the Guillotine*, 27.
43. Jean-Baptiste Du Tertre, *Histoire Generale des Antilles Habitées par les François* (Paris: T. Iolly, 1667), 2:522.
44. See Hart, "James Gillray," 85, on the potential "sublimation" of slavery and the slave trade in this and related prints.
45. Hesiod, *Theogony*, in *Works and Days and Theogony*, trans. Stanley Lombardo (Indianapolis, IN: Hackett Publishing, 1993), lines 180–5.
46. Pythia to Apollo, in Aeschylus, *The Eumenides*, in *The Oresteia: Agamemnon; The Libation Bearers; The Eumenides*, ed. W.B. Stanford, trans. Robert Fagles (1977; New York: Penguin Classics, 1984), line 57.
47. Ibid., l. 263.
48. See also Hart, "James Gillray," 99.
49. Ibid., 97. Hart also notes that, in *Reflections*, Burke deployed "the image of the Furies [...] in his description of the mob's attack on the royal residence at Versailles" (94).
50. Hart, "James Gillray," 100.
51. Hart suggests that the Tory party financed the print ("James Gillray," 77).
52. Hart, "James Gillray," 86.
53. Just over two months earlier, Gillray had published one of relatively few prints depicting black slavery, *Barbarities in the West Indias* [sic] (April 23, 1791). Hart focuses on Fox's support of the abolition of the slave trade ("James Gillray," 77), but I suggest that the print's concerns are much broader.
54. Hart, "James Gillray," 87.
55. Hart writes that "Fox was often depicted as Lucifer or as a demonic figure in satirical prints, or as a particularly hairy and disheveled *sans-culotte*" ("James Gillray," emphasis in original, 97–8), but I propose that hair also hints at *race*—and racial "contamination"—in these depictions.
56. Hart, "James Gillray," 98.
57. For an overview of the August 22, 1791 revolt and its aftermath, see Carolyn E. Fick, *The Making of Haiti: The Saint Domingue Revolution from Below* (Knoxville: University of Tennessee Press, 1990), 91–117.
58. Fick, *The Making of Haiti*, 111; cited in Grigsby, *Extremities*, 18.

59. For the debate context, see Mary Dorothy George and the British Museum Department of Prints and Drawings, *Catalogue of Political and Personal Satires in the British Museum*, vol. 6 (1784–92) (London: By order of the Trustees, 1938).
60. For the identification of these individuals and the "fool's bell," see George, *Catalogue of Political and Personal Satires*, vol. 7 (1793–1800) (London: by order of the Trustees, 1942).
61. In *Vénus Physique* (1745), French naturalist and philosopher Pierre-Louis Moreau de Maupertuis considered "White Negroes" (black people with albinism) and proposed that "it is most likely that the difference between whiteness and blackness, which is so apparent in our eyes, is but a slight thing in nature" (*The Earthly Venus*, ed. George Boas, trans. Simone Brangier Boas [New York: Johnson Reprint Corporation, 1966], 76–7).
62. For the painting as a "double portrait," see Grigsby, *Extremities*, 38.
63. For Belley's and other enslaved men's "freedom" and power through French military service, see Grigsby, *Extremities*, 25–7.
64. Grigsby, *Extremities*, 13.
65. Ibid., 19.
66. Ibid., 40.
67. Through the notion of the "contact zone," Mary Louise Pratt considers colonial relations "in terms of co-presence, interaction, [and] interlocking understandings and practices" that play out "within radically asymmetrical relations of power" (*Imperial Eyes: Travel Writing and Transculturation*, 2nd ed. [1992; New York: Routledge, 2007], 8). Pratt's approach is geographic, but I am proposing hair itself as a contact zone, a fraught terrain in which relations are (re)styled.

Chapter 8

1. James Stewart, *Plocacosmos, or, The Whole Art of Hair Dressing* (London: Printed for the Author, 1782), 205. On Garrick and wigs, see Joseph Roach's famous description of the actor literally flipping his (hydraulic) wig as Hamlet (*The Player's Passion: Studies in the Science of Acting* [Ann Arbor: University of Michigan Press, 1993], 58).
2. Ainsworth's bestselling romance of Jack Sheppard's life, evidently thinking of Thornhill's portrait, made a point of the titular him refusing all his life to wear a wig and preferring his own close-cropped hair.
3. *The London Journal*, November 7, 1724.
4. Marcia Pointon, *Hanging the Head: Portraiture and Social Formation in Eighteenth-Century England* (New Haven, CT: Yale University Press, 1993), 107.
5. See Ibid., 125–6.
6. Margaret K. Powell and Joseph Roach, "Big Hair," *Eighteenth-Century Studies* 38, no. 1 (2004): 80.
7. In Erin Mackie, *Rakes, Highwaymen, and Pirates: The Makings of the Modern Gentleman in the Eighteenth Century* (Baltimore: Johns Hopkins University Press, 2009), Erin Mackie argues that there is a strong division between Sheppard and Macheath, that while Macheath is a continuation of a seventeenth-century model of gallant criminal given an eighteenth-century political update, Sheppard's "mob appeal" is much more rooted in the working population and his artisanal background and abilities (31). It was the increasing presence of British labor unrest that assured Sheppard's continued popularity. Taking her point that gentlemen were not much influenced by Sheppard's example, I nonetheless think it true that his defiance of prescribed social boundaries was a key factor in his mass popularity.

8. Lynn Festa, "Personal Effects: Wigs and Possessive Individualism in the Long Eighteenth Century," *Eighteenth-Century Life* 29, no. 2 (Spring 2005): 70–2.
9. Samuel Pepys, *The Diary of Samuel Pepys*, ed. Henry B. Wheatley (London: George Bell & Sons, 1893).
10. This wig appeared shortly, and was curiously enough more dear than the first wig made of strangers' hair. "After dinner came my perriwigg-maker, and brings me a second periwigg, made of my own haire, which comes to 21s. 6d. more than the worth of my own haire, so that they both come to 4l. 1s. 6d., which he sayth will serve me two years, but I fear it" (Pepys, *The Diary of Samuel Pepys*, November 13, 1663).
11. Other authors in this collection have more thoroughly explored the issue of hygiene, but—not to be facetious—it seems worth a quick note that the choice to wear one's own hair could be very much a choice for or against one's own comfort, depending on one's access to washing. In its "practical Directions for Hair-Dressing," *The Duties of a Ladies Maid* warns, "Some people have a strong prejudice against washing the hair, and imagine that it is productive of very serious evils. Were this prejudice confined to the ignorant and illiterate, I might pass it over without notice." But on the contrary, "When the hair is very long, or when much use is made of hair oils and pomatum, I cannot imagine how hair can be rendered comfortable without frequently washing it" (*The Duties of a Lady's Maid; with Directions for Conduct, and Numerous Receipts for the Toilette* [1825; London: Chawton House Press, 2015], 233). Indeed.
12. It has long been a commonplace that the consumer revolution of the eighteenth century required massive, even formative, female participation; more recently, scholars such as Margot Finn and John Bohstedt have begun to push back against the assumption that men were not also major consumers: "the Hanoverian consumer market included highly acquisitive men as well as compulsively possessive women," and this included ranks of shopkeepers, schoolteachers, and clergymen rather than being limited to the fine and fashionable elites. See Margot Finn, "Men's Things: Masculine Possession in the Consumer Revolution," *Social History* 25, no. 2 (May 2000): 135.
13 Don Herzog, "The Trouble with Hairdressers," *Representations* no. 53 (Winter 1996): 23.
14. Michael Kwass, "Big Hair: A Wig History of Consumption in Eighteenth-Century France," *The American Historical Review* 111, no. 3 (June 2006): 645; Festa, "Personal Effects," 53. It is far less clear that this would extend to women wearing hairpieces, however; Kwass suggests that, broadly speaking, the argument regarding convenience in hairstyles did extend to women (651 n. 87).
15. Kwass, "Big Hair," 653. Kwass begins his piece by recalling Rousseau's famous vow of poverty and reform, which he curiously enacted by renouncing "all finery" of fashion or dress, and swapping out his regular wig for a simple round one (Kwass, "Big Hair," 631). Why, asks Kwass, didn't he just wear his own hair?
16. Festa, "Personal Effects," 68.
17. Ibid., 65–6.
18. Powell and Roach, "Big Hair," 92.
19. Herzog, "The Trouble with Hairdressers," 21–2. He also advances the interesting theory that the barber's shop should be weighed as "an exemplary site of political discussion" to rival the Habermasian coffeehouse. Running with the Revolutionary topic, the nineteenth-century *Duties of a Lady's Maid* educates its reader that late-century "women soon began to erect magnificent edifices upon their heads. But, alas! the empire of fashion, like all other empires, is subject to violent revolutions. A single day was sufficient to destroy a head-dress—to demolish a Bastile!"(211).

20. *Duties*, 200–1.
21. Ibid., 251.
22. Neil McKendrick, John Brewer, and J.H. Plumb, *The Birth of a Consumer Society: The Commercialization of Eighteenth-Century England* (Bloomington: Indiana University Press, 1982), 146.
23. Graham Midgley, *University Life in Eighteenth-Century Oxford* (New Haven, CT: Yale University Press, 1996), 28–9.
24. *God's Dealings with the Reverend George Whitefield*, quoted in Midgley, *University Life in Eighteenth-Century Oxford*, 9; see also Midgley, *University Life in Eighteenth-Century Oxford*, 14–15.
25. John Woodforde, *The Strange Story of False Hair* (London: Routledge and Kegan Paul, 1971), 54.
26. Ibid., 36.
27. Ibid., 32. In the Royal Navy, uniforms were not especially uniform in the eighteenth century, at least until its final years: sailors traditionally wore slops, but their appearance varied widely from ship to ship, even among officers. The first uniform for officers was not instituted until 1748, and it was abolished in 1767 (Robert Wilkinson-Latham, *The Royal Navy 1790–1970* [London: Osprey Publishing, 1977], 4). In 1869, beards were first officially permitted for the "health and comfort of the men" irritated by their at-sea shaves—provided they also wore mustaches and kept it all neatly trimmed (Wilkinson-Latham, *The Royal Navy 1790–1970*, 16–17).
28. Aileen Ribiero, *Dress in Eighteenth-Century Europe, 1715–1789* (New York: Holmes & Meier Publishers, 1985), 94.
29. Woodforde, *The Strange Story of False Hair*, 37.
30. Powell and Roach, "Big Hair," 83.
31. Quoted in Gwenda Morgan and Peter Rushton, *Eighteenth-Century Criminal Transportation: The Formation of the Criminal Atlantic* (New York: Palgrave Macmillan, 2004), 46.
32. *The Proceedings of the Old Bailey, 1674–1913*, Reference No. t16920629-4, https://www.oldbaileyonline.org/ (accessed September 12, 2016).
33. *Old Bailey*, Reference No. t17280828-45.
34. Red hair was generally disliked; men covered it with wigs or dyed their hair with lead-based dyes (Ribiero, *Dress in Eighteenth-Century Europe*, 96). Judas Iscariot was said to be red-bearded. See Paull Franklin Baum, "Judas's Red Hair," *The Journal of English and Germanic Philology* 21, no. 3 (1922): 520–9.
35. *Old Bailey*, Reference No. t16910422-6.
36. *Old Bailey*, Reference No. t16960227-44.
37. Morgan and Rushton, *Eighteenth-Century Criminal Transportation*, 115–16.
38. Ibid., 115–16.
39. Allan Peterkin, *One Thousand Beards: A Cultural History of Facial Hair* (Vancouver: Arsenal Pulp Press, 2001), 34.
40. Peterkin, *One Thousand Beards*, 33, 34.
41. Angela Rosenthal, "Raising Hair," *Eighteenth-Century Studies* 38, no. 1 (Fall 2004): 2.
42. Quoted in Herzog, "The Trouble with Hairdressers," 24.
43. Rosenthal, "Raising Hair," 2.
44. Another paradox of the beard is that it is sometimes cultivated as an important status symbol in cultures that otherwise eschew body hair, such as among ancient Egyptians (Peterkin, *One Thousand Beards*, 17).

45. Londa Schiebinger, *Nature's Body: Gender in the Making of Modern Science* (New Brunswick, NJ: Rutgers University Press, 1993), 120.
46. Ibid., 125.
47. Ribiero, *Dress in Eighteenth-Century Europe*, 75.
48. Rosenthal, "Raising Hair," 3; Peterkin, *One Thousand Beards*, 33.
49. Ribiero, *Dress in Eighteenth-Century Europe*, 76. Outside of Moscow and St. Petersburg, however, beards seem to have remained common for commoners, for the practical reason that they were warmer in the cold Russian winters (Ribiero, *Dress in Eighteenth-Century Europe*, 78).
50. Woodforde, *The Strange Story of False Hair*, 28.
51. Ibid., 99.
52. A Ramillies wig, popular in the military for its practicality, featured a long pigtail tied at its top and bottom with black ribbon. The queue could easily be doubled up and tied to keep it at regulation length and out of the way.
53. Charles Johnson, *A General History of the Pyrates*, ed. Manuel Schonhorn (Mineola, NY: Dover Publications, 1999), 84–5.
54. See, for example, Ian McShane's version of the character in *Pirates of the Caribbean: On Stranger Tides* (Dir. Rob Marshall, 2011).
55. Ibid., 84.
56. Another Barbarossa, the Holy Roman Emperor Frederick I "Barbarossa" (1155–1190: so nicknamed for his conquest of areas in northern Italy), reputedly levied a large fine against any man who plucked a hair from another man's face or head (Schiebinger, *Nature's Body*, 121).
57. Powell and Roach, "Big Hair," 87.
58. Festa, "Personal Effects," 60.
59. Dror Wahrman, *The Making of the Modern Self: Identity and Culture in Eighteenth-Century England* (New Haven, CT: Yale University Press, 2006), 21–8.
60. Woodforde, *The Strange Story of False Hair*, 25, 26.
61. Festa, "Personal Effects," 52.
62. Frances Burney, *Evelina*, ed. Margaret Anne Doody (New York: Penguin, 1994), 167.
63. Penny Howell Jolly, *Hair: Untangling a Social History* (Saratoga Springs, NY: Skidmore College Art Gallery, 2004), 47.
64. *Old Bailey*, Reference No. t17220112-3.
65. Sally O'Driscoll remarks of this image that long hair is "an ambiguous sign of gender," but still identifies it as their most obviously feminine attribute in this image (as compared to the bare-breasted Dutch 1725 version with which the 1724 English engraving is typically contrasted). See Sally O'Driscoll, "The Pirate's Breasts: Criminal Women and the Meanings of the Body," *The Eighteenth Century* 53, no. 3 (2012): 359.
66. Festa, "Personal Effects," 56–7.
67. Woodforde, *The Strange Story of False Hair*, 48–9.
68. Ibid., 48.
69. Though there was a key difference: in the 1760s, upper-class men subjected themselves to extremes of hairdressing to make their hair approximate the glory of the rejected wig, whereas by the turn of the nineteenth century, men were simply favoring easier hairstyles.
70. The tax made hair powder offensive to many for political reasons; for others, hair powder, a luxury largely made of flour, was "a sign of callous indifference to the nation's poor" (Festa, "Personal Effects," 81).

Chapter 9

1. David Hume, *Dialogues Concerning Natural Religion* (1779), ed. J.C.A. Gaskin (Oxford: Oxford University Press, 1993), 60.
2. Joseph Roach and Margaret K. Powell, "Big Hair," *Eighteenth-Century Studies* 38, no. 1 (2004): 80.
3. Ibid., 81.
4. Hume, *Dialogues*, 161.
5. Ibid., 161–2.
6. Alexander Pope, "Essay on Man," in *The Twickenham Edition of the Poems of Alexander Pope*, ed. John Butt et al. (New Haven, CT: Yale University Press, 1939–1969), 3:48.
7. James Boswell, *Boswell's Edinburgh Journals 1767–1786*, ed. Hugh M. Milne (Edinburgh: Mercat Press, 2001), 256.
8. Ibid.
9. Ibid.
10. Ibid., 257.
11. Ibid.
12. Boswell knew how to ask for a lock of hair, although he was more accustomed to asking his love interests for the favor. He badgered Catherine Blaire and Anna Seward for locks of their hair. Catherine Blaire refused. See Peter Martin, *A Life of James Boswell* (New Haven, CT: Yale University Press, 2000), 241. Anna Seward sent hers along bound in a pink ribbon, but she included a short poem that directly refused Boswell's romantic overtures: "By Boswell's hand be the light lock enwove / But never with the dangerous Rose of Love"! See Teresa Barnard, *Anna Seward: A Constructed Life* (New York: Routledge, 2009), 138.
13. I am grateful for the assistance offered by Ralph McLean, Scott Docking, Iain Gordon Brown, and Vicki Hammond for their advice and their work in searching for records and specimens of Hume's hair in the National Library of Scotland, the New College Special Collections at the University of Edinburgh, and the Royal Society of Edinburgh.
14. Edward Bulwer-Lytton, *A Strange Story* (London: S. Low, 1862), 62.
15. Ibid., 467.
16. Ibid.
17. Ibid., 363.
18. Ibid., 360.
19. Ibid., 360–3.
20. Ibid., 467.
21. Ibid., 469.
22. Ibid.
23. Ibid.
24. Ibid., 470.
25. Ibid., 471.
26. Ibid., 460. See also Elizabeth Tucker, *Children's Folklore: A Handbook* (London: Greenwood, 2008), 89–90.
27. Bulwer-Lytton, *A Strange Story*, 469.

28. Ibid., 469–70.
29. Samantha Frost, *Biocultural Creatures* (Durham, NC: Duke University Press, 2016), 26.
30. Ibid., 27.
31. Ibid., 25.
32. Cesare Ripa, *Iconologia: or, Moral Emblems* (London: B. Motte, 1709), 20 (emphases in the original). This early English edition of an Italian work was first published in Rome (1593) without illustrations.
33. Ibid.
34. Caroline Levine, *Forms: Whole, Rhythm, Hierarchy, Network* (Princeton, NJ: Princeton University Press, 2015), 6.
35. Walter Benjamin, "The Storyteller: Reflections on the Works of Nikolai Leskov," in *Illuminations*, ed. Hannah Arendt, trans. Harry Zohn (New York: Schocken Books, 1968), 89.
36. *Aristotle's Book of Problems*, 25th ed. (London, 1710), 2.
37. Ibid.
38. Ibid., 3.
39. Ibid.
40. Ibid., 7.
41. Victor Turner, *The Ritual Process: Structure and Anti-Structure* (1969; London: Transaction Publishers, 2008), 111.
42. Ibid., 103.
43. Ibid., 128.
44. Thomas Gibson, *The Anatomy of Humane Bodies Epitomized* (London: T.W. for Awnsham and John Churchill, 1703), 366.
45. Ibid.
46. Ibid.
47. *Aristotle's Book of Problems*, 5.
48. Ibid.
49. Gibson, *Anatomy*, 365–6.
50. Ibid., 368 (emphases in the original).
51. Robert Hooke, *Micrographia* (1665) (facsimile repr., Lincolnwood: Science Heritage Limited, 1987), 157.
52. Ibid.
53. Other schemas that represent several experiments are intuitively grouped and frequently depict congruent observational experiments. For example, Schema 2 represents a needle, period, and a razor—the subjects of Observations I and II—and all clearly designed to illustrate the microscope's impressive, if basic, function of magnification. Schema 4 represents observations IV and V, both of different types of silk.
54. Hooke, *Micrographia*, 80.
55. Ibid., 46.
56. Ibid., 161–2 (emphasis in the original).
57. Donald F. Bond, ed., *The Spectator* (Oxford: Oxford University Press, 1965), 1:220.
58. Ibid.
59. Ibid.
60. Ibid.
61. Ibid.
62. Jeremiah Wells, *Poems on Divers Occasions* (London: Printed for John Crosley, 1667), 1.

63. Ibid., 3. I am grateful for the assistance of Stewart Tiley at St. John's College, Oxford, for information about this portrait.
64. Johnson's gloss from Locke is as follows: "Shall the difference of *hair* only, on the skin, be a mark of a different internal constitution between a changeling and a drill." See Samuel Johnson, *A Dictionary of the English Language*, 2nd ed. (London: Printed for J. Knapton et al., 1756), 1:958.
65. John Locke, *Essay Concerning Human Understanding*, ed. Peter H. Nidditch (Oxford: Clarendon Press, 1975), 450–1.
66. Nehemia Grew, *Musæum Regalis Societatis* (1681; London: Printed for Thomas Malthus, 1685), 8–9.
67. *A Catalogue of the Rarities to be Seen at Don Saltero's Coffee-House in Chelsea* (London, 1731), 9.
68. *A Catalogue of the Rarities to be Seen at Don Saltero's Coffee-House and Tavern in Chelsea* (London, 1795), 8.
69. *A Catalogue of the Rarities to be Seen at Adams's*, 3rd ed. (London, 1756), 9.
70. Ibid., 6 and 9.
71. Ibid., 8.
72. Ibid., 13.
73. Thomas Hearne, *The History and Antiquities of Glastonbury* (Oxford: Printed at the Theater, 1722), 58.
74. *The Trial of Charles I, King of England* (London, 1740), 260.
75. Ibid.
76. David Hume, *History of England*, ed. William B. Todd (Indianapolis, IN: Liberty Fund, 1983), 5:523.
77. See: Henry Halford, *An Account of What Appeared on Opening the Coffin of King Charles the First* (London: Nichols, Son, and Bentley, 1813). Although some of these locks were returned to the grave in 1888 with other "souvenirs"—which included a tooth and the vertebrae bearing the mark of the executioner's axe—a few remained in circulation and were sold in 1995 for £3,910.00 to the famous hair collector and connoisseur, John Reznikoff. Reznikoff did not respond to an email request for comments and information about the current location of the hair. See "A Little Off the Top for History," *New York Times*, July 13, 2008, http://www.nytimes.com/2008/07/13/fashion/13hair.html (accessed May 9, 2018), and "Lock of Charles I's Hair Sells for £3,910.00," *Independent*, April 6, 1995, http://www.independent.co.uk/news/uk/lock-of-charles-is-hair-sells-for-1633910-1614544.html (accessed May 9, 2018).
78. See the letterpress attached to plates VII, VIII, and IX in the third volume of *Vetusta Monumenta*.
79. Elizabeth Rawdon, "Particulars Relative to a Human Skeleton," *Archaeologia* 7 (1785): 90–110.
80. A representative example can be found in Francis Grose, *The Antiquities of England and Wales* (London, 1773), 3:10.
81. Benjamin, "The Storyteller," 148.
82. Ibid., 94.
83. Ibid., 97.
84. Ibid., 107.
85. Ibid., 96.
86. Alexander Pope, *The Rape of the Lock,* in Butt et al., eds., *The Twickenham Edition of the Poems of Alexander Pope*, 2:142.

BIBLIOGRAPHY

Abelove, Henry. *The Evangelist of Desire: John Wesley and the Methodists.* Stanford, CA: Stanford University Press, 1990.
"An Act to Prevent the Exportation of Wool ...." In *Great Britain. The Statutes of the Realm.* 11 vols. London: Printed by George Eyre and Andrew Strahan, printers to the King, 1810–1828. 7: 524–8.
Adams, George. *An Essay on Electricity.* London: R. Hindsmith, 1792.
Addison, Joseph. *The Spectator.* Edited by Donald F. Bond. 5 vols. Oxford: Clarendon Press, 1965.
Aeschylus. "The Eumenides." In *The Oresteia: Agamemnon; The Libation Bearers; The Eumenides.* 1977. Edited by W.B. Stanford. Translated by Robert Fagles. New York: Penguin Classics, 1984.
Aitken, John. *Principles of Anatomy and Physiology.* 2 vols. London: J. Murray, 1786.
Alaimo, Stacy, and Susan Hekman, eds. *Material Feminisms.* Bloomington: Indiana University Press, 2008.
Albin, Eleazar. *A Natural History of English Insects.* London: Printed for the Author, 1720.
Albin, Eleazar. *A Natural History of Birds.* London: Printed for the Author, 1734.
Allewaert, Monique. *Ariel's Ecology: Plantations, Personhood, and Colonialism in the American Tropics.* Minneapolis: University of Minnesota Press, 2013.
Amussen, Susan Dwyer. *An Ordered Society: Gender and Class in Early Modern England.* New York: Columbia University Press, 1993.
Anderson, Misty G. *Female Playwrights and Eighteenth-Century Comedy: Negotiating Marriage on the London Stage.* New York: Palgrave, 2002.
Anstey, Christopher. *The New Bath Guide: Or, Memoirs of the B-r-d family. In a Series of Poetical Epistles.* 5th ed. London: Printed for J. Dodsley and Fletcher and Hodson, 1767.
Anstey, Peter. *John Locke and Natural Philosophy.* Oxford: Oxford University Press, 2011.
Aravamudan, Srinivas. "Subjects/Sovereigns/Rogues." *Eighteenth-Century Studies* 40, no. 3 (2007): 457–65.
Aristotle. *Aristotle's Book of Problems.* 25th ed. London, 1710.
Arnauld, Antoine and Pierre Nicole. *Logic or the Art of Thinking.* Edited by Jill Vance Buroker. Cambridge: Cambridge University Press, 1996.
Arnold, Janet. *Perukes and Periwigs.* London: Her Majesty's Stationery Office (National Portrait Gallery), 1970.
Austen, R.A., and W.D. Smith. "Private Tooth Decay as Public Economic Virtue: The Slave-Sugar Triangle, Consumerism and European Industrialization." *Social Science History* 14 (1990): 95–115.
Ayers, Michael. *Locke.* 2 vols. London: Routledge, 1991.
Banchetti-Robino, Marina Paola. "The Ontological Function of First-Order and Second-Order Corpuscles in the Chemical Philosophy of Robert Boyle: The Redintegration of Potassium Nitrate." *Foundations of Chemistry* 14, no. 3 (2012): 221–34.
Barad, Karen. *Meeting the Universe Halfway: Quantum Physics and the Entanglement of Matter and Meaning.* Durham, NC: Duke University Press, 2007.
Barber, E.J.W. *Prehistoric Textiles.* Princeton, NJ: Princeton University Press, 1991.

Barker, William. *A Treatise on the Principles of Hair-dressing*. London: J. Rozea, ca. 1785.
Barnard, Teresa. *Anna Seward: A Constructed Life*. New York: Routledge, 2009.
Barrell, John. *The Spirit of Despotism: Invasions of Privacy in the 1790s*. Oxford: Oxford University Press, 2006.
Bashar, Nazife. "Rape in England between 1550 and 1700." In *The Sexual Dynamics of History: Men's Power, Women's Resistance*. Edited by London Feminist History Group, 28–46. London: Pluto, 1983.
Baum, Paull Franklin. "Judas's Red Hair." *The Journal of English and Germanic Philology* 21, no. 3 (1922): 520–9.
Beaumont, Roberts. *Woollen and Worsted: The Theory and Technology of the Manufacture of Woollen, Worsted, and Union Yarns and Fabrics*. London: G. Bell, 1920.
Behn, Aphra. *Oroonoko*. Edited by Janet Todd. London: Penguin Classics, 2004.
Bellamy, George Anne. *An Apology for the Life of George Anne Bellamy*. 4th ed. 5 vols. London: J. Bell, 1786.
Belsey, Catherine. *John Milton: Language, Gender, Power*. Oxford: Blackwell, 1988.
Benedict, Barbara. "Death and the Object: The Abuse of Things in *The Rape of the Lock*." In *Anniversary Essays on Alexander Pope's* The Rape of the Lock. Edited by Donald W. Nichol, 131–49. Toronto: University of Toronto Press, 2016.
Benjamin, Walter. *Illuminations*. Edited by Hannah Arendt. Translated by Harry Zohn. New York: Schocken Books, 1968.
Benjamin, Walter. *The Arcades Project*. Translated by Howard Eiland. Cambridge: Belknap Press, 2002.
Bennett, Jane. *Vibrant Matter: A Political Ecology of Things*. Durham, NC: Duke University Press, 2010.
Berg, Charles. *The Unconscious Significance of Hair*. London: Allen & Unwin, 1951.
Berg, Maxine. *Luxury and Pleasure in Eighteenth-Century Britain*. Oxford: Oxford University Press, 2005.
Bewell, Alan. "Erasmus Darwin's Cosmopolitan Nature." *ELH* 76, no. 1 (2009): 19–48.
Biddle-Perry, Geraldine, and Sarah Cheang, eds. *Hair: Styling, Culture, and Fashion*. Oxford: Berg, 2008.
Bindman, David, Aileen Dawson, and Mark Jones, eds. *The Shadow of the Guillotine: Britain and the French Revolution*. With contribution by John Brewer. London: Published for the Trustees of the British Museum by British Museum Publications, 1989.
Boantza, Victor D. *Matter and Method in the Long Chemical Revolution: Laws of Another Order*. London: Routledge, 2016.
Bobbin, Tim [John Collier]. *The Battle of the Flying Dragon and the Man of Heaton*. Manchester: Printed for the Author, 1775.
Boreman, Thomas. *A Description of a Great Variety of Animals and Vegetables*. London: John Tilly, 1736.
Boswell, James. *Life of Johnson*. Edited by R.W. Chapman. Rev. ed. Oxford: Oxford University Press, 1985.
Boswell, James. *Boswell's Edinburgh Journals 1767–1786*. Edited by Hugh M. Milne. Edinburgh: Mercat Press, 2001.
Boyle, Robert. *Origine of Formes and Qualities*. Oxford: H. Hall, 1667.
Boyle, Robert. *Works of the Honourable Robert Boyle*. Edited by Thomas Birch. 5 vols. London: Printed by A. Millar, 1744.
Brewer, John. "'This Monstrous Tragi-Comic Scene': British Reactions to the French Revolution." In *The Shadow of the Guillotine: Britain and the French Revolution*. Edited

by David Bindman, with Aileen Dawson and Mark Jones, 9–25. London: Published for the Trustees of the British Museum by British Museum Publications, 1989.

Brewer, John. *The Pleasures of the Imagination: English Culture in the Eighteenth Century*. London: Routledge, 1997.

Brooks, Cleanth. *The Well-Wrought Urn: Studies in the Structure of Poetry*. San Diego, CA: Harcourt, Brace, and Company, 1975.

Brown, Laura. *Alexander Pope*. Oxford: Basil Blackwell, 1985.

Brown, Laura. *The Ends of Empire: Women and Ideology in Early Eighteenth-Century English Literature*. Ithaca, NY: Cornell University Press, 1993.

Browne, Peter A. *The Classification of Mankind, by the Hair and Wool of Their Heads: With an Answer to Dr. Prichard's Assertion, That "the Covering of the Head of the Negro Is Hair, Properly so Termed, and Not Wool": Read before the American Ethnological Society, November 3, 1849*. Philadelphia, PA: A. Hart, 1850.

Browne, Thomas. *Pseudodoxia Epidemica*. London: Thomas Harper, 1646.

Buffon, Georges Louis Leclerc, Comte de. *The Natural History of Animals, Vegetables, and Minerals*. Translated by W. Kenrick and J. Murdoch. 6 vols. London: Printed for T. Bell, 1775–1776.

Bulwer, John. *Anthropometamorphosis, Man Transform'd: or, the Artificiall Changling*. London: William Hunt, 1653.

Bulwer-Lytton, Edward. *A Strange Story*. 2 vols. London: S. Low, 1862.

Burke, Edmund. *Reflections on the Revolution in France*. 2nd ed. London: Printed for J. Dodsley, 1790.

Burney, Frances. *Evelina; or the History of a Young Lady's Entrance into the World*. Edited by Margaret Anne Doody. New York: Penguin, 1994.

Burney, Frances. *Evelina; or the History a Young Lady's Entrance into the World*. Edited by Edward Bloom. Introduction by Vivien Jones. Oxford: Oxford University Press, 2008.

Bush-Bailey, Gilli. *Treading the Bawds: Actresses and Playwrights on the Late Stuart Stage*. Manchester: Manchester University Press, 2006.

Butler, Judith. *Gender Trouble: Feminism and the Subversion of Identity*. New York: Routledge, 1999.

Calhoun, Craig, ed. *Habermas and the Public Sphere*. Cambridge, MA: MIT Press, 1993.

Campbell, R. *The London Tradesman*. London: T. Gardner, 1747.

Campbell, Timothy. *Historical Style: Fashion and the New Mode of History, 1740–1830*. Philadelphia: University of Pennsylvania Press, 2016.

Castle, Terry, ed. *The Literature of Lesbianism: A Historical Anthology from Ariosto to Stonewall*. New York: Columbia University Press, 2003.

A Catalogue of the Rarities to be Seen at Adams's. 3rd ed. London, 1756.

A Catalogue of the Rarities to be Seen at Don Saltero's Coffee-House in Chelsea. London, 1731.

A Catalogue of the Rarities to be Seen at Don Saltero's Coffee-House and Tavern in Chelsea. London, 1795.

Cennick, John. *An Account of a Late Riot at Exeter*. London: J. Hart, 1745.

Chapman, John Jay. "Lincoln and Hamlet." *The North American Review* 209, no. 760 (March 1919): 371–9.

"Character of a Macaroni." *The Town and Country Magazine, or Universal Repository* 4. London: Printed for A. Hamilton, 1772.

Charke, Charlotte. *A Narrative of the Life of Mrs. Charlotte Charke*. London: Printed for W. Reeve, A. Dodd, and E. Cook, 1755.

Charke, Charlotte. *A Narrative of the Life of Mrs. Charlotte Charke*. Edited by Robert Rehder. London: Pickering and Chatto, 1999.

Chico, Tita. "The Arts of Beauty: Women's Cosmetics and Pope's Ekphrasis." *Eighteenth-Century Life* 26, no. 1 (2002): 1–23.
Chico, Tita. *Designing Women: The Dressing Room in Eighteenth-Century English Literature and Culture*. Lewisburg, PA: Bucknell University Press, 2005.
Christian, Barbara. "The Race for Theory." *Cultural Critique* no. 6 (1987): 51–63.
Cibber, Colley. *An Apology for the Life of Colley Cibber: With an Historical View of the Stage During His Own Time*. Edited by B.R.S. Fone. Ann Arbor: University of Michigan Press, 1968.
Clabburn, Pamela. *Furnishing Textiles*. New York: Viking, 1988.
Cleland, John. *Memoirs of a Woman of Pleasure*. Edited by Peter Sabor. Oxford: Oxford University Press, 1985.
Cockayne, Emily. *Hubbub: Filth, Noise and Stench in England 1660–1770*. New Haven, CT: Yale University Press, 2007.
Colebrook, Claire. "On Not Becoming Man: The Materialist Politics of Unactualized Potential." In *Material Feminisms*. Edited by Alaimo and Hekman, 52–84.
Colman, George. "Prologue." In David Garrick. *Bon Ton; Or, High Life above Stairs*. Dublin: H. Camberlaine, 1785.
Coma Berenices; or, the Hairy Comet. London: Printed for Jonathan Robinson and John Hancock, 1676.
The Complete Vermin-Killer. 3rd ed. London: Fielding and Walker, 1777.
Coole, Diana, and Samantha Frost, eds. *New Materialisms: Ontology, Agency and Politics*. Durham, NC: Duke University Press, 2010.
Corson, Richard. *Fashions in Hair: The First Five Thousand Years*. Revised ed. London: Peter Owen, 2001.
Cowper, William. *The Letters and Prose Writings of William Cowper*. Edited by James King and Charles Ryskamp. 5 vols. Oxford: Clarendon, 1979–1986.
Crawford, Matthew B. *The World beyond Your Head: On Becoming an Individual in an Age of Distraction*. New York: Farrar, Strauss, and Giroux, 2015.
Crehan, Stewart. "*The Rape of the Lock* and the Economy of 'Trivial Things.'" *Eighteenth-Century Studies* 31, no. 1 (1997): 45–68.
Cross, Louisa. "Fashionable Hair in the Eighteenth Century: Theatricality and Display." In *Hair: Styling, Culture and Fashion*. Edited by Biddle-Perry and Cheang, 15–26.
Curtin, Philip D. *The Rise and Fall of the Plantation Complex: Essays in Atlantic History*. Cambridge: Cambridge University Press, 1984.
Darby, William Dermot. *Wool: The World's Comforter*. New York: Dry Goods Economist, 1922.
Darwin, Erasmus. *The Botanic Garden: A Poem in Two Parts*. London: Printed for J. Johnson, 1791.
De Courtais, Georgine. *Women's Headdress and Hairstyles in England from AD 600 to the Present Day*. Rev. ed. London: Batsford, 1986.
De Vries, Jan. *The Industrious Revolution: Consumer Behavior and the Household Economy, 1650 to the Present*. Cambridge: Cambridge University Press, 2008.
De Zemler, Charles. *Once over Lightly: The Story of Man and His Hair*. New York, 1939.
Deane, Phyllis. "Output of the British Woolen Industry in the Eighteenth Century." *Journal of Economic History* 17, no. 2 (1957): 207–23.
Defoe, Daniel. *A Plan of the English Commerce*. London: Printed for Charles Rivington, 1730.
Defoe, Daniel. *Robinson Crusoe*. Edited by Michael Shinagel. 2nd ed. New York: W.W. Norton, 1993.

Deutsch, Helen. *Resemblance and Disgrace: Alexander Pope and the Deformation of Culture.* Cambridge, MA: Harvard University Press, 1996.
Diderot, Denis, and Jean le Rond d'Alembert, eds. *Encyclopédie, ou dictionnaire raisonné des sciences, des arts et des métiers, etc.* Chicago: University of Chicago and ARTFL Encyclopédie Project, Spring 2016.
Dobranski, Stephen B. "Clustering and Curling Locks: The Matter of Hair in *Paradise Lost*." *PMLA* 125, no. 2 (2010): 337–53.
Donald, Diana. *The Age of Caricature: Satirical Prints in the Age of George III.* New Haven, CT: Yale University Press, 1996.
Donaldson, John. *On the Use of Hair Powder.* 2nd ed. London: T. Cadell and W. Davis, 1795.
Du Tertre, Jean Baptiste. *Histoire Generale des Antilles Habitées par les François.* 4 vols. Paris: T. Iolly, 1667–1671.
Dulaure, Jacques-Antione. *Pogonologia, or, A Philosophical and Historical Essay on Beards.* Exeter: R. Thorn, 1786.
DuPont, Ann. "Captives of Colored Cloth: The Role of Cotton Trade Goods in the North Atlantic Slave Trade (1600–1808)." *Ars Textrina* 24 (1995): 177–83.
The Duties of a Lady's Maid; with Directions for Conduct, and Numerous Receipts for the Toilette. 1825. London: Chawton House Press, 2015.
Elias, Norbert. *The History of Manners.* Translated by Edmund Jephcott. New York: Pantheon Books, 1978.
English Periwig-Maker, An. *A Dissertation upon Head Dress, together with a Brief Vindication of High Coloured Hair and of those Ladies on Which it Grows.* London: Printed for J. Williams, 1767.
Erickson, Amy Louise. *Women and Property in Early Modern England.* London: Routledge, 1993.
Erickson, Peter. "Representations of Blacks and Blackness in the Renaissance." *Criticism* 35, no. 4 (1993): 499–527.
Erwin, Timothy. "William Hogarth and the Aesthetics of Nationalism." *Huntington Library Quarterly* 64 (2001): 383–410.
"An Essay on the Hair, with the Most Proper Methods of Dressing and Preserving It." In *The New London Toilet*, 96–103. London: Printed for Richardson and Urquhart, 1778.
Fawconer, Samuel. *An Essay on Modern Luxury.* London: Printed for James Fletcher and J. Robson, 1765.
"Female Head-gear. Later Eighteenth Century." *The Magazine of Art* no. 9 (1886): 427–43.
Festa, Lynn. "Personal Effects: Wigs and Possessive Individualism in the Long Eighteenth Century." *Eighteenth-Century Life* 29, no. 2 (2005): 47–90.
Fick, Carolyn E. *The Making of Haiti: The Saint Domingue Revolution from Below.* Knoxville: University of Tennessee Press, 1990.
Finn, Margot. "Men's Things: Masculine Possession in the Consumer Revolution." *Social History* 25, no. 2 (2000): 133–55.
Fisher, Will. "The Renaissance Beard: Masculinity in Early Modern England." *Renaissance Quarterly* 54, no. 1 (2001): 155–87.
Flügel, J.C. *The Psychology of Clothes.* London: Hogarth, 1930.
Focillon, Henri. *The Life of Forms in Art.* 1948. Translated by Charles Hogan and George Kubler. Cambridge, MA: MIT Press, 1996.
Folkenflik, Robert. "Gender, Genre, and Theatricality in the Autobiography of Charlotte Charke." In *Representations of the Self from the Renaissance to Romanticism.* Edited by Patrick Coleman, Jayne Lewis, and Jill Kowalik, 97–116. Cambridge: Cambridge University Press, 2000.

Frampton, Mary. *Journal of Mary Frampton from the Year 1779 until the Year 1846*. London: Sampson- Low, 1885.
Fraser, Nancy. "Rethinking the Public Sphere: A Contribution to the Critique of Actually Existing Democracy." *Social Text* no. 25/26 (1990): 56–80.
"The Friend to the Fair Sex. Chapter VI. On Dress." *The Lady's Magazine* 4. London: G. Robinson, December 1773, 637.
Frost, Samantha. *Biocultural Creatures*. Durham, NC: Duke University Press, 2016.
Garrick, David. *The Plays of David Garrick*. 4 vols. Edited by Harry William Pedicord and Frederick Louis Bergman. Carbondale: Southern Illinois University Press, 1981.
Gay, John. "Iolaus Restor'd to Youth." In *Ovid's Metamorphoses*. 2nd ed., 2 vols. Edited by Samuel Garth. London: Printed for J. Tonson, 1720.
Gay, John. *Fables*. London: J. Tonson and J. Watts, 1727.
Gay, John. *Letters of John Gay*. Edited by C.F. Burgess. Oxford: Clarendon, 1966.
Gelbart, Nina Rattner. "The Blonding of Charlotte Corday." *Eighteenth-Century Studies* 38, no. 1 (2004): 201–21.
George, M. Dorothy, ed. *Catalogue of Political and Personal Satires in the Department of Prints and Drawings in the British Museum*. Vols. 5–11. London: By order of the Trustees, 1938–1954.
Gibson, Thomas. *The Anatomy of Humane Bodies Epitomized*. London: T.W. for Awnsham and John Churchill, 1703.
Gikandi, Simon. *Slavery and the Culture of Taste*. Princeton, NJ: Princeton University Press, 2011.
Gilchrist, Peter. *A Treatise on the Hair*. London, 1770.
Gildon, Charles. *A New Rehearsal; or Bays the Younger*. London: Printed for J. Roberts, 1714.
Girten, Kirsten M. "Mingling with Matter; Tactile Microscopy and the Philosophic Mind in Brobdingnag and Beyond." *The Eighteenth Century: Theory and Interpretation* 54, no. 4 (2013): 497–520.
Gissinger, Danielle. "'The Oddity of My Appearance Soon Assembled a Croud': The Performative Bodies of Charlotte Charke and Cindy Sherman." In *The Public's Open to Us All: Essays on Women and Performance in Eighteenth-Century England*. Edited by Laura Engel, 264–7. Newcastle: Cambridge Scholars, 2009.
Goldsmith, Oliver. *The Citizen of the World*. 2 vols. Dublin: Printed for J. Williams, 1769.
Goldsmith, Oliver. *An History of the Earth and Animated Nature*. 2nd ed. 8 vols. London: Printed for J. Nourse, 1779.
Gombrich, E.H. "Imagery and Art in the Romantic Period." *The Burlington Magazine* 91, no. 555 (1949): 153–9.
Goodman, Jordan. *Tobacco in History: Cultures of Dependence*. London: Routledge, 1994.
Gowing, Laura. *Domestic Dangers: Women, Words, and Sex in Early Modern London*. Oxford: Clarendon, 1996.
Graves, Richard. *The Spiritual Quixote: Or, the Summer's Ramble of Mr. Geoffry Wildgoose*. 3 vols. London: Printed for J. Dodsley, 1773.
Graves, Richard. *The Spiritual Quixote: Or, the Summer's Ramble of Mr. Geoffry Wildgoose*. Edited by Clarence Tracy. 3 vols. London: Oxford, 1967.
Greene, Jody. *The Trouble with Ownership: Literary Property and Authorial Liability in England, 1660–1730*. Philadelphia: University of Pennsylvania Press, 2005.
Gregory, Derek. *Regional Transformation and Industrial Revolution: A Geography of the Yorkshire Woollen Industry*. Minneapolis: University of Minnesota Press, 1982.

Grew, Nehemiah. *Musæum Regalis Societatis, Or, A Catalogue and Description of the Natural and Artificial Rarities Belonging to the Royal Society*. 1681. London: Printed for Thomas Malthus, 1685.
Grigsby, Darcy Grimaldo. *Extremities: Painting Empire in Post-Revolutionary France*. New Haven, CT: Yale University Press, 2002.
Grose, Francis. *The Antiquities of England and Wales*. 4 vols. London: Printed for S. Hooper, 1772–76.
Habermas, Jürgen. *The Structural Transformation of the Public Sphere: An Inquiry into a Category of Bourgeois Society*. Translated by Thomas Burger. Cambridge, MA: MIT Press, 1989.
Hacking, Ian. *Representing and Intervening: Introductory Topics in the Philosophy of Natural Science*. Cambridge: Cambridge University Press, 1983.
Hakluyt, Richard. *The Principal Nauigations, Voiages, Traffiques and Discoueries of the English Nation*. 3 vols. London: George Bishop, Ralph Newberie, and Robert Barker, 1598–1600.
Hale, Matthew. *Historia Placitorum Coronae. The History of the Pleas of the Crown. By Sir Matthew Hale ... Published from the Original Manuscripts by Sollom Emlyn. A New Ed.: Carefully Rev. and Cor.; With Additional Notes and References to Modern Cases Concerning the Pleas of the Crown. Together with an Abridgement of the Statutes Concerning Felonies Which Have Been Enacted since the First Publication of this Work. By George Wilson*. 2 vols. London: T. Payne, 1778.
Halford, Henry. *An Account of What Appeared on Opening the Coffin of King Charles the First*. London: Nichols, Son, and Bentley, 1813.
Hall, Rupert, and N.C. Russell, "What about the Fulling-Mill?" *History of Technology* 6 (1981): 113–19.
Hall, Thomas. *Comarum Akosmia. The Loathsomnesse of Long Haire: or, a Treatise Wherein You have the Question Stated, Many Arguments Against It Produc'd, and the Most Materiall Argugments for it Retell'd and Answer'd*. London: J.G. for Nathanael Webb and William Grantham, 1654.
Halsband, Robert. *The Rape of the Lock and Its Illustrations*. Oxford: Clarendon Press, 1980.
Hart, Katherine. "James Gillray, Charles James Fox, and the Abolition of the Slave Trade: Caricature and Displacement in the Debate over Reform." In *No Laughing Matter: Visual Humor in Ideas of Race, Nationality, and Ethnicity*. Edited by Angela Rosenthal and David Bindman, 76–103. Hanover: Dartmouth College Press, 2015.
Haulman, Kate. *The Politics of Fashion in Eighteenth-Century America*. Chapel Hill: University of North Carolina Press, 2011.
Hawking, Stephen W., Malcolm J. Perry, and Andrew Strominger. "Soft Hair on Black Holes." *Physical Review Letters* 116, no. 23 (June 10, 2016): 291301-1-281301-9.
Healey, Jonathan. *The First Century of Welfare: Poverty and Poor Relief in Lancashire 1620–1730*. Woodbridge: Boydell, 2014.
Hearne, Thomas. *The History and Antiquities of Glastonbury*. Oxford: Printed at the Theater, 1722.
Hernandez, Alex Eric. "Commodity and Religion in Pope's *The Rape of the Lock*." *SEL Studies in English Literature, 1500–1900* 48, no. 3 (2008): 569–84.
Herodotus. *The Histories*. Edited by John Marincola. Translated by Aubrey De Sélincourt. Rev. ed. London: Penguin Classics, 2003.
Herzog, Don. "The Trouble with Hairdressers." *Representations* no. 53 (Winter 1996): 21–43.
Hesiod. *Works and Days and Theogony*. Translated by Stanley Lombardo. Indianapolis, IN: Hackett Publishing, 1993.

Hitchcock, Robert. *The Macaroni: A Comedy*. York: A. Ward, 1773.
Hitchcock, Tim. *Down and Out in Eighteenth-Century London*. London: Hambledon and London, 2004.
Hobbes, Thomas. *Elementorum Philosophiae: Sectio Prima, De Corpore*. London: Andreae Crook, 1655.
Hogarth, William. *The Analysis of Beauty*. Edited by Ronald Paulson. New Haven, CT: Yale University Press, 1997.
Holm, Christiane. "Sentimental Cuts: Eighteenth-Century Mourning Jewelry with Hair." *Eighteenth-Century Studies* 38, no. 1 (2004): 139–43.
Hooke, Robert. *Micrographia, or, Some Physiological Descriptions of Minute Bodies made by Magnifying Glasses*. London: Jo. Martyn and Ja. Allestry, 1665.
Hooke, Robert. "The Way of Making Felt." A lecture delivered to the Royal Society in February 1666. Royal Society. GB 117 Classified Papers XX, 3.
Hooke, Robert, ed. "An Extract of a Letter from Norimbergh [sic.], dated April 1680." In Royal Society. *Philosophical Collections* 2: 10–11. London, 1682.
Hooke, Robert. *Micrographia*. 1665. Lincolnwood: Science Heritage, 1987.
Hudson, Pat. "Limits of Wool and the Potential of Cotton in the Eighteenth and Early Nineteenth Centuries." In *The Spinning World*. Edited by Riello and Parthasarathi, 327–50.
Hudson, Pat. *The West Riding Wool Textile Industry: A Catalogue of Business Records from the Sixteenth to the Twentieth Century*. Edington: Pasold Research, 1975.
Hudson, Pat. "Proto-Industrialization: The Case of the West Riding Wool Textile Industry in the 18th and Early 19th Centuries." *History Workshop Journal* 12 (1981): 34–61.
Hudson, Pat, and Steve King. "Two Textile Townships, c. 1660–1820: A Comparative Demographic Analysis." *Economic History Review* 53, no. 4 (2000): 706–41.
Hume, David. *History of England*. 6 vols. Edited by William B. Todd. Indianapolis, IN: Liberty Fund, 1983.
Hume, David. *Dialogues Concerning Natural Religion*. 1779. Edited by J.C.A. Gaskin. Oxford: Oxford University Press, 1993.
Immergut, Matthew. "Manscaping: The Tangle of Nature, Culture, and Male Body Hair." In *The Body Reader*. Edited by Lisa Jean Moore and Mary Kosut, 349–66. New York: New York University Press, 2010.
Ingold, Tim. "The Textility of Making." *Cambridge Journal of Economics* 34, no. 1 (2010): 91–102.
Jameson, Frederic. *Postmodernism: or, the Cultural Logic of Late Capitalism*. Durham, NC: Duke University Press, 1991.
Jenkins, Eugenia Zuroski. "'Nature to Advantage Drest': Chinoiserie, Aesthetic Form, and the Poetry of Subjectivity in Pope and Swift." *Eighteenth-Century Studies* 43, no. 1 (2009): 75–94.
Jenkins, Geraint. *The Wool Textile Industry in Great Britain*. London: Routledge, 1972.
Johnson, Charles. *A General History of the Pyrates*. Edited by Manuel Schonhorn. Mineola, NY: Dover Publications, 1999.
Johnson, Samuel. *A Dictionary of the English Language*. 2 vols. London: W. Strahan, 1755.
Johnson, Samuel. *A Dictionary of the English Language*. 2 vols. 2nd ed. London: Printed for J. Knapton et al., 1756.
Johnson, Thomas. *Discourse Consisting of Motives for the Enlargement and Freedome of Trade*. London: Richard Bishop for Stephen Rowtell, 1645.
Jolly, Penny Howell. *Hair: Untangling a Social History*. Saratoga Springs, NY: Skidmore College Art Gallery, 2004.

Jones, Jennifer. *Sexing la Mode: Gender, Fashion and Commercial Culture in Old Regime France*. London: Bloomsbury Academic, 2004.
Kalm, Pehr. *Kalm's Account of his Visit to England on his Way to America in 1748*. Translated by Joseph Lucas. London: Macmillan, 1892.
Kim, Mi Gyung. "Stabilizing Chemical Reality: The Analytic-Synthetic Ideal of Chemical Species." *Hyle: International Journal for Philosophy of Chemistry* 20, no. 1 (2014): 117–39.
King, Amy May. *Bloom: The Botanical Vernacular in the English Novel*. New York: Oxford University Press, 2003.
King, Thomas A. *The Gendering of Men, 1600–1750*. 2 vols. Madison: University of Wisconsin Press, 2004–2008.
Klein, Herbert S. *The Atlantic Slave Trade*. Cambridge: Cambridge University Press, 1999.
Klein, Ursula, and Wolfgang Lefèvre. *Materials in Eighteenth-Century Science: A Historical Ontology*. Cambridge, MA: MIT Press, 2007.
Kleiner, John. "The Chairs—*Hamlet* and Stage Fright." *Literary Imagination* 17, no. 3 (2015): 276–91.
Kriger, Colleen E. "'Guinea Cloth': Production and Consumption of Cotton Textiles in West Africa Before and During the Atlantic Slave Trade." In *The Spinning World*. Edited by Riello and Parthasarathi, 105–26.
Kroll, Richard. "Pope and Drugs: The Pharmacology of *The Rape of the Lock*." *ELH* 67 (2000): 99–141.
Kuhn, Thomas. *The Structure of Scientific Revolutions*. Chicago: University of Chicago Press, 1962.
Kwass, Michael. "Ordering the World of Goods: Consumer Revolution and the Classification of Objects in Eighteenth-Century France." *Representations* 82, no. 1 (2003): 87–116.
Kwass, Michael. "Big Hair: A Wig History of Consumption in Eighteenth-Century France." *The American Historical Review* 111, no. 3 (2006): 631–59.
Kwass, Michael. *Contraband: Louis Mandrin and the Making of a Global Underground*. Cambridge, MA: Harvard University Press, 2014.
Landes, Joan. *Women and the Public Sphere in the Age of the French Revolution*. Ithaca, NY: Cornell University Press, 1988.
Landes, Joan, ed. *Feminism, the Public, and the Private*. New York: Oxford University Press, 1998.
Laqueur, Thomas. *Making Sex: Body and Gender from the Greeks to Freud*. Cambridge, MA: Harvard University Press, 1990.
La Tour du Pin de Gouvernet, Henriette Lucie Dillon. *Recollections of the Revolution and the Empire*. Edited and translated by Walter Geer. New York: Brentanos, 1920.
The Laureat; or, the Right Side of Colley Cibber, Esq. London: Printed for J. Roberts, 1740.
Leach, Edmund. "Magical Hair." *Journal of the Royal Anthropological Institute* 88, no. 2 (1958): 147–64.
Lee, Mireille M. *Body, Dress, and Identity in Ancient Greece*. New York: Cambridge University Press, 2015.
Lemire, Beverley. *Fashion's Favourite: The Cotton Trade and the Consumer in Britain: 1660–1800*. Oxford: Oxford University Press, 1991.
Leslie, Charles. *The Theological Works of the Reverend Charles Leslie*. 7 vols. Oxford: University Press, 1832.
Levine, Caroline. *Forms: Whole, Rhythm, Hierarchy, Network*. Princeton, NJ: Princeton University Press, 2015.
Lloyd, Evan. "The Methodist. A Poem, by ____ Author of the Powers of the Pen, and The Curate." London: Evan Lloyd, 1766.

Locke, John. *An Essay Concerning Humane Understanding*. London: Eliz. Holt, 1690.
Locke, John. *An Essay Concerning Human Understanding*. Edited by Peter H. Nidditch. Oxford: Clarendon Press, 1975.
Locke, John. *Drafts for the Essay Concerning Human Understanding, and Other Philosophical Writings*. Edited by P.H. Nidditch and G.A.J. Rogers. Oxford: Clarendon Press, 1990.
The London Ladies Vindication of Topknots. London: Printed for P. Brooksey et al. [between 1688 and 1692].
Long, Edward. *The History of Jamaica, Or, General Survey of the Antient and Modern State of That Island*. 3 vols. London: Printed for T. Lowndes, 1774.
"The Louse in Imitation of the Flea." In *A Collection of Miscellany Poems Never before Publish'd*, 23–7. London: Published for the Author, 1737.
Maat, Jan. *Philosophical Languages in the Seventeenth Century*. Dordrecht: Kluwer Academic, 2004.
The Macaroni and Theatrical Magazine, or Monthly Register. London, October 1772, 1.
Mack, Phyllis. *Heart Religion in the British Enlightenment: Gender and Emotion in Early Methodism*. Cambridge: Cambridge University Press, 2008.
Mackie, Erin. "Desperate Measures: The Narratives of the Life of Mrs. Charlotte Charke," *ELH* 58, no. 4 (1991): 841–65.
Mackie, Erin. *Rakes, Highwaymen, and Pirates: The Makings of the Modern Gentleman in the Eighteenth Century*. Baltimore: Johns Hopkins University Press, 2009.
Mandeville, Bernard. *Fable of the Bees: Or, Private Vices, Publick Benefits*. 2 vols. Indianapolis, IN: Liberty Fund, 1988.
Martin, Peter. *A Life of James Boswell*. New Haven, CT: Yale University Press, 2000.
Mather, John. *A Treatise on the Nature and Preservation of the Hair*. London: A. Grant, 1795.
Maupertuis, Pierre Louis Moreau de. *The Earthly Venus*. Edited by George Boas. Translated by Simone Brangier Boas. New York: Johnson Reprint Corporation, 1966.
McCabe, Ina. *A History of Global Consumption: 1500–1800*. London: Routledge, 2014.
McCormick, Ted. *William Petty and the Ambitions of Political Arithmetic*. Oxford: Oxford University Press, 2009.
McGirr, Elaine. *Partial Histories: A Reappraisal of Colley Cibber*. London: Palgrave Macmillan, 2016.
McKendrick, Neil, John Brewer, and J.H. Plumb. *The Birth of a Consumer Society: The Commercialization of Eighteenth-Century England*. Bloomington: Indiana University Press, 1982.
McKeon, Michael. *The Secret History of Domesticity: Public, Private, and the Division of Knowledge*. Baltimore: Johns Hopkins University Press, 2006.
McNeil, Peter. "'That Doubtful Gender': Macaroni Dress and Male Sexuality." *Fashion Theory* 3, no. 4 (1999): 411–48.
Midgley, Graham. *University Life in Eighteenth-Century Oxford*. New Haven, CT: Yale University Press, 1996.
Milton, John. *Paradise Lost*. Edited by Stephen Orgel and Jonathan Goldberg. Introduction by Philip Pullman. Oxford: Oxford World's Classics, 2008.
Mintz, Sidney. *Sweetness and Power: The Place of Sugar in Modern History*. New York: Viking-Penguin, 1985.
"Miscellaneous Articles from the Papers." *The Gentleman's Magazine and Historical Chronicle* 35. London: D. Henry, 1765, 95.
Molineux, Catherine. *Faces of Perfect Ebony: Encountering Atlantic Slavery in Imperial Britain*. Cambridge, MA: Harvard University Press, 2012.

Moore, William. *The Art of Hair-dressing*. Bath: J. Salmon, [1780?].
Morgan, Fidelis. *The Well-Known Troublemaker: A Life of Charlotte Charke*. London: Faber and Faber, 1980.
Morgan, Gwenda, and Peter Rushton. *Eighteenth-Century Criminal Transportation: The Formation of the Criminal Atlantic*. New York: Palgrave Macmillan, 2004.
Nelson, John. *An Extract from John Nelson's Journal, Being an Account of God's Dealing with Him from His Youth to the Forty-Second Year of His Age. Written by Himself*. London: J. Paramore, 1782.
The New London Toilet, or, A Compleat Collection of the Most Simple and Useful Receipts for Preserving and Improving Beauty. London: Printed for Richardson and Urquhart, 1778.
Nichol, Donald W., ed. *Anniversary Essays on Alexander Pope's* The Rape of the Lock. Toronto: University of Toronto Press, 2016.
Nichols, John. "Some Account of the Life of Mrs. Charlotte Charke, Youngest Daughter of Colley Cibber, Esq." *The Gentleman's Magazine and Historical Review* 25 (October 1755): 455–8.
Nussbaum, Felicity. *The Brink of All We Hate: English Satires on Women, 1660–1750*. Bowling Green: University Press of Kentucky, 1984.
Nussbaum, Felicity. *The Autobiographical Subject: Gender and Ideology in Eighteenth-Century England*. Baltimore: Johns Hopkins University Press, 1989.
Nussbaum, Felicity. *The Limits of the Human: Fictions of Anomaly, Race, and Gender in the Long Eighteenth Century*. Cambridge: Cambridge University Press, 2003.
Nussbaum, Felicity. "The Theatre of Empire: Racial Counterfeit, Racial Realism." In *A New Imperial History: Culture, Identity, and Modernity in Britain and the Empire, 1660–1840*. Edited by Kathleen Wilson, 71–90. New York: Cambridge University Press, 2004.
Nussbaum, Felicity. *Rival Queens: Actresses, Performance, and the Eighteenth-Century British Theater*. Philadelphia: University of Pennsylvania Press, 2010.
O'Driscoll, Sally. "The Pirate's Breasts: Criminal Women and the Meanings of the Body." *The Eighteenth Century* 53, no. 3 (2012): 357–79.
O'Quinn, Daniel. "Bread: The Eruption and Interruption of Politics in Elizabeth Inchbald's *Every One Has His Fault*." *European Romantic Review* 18, no. 2 (2007): 149–57.
Ochs, Kathleen H. "The Royal Society of London's History of Trades Program: An Early Episode in Applied Science." *Notes and Records* 39, no. 2 (1985): 129–58.
Ogborn, Miles. "Luxury, Sexuality and Vision in Vauxhall Gardens." *Textual Practice* 11, no. 3 (1997): 445–61.
Oldstone-Moore, Christopher. *Of Beards and Men: The Revealing History of Facial Hair*. Chicago: University of Chicago Press, 2015.
Oliver, Kathleen M. "'With My Hair in Crystal': Mourning Clarissa." *Eighteenth-Century Fiction* 23, no. 1 (2010): 35–60.
"On the Education of the Fair-Sex. Essay X. Argument. Thoughts of a Persian Philospher upon Fashions." *The Lady's Magazine* 4. London: G. Robinson, May 1773, 249–50.
"On the Use of Hair Powder." *Arminian Magazine Consisting of Extracts and Original Treatises on Universal Redemption* 19 (April 1796): 205–6.
Ovid. *Ovid's Metamorphoses*. 1717. Translated by "Mr Dryden … and Mr Gay." 2 vols. London: Samuel Garth, 1720.
Pasanek, Brad. *Metaphors of Mind: An Eighteenth-Century Dictionary*. Baltimore: Johns Hopkins University Press, 2015.
Paulson, Ronald. *Hogarth: High Art and Low, 1732–1750*. New Brunswick, NJ: Rutgers University Press, 1992.

Payne, Deborah C. "Pope and the War against Coquettes; or, Feminism and *The Rape of the Lock* Reconsidered—Yet Again." *The Eighteenth Century: Theory and Interpretation* 32, no. 1 (1991): 3–24.

Payne, Deborah C. "Reified Object or Emergent Professional? Retheorizing the Restoration Actress." In *Cultural Readings of Restoration and Eighteenth-Century English Theater*. Edited by J. Douglas Canfield and Deborah C. Payne, 13–38. Athens: University of Georgia Press, 1995.

Peabody, Sue. *"There are No Slaves in France": The Political Culture of Race and Slavery in the Ancien Régime*. Oxford: Oxford University Press, 1996.

Pearson, Jacqueline. *The Prostituted Muse: Images of Women and Women Dramatists, 1642–1737*. New York: St. Martin's, 1998.

Peavy, Charles D. "The Chimerical Career of Charlotte Charke." *Restoration and Eighteenth-Century Theatre Research* 8, no. 1 (1969): 1–12.

Pepys, Samuel. *The Diary of Samuel Pepys*. Edited by Henry B. Wheatley. 9 vols. London: George Bell and Sons, 1893–1899.

Pepys, Samuel. *The Diary of Samuel Pepys*. Edited by Robert Latham and William Matthews. 11 vols. Berkeley: University of California Press, 1970–1983.

Perry, Bela C. *The Human Hair and the Cutaneous Diseases Which Affect It*. New York: J. Miller, 1865.

Peterkin, Allan. *One Thousand Beards: A Cultural History of Facial Hair*. Vancouver: Arsenal Pulp Press, 2001.

Petty, William. "History of the Making of Cloth from Sheep's Wool." In *The History of the Royal Society of London*. Edited by Thomas Birch. 4 vols. London: Millar, 1661.

Picard, Liza. *Dr. Johnson's London: Life in London 1740–1770*. London: Weidenfeld & Nicolson; New York: St. Martin's Press, 2000.

Pointon, Marcia. *Hanging the Head: Portraiture and Social Formation in Eighteenth-Century England*. New Haven, CT: Yale University Press, 1993.

Pollak, Ellen. "Rereading *The Rape of the Lock*: Pope and the Paradox of Female Power." *Studies in Eighteenth-Century Culture* 10 (1981): 429–44.

Pollak, Ellen. *The Poetics of Sexual Myth: Gender and Ideology in the Verse of Swift and Pope*. Chicago: University of Chicago Press, 1985.

Ponting, Kenneth G. *The Wool Trade: Past and Present*. Manchester: Columbine, 1961.

Pope, Alexander. *The Twickenham Edition of the Poems of Alexander Pope*. Edited by John Butt et al. 11 vols. New Haven, CT: Yale University Press, 1939–1967.

Pope, Alexander. *The Poems of Alexander Pope*. Edited by John Butt. New Haven, CT: Yale University Press, 1974.

Powell, John, and Hans Sloane. "Concerning a Gentlewoman who Voided with her Urine, Hairy Crustaceous Substances." In Royal Society. *Philosophical Transactions* 41 (1739): 452–61.

Powell, Margaret K., and Joseph Roach. "Big Hair." *Eighteenth-Century Studies* 38, no. 1 (2004): 79–99.

Powers, Stephen. *The American Merino: For Wool and for Mutton*. New York: Orange Judd, 1887.

Pratt, Ellis. *The Art of Dressing the Hair: A Poem*. Bath: R. Cruttwell, 1770.

Pratt, Mary Louise. *Imperial Eyes: Travel Writing and Transculturation*. 2nd ed. New York: Routledge, 2007.

Price, Uvedale. *An Essay on the Picturesque*. London: Printed for J. Robson, 1794.

Prynne, William. *The Vnlouelinesse of Loue-lockes*. London, 1628.

Quincy, John. *Lexicon Physico-Medicum.* 5th ed. London: Printed for T. Longman, 1736.
Rauser, Amelia. "Hair, Authenticity, and the Self-Made Macaroni." *Eighteenth-Century Studies* 38, no. 1 (2004): 101–17.
Rauser, Amelia. "Sex and Sensibility: Hair in the Macaroni Caricatures of the 1770s." In *Hair: Untangling a Social History.* Edited by Penny Howell Jolly, 29–38. Saratoga Springs, NY: Skidmore College Art Gallery, 2004.
Rawdon, Elizabeth (Lady Moira). "Particulars Relative to a Human Skeleton." *Archaeologia* 7 (1785): 90–110.
Ribeiro, Aileen. *Dress in Eighteenth-Century Europe, 1715–1789.* New York: Holmes and Meier, 1985.
Ribeiro, Aileen. *Fashion in the French Revolution.* New York: Holmes and Meier, 1988.
Ribeiro, Aileen. *Dress and Morality.* Oxford: Berg, 2003.
Richardson, Jonathan. *Explanatory Notes and Remarks on Milton's Paradise Lost.* London: Printed for James, John, and Paul Knapton, 1734.
Ridley, Glynis. "Making the Perfect Woman: Female Automata from Pandora to Belinda." In *Anniversary Essays on Alexander Pope's* The Rape of the Lock. Edited by Nichol, 53–69.
Riello, Giorgio. "The Globalization of Cotton Textiles: Indian Cottons, Europe, and the Atlantic World, 1600–1850." In *The Spinning World.* Edited by Riello and Parthasarathi, 261–90.
Riello, Giorgio, and Prasannan Parthasarathi, eds. *The Spinning World: A Global History of Cotton Textiles, 1200–1850.* Repr. ed. Oxford: Oxford University Press, 2011.
Ripa, Cesare. *Iconologia: or, Moral Emblems.* London: B. Motte, 1709.
Ritchie, David. *A Treatise on the Hair.* London: Printed for the Author, 1770.
Roach, Joseph. "Garrick, the Ghost and the Machine." *Theatre Journal* 34, no. 4 (1982): 431–40.
Roach, Joseph. "It." *Theatre Journal* 56, no. 4 (2004): 555–68.
Roach, Joseph. *It.* Ann Arbor: University of Michigan Press, 2007.
Roberts, William, ed. *Memoirs of the Life and Correspondence of Mrs. Hannah More.* 4 vols. London: R.B. Seeley and W. Burnside, 1834.
Rochefort, Charles de. *The History of the Caribby-Islands.* Translated by John Davies. London: Printed by J.M. for Thomas Dring and John Starkey, 1666.
Rogers, John. "Transported Touch: The Fruit of Marriage in *Paradise Lost.*" In *Milton and Gender.* Edited by Catherine Gimelli Martin, 115–32. Cambridge: Cambridge University Press, 2004.
Rose, Mark. *Authors and Owners: The Invention of Copyright.* Cambridge, MA: Harvard University Press, 1995.
Rosenthal, Angela, ed. *Hair.* A special issue of *Eighteenth-Century Studies* 38, no. 1 (Fall 2004).
Rosenthal, Angela. "Raising Hair." *Eighteenth-Century Studies,* 38, no. 1 (Fall 2004): 1–16.
Rosenthal, Laura J. *Playwrights and Plagiarists in Early Modern Drama: Gender, Authorship, Literature, Property.* Ithaca, NY: Cornell University Press, 1996.
Royal Society. *Philosophical Transactions and Collections to the End of the Year 1700, Abridged and Disposed under General Heads.* 10 vols. London: Printed for Thomas Bennet et al., 1665–1750.
Rudolph, Julia. "Rape and Resistance: Women and Consent in Seventeenth-Century English Legal and Political Thought." *Journal of British Studies* 39, no. 2 (April 2000): 157–84.
Ryder, M. L. *Sheep and Man.* London: Duckworth, 1983.
Sampson, Henry. "Anatomical Observations on the Body of a Woman about Thirty years Old." In Royal Society. *Philosophical Transactions* 12 (1677): 133–42.

Saumarez-Smith, Charles. *Eighteenth-Century Decoration and the Domestic Interior in England.* New York: Harry N. Abrams, 1993.
Schiebinger, Londa. *Nature's Body: Gender in the Making of Modern Science.* 1993. New Brunswick, NJ: Rutgers University Press, 2004.
Scots Magazine 47. Edinburgh, 1785.
Scott, David. *Conscripts of Modernity: The Tragedy of Colonial Enlightenment.* Durham, NC: Duke University Press, 2004.
Sennert, Daniel. *The Art of Chirurgery Explained in Six Parts.* London: Peter Cole and Edward Cole, 1663.
Sickinger, R.L. "Regulation or Ruination: Parliament's Consistent Pattern of Mercantilist Regulation of the English Textile Trade, 1660–1800." *Parliamentary History* 19, no. 2 (2000): 211–32.
Silver, Sean. *The Mind Is a Collection: Case Studies in Eighteenth-Century Thought.* Philadelphia: University of Pennsylvania Press, 2015.
Smail, John. *Merchants, Markets, and Manufacture: The English Wool Textile Industry in the Eighteenth Century.* Basingstoke: Macmillan, 1999.
Smail, John. "The Sources of Innovation in the Woollen and Worsted Industry of Eighteenth-Century Yorkshire." *Business History* 41, no. 1 (1999): 1–15.
Smith, Alexander. *A Compleat History of the Lives and Robberies of the Most Notorious Highway-Men, Foot-Pads, Shop-Lifts, and Cheats, Of both Sexes.* 2 vols. 5th ed. London: Printed for Sam Briscoe, 1719.
Smith, John. *Memoirs of Wool, Woolen Manufacture, and Trade.* 2 vols. London: Printed for the Author, 1756–1757.
Smith, Justin E.H. *Nature, Human Nature, and Human Difference: Race in Early Modern Philosophy.* Princeton, NJ: Princeton University Press, 2015.
Smith, Sidonie. *A Poetics of Women's Autobiography: Marginality and the Fictions of Self-Representation.* Bloomington: Indiana University Press, 1987.
Smollett, Tobias. *The Adventures of Roderick Random.* 1748. Edited by Paul-Gabriel Boucé. Oxford: Oxford World Classics, 2008.
Society of Antiquaries of London. *Vetusta Monumenta.* 7 vols. London: Society of Antiquaries, 1747–1906.
Southey, Robert. *The Life of Wesley, and the Rise and Progress of Methodism.* 2 vols. London: Longman, Brown, Green, and Longmans, 1846.
Spacks, Patricia Meyer. *Imagining a Self: Autobiography and Novel in Eighteenth-Century England.* Cambridge, MA: Harvard University Press, 1976.
Speight, Alexanna. *The Lock of Hair: Its History, Ancient and Modern, Natural and Artistic.* London: A. Goubaud, 1871.
Staves, Susan. *Married Women's Separate Property in England, 1660–1833.* Cambridge, MA: Harvard University Press, 1990.
Stedman, John Gabriel. *Narrative, of a Five Years' Expedition; against the Revolted Negroes of Surinam, in Guiana.* 2 vols. London: Printed for J. Johnson, 1796.
Steele, Richard, and Joseph Addison. *The Tatler* 151. London, March 25 to March 28, 1710.
Stephanson, Raymond. "'Hairs Less in Sight': Pope, Biology and Culture." In *Anniversary Essays on Alexander Pope's* The Rape of the Lock. Edited by Nichol, 113–30.
Stevens, George Alexander. *The Celebrated Lecture on Heads.* London: Bond, 1765.
Stewart, Alexander. *The Natural Production of Hair.* London: Printed by the Author, 1795.
Stewart, James. *Plocacosmos, or, The Whole Art of Hair Dressing.* London: Printed for the Author, 1782.

Stobart, Jon. *The First Industrial Region: North West England c. 1700–60*. Manchester: Manchester University Press, 2009.
Stone, Lawrence. "Elizabethan Overseas Trade." *Economic History Review* 2, no. 1 (1949): 30–58.
Strange, Sally Minter. "Charlotte Charke: Transvestite or Conjuror?" *Restoration and Eighteenth-Century Theatre Research* 15, no. 2 (1976): 54–9.
Straub, Kristina. *Sexual Suspects: Eighteenth-Century Players and Sexual Ideology*. Princeton, NJ: Princeton University Press, 1992.
Stretton, Tim. *Women Waging Law in Elizabethan England*. Cambridge: Cambridge University Press, 2005.
Stuart, Louisa. *Notes by Lady Louisa Stuart on George Selwyn and His Contemporaries by John Heneage Jesse*. Edited by W.S. Lewis. New York: Oxford University Press, 1928.
Styles, John. *The Dress of the People: Everyday Fashion in Eighteenth-Century England*. New Haven, CT: Yale University Press, 2007.
Styles, John. "Spinners and the Law: Regulating Yarn Standards in the English Worsted Industry: 1550–1800." *Textile History* 44, no. 2 (2013): 145–70.
Swift, Jonathan. *The Essential Writings of Jonathan Swift*. Edited by Claude Rawson and Ian Higgins. New York: Norton, 2010.
The Tatler. Edited by Donald F. Bond. 3 vols. Oxford: Oxford University Press, 1987.
Taylor, Charles. *Sources of the Self: The Making of Modern Identity*. Cambridge, MA: Harvard University Press, 1989.
Thompson, Helen. *Fictional Matter: Empiricism, Corpuscles, and the Novel*. Philadelphia: University of Pennsylvania Press, 2017.
Todd, Janet. "Introduction." In Aphra Behn, *Oroonoko*. Edited by Janet Todd. London: Penguin Classics, 2004.
Tomalin, Claire. *Samuel Pepys: The Unequaled Self*. New York: Knopf, 2002.
Trasko, Mary. *Daring Do's: A History of Extraordinary Hair*. Paris: Flammarion, 1994.
The Trial of Charles I, King of England. London, 1740.
Tucker, Elizabeth. *Children's Folklore: A Handbook*. London: Greenwood, 2008.
Turner, Victor. *The Ritual Process: Structure and Anti-Structure*. 1969. London: Transaction Publishers, 2008.
Uglow, Jenny. *A Gambling Man: Charles II's Restoration Game*. New York: Farrar, Strauss, and Giroux, 2009.
Van Der Wee, Herman, and John Munro, "The Western European Woollen Industries, 1500–1750." In *The Cambridge History of Western Textiles II*. Edited by David Jenkins. Cambridge: Cambridge University Press, 2003.
Vanhaelen, Angela, and Joseph P. Ward. *Making Space Public in Early Modern Europe: Performance, Geography, Privacy*. New York: Routledge, 2013.
Vicary, Thomas. *The Englishemans Treasure, with the True Anatomie of Mans Body*. London: George Robinson, 1586.
Wahrman, Dror. *The Making of the Modern Self: Identity and Culture in Eighteenth-Century England*. New Haven, CT: Yale University Press, 2004.
Wall, Thomas. *Spiritual Armour to Defend the Head from the Superfluity of Naughtiness*. London: Printed for the Author, 1688.
Walpole, Horace. *The Yale Edition of Horace Walpole's Correspondence*. Edited by W.S. Lewis. 48 vols. New Haven, CT: Yale University Press, 1937–83.
Wanko, Cheryl. *Roles of Authority: Thespian Biography and Celebrity in Eighteenth-Century Britain*. Lubbock: Texas Tech University Press, 2003.

Ward, Ned. *The History of the London Clubs: or the Citizens Pastime*. London: Printed for J. Bagnall, 1709.
Warner, Michael. *Publics and Counterpublics*. Brooklyn, NY: Zone Books, 2002.
Weatherill, Lorna. *Consumer Behavior and Material Culture: 1660–1760*. London: Routledge, 1988.
Weber, Caroline. *Queen of Fashion: What Marie Antoinette Wore to the Revolution*. New York: Henry Holt, 2006.
Wells, Jeremiah. *Poems upon Divers Occasions*. London: Printed for John Crosley, 1667.
Wesley, John. *Minutes of Several Conversations Between the Rev. John Wesley, A.M. and the Preachers in Connection with Him*. London: G. Whitfield, 1779.
[Wesley, John]. *The Arminian Magazine* 19. London, April 1796, 205–6.
Wesley, John. "An Account of his Residence at Oxford." In *The Life and Journal of the Rev. John Wesley, A.M.* Vol. 1. Edited by Joseph Benson. New York: Harper, 1827.
Wesley, John. *The Journal of the Rev. John Wesley*. Introduction by F.W. MacDonald. 4 vols. London: J. Dent, 1906.
Wesley, John. *The Journal of the Rev. John Wesley, A.M.* Edited by Nehemiah Curnock. 8 vols. London: R. Culy, 1909–1916.
Wheeler, Roxann. *The Complexion of Race: Categories of Difference in Eighteenth-Century British Culture*. Philadelphia: University of Pennsylvania Press, 2000.
Whitefield, George. *A Short Account of God's Dealings with the Reverend Mr. George Whitefield*. London: W. Strahan, 1740.
Wilkins, John. *An Essay Towards a Real Character, and a Philosophical Language*. London: Printed for Sa. Gellibrand and John Martyn, 1668.
Wilkinson-Latham, Robert. *The Royal Navy 1790–1970*. London: Osprey, 1977.
Willis, Thomas. *Two Discourses Concerning the Soul of Brutes*. London: Th. Dring, Ch. Harper, and John Leigh, 1683.
Wilson, Bronwen, and Paul Yachnin, eds. *Making Publics in Early Modern Europe: People, Things, Forms of Knowledge*. New York: Routledge, 2010.
Wilson, Elizabeth. *Adorned in Dreams: Fashion and Modernity*. Rev. ed. New Brunswick, NJ: Rutgers University Press, 2003.
Withey, Alun. *Technology, Self-Fashioning and Politeness in Eighteenth-Century Britain: Refined Bodies*. Basingstoke: Palgrave Macmillan, 2016.
Wolcot, Jon. *The Works of Peter Pindar, Esq*. 5 vols. London: J. Walker, 1812.
Woodforde, John. *The Strange Story of False Hair*. London: Routledge and Kegan Paul, 1971.
Worden, Blair. *The English Civil Wars, 1640–1660*. London: Penguin, 2009.
Wrigley, E.A. "Explaining the Rise in Marital Fertility in England in the 'Long' Eighteenth-Century." *Economic History Review* 51, no. 3 (1998): 435–64.
Yonge, James. "An Account of Balls of Hair taken from the Uterus and Ovaria of Several Women." In Royal Society. *Philosophical Transactions* 25 (1706–1707): 2387–92.
Yonge, James. "An Extract of Another Letter upon the Same Subject." In Royal Society. *Philosophical Transactions* 26 (1708): 313–24.
Young, Arthur. *Political Essays Concerning the Present State of the British Empire*. London: Printed for W. Strahan and T. Cadell, 1772.

CONTRIBUTORS

Misty G. Anderson is Lindsay Young Professor of English and Affiliate Professor of Theatre at the University of Tennessee, Knoxville. She is the author of *Imagining Methodism* (2012) and *Female Playwrights and Eighteenth-Century Comedy: Negotiating Marriage on the London Stage* (2002), and one of the coeditors of *The Routledge Anthology of Restoration and Eighteenth-Century Drama* (2017).

Julia H. Fawcett is Assistant Professor of Theater, Dance, and Performance Studies at the University of California, Berkeley. Her first book, *Spectacular Disappearances: Celebrity and Privacy, 1696–1801*, was published in 2016. She is currently at work on a second book, *Unmapping London: Performance and Urbanization after the Great Fire of 1666*.

Lynn Festa is Associate Professor of English at Rutgers University, New Jersey. She is the author of *Sentimental Figures of Empire in Eighteenth-Century Britain and France* (2006) and coeditor (with Daniel Carey) of *The Postcolonial Enlightenment: Eighteenth-Century Colonialism and Postcolonial Theory* (2009). She has recently completed a book on the role of fiction in elaborating definitions of the human in early Enlightenment thought.

Crystal B. Lake is Associate Professor of English at Wright State University in Dayton, Ohio. Her research has appeared in *ELH*, *Modern Philology*, *RES*, and *Word & Image*, among other publications, supported by fellowships from the Lewis Walpole Library, the Yale Center for British Art, and the NEH. She is currently completing a book on the artifacts that were dug up in England during the long eighteenth century.

Jayne Lewis is Professor of English at the University of California, Irvine. She is the author, most recently, of *Air's Appearance: Literary Atmosphere in British Fiction, 1660–1794* (2012) and the editor of the anthology *Religion in Enlightenment England* (2017).

Manushag N. Powell is Associate Professor of English and University Faculty Scholar at Purdue University, Indiana. Major publications include *Performing Authorship in 18th-Century English Periodicals* (2012); (with Frederick Burwick) *British Pirates in Print and Performance* (2014); and the coedited volume (with Jennie Batchelor) *Women's Periodicals and Print Culture in Britain, 1690–1820s* (2018). Her edition of Defoe's *Captain Singleton* will appear in 2019.

Margaret K. Powell is the former W.S. Lewis Librarian and Executive Director of the Lewis Walpole Library, Yale University, Connecticut, where her exhibition of caricatures depicting hair in the eighteenth century inspired an essay with Joseph Roach: "Big Hair" (*Eighteenth-Century Studies* 38, no. 1 [2004]: 79–99).

Joseph Roach is Sterling Professor of Theater at Yale University, Connecticut, and the author of *The Player's Passion: Studies in the Science of Acting* (1985), *Cities of the Dead:*

Circum-Atlantic Performance (1996), and *It* (2007), a study of charismatic celebrity and ageless glamour.

Sean Silver is Associate Professor of English at the University of Michigan. His last project, entitled *The Mind Is a Collection* (2015), is the exhibit catalogue of a virtual museum of seventeenth- and eighteenth-century British cognitive models. Please visit www.mindisacollection.org.

Heather V. Vermeulen is Lecturer in African American Studies at Yale University, Connecticut, where she received her doctorate in African American Studies and American Studies. Her current research relates eighteenth- and nineteenth-century archival documents from the Anglophone Caribbean to literature and arts of the African Diaspora, with a focus on slavery, ecology, and queer kinship. She has cocurated exhibitions on transatlantic slavery and the British Empire at Yale University's Lewis Walpole Library. An article on Thomas Thistlewood is forthcoming in *Small Axe*.

INDEX

Abelove, Henry 30, 32
Abigails 66
Abington, Frances 108
abjection, social 14
actors and actresses 44, 47, 104, 155
Adams, George 122
addictive substances 76
Addison, Joseph 64, 66, 110, 185, 188
advertising 162
Aeschylus 148
aesthetics 72, 177
Age of Reason 1
albinism 152
American hairstyles 57
Anglomania (in France) 61
Anstey, Christopher 29
antiquarianism 15, 172, 187–9
Aravamudan, Srinivas 17
Aristotle 180
The Arminian Magazine 31–2
"authenticity" 64

bagwigs 58
baldness 19, 56, 92, 100, 122, 124, 159
Barad, Karen 119–20
Barbarossa brothers 167
Barker, William 72, 108, 126
Barthes, Roland 72
beards 7, 14, 61–2, 122, 125, 162–3, 166–7, 170, 180
"bear's grease" 92, 99
Beauclerk, Topham 99, 108
Beaumont, Mademoiselle de 116
The Beggar's Opera 157, 159
Behn, Aphra 141–2, 147
Bellamy, George Anne 6–7, 44–51
Belley, Jean-Baptiste 152–4
Belsey, Catherine 22
Benjamin, Walter 54–6, 72, 172, 180, 189
Bennett, Jane 119
biblical references 38
Bickham, George 27
"big hair" 53, 100, 137, 139, 158–9, 171
"bigwigs" 155

Bindman, David 145
"biocultural creatures" 171, 178, 180
black hair 137
black holes 133
Blackbeard 14, 164–7
Blake, William 157
Bluebeard 167
bob wigs 58
Bolton, Robert 19
Bonny, Anne 14, 168–9
Boswell, James 40, 46, 174–5
Boyle, Robert 12, 81, 85, 122
bread shortages 31
Brewer, John 144
broadcloths 78–9
Browne, Peter A. 136
bubonic plague 97
Buffon, Georges Louis Leclerc 125
Bulwer, John 56
Bulwer-Lytton, Edward 171–2, 175–7, 182
Burke, Edmund 145–6, 150
Burney, Frances 131–2, 168
Butler, Judith 115
Byron, Lord 37–8

cadogans 58
Callimachus 117
Campbell, Robert 60
Canning, Elizabeth 168–9
Castle, Terry 46
Catholicism 27
  opposition to 48
Cavaliers 4, 19–20, 56
Cennick, John 32
Cervantes, Miguel de 5
Chapman, Graham 167
charismatic leaders 15
Charke, Charlotte 6, 41, 44–51, 115–17
Charles I, King 172, 185–8
Charles II, King 26, 44, 56–7, 137, 159, 185, 188
Cheviot sheep 78–9
Chico, Tita 95
children's hair 162

Christianity 17–18, 57, 172
  "primitive" 38
Cibber, Colley 6, 41–7, 58
Cipriani, Giovanni Battista 24
Clarke, Adrian 32
Clarke, Timothy 103
class distinctions 54–6
cleanliness 98–9, 104–5
Cole, B. 166, 169
Colebrook, Claire 119–20
Coleridge, Samuel Taylor 37
colonialism 136–9
combs and combing 94–5, 98, 104–5
commercial production of hair 8
commercial prosperity 56
complexity, concept of 75, 81–3, 88–9
Congreve, William 44
conscience 17
conspicuous consumption 76
consumer revolution 7–8, 15, 56, 76
consumerism 76
contamination, fears of 137, 139
Cooper, Samuel 20
corpuscularianism 85, 88
Cowper, William 60
Crewe, Emma 128–9
criminality 162–70
Cromwell, Oliver 18, 20, 22
cropped hair 18, 20, 92, 97–8, 156, 170
Cruikshank, Isaac 151
curiosity 178–80
curling irons 92–3
Curnock, Nehemiah 30

dandruff 92
dandyism 62
Darly, M. 110, 122, 126, 128, 131–2
Darwin, Charles 128
Darwin, Erasmus 122
Davies, John 141
Davies, Moll 104
Dawe, Philip 140
death
  associations with 12, 14
  hair continuing to grow afterwards 118, 133, 181, 189
Defoe, Daniel 14, 77, 142
Democritus 110
Dent, William 144–5
depilation 110
Derby, Lord 152
Descartes, René 184

difference marking, hair used for 139, 163–4, 169–71
Digges, West 46
diseases associated wth hair 10, 92
Dissenters 32
Dobranski, Stephen 20, 22
domestic service 14
Donald, Diana 69
Donaldson, John 100
Donne, John 117
Du Bose, Claude 110, 112
Du Guernier, Louis 110, 112
Dulaure, Jacques-Antoine 62
Du Tertre, Jean-Baptiste 146–7
dyeing
  of hair 161
  of yarns 79

Edward IV, King 188
"election" (in religious terms) 33
Elias, Norbert 54
empiricism 1, 15
Enlightenment thought 1, 4, 14–15, 53, 61, 73, 88–9, 97, 118, 137, 143–4, 149, 171–2, 178
entrepreneurship 15
d'Eon, Chevalier 115–16
Equiano, Olaudah 145, 168
eroticism 26
ethnic divides 163–4
excrement, forms of 19, 94, 124–5, 181
exports 75

factory system 77
Fairfax, Sir Thomas 20, 23
Faithorne, William 20, 23–4
false hair 5–7, 47, 57, 159, 168
  sources of 160
Farley, Elizabeth 104
fashion 18, 53–6, 60–1, 64, 68–9, 72, 139, 161
  etymological origin of the word 53
Fawconer, Samuel 61
felting process 78–9
feminism 41, 109, 117, 119
feminization 61
Fenwick, Allen 175–6
Fermor, Arabella 3, 49, 109
Festa, Lynn 39–42, 115, 159, 167
fideism 173
Fielding, Henry 35
fire risk to hair 91–2

fleas 95–9, 103
  traps for 100
Fletcher, John 104
Flügel, J.C. 60, 117
Focillon, Henri 68
Ford, Charles 109
Fox, Charles James 146–7, 150–2
Frampton, Mary 69
French Revolution 72, 137, 141–5, 148–52
French style and French ways 57, 61, 135–8, 141
"Friday" (in *Robinson Crusoe*) 142
frizzed hair 137
Frost, Samantha 171–2, 178
Fuseli, Henry 114, 128, 130, 164

Garden, Frances 43
Garrick, David 14, 30, 58, 108, 115, 142–3, 155
Gay, John 14, 109, 126, 135–6, 159
Gelbart, Nina Rattner 72
gender differences 12, 115, 121–4
The Gentleman's Magazine 46
gentlemanly status 58
George II, King 31
George III, King 60, 97–8, 149
Gibson, Thomas 126, 181–2
Gilchrist, Peter 66, 93–4
Gildon, Charles 109
Gillray, James 12–13, 57, 148–52
Girodet, Anne-Louis 152–4
glamour 30
Goffman, Erving 64
Goldsmith, Oliver 60, 125
Gombrich, E.H. 143
Grand Tour 62
Graves, Richard 4, 33–6, 54
gray hair 94, 114, 159–60, 180, 188
Grew, Nehemia 187
Grigsby, Darcy 136, 144, 152–3
grooming 14, 54, 92, 103, 105
group norms 60
Gulliver's Travels 7
Gwynne, Nell 104

Habermas, Jürgen 39, 41, 49
Hacking, Ian 75, 110
hairpieces 39
"hairscaping" 126
"hairstories" 15, 171–2, 178–80, 190
Haitian Revolution 137, 141–2, 145, 149
Hakluyt, Richard 77

Hale, Sir Matthew 44
Hall, Thomas 18–19, 57, 117
Halsband, Robert 109
Hamilton, Mary 29
Hamlet 6, 13, 142–3
Hart, Katherine 148–9
Haulman, Kate 56–7
Hawking, Stephen 133
headdresses 7, 62–72, 160
"healthy" hair 93–4
Hearne, Thomas 187
Hedges, Edward 147
Herbert, George 185
Herodotus 136
Herzog, Don 160
Hesiod 148
hierarchies
  racial 145, 149
  social 14, 56, 160
highwaymen 163
Hinchinbrooke, Lady 103
Hitchcock, Robert 64
Hitchcock, Tim 106
Hobbes, Thomas 39
Hogarth, William 27–8, 40, 46–7, 57–9, 124, 138, 157
Holm, Christiane 120
Holy Club, Oxford 26–7
Homer 177
Hooke, Robert 1–3, 8–9, 15, 81, 84–8, 110, 118, 172, 181–9
  Micrographia 1, 3, 15, 84–8, 110, 172, 182–9
Horne, Margaret 32
horripilation 14
Hume, David 14, 171–8, 181, 187–8
hygiene 94–5, 100, 103

"Ideas" distinct from "ideas" 10–12
identity
  constructionist models of 119
  individual 47, 53–4, 60
  misrepresentation of 60
  racial 137
  sexual 57, 121
  social and corporate 53–4
  stable 62
Inchbald, Elizabeth 31

James, King (Sixth of Scotland, First of England) 18
Jameson, Frederic 17

Jesus Christ 32, 35, 38, 187–8
Johnson, Samuel 40, 47, 125, 174–5, 187
Jolly, Penny Howell 168

Kalm, Pehr 57
Kant, Immanuel 1
Kauffman, Angelica 72
Kelly, John 80
King, Thomas A. 45
Knepp, Mary 104
Kuhn, Thomas 75

The Lady's Magazine 61, 68
Laqueur, Thomas 115
Latour, Bruno 75
Laud, William 18, 20, 30
lawyers 164
Leslie, Charles 57
Levine, Caroline 172
liberalism 17
lice 97–100, 103–7
liminality of hair 14–15, 181
Linnaeus, Carl 135–6
Lock, William 114
Locke, John 39, 79–81, 85, 88, 110, 187
locks of hair 175, 189
Long, Edward 12, 139, 149
long hair 27–30, 36–7, 56, 168
long-staple wool 79
loose hair 14, 39, 92, 121, 168
Louis XIII, King of France 56, 159
Louis XIV, King of France 56, 137, 159
Louis XVI, King of France 145
Lowthorp, John 118–19, 122
Lucretius 175
Luther, Martin 17–18
luxury goods 76
Lycidas 20

Macaronis 7, 62–4, 117
Macaulay, Catherine 132
Mackie, Erin 46
Macpherson, C.B. 39
malleability of hair 58, 60
Mandeville, Bernard 39, 56
manuals of hair care 160–1
Marat, Jean Paul 37
Marie Antoinette, Queen to Louis XVI of France 69
maroons 145
Marvell, Andrew 20
Mary Magdelene 49
Mary the Mother of Jesus 49, 187–8

masculinity and masculine authority 57–60, 66, 69, 164
materials science 82
Mather, John 125
Medusa myth 20, 146–9
"memory miniatures" 120–1
mercantilism 77
merkins 7, 47–50
metaphorical significance of hair 141
Methodism 38
"Methodist hair" 4, 26–37
microscopes, uses of 1, 8–9, 84–7, 110, 172, 181
military hairstyles 162–4
Milton, John 4, 20–5, 36, 117, 121, 124
The Mischief of Methodism 37
modesty 56
Molineux, Catherine 137
Montagu, Elizabeth 137
Moore, William 95, 99, 106
More, Hannah 126
mourning jewelry 117–20
mustaches 163–4

Napoleon 37
narcissism 64
"natural" hair and hairstyles 28–31, 36, 72, 117
natural philosophy of hair 92–6
nature itself made into a fashion 60
The New London Toilet 93
Newton, Richard 7–8
Nussbaum, Felicity 44, 46, 137

Ogborn, Miles 64
O'Quinn, Daniel 31
ornamentation 15, 54
Ovid 126
Oxford colleges 162

Paine, Thomas 146
Paradise Lost 121
Paul, St. 17
Peden, Alexander 18
Pepys, Elizabeth 103–5, 168
Pepys, Samuel 26, 92, 103–7, 159–60, 168
"performance" of hair 53
periwigs 5–6, 26, 36, 40, 45, 57–9, 103, 159–60
Perry, John 164
perukes 57–61, 69, 103, 156
Peter, St., "beard" of 48–9
Peter the Great 164

Peterkin, Allan 163
Petre, Robert Lord 3
Petty, William 10, 81–2, 87–8
phallic symbols 20, 36, 140
philosophical issues 14–15, 83
pigtails 162–3, 168, 170
Pindar, Peter 97–8
pirates 14, 164–70
    female 168–9
Pitt, William 72, 110, 150–1
plague 97, 103
Plocacosmos 155–60
poetry 39
Pointon, Marcia 57–8, 115, 157, 160
Polish hairstyles 19–20
politicians 40
pomatum 66, 69, 94, 98–9
Pope, Alexander 1–3, 7, 10, 49–51, 62, 93, 109–14, 117–19, 137, 157, 173, 190
pornography 29
Portland, Duke of 146–7
poufs 69
powdering of hair 14, 26, 31, 72, 110, 160, 170
Powell, Margaret K. 53, 64, 115, 137, 158, 162, 171
Pratt, Ellis 62
preaching 30–3, 37
Price, Uvedale 126
private life 39
professional hairdressers
    attitudes to 10, 108, 145
    increase in expertise and status of 3, 10, 15, 66
    number of 3, 10, 15, 66
    remedial treatment given by 92–3, 98–9
properties of hair as s substance 12–15
property laws 43–4
prostitution 44–7, 51
protectionism 77
Protestantism 18
pubic hair 10, 51, 109, 180
public sphere and public discourse 39–41, 45–50, 64, 119
"Puritan hair" 4, 18–26, 56, 167

Quincy, John 124

racism 4, 12, 136, 149
rape 43–4
The Rape of the Lock 1–3, 7, 10, 49–50, 62, 93, 109–14, 119, 137, 190

rats-bane 106
Rauser, Amelia 62, 64
Raynal, Guillaume-Thomas 153–4
razors 61, 162
Read, Mary 14, 168–9
Redbeard 167
the Reformation 17–18
The Relapse 6, 41
religion 4, 15
the Renaissance 38
the Restoration 20, 26
revolutionary politics 141, 145, 149–52
Reynolds, Joshua 72
Richardson, Jonathan 121
rights of individuals 51
Ripa, Cesare 178–80
Ritchie, David 53, 61, 109, 121, 124
rites of passage 181
Roach, Joseph 30, 53, 64, 115, 137, 142, 158, 162, 171
robbery 162–3
Roberts, Bartho 164–5
Robinson Crusoe 142
Rochefort, Charles de 141
Roe, Hester Anne 29
Rogers, John 22
Romanticism 54
Roundheads 18, 20, 30, 56
Rousseau, Jean-Jacques 39, 61–2
Rowlandson, Thomas 4, 57, 91–2, 95–102, 106–7
Royal Society 1, 8–9, 12, 79, 81, 88, 118–19, 172, 177, 180, 187
runaway servants 163

sailors 162, 168, 170
Saltero, Don 187
satires 62, 66–9, 137, 160
Sayers, James 146–7
Schiebinger, Londa 115, 164
sciences and scientific principles, application of 3–4, 75. *See also* textile science
scurvy 92
sedan chairs 67–9
self-expression 73
selvage 88
Sennart, Daniel 125
servitors 162
sexual difference 121, 124
Shakespeare, William 177
Shapin, Steven 75
Sharp, Granville 145
shaving 7, 92, 162

Sheppard, Jack 14, 155–9, 162
Sheridan, Richard Brinsley 150
short hair 18, 20, 29, 98, 156, 160, 170
Siddons, Sarah 108
silk, watering of 85–7
Simon, John 42
skin, properties of 87–8
slavery 12, 14, 76, 141–6, 149–51
Smith, Adam 39
Smith, Alexander 7, 48–9
Smith, John 77
Smollett, Tobias 97–8
social climbing 56
"social hair" 115
Society of Antiquaries 15, 172, 187–8
society in relation to self 39–41
society's view of hair 92
Southey, Robert 30
spectacularization of male bodies 64
Speight, Alexanna 128
split ends 92, 94
Squires, Mary 168–9
Stanhope, Earl of 149
Stedman, John Gabriel 139–40
Stevens, George 33, 60, 69
Stewart, Alexander 94, 99–100, 106, 115, 122
Stewart, James 6, 94
Stewart, Lady Louisa 99
Stone, Lawrence 77
Stothard, Thomas 114
straightened hair 141
A Strange Story 171, 175–7
Stretton, Tim 44
Swift, Jonathan 7, 94–5, 98
symbolism of hair 40, 72.
  See also phallic symbols
syphilis 47

taboos about hair 1
The Tatler 64
taxonomies related to hair 12–15
Teach, Edward 14. *See also* Blackbeard
technical advances affecting hair care 61
terror induced by hair 14
Tête de mouton style 66
textile manufacture 8–10, 15, 75–6
textile science 82–9
Thatch, Edward. *See* Blackbeard
theatrical entertainment 33, 155
theft of wigs 162, 168
"thing-ness" of hair 17, 115, 117, 172
thinning hair 160

Thornhill, William 156–8
Tillotson, John 27
"Titus" cut 72
tonsure 27, 29
trade
  general patterns of 8, 15, 54
  in hair 8
  triangles of 76
treatises from hairdressers 92, 108
Turner, Victor 172, 180–1
tyewigs 58
typhus 97
"typologies" 135–6
Tyson, Edward 118, 125

Vanbrugh, Sir John 6, 41
Veblen, Thorstein 56, 69
"vegetal" hairstyles 127–8
vegetative life 181–3
Vicary, Thomas 125

Wade, Samuel 113–14
Wahrman, Dror 115
Walker, Robert 20, 22
Walpole, Horace
Wanko, Cheryl 46
Ware, Ned 106
warp and *weft* yarns 78
The Way of the World 44
weaving techniques 78, 81–2, 85–9
  as a metaphor for the construction
  of natural materials 87
Wells, Jeremiah 185
Wells, Susannah 169
Wesley, Charles 4, 26
Wesley, John 4, 26–38
  hair of 29–33
  Journals of 32
Whistle, Mary 106–8
Whitefield, George 4–5, 26–35, 162
wigs 1, 5–6, 18, 26, 36–7, 39–40, 53, 56–62,
  72, 98, 115, 117, 137, 159
  absence of 157
  code of manners for wearing of 170
  cost of 57–8
  full-bottomed 57–8, 164
  impressions made by 60
  in the military and at sea 162
  smaller sizes of 58
  styles of 6, 58, 162, 167
  worn by women 6, 41, 44–51
  worn by young people 162

Wilberforce, William 145
Wilkins, John 83–4
Willet, Deb 104–5
Wilson, Elizabeth 60, 72
Wilson, Thomas 133
Wiltshire, Mary 163
Withey, Alun 61
Woodforde, John 164
Wool Act (1699) 8, 77

"wool" of Africans 12, 136, 139
wool and woolens, trade in 76–8
Wordsworth, William 37
worsted fabrics 78–9

xenophobia 12

Yellowbeard 167
Young, Arthur 77

www.ingramcontent.com/pod-product-compliance
Ingram Content Group UK Ltd.
Pitfield, Milton Keynes, MK11 3LW, UK
UKHW050007230326
469204UK00010B/322